Geospatial Data Analytics on AWS

Discover how to manage and analyze geospatial data
in the cloud

Scott Bateman

Janahan Gnanachandran

Jeff DeMuth

<packt>

BIRMINGHAM—MUMBAI

Geospatial Data Analytics on AWS

Publishing Product Manager: Reshma Raman
Book Project Manager: Kirti Pisat
Content Development Editor: Joseph Sunil
Technical Editor: Sweety Pagaria
Copy Editor: Safis Editing
Proofreader: Safis Editing
Indexer: Subalakshmi Govindhan
Production Designer: Ponraj Dhandapani
DevRel Marketing Coordinator: Nivedita Singh

First published: June 2023

Production reference: 1280623

Published by Packt Publishing Ltd.
Livery Place
35 Livery Street
Birmingham
B3 2PB, UK.

ISBN 978-1-80461-382-5

www.packtpub.com

This book is dedicated to my father, Orren, for instilling my passion for both computers and maps. To the memory of my mother, Jolene, for teaching me the persistence and patience needed to get my thoughts on the page. To my wife, Angel, and wonderful children Jackson and Emily for the support and encouragement to bring this book to life.

Scott Bateman

This book is dedicated to my parents, Gnanachandran and Rajaletchumy, for guiding me through life's challenges and celebrating my successes. To my amazing wife, Dilakshana and lovely children, Jashwin, and Dhruvish, for your unwavering support and belief in me. Finally, to the team at Amazon Web Services (AWS), whose relentless pursuit of excellence has transformed the way we harness technology. Thank you for inspiring this work and for your commitment to empowering businesses worldwide.

Janahan (Jana) Gnanachandran

Contributors

About the authors

Scott Bateman is a Principal Solutions Architect at AWS focused on customers in the energy industry. Prior to joining the AWS Houston office in 2019, he was Director of business applications at bpx energy and has worked for over a quarter century innovating with technology to solve the toughest energy business problems. As part of the Geospatial Technical Field Community (TFC) group within AWS, Scott is able to speak with customers about common challenges gathering geospatial data, tracking assets, optimizing driving routes, and better understanding facilities and property through remote sensing. When not working or writing, Scott enjoys snowboarding, flying drones, traveling to unknown destinations, and learning something new every day.

Janahan (Jana) Gnanachandran is a Principal Solutions Architect at AWS. He partners with customers across industries to increase speed, agility, and drive innovation using the cloud for digital transformation. Jana holds a BE in Electronics and Communication Engineering from Anna University, India, and an MS in Computer Engineering from the University of Louisiana at Lafayette. Alongside designing scalable, secure, and cost-effective cloud solutions, Jana conducts workshops, training sessions, and public speaking engagements on cloud best practices, architectural best practices, and data and AI/ML strategies. When not immersed in cloud computing, he enjoys playing tennis or golf, photography, and traveling with his wife and their 2 kids.

Jeff DeMuth is a solutions architect who joined Amazon Web Services (AWS) in 2016. He focuses on the geospatial community and is passionate about geographic information systems (GIS) and technology. Outside of work, Jeff enjoys travelling, building Internet of Things (IoT) applications, and tinkering with the latest gadgets.

About the reviewers

Faizan Tayyab is a GIS Professional with over 16 years of experience in the oil and gas industry. He holds a master's degree and has several certifications covering various technologies including web & cloud technologies. He is also a software trainer, teaching courses to worldwide audience on technologies through Udemy, a popular online training platform. He is well-versed with various technologies and actively contributes to open source geospatial community through development and distribution of software components available free for use by other geographers and developers.

Angela Orthmeyer is currently the Lead Geospatial Data Analyst at RapidSOS, the world's leading intelligent safety platform. Angela is a creative problem solver with experience in GIS, data science and project management. Prior to her position at RapidSOS, she was a Data Scientist at CKM Analytix, a Natural Resources Social Scientist at the National Oceanic and Atmospheric Administration, and a Peace Corps Volunteer in Panama. Her education spans the social and natural sciences. Angela received a Master of Environmental Management from Yale University, a B.S. in Biology from the University of Richmond, and a certificate in Data Analytics from Principal Analytics Prep.

Rohit Mendadhala is a Geospatial Data Scientist and an FAA Certified Drone Pilot with over 7 years of professional experience in developing, managing, and implementing geospatial solutions at scale for organizations across a wide range of industries such as government, environmental, transportation, software, telecom, real-estate research. His core areas of expertise include Geospatial Data Analytics, Data Visualization, Spatial Analysis and Mapping, Spatial Data Science, GIS Development, Web and Enterprise GIS, Market Research and Analysis using ArcGIS and open-source geospatial platforms. He enjoys discovering underlying patterns in large datasets with a spatial context and curating answers to critical thought-provoking questions.

Shital Dhakal is a seasoned GIS professional with over seven years' experience in the field of GIS and remote sensing. He has acquired industry and research experience in North America, Europe, and Asia. Currently, he works at a San Francisco Bay Area-based start-up and helps local government to implement enterprise GIS strategies. He is a certified GIS Professional (GISP) and has an MSc from Boise State University, Idaho. When he is not playing with spatial data, writing blogs, or making maps, he can be found hiking in the Sierra Nevada and, occasionally, in the Himalayas.

Table of Contents

Preface   xiii

Part 1: Introduction to the Geospatial Data Ecosystem

1

Introduction to Geospatial Data in the Cloud   3

Introduction to cloud computing and AWS	3	People, processes, and technology are equally important	9
Storing geospatial data in the cloud	5	Cost management in the cloud	9
Building your geospatial data strategy	6	Right-sizing, simplified	10
Preventing unauthorized access	7	The elephant in the server room	10
The last mile in data consumption	7	Bird's-eye view on savings	11
Leveraging your AWS account team	8	Can't we just add another server?	11
		Additional savings at every desk	12
Geospatial data management best practices	8	Summary	13
Data – it's about both quantity and quality	9	References	13

2

Quality and Temporal Geospatial Data Concepts   15

Quality impact on geospatial data	15	Considering temporal dimensions	21
Transmission methods	17	Summary	22
Streaming data	18	References	22
Understanding file formats	18		
Normalizing data	20		

Part 2: Geospatial Data Lakes using Modern Data Architecture

3

Geospatial Data Lake Architecture   25

Modern data architecture overview	25	Data collection and ingestion layer	29
The AWS modern data architecture pillars	26	Data storage layer	33
		Data processing and transformation	34
Geospatial Data Lake	27	Data analytics and insights	37
Designing a geospatial data lake using modern data architecture	27	Data visualization and mapping	40
		Summary	41
		References	41

4

Using Geospatial Data with Amazon Redshift   43

What is Redshift?	44	Redshift geospatial support	47
Understanding Redshift partitioning	44	Launching a Redshift cluster and running a geospatial query	48
Redshift Spectrum	45		
Redshift geohashing support	46	Summary	55
Redshift AQUA	46	References	56

5

Using Geospatial Data with Amazon Aurora PostgreSQL   57

Lab prerequisites	57	Architectural considerations	78
Setting up the database	58	Summary	78
Connecting to the database	65	References	79
Installing the PostGIS extension	66		
Geospatial data loading	69		
Queries and transformations	72		

6

Serverless Options for Geospatial   81

What is serverless?   81
Serverless services   81
Object storage and serverless websites with S3   82

Geospatial applications and S3 web
hosting   82

Serverless hosting security and performance
considerations   83

Python with Lambda and API Gateway 83
Deploying your first serverless
geospatial application   84
Summary   91
References   91

7

Querying Geospatial Data with Amazon Athena   93

Setting up and configuring Athena   93
Geospatial data formats   97
WKT   97
JSON-encoded geospatial data   97

Spatial query structure   99

Spatial functions   100
AWS service integration   102
Architectural considerations   103
Summary   104
References   104

Part 3: Analyzing and Visualizing Geospatial Data in AWS

8

Geospatial Containers on AWS   107

Understanding containers   107
Scaling containers   108
Container portability   109
GDAL   109
GeoServer   110
Updating containers   110

AWS services   110

Deployment options   111

Deploying containers   111
Summary   114
References   114

9

Using Geospatial Data with Amazon EMR   115

Introducing Hadoop	115	Geospatial with EMR	117
Introduction to EMR	116	Launching EMR	118
Common Hadoop frameworks	117	Summary	126
EMRFS	117	References	126

10

Geospatial Data Analysis Using R on AWS   127

Introduction to the R geospatial data analysis ecosystem	127	Analyzing and visualizing geospatial data using RStudio	153
Setting up R and RStudio on EC2	129	Summary	156
RStudio on Amazon SageMaker	138	References	156

11

Geospatial Machine Learning with SageMaker   159

AWS ML background	159	First-time use steps	164
AWS service integration	160	Geospatial data processing	166
Common libraries and algorithms	161	Geospatial data visualization	172
Introducing Geospatial ML with SageMaker	162	Architectural considerations	174
		Summary	174
Deploying a SageMaker Geospatial example	163	References	174

12

Using Amazon QuickSight to Visualize Geospatial Data   177

Geospatial visualization background	177	Configuring Athena	181
Amazon QuickSight overview	180	Configuring QuickSight	183
Connecting to your data source	180	Visualization layout	187

Features and controls   188
Point maps   190
Filled maps   194

Putting it all together   196

Reports and collaboration   198
Summary   198
References   198

Part 4: Accessing Open Source and Commercial Platforms and Services

13

Open Data on AWS   201

What is open data?   201
Bird's-eye view   201
Modern applications   203

The Registry of Open Data on AWS   204
Requester Pays model   204

Analyzing open data   206

Using your AWS account   206
Analyzing multiple data classes   207

Federated queries with Athena   208
Open Data on AWS benefits   209
Summary   210
References   210

14

Leveraging OpenStreetMap on AWS   211

What is OpenStreetMap?   211
OSM's data structure   211
OSM benefits   214

Accessing OSM from AWS   214
Application – ski lift scout   218
The OSM community   222

Architectural considerations   222
Summary   223
References   223

15

Feature Servers and Map Servers on AWS 225

Types of servers and deployment options	226	Deploying a container on AWS with ECR and EC2	228
Capabilities and cloud integrations	226	Summary	235
		Further reading	235

16

Satellite and Aerial Imagery on AWS 237

Imagery options	237	Demonstrating satellite imagery using AWS	239
Sentinel	237		
Landsat	238	Summary	243
NAIP	238	References	243
Architectural considerations	239		

Index 245

Other Books You May Enjoy 254

Preface

This book will provide a comprehensive overview of geospatial data and analytics in the cloud. You will learn how to optimize your geospatial data asset by using the Amazon Web Services (AWS) cloud. You will be shown examples and exercises depicting how to ingest and manage geospatial data from a variety of sources using AWS services like Amazon S3, Amazon DynamoDB, Amazon RDS, Amazon Redshift, and Amazon Athena. The concepts and patterns outlined in this book can help to build a new Geographic Information System (GIS) for you and your organization. It will also be helpful to identify areas of an existing GIS that are candidates for migration to or modernization in the AWS cloud.

Each chapter will give you a basic understanding about what you can do in the cloud for a specific technical area and point you in the right direction for additional resources. The earlier chapters are general and read somewhat like a narrative. Later chapters have lab exercises and samples with prescriptive steps to walk you through how to do specific tasks. We know that everyone learns differently and sometimes it is just about knowing enough to start asking the right questions. Frank Lloyd Wright said that an expert is someone who has "stopped thinking because he 'knows.' If you are a cloud-native geospatial expert much of this book's content will be a refresher, but I invite you to read it cover to cover and you'll find some new topics and ideas. Warren Berger realized "As expertise loses its 'shelf life,' it also loses some of its value" and the AWS cloud has brought that to GIS. If you knew everything there was about creating highly available web mapping services 10 years ago, most of that expertise is due for a reboot.

We hope you appreciate the years of expertise, experimentation, failures, and successes that went into the creation of this book. The geospatial ecosphere on AWS is continually evolving, and future revisions of this title will include sections to cover new services and features that will make your life easier. Using the AWS cloud for geospatial data management and analysis provides substantial benefits over an on-premises deployment. As you reflect on your GIS environment and identify areas for improvement, we hope this book serves as a trusted guide to inspire you to build and explore. We love all forms of feedback, so please reach out if there are topics or use cases that would be particularly helpful for you and your organization.

Who this book is for

Geospatial practitioners who work primarily in local or on-premises environments are the primary audience for this book. Data scientists, analysts, engineers, surveyors, and property managers will also find the contents of this book insightful. Having a basic understanding of GIS or cloud technology is helpful, but fundamentals are explained in each chapter.

No matter who you are, you will find most of the chapters in this book helpful. The readers who will get the most out of this book are technologists that have 2-5 years of cloud and/or GIS experience. Knowledge of either cloud or GIS, but not both, will amplify the value you'll get reading this book. We don't dive too deep into either cloud or geospatial, and if you have a firm footing in either one, you're going to learn a lot. If you know how to use geospatial data to make beautiful maps but are frustrated by some of the technical limitations you face, this book is for you. Even if you didn't know that geospatial was a word until reading this book, I think the following 16 chapters will still be enjoyable and help you understand the power of analyzing geospatial data in the AWS cloud.

What this book covers

Chapter 1, Introduction to Geospatial Data in the Cloud, shows us how to work with Geospatial Data in the cloud, and the economics of storing and analyzing the data in the cloud.

Chapter 2, Quality and Temporal Geospatial Concepts, explores the different quality characteristics of geospatial data. Additionally, concepts will be presented that show how the time-specific (temporal) aspects of data can be captured and designated in the data structure.

Chapter 3, Geospatial Data Lake Architecture, talks about designing and building a Data Lake architecture to ingest, store manage, analyze, and visualize the geospatial data in AWS

Chapter 4, Using Geospatial data with Redshift, shows an overview of Amazon Redshift and how to store and analyze geospatial data using Amazon Redshift

Chapter 5, Using Geospatial Data with Amazon Aurora PostgresSQL, provides an overview of Amazon Aurora PostgreSQL along with the PostGIS extension. We will also understand how to store and analyze geospatial data using Amazon Aurora PostgreSQL with hands-on examples

Chapter 6, Serverless Options for Geospatial, provides an overview AWS serverless technologies and how to use AWS Lambda and other managed services to collect, store, and analyse geospatial data. We will also learn about event-driven mechanisms for both on-demand and scheduled workloads.

Chapter 7, Querying Geospatial Data with Amazon Athena, Amazon Athena provides scalable, robust access to a wide range of geospatial data sources on AWS. Powerful geospatial functions allow for on-the-fly analysis and transformation capabilities that can be applied in a scalable and cost-effective manner. This chapter will explore geospatial use patterns with Athena to gain insights and create new datasets.

Chapter 8, Geospatial Containers on AWS, covers what containers are and how they benefit geospatial workloads on the cloud.

Chapter 9, Using Geospatial Data with Amazon EMR, explores Elastic MapReduce (EMR). We will walk through a demo of Hadoop, EMR and visualize geospatial data using them.

Chapter 10, Geospatial Analysis using R on AWS, explores use of the R programming language to construct commands and procedures for geospatial analysis on AWS

Chapter 11, Geospatial Machine Learning with SageMaker, SageMaker is the cornerstone AWS service for statistical and machine learning computing. This chapter provides readers with step by step guidance to import, analyze, and visualize geospatial data on AWS using SageMaker

Chapter 12, Using Amazon QuickSight to Visualize Geospatial Data, delves into how geospatial data on AWS can be converted into visualizations that can be shared with others and combined with web maps and other geospatial visualizations.

Chapter 13, Open Data on AWS, Open Data on AWS offers public data made available through AWS services from across the globe. Whether directly interacting with the source or downloading for analysis and transformation, datasets on demographics, public health, industry, and environment are ready to use.

Chapter 14, Leveraging OpenStreetMap, OpenStreetMap has more crowdsourced updates than any other geospatial dataset on the planet. From roads and buildings to businesses and parks, millions of places can be found on OpenStreetMap. This chapter will show what data can be leveraged using Amazon Athena queries directly against the latest updates.

Chapter 15, Map and Feature Services on AWS, looks at tools and services available on AWS to create a durable, scalable platform optimized for the cloud.

Chapter 16, Satellite Imagery on AWS, talks about how to find and use this data and use Amazon SageMaker for incorporating near real-time machine learning into your applications.

To get the most out of this book

While neither geospatial expertise nor familiarity with the AWS cloud are prerequisites, having a technical foundation in working with spatial data will help accelerate reading and using this book. It is recommended to create an AWS account to experiment and practice using the exercises in this book.

Software/hardware covered in the book	Operating system requirements
Python 3	Windows or Linux
Structured Query Language (SQL)	Any platform
Command Line Terminal	Windows of Linux
AWS Console	Modern web browser

If you are using the digital version of this book, we advise you to type the code yourself or access the code from the book's GitHub repository (a link is available in the next section). Doing so will help you avoid any potential errors related to the copying and pasting of code.

Download the example code files

The examples used in this book will contain links or examples of code used. There is not a separate code repository provided. Any future updates or additions will be included in revisions of this book.

We also have other code bundles from our rich catalog of books and videos available at `https://github.com/PacktPublishing/`. Check them out!

Conventions used

There are a number of text conventions used throughout this book.

Code in text: Indicates code words in text, database table names, folder names, filenames, file extensions, pathnames, dummy URLs, user input, and Twitter handles. Here is an example: " This lets you run a command like `spark.read().text(s3://myfile);` and Hadoop can natively read that file as if it was local."

A block of code is set as follows:

```
#!/bin/bash
sudo python3 -m pip install jupyter
mkdir /home/hadoop/.jupyter
touch /home/hadoop/.jupyter/jupyter_notebook_config.py
```

When we wish to draw your attention to a particular part of a code block, the relevant lines or items are set in bold:

```
echo "c.NotebookApp.port = 8887" >> /home/hadoop/.jupyter/jupyter_
notebook_config.py
/usr/local/bin/jupyter notebook --config /home/hadoop/.jupyter/
jupyter_notebook_config.py
```

Bold: Indicates a new term, an important word, or words that you see onscreen. For instance, words in menus or dialog boxes appear in bold. Here is an example: " Click **Create Cluster** in the Top Right Corner."

> Tips or important notes
> Appear like this.

Get in touch

Feedback from our readers is always welcome.

General feedback: If you have questions about any aspect of this book, email us at `customercare@packtpub.com` and mention the book title in the subject of your message.

Errata: Although we have taken every care to ensure the accuracy of our content, mistakes do happen. If you have found a mistake in this book, we would be grateful if you would report this to us. Please visit `www.packtpub.com/support/errata` and fill in the form.

Piracy: If you come across any illegal copies of our works in any form on the internet, we would be grateful if you would provide us with the location address or website name. Please contact us at `copyright@packt.com` with a link to the material.

If you are interested in becoming an author: If there is a topic that you have expertise in and you are interested in either writing or contributing to a book, please visit `authors.packtpub.com`.

Share Your Thoughts

Once you've read *Geospatial Data Analytics on AWS*, we'd love to hear your thoughts! Scan the QR code below to go straight to the Amazon review page for this book and share your feedback.

`https://packt.link/r/1-804-61382-7`

Your review is important to us and the tech community and will help us make sure we're delivering excellent quality content.

Download a free PDF copy of this book

Thanks for purchasing this book!

Do you like to read on the go but are unable to carry your print books everywhere?

Is your eBook purchase not compatible with the device of your choice?

Don't worry, now with every Packt book you get a DRM-free PDF version of that book at no cost.

Read anywhere, any place, on any device. Search, copy, and paste code from your favorite technical books directly into your application.

The perks don't stop there, you can get exclusive access to discounts, newsletters, and great free content in your inbox daily

Follow these simple steps to get the benefits:

1. Scan the QR code or visit the link below

https://packt.link/free-ebook/9781804613825

2. Submit your proof of purchase

3. That's it! We'll send your free PDF and other benefits to your email directly

Part 1: Introduction to the Geospatial Data Ecosystem

In this part we will learn how to work with Geospatial Data in the cloud, and the economics of storing and analyzing the data in the cloud.

This part has the following chapters:

- *Chapter 1, Introduction to Geospatial Data in the Cloud, shows us how to work with Geospatial Data in the cloud,* and the economics of storing and analyzing the data in the cloud.

- *Chapter 2, Quality and Temporal Geospatial Concepts,* explores the different quality characteristics of geospatial data. Additionally, concepts will be presented that show how the time-specific (temporal) aspects of data can be captured and designated in the data structure.

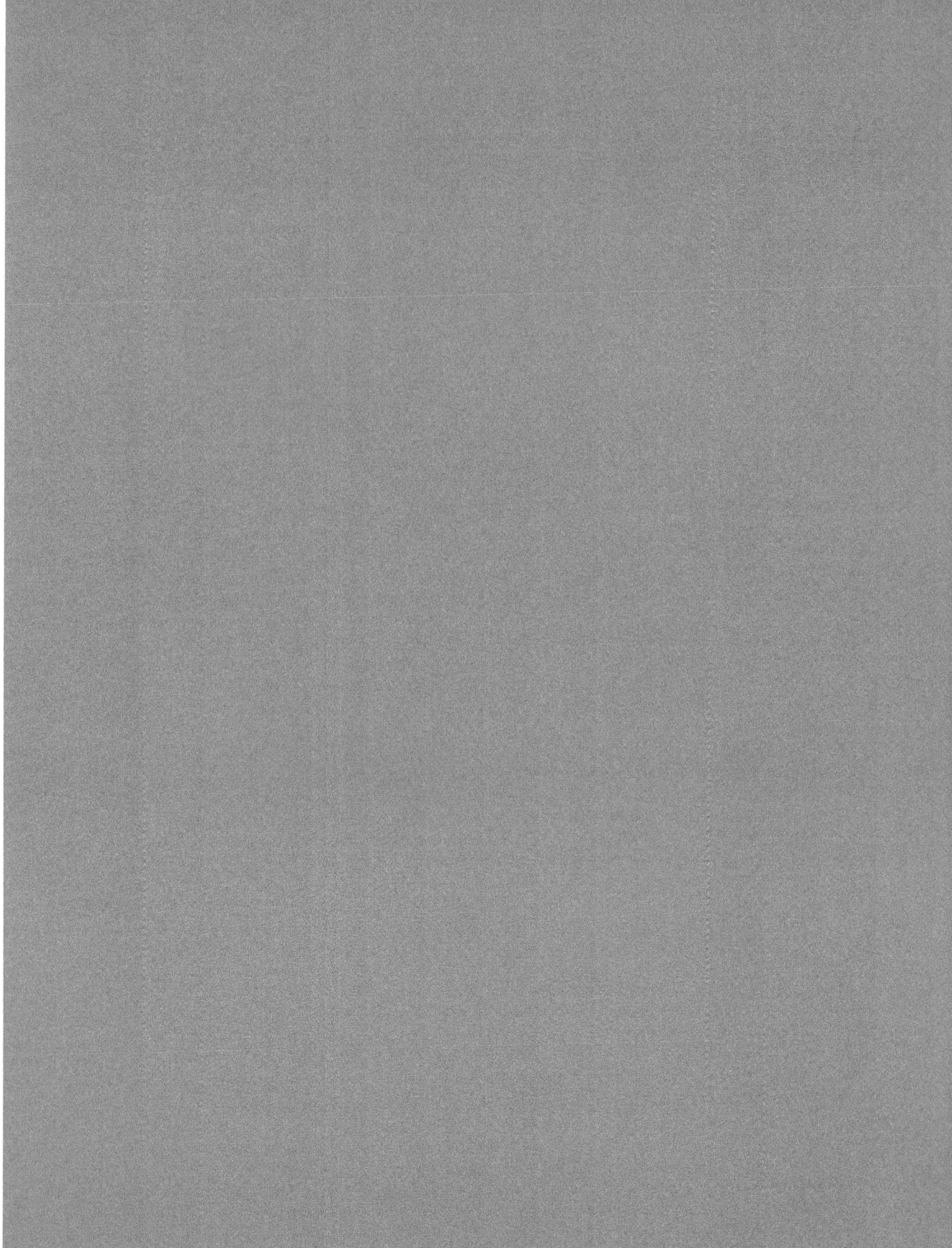

1

Introduction to Geospatial Data in the Cloud

This book is divided into four parts that will walk you through key concepts, tools, and techniques for dealing with geospatial data. Part 1 sets the foundation for the entire book, establishing key ideas that provide synergy with subsequent parts. Each chapter is further subdivided into topics that dive deep into a specific subject. This introductory chapter of Part 1 will cover the following topics:

- Introduction to cloud computing and AWS

- Storing geospatial data in the cloud

- Building your geospatial data strategy

- Geospatial data management best practices

- Cost management in the cloud

Introduction to cloud computing and AWS

You are most likely familiar with the benefits that geospatial analysis can provide. Governmental entities, corporations, and other organizations routinely solve complex, location-based problems with the help of geospatial computing. While paper maps are still around, most use cases for geospatial data have evolved to live in the digital world. We can now create maps faster and draw more geographical insights from data than at any point in history. This phenomenon has been made possible by blending the expertise of geospatial practitioners with the power of **Geographical Information Systems (GIS)**. Critical thinking and higher-order analysis can be done by humans while computers handle the monotonous data processing and rendering tasks. As the geospatial community continues to refine the balance of which jobs require manual effort and which can be handled by computers, we are collectively improving our ability to understand our world.

Geospatial computing has been around for decades, but the last 10 years have seen a dramatic shift in the capabilities and computing power available to practitioners. The emergence of the cloud as a fundamental building block of technical systems has offered needle-moving opportunities in compute, storage, and analytical capabilities. In addition to a revolution in the infrastructure behind GIS systems, the cloud has expanded the optionality in every layer of the technical stack. Common problems such as running out of disk space, long durations of geospatial processing jobs, limited data availability, and difficult collaboration across teams can be things of the past. AWS provides solutions to these problems and more, and in this book, we will describe, dissect, and provide examples of how you can do this for your organization.

Cloud computing provides the ability to rapidly experiment with new tools and processing techniques that would never be possible using a fixed set of compute resources. Not only are new capabilities available and continually improving but your team will also have more time to learn and use these new technologies with the time saved in creating, configuring, and maintaining the environment. The undifferenced heavy lifting of managing geospatial storage devices, application servers, geodatabases, and data flows can be replaced with time spent analyzing, understanding, and visualizing the data. Traditional *this or that* technical trade-off decisions are no longer binary proposals. Your organization can use the right tool for each job, and blend as many tools and features into your environment as is appropriate for your requirements. By paying for the precise amount of resources you use in AWS, it is possible to break free from restrictive, punitive, and time-limiting licensing situations. In some cases, the amount of an AWS compute resource you use is measured and charged down to the millisecond, so you literally don't pay for a second of unused time. If a team infrequently needs to leverage a capability, such as a monthly data processing job, this can result in substantial cost savings by eliminating idle virtual machines and supporting technical resources. If cost savings are not your top concern, the same proportion of your budget can be dedicated to more capable hardware that delivers dramatically reduced timeframes compared to limited compute environments.

The global infrastructure of AWS allows you to position data in the best location to minimize latency, providing the best possible performance. Powerful replication and caching technologies can be used to minimize wait time and allow robust cataloging and characterization of your geospatial assets. The global flexibility of your GIS environment is further enabled with the use of innovative end user compute options. Virtual desktop services in AWS allow organizations to keep the geospatial processing close to the data for maximum performance, even if the user is geographically distanced from both. AWS and the cloud have continued to evolve and provide never-before-seen capabilities in geospatial power and flexibility. Over the course of this book, we will examine what these concepts are, how they work, and how you can put them to work in your environment.

Now that we have learned the story of cloud computing on AWS, let's check out how we can implement geospatial data there.

Storing geospatial data in the cloud

As you learn about the possibilities for storing geospatial data in the cloud, it may seem daunting due to the number of options available. Many AWS customers experiment with **Amazon Simple Storage Service (S3)** for geospatial data storage as their first project. Relational databases, NoSQL databases, and caching options commonly follow in the evolution of geospatial technical architectures. General GIS data storage best practices still apply to the cloud, so much of the knowledge that practitioners have gained over the years directly applies to geospatial data management on AWS. Familiar GIS file formats that work well in S3 include the following:

- Shapefiles (`.shp`, `.shx`, `.dbf`, `.prj`, and others)
- File geodatabases (`.gdb`)
- Keyhole Markup Language (`.kml`)
- Comma-Separated Values (`.csv`)
- Geospatial JavaScript Object Notation (`.geojson`)
- Geostationary Earth Orbit Tagged Image File Format (`.tiff`)

The physical location of data is still important for latency-sensitive workloads. Formats and organization of data can usually remain unchanged when moving to S3 to limit the impact of migrations. Spatial indexes and use-based access patterns will dramatically improve the performance and ability of your system to deliver the desired capabilities to your users.

Relational databases have long been the cornerstone of most enterprise GIS environments. This is especially true for vector datasets. AWS offers the most comprehensive set of relational database options with flexible sizing and architecture to meet your specific requirements. For customers looking to migrate geodatabases to the cloud with the least amount of environmental change, **Amazon Elastic Compute Cloud (EC2)** virtual machine instances provide a similar capability to what is commonly used in on-premises data centers. Each database server can be instantiated on the specific operating system that is used by the source server. Using EC2 with **Amazon Elastic Block Store (EBS)** network-attached storage provides the highest level of control and flexibility. Each server is created by specifying the amount of CPU, memory, and network throughput desired. **Relational database management system (RDBMS)** software can be manually installed on the EC2 instance, or an **Amazon Machine Image (AMI)** for the particular use case can be selected from the AWS catalog to remove manual steps from the process. While this option provides the highest degree of flexibility, it also requires the most database configuration and administration knowledge.

Many customers find it useful to leverage **Amazon Relational Database Service (RDS)** to establish database clusters and instances for their GIS environments. RDS can be leveraged by creating full-featured database Microsoft SQL Server, Oracle, PostgreSQL, MySQL, or MariaDB clusters. AWS allows the selection of specific instance types to focus on memory or compute optimization in a variety of configurations. Multiple **Availability Zone (AZ)**-enabled databases can be created to establish fault tolerance or improve performance. Using RDS dramatically simplifies database administration, and decreases the time required to select, provision, and configure your geospatial database using the specific technical parameters to meet the business requirements.

Amazon Aurora provides an open source path to highly capable and performant relational databases. PostgreSQL or MySQL environments can be created with specific settings for the desired capabilities. Although this may mean converting data from a source format, such as Microsoft SQL Server or Oracle, the overall cost savings and simplified management make this an attractive option to modernize and right-size any geospatial database.

In addition to standard relational database options, AWS provides other services to manage and use geospatial data. **Amazon Redshift** is the fastest and most widely used cloud data warehouse and supports geospatial data through the `geometry` data type. Users can query spatial data in Redshift's built-in SQL functions to find the distance between two points, interrogate polygon relationships, and provide other location insights into their data. **Amazon DynamoDB** is a fully managed, key-value NoSQL database with an SLA of up to 99.999% availability. For organizations leveraging MongoDB, **Amazon DocumentDB** provides a fully managed option for simplified instantiation and management. Finally, AWS offers the **Amazon OpenSearch Service** for petabyte-scale data storage, search, and visualization.

The best part is that you don't have to choose a single option for your geospatial environment. Often, companies find that different workloads benefit from having the ability to choose the most appropriate data landscape. Combining **Infrastructure as a Service** (**IaaS**) workloads with fully managed databases and modern databases is not only possible but a signature of a well-architected geospatial environment. Transactional systems may benefit from relational geodatabases, while mobile applications may be more aligned with NoSQL data stores. When you operate in a world of consumption-based resources, there is no downside to using the most appropriate data store for each workload. Having familiarity with the cloud options for storing geospatial data is crucial in strategic planning, which we will cover in the next topic.

Building your geospatial data strategy

One of the most important concepts to consider in your geospatial data strategy is the amount of change you are willing to accept in your technical infrastructure. This does not apply to new systems, but most organizations will have a treasure trove of geospatial data already. While lifting and shifting on-premises workloads to the cloud is advantageous, adapting your architecture to the cloud will amplify benefits in agility, resiliency, and cost optimization. For example, 95% of AWS customers elect to use open source geospatial databases as part of their cloud migration. This data conversion process, from vendor relational databases such as Oracle and Microsoft SQL Server to open source options such as PostgreSQL, enjoys a high degree of compatibility. This is an example of a simple change that can be made to eliminate significant license usage costs when migrating to the cloud. Simple changes such as these provide immediate and tangible benefits to geospatial practitioners in cloud architectures. Often, the same capabilities can be provided in AWS for a significantly reduced cost profile when comparing the cloud to on-premises GIS architectures.

All the same concepts and technologies you and your team are used to when operating an on-premises environment exist on AWS. Stemming from the consumption-based pricing model and broad set of EC2 instances available, AWS can offer a much more flexible model for the configuration and consumption of compute resources. Application servers used in geospatial environments can be migrated directly by selecting the platform, operating system, version, and dependencies appropriate for the given workload. Additional consideration should be given in this space to containerization where feasible. Leveraging containers in your server architecture can speed up environment migrations and provide additional scaling options.

Preventing unauthorized access

A key part of building your geospatial data strategy is determining the structure and security of your data. AWS **Identity and Access Management** (**IAM**) serves as the foundation for defining authorization and authentication mechanisms in your environment. **Single Sign-On** (**SSO**) is commonly used to integrate with existing directories to leverage pre-existing hierarchies and permission methodologies. The flexibility of AWS allows you to bring the existing security constructs while expanding the ability to monitor, audit, and rectify security concerns in your GIS environment. It is highly recommended to encrypt most data; however, the value of encrypting unaltered public data can be debated. Keys should be regularly rotated and securely handled in accordance with any existing policies or guidelines from your organization.

As changes take place within your architecture, alerts and notifications provide critical insight to stewards of the environment. **Amazon Simple Notification Service** (**SNS**) can be integrated with any AWS service to send emails or text messages to the appropriate teams or individuals for optimized performance and security. Budgets and cost management alerts are native to AWS, making it easy to manage multiple accounts and environments based on your organization's key performance indicators. Part of developing a cloud geospatial data strategy should be to internally ask where data issues are going unnoticed or not being addressed. By creating business rules, thresholds, and alerts, these data anomalies can notify administrators when specific areas within your data environment need attention.

The last mile in data consumption

Some commonly overlooked aspects of a geospatial data management strategy are the desktop end user tools that are necessary to manage and use the environment. Many GIS environments are dependent on high-powered desktop machines used by specialists. The graphics requirements for visualizing spatial data into a consumable image can be high, and the data throughput must support fluid panning and zooming through the data. Complications can arise when the user has a high-latency connection to the data. Many companies learned this the hard way when remote workers during COVID tried to continue business as usual from home. Traditional geospatial landscapes were designed for the power users to be in the office. Gigabit connectivity was a baseline requirement, and network outages meant that highly paid specialists were unable to do their work.

Virtual desktops have evolved, and continue to evolve, to provide best-in-class experiences for power users that are not co-located with their data. Part of a well-architected geospatial data management strategy is to store once, use many times. This principle takes a backseat when the performance when used is unacceptable. A short-term fix is to cache the data locally, but that brings a host of other cost and concurrency problems. Virtual desktops or **Desktop-as-a-Service** (**DaaS**) address this problem by keeping the compute close to the data. The user can be thousands of miles away and still enjoy a fluid graphical experience. **Amazon WorkSpaces** and **Amazon AppStream** provide this capability in the cloud. WorkSpaces provides a complete desktop environment for Windows or Linux that can be configured exactly as your specialists have today. AppStream adds desktop shortcuts to a specialist's local desktop and streams the application visuals as a native application. Having access to the native geospatial data management tools as part of a cloud-based architecture results in a more robust and cohesive overall strategy.

Leveraging your AWS account team

AWS provides corporations and organizational customers with a dedicated account team to help navigate the details of using cloud services. When it comes to migrating existing geospatial data, numerous incentive programs exist. Your AWS account team can help you identify areas where credits and other strategic incentives may apply to your situation. In addition to financial assistance, AWS has developed a robust methodology and processes for migrating data and workloads to the cloud. The **AWS Migration Accelerate Program** (**MAP**) draws on experience gained from thousands of enterprise customer migrations. MAP educates customers on the methodology, tools, partners, professional services, and investments that are available to customers. Whether AWS or a **systems integrator** (**SI**) partner provides the guidance, it is highly recommended to leverage this experience in your cloud data management strategy.

Now that we've covered the strategic side of things, let's look at some best practices you can incorporate into your tactics for establishing a geospatial cloud landscape.

Geospatial data management best practices

The single most important consideration in a data management strategy is a deep understanding of the use cases the data intends to support. Data ingestion workflows need to eliminate bottlenecks in write performance. Geospatial transformation jobs need access to powerful computational resources, and the ability to cache large amounts of data temporarily in memory. Analytics and visualization concerns require quick searching and the retrieval of geospatial data. These core disciplines of geospatial data management have benefitted from decades of fantastic work done by the community, which has driven AWS to create pathways to implement these best practices in the cloud.

Data – it's about both quantity and quality

A long-standing anti-pattern of data management is to rely primarily on folder structures or table names to infer meaning about datasets. Having naming standards is a good thing, but it is not a substitute for a well-formed data management strategy. Naming conventions invariably change over time and are never fully able to account for the future evolution of data and the resulting taxonomy. In addition to the physical structure of the data, instrumenting your resources with predefined tags and metadata becomes crucial in cloud architectures. This is because AWS inherently provides capabilities to specify more information about your geospatial data, and many of the convenient tools and services are built to consume and understand these designations. Enriching your geospatial data with the appropriate metadata is a best practice in the cloud as it is for any GIS.

Another best practice is to quantify your data quality. Simply having a hunch that your data is *good* or *bad* is not sufficient. Mature organizations not only quantitatively describe the quality of their data with continually assessed scores but also track the scores to ensure that the quality of critical data improves over time. For example, if you have a dataset of addresses, it is important to know what percentage of the addresses are invalid. Hopefully, that percentage is 0, but very rarely is that the case. More important than having 100% accurate data is having confidence in what the quality of a given dataset is… today. Neighborhoods are being built every day. Separate buildings are torn down to create apartment complexes. Perfect data today may not be perfect data tomorrow, so the most important aspect of data quality is real-time transparency. A threshold should be set to determine the acceptable data quality based on the criticality of the dataset. High-priority geospatial data should require a high bar for quality, while infrequently used low-impact datasets don't require the same focus. Categorizing your data based on importance allows you to establish guidelines by category. This approach will allow finite resources to be directed toward the most pressing concerns to maximize value.

People, processes, and technology are equally important

Managing geospatial data successfully in the cloud relies on more than just the technology tools offered by AWS. Designating appropriate roles and responsibilities in your organization ensures that your cloud ecosystem will be sustainable. Avoid single points of failure with respect to skills or tribal knowledge of your environment. Having at least a primary and secondary person to cover each area will add resiliency to your people operations. Not only will this allow you to have more flexibility in coverage and task assignment but it also creates training opportunities within your team and allows team members to continually learn and improve their skills.

Next, let's move on to talk about how to stretch your geospatial dollars to do more with less.

Cost management in the cloud

The easiest benefit to realize in a cloud-based geospatial environment is cost savings. While increased agility, hardened resiliency, improved performance, and reduced maintenance effort are also key benefits, they generally take some time to fully realize. Cost reductions and increased flexibility are immediately apparent when you leverage AWS for geospatial workloads. Charges for AWS resources are continuously visible in the AWS console, and the amount of expenditure can be adjusted in real time based on your business needs. In this section of the chapter, we will examine cost management tactics for the following areas:

- Hardware provisioning
- Geodatabase servers
- File-based data
- Geospatial application servers
- End user compute services

Right-sizing, simplified

I recall many times in my career when I consternated for days over which server to buy. Buying a server is a big decision, and buying the wrong one can have real consequences. What if we're more successful than projected and our user count doubles? What if we have more data than estimated? What if my processes consume more resources than expected? These are just a few of the questions that compel organizations to buy bigger servers than necessary. Of course, it makes sense to plan for the future, but what doesn't make sense is paying for things you don't use. This problem is only amplified when you bring resiliency and **disaster recovery** (**DR**) into the picture. I've designed enterprise GIS systems that have completely dormant standby instances for very expensive servers. In an on-premises data center, your "just-in-case" hardware has to be paid for even though it is not used. AWS provides a full range of DR capabilities without additional license or hardware overhead costs.

The elephant in the server room

One of the largest costs in a geospatial environment for many organizations is the relational geodatabase infrastructure. Hefty enterprise license costs, expensive hardware, and dedicated time from a specialist **database administrator** (**DBA**) and supporting resources add up quickly. Remember that having a cloned standby environment for critical systems may be required for production workloads. Power, cooling, and networking charges apply for on-premises environments.

A typical concern surrounding RDBMS migration to the cloud is performance, specifically as it relates to scale. The same week that I began working at AWS, a multi-year effort across all Amazon companies was wrapping up. All of Amazon's internal databases were modernized, many of which were converted from Oracle. Alexa, Amazon Prime, Amazon Prime Video, Amazon Fresh, Kindle, Amazon Music, Audible, Shopbop, Twitch, and Zappos were the customer-facing brands that were part of the migration, resulting in Amazon turning off its final Oracle database in October 2019. The scale of internal databases at Amazon is mind-boggling, but the migration of 75 petabytes was realized with little or no downtime. Resulting reductions in database costs were over 60%, coupled with latency performance improvements of 40%. This project was enormous in scale, and the cost savings have been enormous as well.

Bird's-eye view on savings

Raster data is being collected with increasing frequency and resolution. Sentinel-2 provides satellite imagery data all over the globe within the most recent 5 days. The quality of the images continues to improve, as does the file size. Storing long histories of file-based data is commonplace as historical images and data may someday be needed. Corporations may have legal obligations to retain the data. Whatever the reason, storing data generates costs. Those costs increase as the size and volume of data increase. Raster geospatial data is notoriously large and commonly stored in enterprise filesystems. When organizations have multiple copies of data for different purposes or departments, the sustained long-term expenses can be exorbitant.

The costs associated with storing large volumes of file-based data in AWS are completely under the customer's control. Amazon S3 is simple to use and compatible with any geospatial data format. In fact, some formats that we'll talk more about later in this book perform best in the cloud. Consolidating geospatial data to a platform with fine-grained life cycle options can be a cost game-changer. The data for both performance and cost can be optimized at the same time using an S3 Lifecycle configuration. These storage classification rules will price data differently based on the usage pattern. A great example of geospatial data is **Extract, Transform, and Load** (ETL) staging datasets. Processing jobs may leave behind transient datasets as large as the source data, and possibly multiple copies of them for each process run. Historical data may be accessed frequently for dates within the most recent month, but rarely for older data. Another great use case for an S3 Lifecycle configuration is data that is meant to be archived initially for the lowest long-term storage cost.

Amazon S3 provides automated rules that move files between various pricing models. The rules are customer-defined and can be changed at any time in the AWS console. Using just a few simple clicks, it is possible to realize massive storage cost savings. Most geospatial data brought into AWS starts in the **S3 Standard** storage class. This feature-rich, general-purpose option provides 99.999999999% (11 9s) of durability for a few cents per GB per month. While this is affordable, the **S3 Glacier Deep Archive** storage class is designed for long-term archives accessed infrequently for just 0.00099 per GB per month. IT backups of geospatial databases and filesystems are prime candidates for S3 Glacier Deep Archive. Details of each storage class in between, associated use cases, and pricing are available on the S3 pricing page. There is also an "easy button" to optimize your S3 Lifecycle using **Intelligent-Tiering**. The key takeaway is that file-based storage, mainly raster geospatial data, can be stored in the cloud for a fraction of on-premises costs. When it comes to geospatial cost management strategy, file-based data storage classification can yield tremendous cost savings.

Can't we just add another server?

Application servers are the workhorse of a robust GIS architecture. Specialized servers deliver web map services, imagery, geoprocessing, and many other compute-intensive capabilities. While the number of application servers in an architecture generally outnumbers database servers, the storage and networking performance requirements tend to be lower. These are cheaper machines that perform specific tasks. Horizontal scaling is commonly used by providing multiple servers that can each execute independent, parallel tasks. Resource demands and traffic patterns tend to be erratic and spiky, resulting in underutilized CPU and GPU cores.

Launching geospatial application server capabilities on AWS can be done in a number of ways, but the most common is EC2 migration. If you have a geoprocessing server that supports horizontal scaling, it may be possible to add processing nodes in AWS to your existing server pool. Over time, you can adjust the utilization of servers based on the requirements and cost profile. Cloud servers can be deactivated when not in use to stop compute charges, and the EC2 spot pricing option provides a flexible way to get instances at a discount of up to 90% compared to on-demand prices. **AWS Auto Scaling** provides multiple options to control how and when servers start up and shut down based on demand requirements. If you have a server dedicated to a monthly process that takes 8 hours, 91% of your server capacity is unutilized. Understanding the steady-state processing profile of your geospatial environment allows you to identify where cost-saving compute opportunities exist. By leveraging AWS applied to these compute profiles, you'll be able to get more processing done in less time, and at a lower cost.

Additional savings at every desk

I worked in the energy technology industry since before Y2K was in the headlines. One interesting cultural phenomenon I've seen in the workplace occurs among geoscientists, engineers, technical SMEs, and others who do specialized compute-intensive work. The power of your work machine is a badge of honor, where the highest regarded professionals are awarded more CPUs or an additional monitor. While this philosophy attracted the best petrophysicists, geologists, and other specialists, it generated significant costs. Infrequently utilized workstations sat idle, not returning any value for their purchase. This scenario is highly likely in volatile industries where layoffs are frequent and contractor usage is high. Imagine the waste if the machine is turned on 24/7, even if it is only used for a few hours a week.

DaaS provides a flexible cost-saving solution for underutilized workstations. By provisioning your workstation in the cloud, you can take advantage of larger amounts of processing power and only pay for the hours consumed. Windows license portability applies in some cases, and you can select configurations such as the GraphicsPro bundle, which packs a whopping 16 vCPU with an additional GPU, 8 GiB of video memory, and 122 GiB of general memory. At the time of writing, that machine would cost around $100 per month if only used for a few hours of monthly geospatial analysis (including the Windows license). Additional savings can be realized through reduced IT administration. AWS manages the hardware and service management, leaving the customer in charge of machine images, applications, and security administration.

As described in the preceding paragraph, the AWS cloud provides powerful and flexible services that help costs align with your geospatial activities. It all starts by building the right cloud strategy and establishing an empowered team to discover and operationalize digital innovation. Endorsement or sponsorship from forward-looking executives has proven to be correlated with success in cloud technology projects. There are new ways to get things done in the cloud that can be a fraction of the cost of traditional methods. All of these concepts factor into your evergreen geospatial computing strategy and result in better geospatial data and insights delivered to your end users.

Summary

Throughout this overview chapter, you have learned how the cloud can be a beneficial approach or addition to your geospatial environment. The intent of this chapter is to outline key concepts that will help you be successful in creating a technical landscape in AWS for geospatial analytics. We've covered high-level technologies that will be further explained with examples later in this book. In *Chapter 2, Quality and Temporal Geospatial Data Concepts*, we will finish up Part 1 with a deeper look into the importance of high-quality geospatial data over time. More specifically, we will explain how the AWS cloud removes barriers to working with the richest, most complete geospatial datasets.

References

- *Evolution of Geospatial Workloads on AWS* (2017): https://www.youtube.com/watch?v=0Q27eYt5QH8&t=407s

- *Migration Complete – Amazon's Consumer Business Just Turned off its Final Oracle Database* (2019): https://aws.amazon.com/blogs/aws/migration-complete-amazons-consumer-business-just-turned-off-its-final-oracle-database/

- *Amazon S3 Pricing* (2022): https://aws.amazon.com/s3/pricing

- *Amazon EC2 Spot Instances* (2022): https://aws.amazon.com/ec2/spot

- *What is AWS Auto Scaling? And When Should You Use It?* (2021): https://www.cloudzero.com/blog/aws-auto-scaling

Quality and Temporal Geospatial Data Concepts

Geospatial data is everywhere, in every industry, and in nearly every file format. The good news is that this broad range of data can be stored, transformed, analyzed, and visualized on AWS. In this chapter, we will talk about some of the different scenarios, file formats, workflows, and data normalization challenges that are common in geospatial data. Whether you are in oil and gas, healthcare, retail, power and utility, agriculture, or mining, to name a few, you have probably already done some work with GIS data. GIS data is ubiquitous in everyday applications, so it's highly likely you have worked with geospatial data and didn't even know it. In this chapter, you will learn about the importance of quality and time dimensions in your geospatial data through the following topics:

- Quality impact on geospatial data
- Transmission methods
- Streaming data
- Understanding file formats
- Normalizing data
- Considering temporal dimensions

Quality impact on geospatial data

Historically, high-fidelity geospatial data has been challenging to acquire and use. In theory, everyone would agree that the highest-quality data is ideal. In practice, data transfer bandwidth and other technical limitations often handicap initiatives from using the highest-quality geospatial data. An important mindset that should be adopted when using geospatial data in the cloud is that you do not need to sacrifice data quality to keep your projects within budget. Throughout this book, we will show ways in which you can have it all: massive amounts of high-quality geospatial data and a reasonable, controllable cost profile.

A common scenario where data quality can be tainted is a loss of precision in coordinate values. Whether done intentionally to save bytes or accidentally due to repeated transformation, latitude and longitude data tends to become less accurate the more it is used and shared. Using five decimal points of precision instead of eight is never going to provide a more accurate description of a location on Earth. Sometimes, organizations are tempted to make this trade-off in order to save on disk space or reduce the time it takes to move geospatial data from one place to another. The diagram in *Figure 2.1* shows how significantly the accuracy changes when removing a few decimal points. For example, moving from eight to five drops your accuracy from 1 millimeter to 1 meter; 1 meter might be fine for ship navigation, but wouldn't work for BIM integrations or Building Information Management where CAD-level drawings are imported into geospatial software.

Accuracy versus decimal places

decimal places	degrees	distance
0	1.0	111 km
1	0.1	11.1 km
2	0.01	1.11 km
3	0.001	111 m
4	0.0001	11.1 m
5	0.00001	1.11 m
6	0.000001	0.111 m
7	0.0000001	1.11 cm
8	0.00000001	1.11 mm

Figure 2.1 – Accuracy for each number of decimal places

So, exactly how many digits of precision should you target in your geospatial coordinate data? The answer is largely dependent on the accuracy that is required by your intended use. If you are tracking general address locations, four decimals may be enough to identify each land parcel. A good frame of reference to keep in mind is that four decimal places of precision will be sufficient to differentiate one tract of land from another. This is generally the accuracy recorded by common GPS devices. Adding one additional decimal place of precision to capture five numbers after the decimal point will let you identify individual trees or buildings. Detailed lines and polygons for features such as local municipal boundaries or roads will benefit from having six digits of precision. Eight-digit precision is extremely accurate, but not often within the technical capabilities of data-gathering equipment, as this range is only obtainable by high-precision, survey-grade devices.

Transmission methods

An important topic we should touch on is transmission methods for transmitting data from remote operations into your data center or cloud. There are several mediums and methods, and each has pros, cons, and varied characteristics. A common scenario is if you have a GPS tracker on a truck or a ship; as your asset moves around the world, it streams its coordinates back to your system. It might even be a piece of hardware with multiple sensors such as GPS, temperature, vibration, and maybe different atmospheric readings all sending data at a specified frequency. An example of this could be some type of weather balloon or a tracker used to track endangered species.

When you have sensors deployed in the field, the common network solutions are Wi-Fi, LoRaWAN, cellular, and satellite. Wi-Fi is generally the cheapest and most effective solution but isn't always an option in certain environments. Some environments, depending on building materials, can be difficult for Wi-Fi to penetrate and get a strong signal to all of your sensors. Wi-Fi is a fairly common method used in many urban locations, even when the area might have partial dead spots. When you start to get to the city scale, you see more sensors start to switch to cellular and LoRaWAN. Cellular is more expensive but can handle high-bandwidth applications and even have more availability and range compared to LoRaWAN, given the existing cellular infrastructure deployed. It's also beneficial for sensors that are highly mobile in cars, trucks, and low-altitude aviation.

LoRaWAN is cheaper by comparison, but, because of its low network throughput and shared bus, the use cases outside of sensors that just wake up and send their current readings have seen limited adoption. More vendors are looking to push software updates **over the air** (**OTA**), which, depending on the package size, can consume a lot of LoRaWAN resources. This is especially pertinent when you are updating thousands of devices. However, I'm still a believer in LoRaWAN and am hoping to see more expansion of citywide LoRaWAN deployments. One area where LoRaWAN has an advantage is battery consumption. LoRaWAN receivers, combined with the low processing power of the MQTT protocol, which we will talk a bit about shortly, can create very energy-efficient solutions. When you have a sensor deployed in hard-to-reach areas, you may use a small battery to power the appliance. It's not uncommon to have an appliance with just a sensor and a battery run for upward of a year off that single battery.

Lastly, some very remote operations only have the option to use satellite connections. These are the most expensive solutions but provide an unparalleled range; even the most remote parts of the planet can be accessed through satellite communication. These solutions also have varying network speeds, from a low throughput of couple of kilobytes per second to even high-speed connections in the 10s to 100s of megabytes per second, depending on the satellite provider and where on the planet you are in relation to the satellites. With the expansion of **low Earth orbit** (**LEO**) satellites for data communications, this may become increasingly accessible and cost-effective in the fullness of time.

Streaming data

One type of data that is becoming increasingly prevalent in GIS data is IoT data. IoT data is closely integrated with geospatial data and has had a major boom in adoption and implementation. All of these IoT sensors from farm equipment, medical sensors, pressure sensors from pipes and various tanks, and voltage, vibration, and temperature sensors are streaming in their coordinates and timestamps, also known as their spatiotemporal attributes.

I think it's important to point out that there are various forms of streaming data, and there is a lot of confusion around real time. I have yet to see a formal definition of what constitutes real-time data, but it seems the general consensus is that real time is streaming data that is actionable within its frequency. For power and electric sensors, that might mean nanoseconds to respond, but in other sectors, that could mean milliseconds to seconds to even minutes for disaster response and public safety scenarios. Generally, anything above a few minutes is typically referred to as near real time. Across industries, we don't always have access to network mediums conducive to real time and near real time. Some of these remote operations, which rely on satellite connectivity or remote sensors that cannot always be serviced in a timely manner, may only update their data on an hourly or daily basis. These sensors may even lose connectivity for long periods of time, but we still need the capability to query them to get their latest known state. Well, good news: AWS has a service for that! We will dive into that in a later chapter, but services such as **IoT Device Shadow** will record the last known state of a device and respond to queries on behalf of that device.

Now that we have the frequency of streaming data out of the way, we can start to talk about mechanisms for streaming. An up-and-coming protocol in the IoT world is MQTT, which not many SCADA systems are using today, but most new applications and deployments are. It's a lightweight protocol specifically designed for low-power sensors that are deployed in remote areas. Not only are they conservative in terms of battery resources but they are also conservative in terms of network resources. It has a simple **Quality of Service (QOS)** capability so that it can transmit and retransmit data if the original packets did not reach their destination, without all of the protocol overhead of something such as HTTP/S. AWS typically will deploy a Greengrass instance to bridge the gap between SCADA systems with MQTT to transmit the data back to AWS. This software is very lightweight and easily runs on hardware such as a Raspberry Pi.

Understanding file formats

Now, let's talk a bit about the different data formats used in these workflows. GIS is still consumed with the ubiquitous shapefile, but there are a lot of up-and-coming big data formats with promising potential. Shapefiles work great on AWS and Redshift, which is an AWS-managed data warehouse service that actually has full support to ingest shapefiles natively. This is an incredibly powerful way to work with geospatial data in shapefiles. You can easily script ETL jobs to run on AWS so that when a shapefile is uploaded to S3, our simple object storage service, S3 triggers an event, and those shapefiles are picked up and ingested into Redshift for processing. The shapefiles are then immediately queryable and available to other analytic applications and services.

Next to shapefiles, I am seeing JSON and GeoJSON as preferred formats. Many users are familiar with the easy-to-read and write JSON syntax. There has been some standardization done in the geospatial industry to create a GeoJSON format, which makes working with geospatial data in JSON even easier. The main benefit of JSON is its ease of use for user interaction. It also allows for nearly unlimited metadata or attributes to be added to an object. Another benefit is that because the file is text-based in nature, many applications are able to read and modify the file. Updating a GeoJSON file is as easy as opening the file in Notepad and doing a find-and-replace, or manually typing in and adding fields. The text representation, however, can also be somewhat of a drawback. GeoJSON files are much larger than their binary alternatives such as Parquet, AVRO, and ORC, which I'll talk about next.

This SQL code snippet shows the creation of a geospatially enabled table from a text-based GeoJSON object (see `https://docs.aws.amazon.com/athena/latest/ug/geospatial-example-queries.html`):

```
"
CREATE external TABLE IF NOT EXISTS MyGeoJsonTable
(
Name string,
BoundaryShape binary
)
ROW FORMAT SERDE 'com.esri.hadoop.hive.serde.JsonSerde'
STORED AS INPUTFORMAT 'com.esri.json.hadoop.EnclosedJsonInputFormat'
OUTPUTFORMAT 'org.apache.hadoop.hive.ql.io.
HiveIgnoreKeyTextOutputFormat'
LOCATION 's3://MyGeoJsonBucket/';
```

Some of the up-and-coming formats in big data, although they have been around for a while, are Parquet, AVRO, and ORC. These combined with WKT, WKB, and Geohash formats can be very powerful and efficient for reading and working with geospatial data. These formats are binary and are optimized so that individual columns can be read through byte-range requests to large files without having to move the rest of the file column bytes across the wire. This sounds very complicated, but what it boils down to is that if you have a file that is 10 GB with 100 columns, you can write a query against that file to only read the first column, and 1/100 of the data needs to be read off the disk to get your results. There is currently development on a project called GeoParquet that will deliver even more promising geospatial performance within Parquet files. Two big goals of the project are to allow geospatial partitioning of the data as well as geospatial indexes.

Some current areas of exploration are the merging of point cloud formats with these big data formats. LAZ is probably the most common point cloud format that is deployed on AWS, but it is still a quickly evolving format. There is currently work to make LAZ more cloud-native, similar to how **Cloud Optimized GeoTiff** (**COG**) files work, which I will talk about later in the chapter. Essentially, if optimizing the file format so an HTTP range request can be used initially to read the metadata at the top of the file, subsequent HTTP range requests can be used to pull specific bits from the file without reading the entire file. Sound familiar? It should, because this is the same way the aforementioned big data formats work, such as Parquet! COPC.io is actively developing this cloud-optimized point cloud, which is actually what the COPC acronym stands for. The goal of COPC is to create a *"Range-readable, compressed, geospatial organized LAZ specification."* Working with point clouds, either on-premises or in the cloud, is one of the most challenging geospatial workflows today because of their massive file size. Raster file sizes are not far behind, but an orthomosaic of a city block might be in the tens of megabytes to hundreds of megabytes. However, an equivalent point cloud for the same thing can easily reach gigabytes to tens of gigabytes.

Lastly, on file formats, I want to spend some time on COGs. Imagery formats have come a long way, from JPG to JPG2000, to GeoTIFF to MRF, and now COG. All of these formats are still widely in use for various workflows but COGs are starting to see widespread adoption. I am seeing a lot of the new satellite data that is streaming into AWS as COG formats, such as Landsat and Sentinel-2. So, why are COGs becoming so popular? As I mentioned earlier, the big differentiator is the way COGs store and organize their bytes inside the file. The metadata for the file is stored at the top of the file so the original read to the file just grabs the top of the file like a header. Then, from this data, the application can issue a subsequent query and grab a bounding box of pixels out of a larger image. If you have an image that is 1 gigabyte, you can have a higher zoom level that is 1/100 of the larger image and you will only read that 1/100 of the image off the disk, as well as deliver that 1/100 of the file over the network.

Normalizing data

There is a well-known saying in the data analytics world that "90% of the work is normalizing the data." There is also a well-known saying at Amazon that "everything fails all the time" (Verner Vogels). This is also true for geospatial data sources. No matter what the data source, there is always the possibility of missing or inaccurate data. It's common on devices that need high precision to deploy three or more sensors from different manufacturers, all measuring the same attribute, and to then compare the readings against each other. Ideally, all of the sensors will report similar readings, but it's much easier to identify whether one of the sensors needs to be recalibrated if two of the readings are significantly different from the third. Municipal boundary polygons you may find from public sources can vary widely in terms of spatial accuracy, depending on who digitized them. Incorrect or misaligned coordinates or postal addresses can cause hours of data cleanup work, and public road networks struggle to keep up with new construction and other changes that are constantly occurring around the world.

I use a recent example to describe some of the challenges with normalizing data. Not that long ago, I was deploying a machine learning algorithm that did predictive health maintenance. This was powered by an AWS service called **Amazon Lookout for Equipment (L4E)**. This service requires six months of data for training as well as failure data. I was working with a dataset from a pump that had voltage and pressure, and was trying to predict when the pump would fail by looking at how these values varied over time. To start with, my dataset had large gaps in the data where I was either missing voltage for a certain period of time or I was missing pressure. L4E is actually pretty intelligent about common datasets and the service automatically compensates for scenarios such as this. L4E does what's known as imputing or forward-filling the last known value from the sensor across all the missing rows.

Forward-filling data may sound like an easy fix at first but it can have some undesirable consequences. For example, what if the last sensor reading was erroneous, maybe during a power blip that caused a voltage spike or drop? Carrying that value across minutes, hours, or days of data would significantly alter the average of the dataset. An alternative approach would be to take some averages across the dataset and forward-fill with that value. However, depending on the highs and lows the values can swing between, even that could adversely impact the service's ability to understand what a normal operating range for the sensor should be. Lastly, if you know what the normal operating range is for the sensor, you can simply forward-fill with that value, assuming you also know that there was no impact to the equipment during that time, and any relationship to other sensors at the time of that reading was not outside of normal levels either.

This point is important because the best insights are found through correlations in the data, and data anomalies in one dataset may impact other datasets in unintended ways. A drop in temperature and barometric pressure may mean that rain is in the forecast. If you forward-fill the barometric data while there is a temperature drop, the accuracy of the forecast for each geospatial location will be tainted. As you plan your geospatial data environment, be sure to consider at what stage normalization may be helpful, and define data quality rules to help notify of anomalies. More than one AWS service can be used for data preparation and normalization. Throughout this book, we will look at options and show how they can be used with your geospatial data.

Considering temporal dimensions

All of the concepts we have reviewed in this chapter become amplified by the dimension of time. For example, imagine you are ingesting and storing location-based data for marathon runners in the United States. Let's say this number is around 500,000. Creating a heat map to show concentrations of where marathon runners live already means dealing with a reasonably large dataset. Now, consider the locations of each race that the runners participated in over the course of a year. You get even better location insights into the marathon activity over the year, but you are likely dealing with millions of data points. The data grows exponentially when you start to look at GPS data from fitness trackers along the marathon routes. There are over 1,000 marathons each year in the US, and the largest marathons have over 10,000 finishers. Multiply that by the GPS location of each runner, and even at 10-second intervals, the data volumes become enormous. Conventional GIS environments may be tempted to store lower-granularity temporal data to minimize cost and time, but the AWS cloud enables you to capture and store unlimited amounts of data for the highest-quality geospatial analysis.

Another example where time is a crucial dimension of geospatial data can be found in weather forecast data. Weather forecasts are generated for generalized locations with the temporal aspect of what conditions will be at that point for a particular point in time. Without the time dimension, it is easy to see how weather forecast geospatial data becomes significantly less useful.

The purpose of highlighting the importance of time in your geospatial data is to help you plan the eventual outcomes of your geospatial data environment on AWS. Think about the data-driven insights you and your organization hope to derive from the data. Having concrete, outcome-based goals and working backward from them to design and build your geospatial data management strategy will help make your project successful.

Summary

In this chapter, we discussed in-depth considerations for quality and temporal data concepts. All of the concepts we discussed have trade-offs, and it's always worth taking a step back to confirm your requirements before making a design decision. Lat/long data quality, transmission methods, streaming versus batch, and big data file formats are core architecture decisions. Jeff Bezos has a famous theory about one-way doors and two-way doors: invest time in one-way door decisions, or essentially, design decisions that would be very disruptive to go back and change. Two-way doors are design decisions that are easy to change later. Many of the concepts in this chapter are one-way doors. If you collected all of your sensor data at 1-meter accuracy and you later realize you need 0.1-meter accuracy, it is probably not trivial to redeploy all your sensors to get more accurate readings.

Lastly, two more takeaways. Always keep in mind the 80/20 rule for analyzing and normalizing data. It's highly likely you will spend 80% of your time normalizing and correcting errors in your data and 20% of your time doing actual analysis. Finally, temporal considerations: changing your frequency of data sampling from 10 seconds to 1 second exponentially increases your data size by a factor of 10. Storage for this data may be cheap, but you will also spend a significant number of CPU cycles and RAM reading in and filtering this additional data.

In the next chapter, we will discuss geospatial data lake architectures. We will talk about what a data lake is and how it benefits geospatial data. We will discuss the different strategies and technologies for storing data in a data lake, as well as the benefits and limitations of the various storage architectures and geospatial file formats.

References

- GeoParquet specifications: `https://github.com/opengeospatial/geoparquet`

- COPC specification: `https://copc.io/`

- AWS L4E overview: `https://aws.amazon.com/lookout-for-equipment/`

- AWS L4E data specifications: `https://docs.aws.amazon.com/lookout-for-equipment/latest/ug/the-right-data.html`

- Latitude and longitude accuracy discussion: `https://gis.stackexchange.com/questions/8650/measuring-accuracy-of-latitude-and-longitude/8674`

Part 2: Geospatial Data Lakes using Modern Data Architecture

In this chapter, we will learn about designing and building a Data Lake architecture to ingest, store, manage, analyze, and visualize the geospatial data in AWS.

This part has the following chapters:

- *Chapter 3, Geospatial Data Lake Architecture*, talks about designing and building a Data Lake architecture to ingest, store manage, analyze, and visualize the geospatial data in AWS

- *Chapter 4, Using Geospatial data with Amazon RedShift*, shows an overview of Amazon Redshift and how to store and analyze geospatial data using Amazon Redshift

- *Chapter 5, Using Geospatial Data with Amazon Aurora PostgresSQL*, provides an overview of Amazon Aurora PostgreSQL along with the PostGIS extension. We will also understand how to store and analyze geospatial data using Amazon Aurora PostgreSQL with hands-on examples

- *Chapter 6, Serverless Options for Geospatial*, provides an overview AWS serverless technologies and how to use AWS Lambda and other managed services to collect, store, and analyse geospatial data. We will also learn about event-driven mechanisms for both on-demand and scheduled workloads.

- *Chapter 7, Querying Geospatial Data with Amazon Athena*, Amazon Athena provides scalable, robust access to a wide range of geospatial data sources on AWS. Powerful geospatial functions allow for on-the-fly analysis and transformation capabilities that can be applied in a scalable and cost-effective manner. This chapter will explore geospatial use patterns with Athena to gain insights and create new datasets.

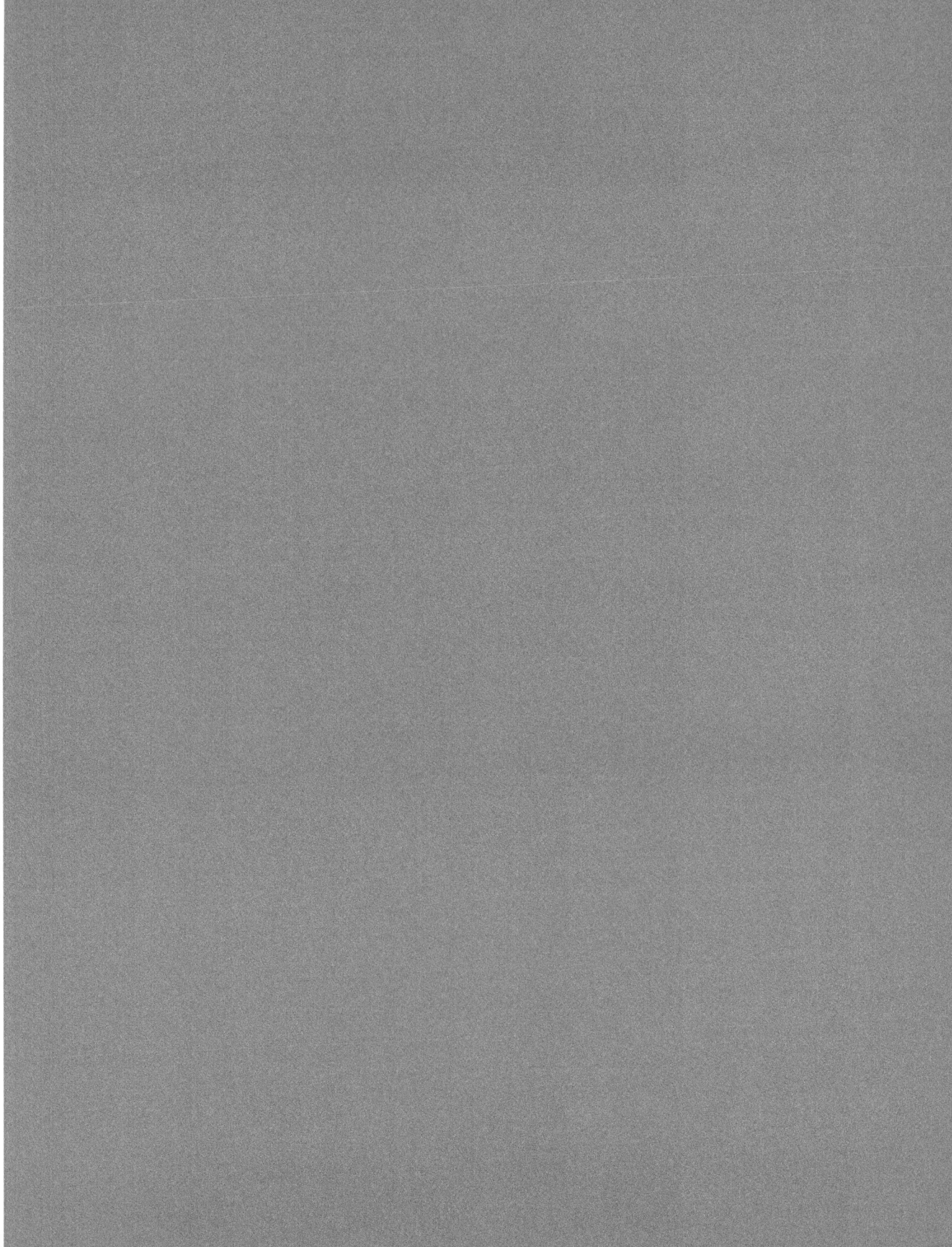

3
Geospatial Data Lake Architecture

Geospatial data combined with spatial analytics help companies across all industries answer a wide range of business questions. The sheer volume of geospatial data collection and analytical capabilities present many challenges for organizations to take full advantage of geospatial data by turning data into useful insights to solve a specific problem. This chapter will outline the designing and building of a Data Lake architecture to ingest, store, manage, analyze, and visualize the geospatial data in AWS. In this chapter, you will learn about the geospatial data management methodologies through the following topics:

- Modern data architecture overview
- Designing and building a geospatial data lake
- Geospatial data ingestion overview
- Extract, transform, and load geospatial data
- Storing geospatial data
- Building a search service on a geospatial data lake
- Security and governance

Modern data architecture overview

With the evolution of technology, the data generated from various geospatial sources is increasingly diverse and growing exponentially. Data of any type is captured and stored across various data stores. Companies want to collect, store, and analyze geospatial data as quickly as possible to derive insights from it for business operation improvements and better customer experience, which will help them stay ahead of their competitors. With the diverse types of geospatial data, a one-size-fits-all data strategy would have many challenges in geospatial data management. You should be able to capture and store any volume of geospatial data at any velocity using flexible data formats. This requires a highly scalable, available, secure, and centrally governable data store or a data lake that can handle huge geospatial datasets. You also need the right tools to run analytics services against this data. This requires moving the data between the data lake and the analytics services in all directions, from the inside out, outside in, and around the outside.

Modern data architecture allows you to rapidly build a scalable data lake that can leverage a broad collection of purpose-built data services to analyze the data for use cases such as interactive dashboards, log analytics, big data processing, data warehousing, and machine learning. AWS's modern data architecture consists of five pillars, which we will explore in the next section. It also enables data movement between the data lake and purpose-built data services along with unified governance and compliance.

The AWS modern data architecture pillars

The AWS modern data architecture allows you to unify the enterprise data landscape by breaking down data silos to derive business value across databases, data lakes, analytics, and machine learning. You can store and move data seamlessly and securely with the right governance control. It consists of five pillars:

- Scalable data lakes

- Purpose-built analytics services

- Unified data access

- Centralized governance

- Performance and cost

A data lake should be scalable to allow an organization to collect and store any volume of data from disparate data sources at different acquisition rates in a centralized data store with high reliability and availability. Amazon's **Simple Storage Service** (**S3**) object storage service could be used to build a data lake with 11 nines of durability and 4 nines of availability. Based on the business and functional requirements, different storage classes of Amazon S3 could be leveraged to store the data cost-efficiently and reliably. The objects in an Amazon S3 bucket could be encrypted using **server-side encryption** (**SSE**) with either Amazon S3 managed keys (SSE-S3) or AWS KMS keys stored in **AWS Key Management Service** (**AWS KMS**)/(**SSE-KMS**) or with customer-provided keys (SSE-C). Amazon S3 will also provide compliance and audit capabilities with object-level audit logging and access control. Building a data lake requires ingesting and cataloging data from diverse sources, and then transforming and enriching it to derive meaningful insights. AWS Lake Formation would enable you to build, manage, and secure data lakes quickly with an integrated console that makes it easy for you to discover, ingest, transform, clean, catalog, and secure your data and make it available for downstream analysis. You could leverage AWS Lake Formation to define and manage fine-grained authorization policies to access databases, tables, and columns in the data lake via the AWS Glue Data Catalog.

Once the data lake is built, you can leverage the wide range of purpose-built data analytics services to analyze the underlying data. Amazon Athena is an interactive serverless analytics engine that allows you to query the data in Amazon S3 using standard SQL or Python with no resource provisioning or configuration requirements. Geospatial functions in Athena engine version 2 are based on the open source Presto. Athena engine version 3 leverages the open source Trino framework (Presto is an open source distributed SQL query engine for data of any size that allows users to query against multiple data sources such as Hadoop, Cassandra, Kafka, AWS S3, MySQL, MongoDB, and many more. In December 2020, Presto was rebranded as Trino.) Athena also supports the open source Apache Spark distributed processing system, which allows you to run interactive Apache PySpark applications in the Athena console using notebooks or through Athena APIs.

In this section, we discussed the key aspects of AWS's modern data architecture, which enables organizations to integrate and optimize their data landscape for improved business outcomes. The architecture is built on five pillars that ensure scalability, analytics capabilities, unified data access, centralized governance, and optimal performance and cost management. In the next section, we will review the foundations of building a geospatial data lake using the AWS modern data architecture.

Geospatial Data Lake

Geospatial data is used to describe collective information about objects, events, or other features along with geographic or location components. Traditionally, companies use **Enterprise Data Warehouses (EDWs)** to store data from multiple sources using various data integration services. This requires complex data transformations and conformed data models. Companies must invest a significant amount of time and effort to achieve these. Compute and storage improvements over the years allow the capturing and sharing of any amount of geospatial data at any velocity. Geospatial data is collected in many ways and stored in different formats. Modern geospatial data products and applications require agile approaches and faster time to market. Data Lakes allow us to store both structured and unstructured geospatial data at any scale in a centralized repository. They are designed for low-cost storage and analytics that allow you to collect, process, store, and serve both vector and raster data of any format. With a data lake, you can also tag the data in a central, searchable catalog. This helps us to break down the data silos across various data storages and incorporate spatial analytics to get business insights with minimal data movements. Let's now dive into actually designing the data lake.

Designing a geospatial data lake using modern data architecture

You need to build and scale your geospatial infrastructure for the growing demand for efficiency and agility. Defining the modern data architecture building blocks and designing a data lake requires a data discovery exercise. This discovery process is the first step and includes several discussions with both business and IT stakeholders in an organization. Start working backward from defining the business value. It will be either about solving a specific business problem or about modernizing the enterprise data landscape. Some customers also use geospatial data to solve business, social, environmental, and economic problems. Identify the data consumers such as business analysts, external customers, data engineers, data scientists, and other downstream applications. Find out the consumption mechanisms for these channels. Then, list down all the data sources that are required to attain business value and define the frequencies and means to ingest them into the data lake. Finally, focus on data storage, management, and processing requirements.

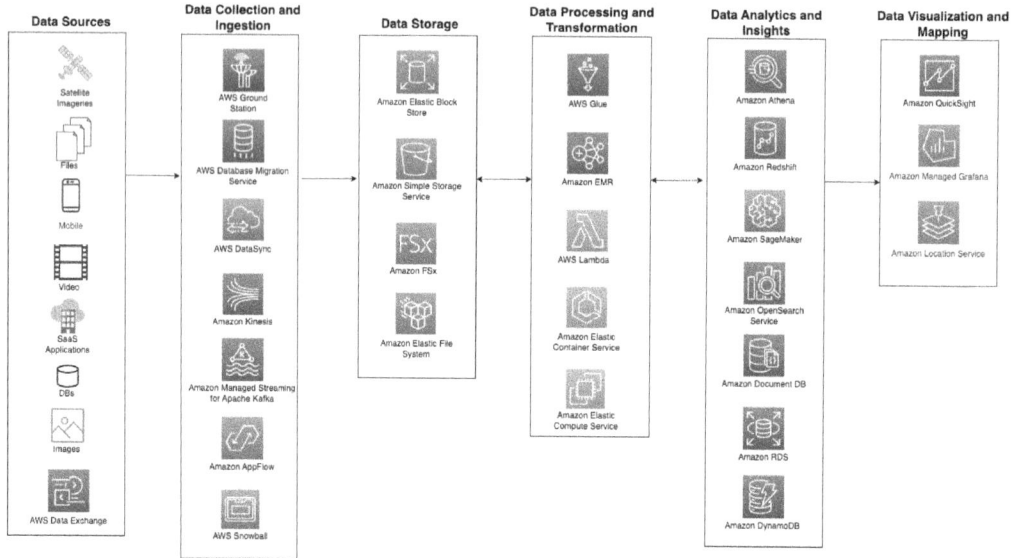

Figure 3.1: Geospatial data lake architecture

The core building blocks of a geospatial data lake could be categorized under data collection and ingestion, data storage, data processing and transformation, data analytics and insights, and data visualization and mapping, as shown in *Figure 3.1*. You should also consider security, governance, and orchestration aspects while designing a geospatial solution. The data ingestion layer would allow you to bring any volume of data into the data lake in both batch and real time at any time interval. The storage layer enables you to persist the raw data in a geospatial-native file format. The transformed data is stored in an open data format for downstream consumption and analytics. The data processing module comprises all tools and techniques to process and transform the geospatial data into a desired format. Security and governance frameworks allow you to ingest, store, and serve data securely and catalog both business and technical metadata. You could further extend data lineage, data quality, and data auditing capabilities in this layer. The orchestration layer helps you to design and orchestrate end-to-end geospatial data processing and analysis pipelines. Finally, the data consumption block would provide the tools and techniques to serve the enriched geospatial data to the end users and the downstream applications. This can be represented as follows:

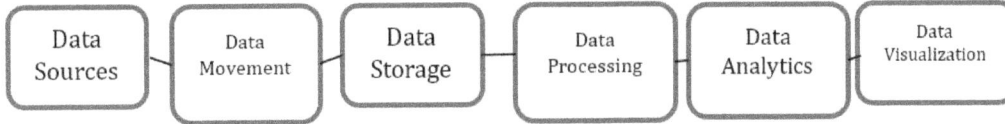

Figure 3.2: The order of designing a geospatial data lake

Data collection and ingestion layer

Geospatial data could be collected from sources that are owned by your enterprise or from a third-party data provider. Substantial amounts of geospatial data collected by public and private organizations are available via various channels such as **Public Geodata**, **OpenStreetMap**, **GeoPlatform**, and many others. AWS Data Exchange is a single global data catalog service that can be used to securely find, subscribe, and use third-party geospatial data in the AWS cloud. The AWS Data Exchange catalog contains over 3,500 data products from a broad range of domains and can be accessed as data files, data tables, and data APIs. You could consolidate your geospatial data ingestion across different third-party data providers and ingest your data from a single source. The **Amazon Sustainability Data Initiative (ASDI)** (`https://sustainability.aboutamazon.com/environment/the-cloud/amazon-sustainability-data-initiative`) also provides users with petabytes of geospatial data, including weather observations, ocean temperatures, climate projection data, and satellite imagery, along with the tools and technical expertise needed to accelerate sustainability research and innovation. The data is hosted on the Registry of Open Data on AWS (`https://registry.opendata.aws/collab/asdi/`). Now, this Registry of Open Data on AWS is also available on AWS Data Exchange. The number of data sources that produce and transmit geospatial information is growing, and this creates new possibilities for real-time geospatial analytics and visualization. If the data needs to be ingested from streaming spatial-temporal data sources, Amazon Kinesis Data Streams and Amazon Managed Streaming for Apache Kafka could be used as stream storage services, and the Amazon Kinesis Data Firehose can be leveraged to deliver this streaming data into the data lake on Amazon S3.

Apache Kafka is a distributed, high-performance, fault-tolerant event streaming platform for data processing and application. **Amazon Managed Streaming for Apache Kafka** (**Amazon MSK**) is a managed service from AWS that takes care of the undifferentiated heavy lifting of managing the infrastructure and operations of the open source Apache Kafka along with seamless built-in connectivity with other AWS services. You could use Kafka Connect to connect Apache Kafka with external SQL and NoSQL databases, search databases, and other filesystems. There is an MSK Serverless cluster type option available for Amazon MSK, which makes it easier to run Apache Kafka applications without having to manage or configure storage or compute of the cluster.

Amazon Kinesis Data Streams is a serverless data streaming service for processing and analyzing streaming data. The data will be available for the downstream applications within seconds. Amazon Kinesis Data Streams manages the underlying infrastructure and configuration that is required to stream high throughput data from clickstreams, application logs, social media, and many other geospatial sources. It also provides synchronous data replication across three Availability Zones. It offers two types of provision modes (on-demand mode and provisioned mode) that could be used for unpredictable traffic patterns and predictable traffic patterns, respectively. You could use `PutRecord` and `PutRecords` operations, Amazon **Kinesis Producer Library (KPL)**, or Amazon Kinesis Agent to add data to a Kinesis data stream. In addition to these data sources, you could also stream data to Amazon Kinesis Data Streams from native AWS services such as Amazon DynamoDB, Amazon Aurora, Amazon CloudWatch, and AWS IoT Core. The data from Amazon Kinesis Data Streams and MSK can also be directly ingested into the data warehouse service Amazon Redshift for real-time data analysis requirements without the need to stage in Amazon S3.

Suppose you need to stream videos from geospatial and time-encoded data sources. In that case, you could use Amazon Kinesis Video Streams, which enables scalable secured stream video ingestion from any stream video devices that could use Kinesis Video Streams SDKs. It also supports the WebRTC open source project for ultra-low latency, two-way, real-time communication between the source and your applications. The streamed data could be consumed by Amazon Rekognition, Amazon SageMaker, and any custom or third-party applications built using Amazon Kinesis Video Streams APIs and SDKs.

Amazon Kinesis Data Firehose can be used for streaming **extract, load, transform (ELT)** to process and load data in real time into Amazon S3 data lakes, Amazon Redshift data warehouses, Amazon OpenSearch Service, third-party log analytics service providers, and HTTP endpoints. By using Kinesis Data Firehose, you could convert and compress the input data in flight to Apache Parquet and Apache ORC data formats and GZIP, ZIP, and SNAPPY compression formats.

The AWS Snow Family could be used for secure offline data transfers into and out of a data lake on AWS. It's a collection of physical devices that is ideal for transferring up to 100 PB data from sources where you have no or low network bandwidth. The AWS Snow Family consists of AWS Snowcone, AWS Snowball Edge, and AWS Snowmobile. AWS Snowcone is a compact, ruggedized, secure, and ultra-portable data transfer device that weighs around 4.5 pounds. It comes with 14-TB SSD or 8-TB HDD options with 4 usable vCPUs and 4 GB of memory. It doesn't include a power supply. Customers can run the device via a plug-in power source or an external battery. The data collected from a Snowcone device could be transferred to AWS with the AWS DataSync service, or it could be shipped to AWS for an offline transfer. AWS Snowcone could be used for collecting and processing data from edge locations for gathering real-time insights at the edge. It can also be used for light remote location application deployment with minimal power and CPU usage. It also supports a wired network interface for data collection. AWS Snowball Edge is an edge computing and data transfer device that is used for edge data processing and collection in disconnected remote environments. It comes in two options: Storage Optimized and Compute Optimized. The Storage Optimized option comes with 80 TB of usable HDD storage, 40 vCPUs, 1 TB of SATA SSD storage, and up to 40 Gb of network connectivity for large-scale remote edge data processing and data transfer. The Compute Optimized option provides 104 vCPUs, 28 TB of NVMe SSD, and up to 100-GB networking for powerful edge computing and processing use cases such as real-time process optimization, edge machine learning inferences, video and audio processing, and Internet of Things data analytics. Snowball Edge devices also come with a **Hadoop Distributed File System (HDFS)** client to move data directly from Hadoop clusters into an Amazon S3 data lake. Learn more about different snowball options from the link provided in the *Reference* section[3]. AWS OpsHub is a free user interface that is available globally to set up and manage the Snow Family of devices and deploy applications at the edge. You could unlock and configure snow devices, drag-and-drop data to devices, launch and manage EC2 instances or **Amazon Machine Images** (**AMIs**) within Amazon EC2 on devices, or monitor device metrics using AWS OpsHub. Finally, the AWS Snowmobile could be used for Exabyte-scale data migration needs. It is a 45-foot-long ruggedized shipping container that is pulled by a semi-trailer truck, and it can migrate up to 100 PB at a time.

AWS Glue is a serverless data integration service that provides a single interface to ingest, catalog, transform, and integrate data from multiple sources for downstream data analytics. It consists of three major components: a data cataloging service, an ETL engine, and a flexible job scheduler. You could use the built-in JDBC connections to move the data from Amazon Redshift, Amazon Aurora, Microsoft SQL Server, MySQL, MongoDB, and PostgreSQL using AWS Glue. You could also build or use custom JDBC drivers in your ETL jobs or subscribe to several third-party connectors available in AWS Marketplace. Glue streaming ETL can be used to consume and ingest data from streaming sources such as Amazon Kinesis Data Streams, Apache Kafka, and Amazon MSK. These jobs could run continuously to read and transform the data, and then load the results into Amazon S3 data lakes or any other JDBC data stores. By default, the streaming data is written out in 100-second intervals, but this could be modified based on your needs. Checkpoints are used to track the data that has already been in AWS Glue streaming jobs. We'll investigate the other key AWS Glue features in the *Data transformation* section.

If you have requirements to move and sync data securely between on-premises and Amazon S3 data lake, AWS DataSync could be an option to ingest data from on-premises storages such as **Network File System** (**NFS**), **Server Message Block** (**SMB**), Hadoop clusters, or third-party object stores. It provides an out-of-the-box data integrity validation module to validate the data transfer. You could also use AWS DataSync to move data from and to a storage service in another AWS account. AWS DataSync Discovery simplifies and accelerates data migration to AWS. Using DataSync Discovery, you can automatically collect data about your on-premises storage systems and view the aggregated results in the DataSync console. If you just want to ingest data from on-premises Hadoop clusters without using any native AWS data transfer services, you could use the native open source Apache Hadoop **distributed copy** (**DistCp**) command that is supported by Amazon S3. If you have to move geospatial data between you and your customers or partners, the AWS Transfer Family can be used to ingest files into and out of Amazon S3 or Amazon EFS over FTP, FTPS, SFTP, and AS2 protocols. It is a fully managed **business-to-business** (**B2B**) file transfer service that allows you to automate and monitor your data migration while keeping the existing client-side configurations.

Sometimes, customers want to process their geospatial data on their on-premises clusters but need a cost-effective storage mechanism to manage the data. The AWS Storage Gateway is a set of hybrid storage services that provide cloud storage for such use cases without setting up any new storage hardware. It provides applications that run on-premises with low-latency access to cloud-backed storage. There are three different Storage Gateway services: File Gateway, Volume Gateway, and Tape Gateway. The File Gateway is used for moving file data types between AWS and on-premises. The Amazon S3 File Gateway gives a file interface to any applications, devices, and workflows to store the files as objects in Amazon S3 using both NFS (v3 and v4.1) and SMB (v2 and v3) protocols. **Active Directory (AD)** users could be used to authenticate users' access to SMB file shares. The Amazon S3 File Gateway also allows you to leverage S3 Standard, S3 Intelligent-Tiering, S3 Standard - Infrequent Access (S3 Standard-IA), and S3 One Zone-IA storage classes to optimize the storage cost. The other option of the File Gateway, called Amazon FSx File Gateway, can be used for low-latency Windows File Server read/write requirements while minimizing the amount of data transfer. It's a fully managed, scalable, and highly reliable file storage in AWS that provides a local cache for frequently used data and to set up Windows file shares on Amazon FSx with background data synchronization. This is a great option to consider before extending your existing on-premises storage without impacting your existing applications or networks. The Tape Gateway can be used for data backup requirements to replace physical on-premises tapes with virtual tapes in AWS. It supports many leading backup software tools on the market without major changes to existing workflows and VTL configurations. The data can be transferred to Amazon S3 Glacier Flexible Retrieval or Amazon S3 Glacier Deep Archive, and the data could be compressed and encrypted between the gateway and AWS. A virtual tape should be at least 100 GiB and can be up to 15 TiB. The maximum number of virtual tapes that a Tape Gateway can have is 1,500, with an aggregated capacity of 1 PB. The Volume Gateway provides an **Internet Small Computer Systems Interface (iSCSI)** cloud block storage interface to the on-premises applications and devices. iSCSI is an IP-based standard that defines how data is transferred between host systems and storage devices over a TCP/IP network. The Volume Gateway consists of two modes: cached mode and stored mode. The cached Volume Gateway mode retains frequently accessed data locally while the primary data is stored in Amazon S3, whereas the stored Volume Gateway mode stores the entire dataset on-premises for latency-sensitive applications, and asynchronously backs up the data in Amazon S3. In cached mode, you could store up to 32 TB for a maximum of 1 PB of data per gateway. In stored mode, the maximum storage per volume is 16 TB for a maximum of 512 TB of data per gateway. For both volume gateway options, you can take point-time Amazon EBS snapshots. AWS Backup along with Volume Gateway can be used for backing up and recovering on-premises applications. Storage Gateway can be hosted on-premises on VM appliances or hardware appliances, or in AWS as an Amazon EC2 instance. AWS Direct Connect can also be used for such hybrid workload requirements. AWS Direct Connect provides dedicated network connectivity between the on-premises network and AWS. It connects the internal on-premises network to an AWS Direct Connect location over a standard Ethernet fiber optic cable. The network traffic transits through the AWS global network and never uses the public internet. Using the dedicated connection, you can reduce the latency bottlenecks. You could create a virtual interface directly with Amazon S3 for secure data transfer between on-premises data stores and geospatial data lakes.

AWS Database Migration Service (AWS DMS) can be leveraged when there is a need to move or replicate data from another database service with minimal downtime and in-built monitoring. This can be a great tool to hydrate your geospatial data lake by ingesting data from multiple data sources into Amazon S3. AWS DMS supports one-time full data load or ongoing data movements along with change data capture (CDC). It could be used for both homogenous (same source and destination) and heterogeneous (different source and destination) data migrations. It automatically discovers and converts the source database schemas that are compatible with the target database using the **Schema Conversion Tool** (**SCT**), provides a replication server along with source and destination endpoints for the data stores, and creates a migration task(s) to move the data. The source data could be from databases such as Oracle, Microsoft SQL Server, MySQL, MariaDB, PostgreSQL, SAP **Adaptive Server Enterprise** (**ASE**), MongoDB, and IBM DB2 that run on-premises or on Amazon EC2 or Amazon RDS instances, Amazon DocumentDB (with MongoDB compatibility), and Amazon S3. You could also move data from Microsoft Azure SQL Database and Google Cloud for MySQL. The targets could be the same as the sources that were mentioned previously. In addition to these targets, AWS DMS can also ingest the data into Amazon Redshift, Amazon DynamoDB, Amazon OpenSearch Service, Amazon ElastiCache for Redis, Amazon Kinesis Data Streams, Amazon Neptune, and Apache Kafka. There is a fully managed version of AWS DMS called AWS DMS Fleet Advisor, which is a free service to automate migration planning and migration to AWS with minimal effort for many databases and analytics fleets.

Data storage layer

Data storage and management is the foundation for building a geospatial data lake. Storing, managing, and analyzing geospatial data requires special considerations so that the platform is optimized to represent the objects defined in the complex geospatial vector and raster data. Geospatial data is generated in all shapes and sizes. **Open Geospatial Consortium** (**OGC**) provides a basic data model for representing geographic information and interoperability. Shapefiles, GeoJSON, GeoTiff, GeoPackage, **Geography Markup Language** (**GML**), and many other geospatial data formats are used to describe geo-coordinates and other geo-referencing information. The raw geospatial data can be stored in Amazon S3. Amazon S3 is a petabyte-scale object storage service with scalability, data availability, security, and performance. You could start storing your geospatial data without any upfront hardware setup or investment. It also provides industry-leading security, compliance, and audit capabilities. AWS purpose-built analytics services could be used for downstream data analytics and insights.

Geospatial data could also be stored and cached in a high-performance block-storage system based on **Amazon Elastic Block Store (Amazon EBS)**. Amazon EBS volumes are highly available, reliable, and durable, and attached to Amazon **Elastic Compute Cloud** (**EC2**) instances. It consists of two storage categories: SSD-backed storage, which is used for latency-sensitive high IOPS and transactional workloads, and HDD-backed storage, which is used for throughput-heavy workloads. The data stored in an Amazon EBS volume can persist independently of the lifespan of the EC2 instance. You are charged for the EBS storage you hold, whereas in Amazon S3, you are charged for the storage you consume. You can create incremental snapshots of EBS volumes that act as backups stored on Amazon S3 buckets. Amazon EBS provides data-at-rest security encryption for its data volumes, boot volumes, and snapshots, without needing to manage a key management infrastructure. The data is encrypted either using Amazon-managed keys or keys you create and manage using AWS KMS.

The Amazon FSx service could be used if you need highly performant file storage for geospatial machine learning, analytics, and HPC applications. Amazon FSx is a fully managed, high-performance storage service that provides sub-millisecond latency and high throughput. It also provides data deduplication and data compression features out of the box and allows you to scale throughput performance independently from storage capacity. Amazon FSx could be used for hybrid workloads, allowing you to store the data in AWS, and provide low-latency on-premises local access by using Amazon FSx File Gateway and NetApp ONTAP's Global File Cache. Similarly, you could back up, archive, or replicate your on-premises geospatial files to AWS for regulatory, data retention, or disaster recovery requirements using Amazon FSx. It also offers SSD or HDD storage options and lets you select between four industry-leading filesystems: NetApp ONTAP, OpenZFS, Windows File Server, and Lustre. Amazon FSx also integrates with Amazon S3. Amazon FSx for NetApp ONTAP is a fully managed shared storage service that provides data access and management capabilities of NetApp's ONTAP filesystem. It offers virtually unlimited elastic storage and supports NFS, SMB, and iSCSI protocols. Amazon FSx for OpenZFS provides fully managed shared file storage built on the OpenZFS filesystem that allows you to move workloads running on ZFS or other Linux-based file servers. It provides up to 21 **gigabytes per second** (**GB/s**) of throughput and over 1 million IOPs for the cached data and delivers up to 10 GB/s and up to 350,000 IOPS for persistent disk data access. Amazon FSx for Windows File Server provides fully managed shared storage built on Windows Server that helps you to move Windows-based workloads to the cloud while maintaining application compatibility. It can be used with Amazon FSx File Gateway to provide low-latency, on-premises Windows file share access. Amazon FSx for Lustre is built on the open source Lustre filesystem and is used for compute-intensive workloads such as machine learning, **high-performance computing** (**HPC**), video processing, financial modeling, and genome sequencing. Lustre provides two deployment options: scratch filesystems, which are used for short-term temporary storage and data processing where data does not persist if a file server fails, and persistent filesystems, which are used for longer-term storage and workloads.

Amazon **Elastic File System** (**EFS**) is a serverless, fully elastic file storage service that provides petabyte-scale storage without needing to provision, deploy, patch, and manage the underlying storage hardware. It allows you to create filesystems that can be accessed by Amazon EC2 instances, Amazon container services (Amazon **Elastic Container Service** (**ECS**), Amazon **Elastic Kubernetes Service** (**EKS**), and AWS Fargate), and AWS Lambda functions. You could also concurrently connect to thousands of EC2 instances from a single Amazon EFS. It also supports strong consistency and file locking. EFS provides two types of throughput options: elastic throughput, which is used for spiky applications where throughput performance automatically scales with your workload activity and you only pay for the throughput you use, and provisioned throughput, which is used for workloads with predictable throughput requirements. Provisioned throughput provides a predictable billing experience.

Data processing and transformation

AWS Glue's ingestion and integration features were discussed earlier in the *Data collection* section. AWS Glue could also be used for geospatial data processing and transformation of shapefiles, GeoJSON, KML, and CSV files. You can use AWS Glue to convert geospatial data to a common format for further processing and analysis. AWS Glue also supports custom data transformations using Apache Spark that can be used for spatial joins of geospatial data as needed. You could use any geospatial APIs from other services as part of the AWS Glue job. For example, the geocoding API from Amazon Location Service can be used along with AWS Glue custom transformation to convert physical addresses from input data into latitude and longitude. Amazon EventBridge can be used to run ETL scripts on a scheduled basis or as event-driven jobs. You can use the AWS Glue Python shell to run simple Python data integration jobs that run on a single Amazon EC2 instance. These jobs have the limitation to that specific EC2 instance's CPU and memory capacity. To scale native Python jobs, AWS Glue now supports Ray, which is a unified framework for scaling Python applications. AWS Glue for Ray allows you to scale up Python workloads without the need for learning and investing in Apache Spark. Ray enables you to automatically scale your Python code by distributing the load of the Python job processing across a cluster of machines that it reconfigures in real time. You could also use AWS Glue to measure and monitor the data quality during the ingestion and at rest. It provides a set of pre-built data quality rules that you can use to detect common data quality issues, such as column count, completeness, data freshness, and missing values. The data quality can also be measured based on the rules you define. AWS Glue Data Quality has the option to recommend a set of data quality rules based on the computed statistics of your data. You can use AWS Glue Data Quality to ensure that the data is of high quality and fit for use in downstream applications.

Amazon EMR could be used to build scalable data pipelines and run geospatial data analytics at scale. It is a big data platform for running distributed data ingestion and processing jobs, interactive SQL queries, and machine learning applications in the cloud. It supports major open source frameworks such as Apache Spark, Apache Hive, and Presto. You could also build fault-tolerant batch and streaming data pipelines to analyze geospatial streaming events at any velocity. Amazon EMR is filesystem agnostic, meaning you could store and process geospatial data from multiple data stores such as HDFS, Amazon S3, and Amazon DynamoDB. By integrating with geospatial libraries and tools, EMR can be used for geospatial data processing and analysis at any scale. Spatial data can be processed using Apache Spark with a rich ecosystem of geospatial libraries, including Apache Sedona. Sedona extends cluster computing services such as Apache Spark and Apache Flink with a set of out-of-the-box distributed spatial datasets and spatial SQL to load, process, and analyze large-scale spatial data across a cluster. EMR can also be used with the GIS Tools for Hadoop, which are a collection of GIS tools for Hadoop for geospatial data analysis. It provides access to the Hadoop system from the ArcGIS geoprocessing environment. Presto is an open source, distributed SQL query engine designed for fast, interactive queries on data in HDFS and other storage systems. The Presto engine of EMR, along with Presto geospatial functions, can be used to enrich geospatial data and get geographical insights. Presto geospatial functions only support the **Well-Known Text** (**WKT**) and **Well-Known Binary** (**WKB**) file formats. Presto can be used to join geospatial data with non-spatial data to perform an analysis that combines geospatial and non-spatial attributes. Apache Hive is a distributed, fault-tolerant data warehouse system that runs on HDFS and provides SQL-like query capabilities to analyze data, including geospatial data. You can create Hive tables using a spatial data format such as GeoJSON, WKT, or WKB, and partition them by geospatial attributes such as location, time, or geometry type to enable faster querying and processing. **Hive Query Language** (**HiveQL**), which is a query language for Hive to process and analyze structured data, provides out-of-the-box functions to manipulate geospatial data, such as `ST_Contains`, `ST_Intersects`, and `ST_Distance`. Hive's built-in statistical functions can be used to analyze geospatial data, such as computing the mean, median, or standard deviation of geospatial attributes.

EMR Studio, which is an **integrated development environment** (**IDE**) can be leveraged to develop, visualize, and debug geospatial data processing and analyses written in R, Python, Scala, and PySpark. You could deploy your geospatial workloads using different deployment options such as EMR on Amazon EC2, EMR Serverless EMR on Amazon EKS, or EMR on AWS Outposts (AWS Outposts is a deployment of a suite of fully managed AWS services to an on-premises or edge location).

AWS Lambda is a serverless compute service that runs your code without provisioning or managing servers. It takes care of performing all administrative tasks of the compute resources, including server and operating system maintenance, scaling, logging, and capacity provisioning. Users pay only for the compute time they consume. A Lambda function can be triggered to process geospatial data when it is uploaded to Amazon S3 or another storage service. The Lambda function can perform common geospatial processing operations such as data conversion, data filtering, data aggregation, data enrichment, geocoding, format validation, and data normalization. AWS Lambda along with AWS IoT services can be used to ingest and process real-time geospatial data from IoT devices such as drones, sensors, and location trackers. AWS AppSync is a fully managed serverless GraphQL API service for real-time data queries. You can use AWS AppSync and AWS Lambda to build geospatial data applications. AppSync can be used with a Lambda function that processes and aggregates geospatial data and provides it to the frontend application in a format that can be displayed on a map or table. AppSync also allows you to interact with multiple data sources such as SQL, NoSQL, search data, REST endpoints, and microservices with a single network call. AWS Lambda is the best option for you to integrate third-party APIs such as Google Maps or Mapbox into your geospatial workflow. You could write a Lambda function to receive input parameters such as addresses or coordinates and use the third-party API to return the corresponding geocoded information such as latitude and longitude. You can orchestrate a series of geospatial workflows that are written as Lambda functions using AWS Step Functions, a serverless workflow service. AWS Lambda can be a powerful tool for geospatial data processing, leveraging the flexibility and scalability of serverless computing to process, analyze, and visualize data in batch or real time.

Amazon ECS is a highly scalable, high-performance, and fully managed container management and orchestration service that makes it easy for you to deploy, manage, and scale containerized applications. It removes the need for users to install, operate, and scale their own cluster management infrastructure. AWS Fargate is a technology that can be used with Amazon ECS to run Docker containers without having to manage servers or clusters of Amazon EC2 instances. With Fargate, users do not have to provision, configure, or scale clusters of virtual machines to run their containers, and it eliminates the need to configure and manage control planes, nodes, and instances. Using Amazon ECS, you can plan, schedule, and execute long-running batch geospatial workload Docker containers across the full range of AWS services, including Amazon EC2, Fargate, and Amazon EC2 Spot Instances. The geospatial data processing application can be defined in a Dockerfile, which describes the dependencies and steps needed to build your application. Ensure that the Dockerfile includes all the necessary geospatial libraries and tools required for your application. Docker build can be used to build this Docker image, and then push it to a container registry such as Amazon ECR or Docker Hub. This image will be used to create and run containers on your ECS cluster, allowing you to process large amounts of geospatial data at scale. You can configure your ECS cluster to automatically scale up or down based on demand and to load balance traffic across the instances of your task.

Data analytics and insights

Amazon Athena is an interactive analytic query service that makes it easy to analyze petabyte-scale data directly in Amazon S3 and other data sources using standard SQL or Python. It is built on open source Trino and Presto engines and Apache Spark frameworks. Users pay only for the queries that they run with no infrastructure provisioning or configuration effort required. You will need to have your geospatial data stored in WKT (represented as a `varchar` data type) and JSON-encoded geospatial data that is compatible with Athena. It handles geospatial queries with the support of specialized geometry data types such as `point`, `line`, `polygon`, `multiline`, and `multipolygon`. Athena supports many SQL functions for working with geospatial data such as `ST_AsText`, `ST_Polygon`, and `ST_Contains`. The geospatial queries in Amazon Athena can also be extended with **User-Defined Functions** (**UDFs**) and AWS Lambda. You can use Athena queries with visualization tools such as QGIS to display your geospatial data to create maps and visualizations. QGIS is a free and open source, cross-platform, desktop geographic information system application used for viewing, editing, printing, and analyzing geospatial data. Make sure to partition your geospatial data to optimize the performance of your geospatial queries in Athena. You can also use columnar storage formats such as **Optimized Row Columnar** (**ORC**) or Parquet to reduce query latency and improve the speed of your queries.

Amazon Redshift lets you analyze structured and semi-structured data using SQL across data warehouses, operational databases, and data lakes. Amazon Redshift supports GeoJSON, shapefile, WKT, **Extended WKT** (**EWKT**), WKB, and **Extended WKB** (**EWKB**) data formats with the GEOMETRY and/or GEOGRAPHY data types, which contain spatial data such as `point`, `linestring`, `polygon`, `multipoint`, `multilinestring`, `multipolygon`, and `geometrycollection`. To query spatial data using Amazon Redshift, the geospatial data must be stored in Amazon S3, and you can use the COPY command in Redshift to load it from S3 into Redshift. The appropriate data type for the geospatial columns, such as GEOMETRY or GEOGRAPHY, must be specified while loading geospatial data to Redshift. The table partitioning, column compression, and distribution styles can be used to optimize the performance of the geospatial queries in Redshift to reduce query latency and improve the speed of the queries. Partitioning vector data by Geohash in Amazon S3 with Amazon Redshift will also enhance the query performance. Amazon Redshift Spectrum is a service that allows you to efficiently query and retrieve structured and semistructured data from files in Amazon S3 without having to load the data into Amazon Redshift tables. Amazon Redshift Spectrum doesn't natively support spatial data.

Amazon SageMaker is a fully managed **machine learning** (ML) service that provides you with ways to build, train, and deploy ML models along with capabilities to label and prepare your data, choose from over 15 algorithms, train the model, tune and optimize it for deployment, make predictions, and take action. You could use Amazon SageMaker Studio, which is an IDE that provides a single web-based visual interface to build end-to-end ML workflows. SageMaker Autopilot enables you to automatically build, train, and tune the best ML models based on your data while maintaining full control and visibility of the model. If you don't have any prior ML experience, you can use Amazon SageMaker Canvas, which provides a visual interface to generate accurate ML predictions on your own without needing to write a single line of code. Amazon SageMaker supports geospatial ML capabilities by providing access to geospatial data sources such as satellite imagery, maps, and location data. It consists of purpose-built processing operations such as resampling, mosaicking, and reverse geocoding. You could also leverage pre-trained deep neural network ML models such as land cover segmentation and cloud masking for common uses in agriculture, real estate, insurance, and financial services domains. It allows you to visualize predictions layered on a map with the built-in visualization tool, which is powered by Foursquare Studio. You can either use the SageMaker geospatial capability through the SageMaker geospatial UI from the Amazon SageMaker Studio UI or through SageMaker notebooks with a SageMaker geospatial image. You could also bring your own geospatial data.

Amazon OpenSearch Service is an open source, secure, and managed search and analytics service that allows you to perform interactive operations such as log analytics, real-time application monitoring, and website search. It is derived from Elasticsearch. You can use OpenSearch for standard search queries along with parameters to filter, sort, and aggregate your data. OpenSearch can also perform advanced search operations such as fuzzy matching, proximity matching, and Boolean queries. In addition to its full search capabilities, it can store and query geospatial data. Amazon OpenSearch Service offers geospatial visualization capabilities powered by OpenSearch Dashboards and Kibana. It supports `geo_point` and `geo_shape` geographic field types. It also supports the Cartesian `xy_point` and `xy_shape` field types to index and search points and shapes in a two-dimensional Cartesian coordinate system. The **Hexagonal Hierarchical Geospatial Indexing System** (H3) partitions the Earth's areas into identifiable hexagonal cells. The H3 grid system works well for proximity applications. Amazon OpenSearch supports GeoHex Grid aggregation that groups geopoints into grid cells for geographical analysis. You can also use OpenSearch Serverless options, which provide core components including a search engine (OpenSearch) and a visualization interface (OpenSearch Dashboards) without needing to provision, configure, and tune clusters.

Amazon DocumentDB is a fully managed, highly available, and secure document database service that supports storing, querying, and indexing JSON data. It is compatible with MongoDB and offers flexible schemas and extensive query capabilities. Amazon DocumentDB only uses the `point` GeoJSON type to store geospatial data where each GeoJSON document contains two fields: `type` (the shape being represented, which informs Amazon DocumentDB how to interpret the `coordinates` field), and `coordinates` (latitude and longitude information represented as an object in an array). Note that Amazon DocumentDB does not support data types such as `Polygons`, `LineString`,

`MultiPoint`, `MultiPolygon`, `MultiLineString`, and `GeometryCollection`. It uses 2dsphere indexes to index geospatial data and supports proximity querying using the MongoDB APIs such as `$nearSphere`, `$geoNear`, `$minDistance`, and `$maxDistance`. You can also use Amazon DocumentDB for inclusion and intersection querying of geospatial data.

Amazon DynamoDB is a fully managed, secure, serverless, key-value NoSQL database that allows you to run applications with single-digit milliseconds performance at any scale. DynamoDB offers out-of-the-box automatic scaling, continuous backups, automated replication, in-memory caching, and data import and export tools with 99.999% availability. Geo Library for Amazon DynamoDB supports geospatial indexing on Amazon DynamoDB datasets to build location-based applications on AWS. Geohashing is a popular public-domain geocode system that converts geographic information into an alphanumeric hash. The Geo Library takes care of creating and managing Geohash indexes in Amazon DynamoDB. You can use these Geohash indexes to efficiently query location-based data in DynamoDB. Geo Library can be used for basic **create, retrieve, update, and delete (CRUD)** operations on geospatial data items or box queries that return all of the items that fall within a pair of geo points, or radius queries that return all of the items that are within a given radius of a geo point.

Amazon Relational Database Service (**Amazon RDS**) is a collection of managed services that makes it simple to set up, operate, and scale popular database engines such as Amazon Aurora with MySQL compatibility, Amazon Aurora with PostgreSQL compatibility, MySQL, PostgreSQL, MariaDB, Oracle, and SQL Server. You could leverage the PostGIS extension for your PostgreSQL database to add support for geographic objects, allowing spatial indexing and efficient location queries to be run in SQL. PostGIS supports several geospatial data types, including `Point`, `LineString`, `Polygon`, `MultiPoint`, `MultiLineString`, `MultiPolygon`, and `GeometryCollection`. Create a PostgreSQL table with a spatial column that uses one of the geospatial data types and then insert geospatial data into the table using SQL statements or import data from external sources using tools such as ogr2ogr or shp2pgsql. A spatial index is a type of extended index that allows you to index a spatial column, and it reduces search space to enable faster querying. A spatial column is a table column that contains data of a spatial data type, such as geometry or geography. Amazon Aurora PostgreSQL-Compatible edition also supports PostGIS. You can use MySQL Spatial Extensions to analyze geospatial data in MySQL. It supports geospatial data types such as `Point`, `LineString`, `Polygon`, `MultiPoint`, `MultiLineString`, `MultiPolygon`, and `GeometryCollection`. Specify the spatial column when you create a table with appropriate geospatial data types. You can then insert geospatial data into the table using SQL statements or import data from external sources using tools such as ogr2ogr or shp2mysql. It supports various geospatial functions including `ST_Latitude`, `ST_Longitude`, `ST_SwapXY`, and `ST_Transform`. MariaDB also uses the same spatial extension as MySQL for analyzing geospatial data. Amazon RDS supports Oracle Spatial through the `SPATIAL` option in Oracle **Enterprise Edition** (**EE**) and Oracle **Standard Edition 2** (**SE2**). Oracle Spatial provides a SQL schema and functions that facilitate the storage, retrieval, update, and querying of collections of spatial data in an Oracle database. SQL Server supports spatial data and spatial indexes. SQL Server spatial tools is a Microsoft-sponsored open source collection of tools for use with the spatial types in SQL Server.

Data visualization and mapping

Amazon QuickSight is a cloud-native, scalable, embeddable, ML-powered business analytics service that makes it easy to build interactive visualizations and perform ad hoc analysis to get business insights. Amazon QuickSight also provides **SPICE**, a **Super-fast, Parallel, In-memory Calculation Engine** that uses a combination of columnar storage and in-memory technologies to run super-fast interactive queries. QuickSight is also available as a mobile app on iOS and Android to access your business intelligence dashboards on any device. QuickSight can connect to AWS data sources including Amazon RDS, Amazon Aurora, Amazon Redshift, Amazon Athena, AWS IoT, Amazon OpenSearch Service, and Amazon S3, and can also connect to on-premises databases such as SQL Server, MySQL, and PostgreSQL. It allows you to upload Excel spreadsheets or flat files (CSV, TSV, CLF, and ELF) or JSON files. You can import data from third-party services such as Databricks, Snowflake, Salesforce, Jira, and ServiceNow as well. There are two types of maps you could create in Amazon QuickSight: point maps that show the difference between data values for each location by size, and filled maps that show the difference between data values for each location by varying shades of color. QuickSight maps require the dataset to contain location data with latitudinal and longitudinal values, and those location data fields are marked as geospatial data types. QuickSight can also geocode place names to latitude and longitude coordinates. It also recognizes geographic components such as country, state or region, county or district, city, and ZIP code or postal code.

Grafana is an open source, multi-platform, interactive data visualization and operational dashboarding solution. Amazon Managed Grafana is a fully managed, scalable, and enterprise-secure version of open source Grafana with added features such as single sign-on via SAML 2.0 and AWS Single Sign-On, audit logging, and team sync. By using an Amazon Managed Grafana workspace, you create a logically isolated Grafana server, then integrate it with data sources for querying and visualizing metrics, logs, and traces. You could use the Geomap panel visualization to view and customize the world map using geospatial data. Overlay styles and map views can be configured to view important geospatial characteristics of the data. A base map layer provides the visual foundation for a mapping application, and there are four base map layer types to choose from in the Geomap visualization: OpenStreetMap (to add maps from the free geographic world database), CARTO (the default base layer that allows you to add a layer from CARTO Raster base maps), ArcGIS (to add layers from an ESRI ArcGIS MapServer), and XYZ (to add a map from a generic tile layer). The data layer in the Geomap panel needs a source of geographical data and determines how you visualize geospatial data on top of the base layer. There are four mapping options for the data layer: Auto (automatically searches for location data), Coords (specifies that your query holds coordinate data), Geohash (specifies that your query holds Geohash data), and Lookup (specifies that your query holds location name data that needs to be mapped to a value). Use the markers layer to display data points in different marker shapes such as circles, squares, triangles, stars, and so on, and use the heatmap layer to visualize locations with different densities.

Amazon Location Service is a cloud-based geospatial service to add location functionality, such as maps, points of interest, geocoding, routing, tracking, and geofencing to geospatial applications. It provides a suite of APIs and SDKs that allow developers to easily integrate location-based services into their applications, such as displaying maps, route optimizations, and asset tracking in real time.

Amazon Location Service resources are the entities that will be used for all location API requests. The Amazon Location Service Map resource is combined with a rendering library such as MapLibre to display a map in any application. To search for points of interest or geocode or reverse geocode, you could use a geographical search engine such as the Amazon Location Place Index resource. The Place Index also allows you to pick the data provider for the search process, auto-complete, and other operations. An Amazon Location Service Route Calculator resource is used for calculating driving routes, requesting driving directions, driving time, and driving distance between geographical locations. The Amazon Location Tracker resource can be used for geofencing use cases.

Summary

In this chapter, we presented a comprehensive overview of the geospatial data lake architecture and its implementation using AWS services. We went through the technical details of building and managing a geospatial data lake, covering topics such as data collection and ingestion, data storage, data processing and transformation, data analytics and insights, and data visualization and mapping. You could also use other AWS services for security, privacy, governance, and orchestration requirements of your geospatial data lake. You can use Amazon CloudWatch and other monitoring tools to monitor your application's performance and troubleshoot any issues that arise. This reference architecture would enable you to efficiently store and manage large volumes of geospatial data and to perform advanced analytics and ML on the data to gain insights and make informed decisions. In the next chapter, we will explore how we can use Redshift for geospatial tasks.

References

1. How to partition your geospatial data lake for analysis with Amazon Redshift: `https://aws.amazon.com/blogs/publicsector/how-partition-geospatial-data-lake-analysis-amazon-redshift/`

2. AWS Modern Data Architecture: `https://aws.amazon.com/big-data/datalakes-and-analytics/modern-data-architecture/`

3. AWS Snowball Edge device differences: `https://docs.aws.amazon.com/snowball/latest/developer-guide/device-differences.html`

4. Amazon Sustainability Data Initiative: `https://sustainability.aboutamazon.com/environment/the-cloud/amazon-sustainability-data-initiative`

5. Open Geospatial Consortium: `https://en.wikipedia.org/wiki/Open_Geospatial_Consortium`

6. Ray is a unified framework for scaling AI and Python applications: `https://github.com/ray-project/ray`

7. Apache Sedona: `https://sedona.apache.org/latest-snapshot/`

8. gis-tools-for-hadoop: `https://github.com/Esri/gis-tools-for-hadoop`

9. Presto Geospatial functions: `https://github.com/trinodb/docs.trino.io/blob/master/313/_sources/functions/geospatial.rst.txt`

10. Athena V3 geospatial functions: `https://trino.io/docs/current/functions/geospatial.html`

11. Extend geospatial queries in Amazon Athena with UDFs and AWS Lambda: `https://aws.amazon.com/blogs/big-data/extend-geospatial-queries-in-amazon-athena-with-udfs-and-aws-lambda/`

12. How to partition your geospatial data lake for analysis with Amazon Redshift: `https://aws.amazon.com/blogs/publicsector/how-partition-geospatial-data-lake-analysis-amazon-redshift/`

13. GeoHex grid aggregations: `https://opensearch.org/docs/latest/aggregations/geohexgrid/`

14. PostGIS: `https://postgis.net/`

15. Oracle Spatial Concepts: `https://docs.oracle.com/database/121/SPATL/spatial-concepts.htm#SPATL010`

16. SQLServer Spatial Tools: `https://github.com/Microsoft/SQLServerSpatialTools`

## 4

Using Geospatial Data with Amazon Redshift

Querying geospatial data in a data warehouse isn't anything new, but the advantage of doing so in the cloud has opened the door to unparalleled performance and insight. I have heard from numerous customers who said that when they moved from their on-premises data warehouse to Redshift, they not only saved money but were also able to store and analyze more data exponentially. When you combine the cheap and efficient storage of S3 with the power of Redshift, where you can create up to 128 Redshift instances in a cluster, you can unlock powerful analytics. Also, like everything on AWS, you can then turn off those 128 instances after your query has completed and pay next to nothing. In this chapter, we will cover Redshift features as well as offer a demonstration of setting up and running geospatial queries on Redshift.

The chapter covers the following topics:

- What is Redshift?
- Understanding Redshift partitioning
- Redshift Spectrum
- Redshift geohashing support
- Redshift AQUA
- Redshift geospatial support
- Tutorial

What is Redshift?

Redshift is a column-based data warehouse. So, what is a columnar database, you might ask? Most of the databases you will come across would be considered row-based databases. These architectures are common in transactional databases, also known as **Online Transaction Processing (OLTP)**, which provide the backend for most enterprise applications. When a query is sent to a row-based database, it will read through its table one row at a time, reading all the attributes from all of the columns in that row, before moving on to the next row of data. These databases are good at reading tables that may have many columns and fewer rows. When I say fewer rows, I typically mean under a billion, but that exact number can depend on a few variables.

Where columnar databases differ is that when they read a table, they read it column by column. They first read every value within the first column before reading data from the second column. So, if I want to only read the first column of my table and I have several billion rows of data, a column-based database will exponentially outperform a row-based database. Another example where column-based databases shine is if you want to do a `sql count` function. Typically, you would perform a count on a single column, which a column-based database can return very quickly. The alternative to this though is running a `select *` query on a table. Column-based databases will have significantly impacted performance with a `select *` query because the database will read every value from the first column, before moving on to the next column. So, if you have a `select *` query where the column ID is 1, reading the first row would basically be the worst-case scenario for a column-based database.

Where we see these databases deployed primarily is in analytics workloads or **Online Analytical Processing (OLAP)**, which we do quite a bit of in the geospatial world. A good distinction from a geospatial standpoint might be a scenario where you serve a feature service to tens of thousands of users that might use a row-based database. Trying to understand your data and wanting to run a few queries against a database without causing it to melt down is a great scenario for an analytics database. In analytics workflows, it's common to scan tables and pull in large amounts of data because you can't always answer a question with a subset of the information. These types of queries can strain a database that simultaneously serves web users, and they are better suited to a replica of a database loaded in a data warehouse, such as Redshift.

In the next section, you will see how a columnar database can be efficiently queried when combined with a distributed backend storage system. Similar to database sharding techniques, Redshift makes use of data partitioning to improve performance and optimize the amount of data that is read when a table is queried.

Understanding Redshift partitioning

Redshift supports a couple of different partitioning models or, as Redshift calls them, distribution styles in a table – **AUTO**, **EVEN**, **KEY**, and **ALL**. Many first-time Redshift users simply ignore this optional parameter when they create their first tables, but this option can be the single most important attribute in your entire cluster. When you create a table, if this parameter is not set, it will default to

AUTO, and Redshift will try and guess the correct style. So, let's dive into these different distribution styles and their considerations.

One of the easiest to understand but potentially the most impactful distribution style is the ALL option. The significance of choosing the ALL option is that it will replicate the entire dataset across every node. A Redshift database can have up to 128 nodes in a cluster. If you have a table that is one petabyte in size and you choose the ALL option, you now have a 128-PB dataset. This is pretty similar to how read replicas operate, and you are now able to split your queries across all the nodes for a 128x increase in read throughput. Unlike read replicas, these nodes are writable, and every write has to be replicated 128 times. The main benefit of ALL is that it's relatively easy to enable and see huge performance in queries, since each node can work with its subquery to fetch, compile, aggregate, and return its results.

The next option is EVEN, which is also a relatively simple style because, as data is written, the database will essentially round-robin the data across the nodes in a cluster. If you have a table with 10 columns and a cluster with 2 nodes, then 1 node might get 5 columns and the other node the other 5. When you issue a `select  *` query for that table, the query will be split, and node one will read its five columns, and node two will read its five columns. Redshift then has a concept of a leader node, which essentially oversees the sub-queries, takes two of them, combines them, and returns the 10 columns to the requester.

Finally, we save the best for last, the KEY distribution style. KEY is similar to EVEN in that it will divide data up across the nodes in a cluster, but it gives you more flexibility in how that data is divided. With KEY, you choose a column from the table, and Redshift will divide that column up by the unique attributes across the nodes. This design is an amazing fit for geospatial queries – for example, if you have a table with zip codes, you could set them as the KEY. Now, if you run `select population where city = Austin,  TX`, your query will be divided up by zip code, and the reads will be spread across however many nodes are in the cluster. If this were a traditional row-based database and you had billions of rows in that table, you might want to leave the office for lunch, and if you were lucky, the query would be complete by the time you got back. Now, let's take a look at Redshift Spectrum, which is the bridge between our Redshift database and S3 object storage.

Redshift Spectrum

Another topic I want to introduce before we dive into Redshift's geospatial support is a feature called Spectrum. This is a powerful feature that lets Redshift seamlessly integrate with your data lake on S3. Spectrum allows Redshift to query data sitting in your S3 data lake as if it were sitting locally in the cluster. This provides massive efficiencies because you can have petabytes of data sitting on cheap S3 storage instead of sitting on expensive disk storage in your database. Not only does it allow you to query data from S3, but it also allows you to seamlessly write SQL joins against the data, both on S3 as well as the data local to the cluster.

Spectrum is also set up to take advantage of partitioning, similar to what we mentioned in the previous section. It's not the same as the ALL, EVEN, and KEY-based partitioning but is instead a simpler folder-based partitioning. Like our previous example, where we queried for the city name, you can divide your data up in S3 into folders with city names. When you write your SQL query against your S3 table and say `where city equals Austin`, Redshift will only read the data under the `Austin` folder. This improves speed because the cluster is reading in less data and, thus, is able to execute the query faster, but it also reduces network throughput costs. In the next section, we will take a look at how geohashing can be used to optimize our geospatial queries.

Redshift geohashing support

Now, let's look at how Redshift Spectrum partitioning can be combined with geospatial data to efficiently query data. So, what is geohashing? Geohashing essentially takes the world and divides it into grids. By hashing latitude and longitude coordinates, we can create a hashmap that is assigned to those grids and group data into these grids. This grouping can then be used in conjunction with database partitioning. This is a powerful approach to segmenting and storing data in a data lake. Redshift supports geohashing, giving you the ability to write a SQL query and generate a geohash for latitude and longitude, which can then be used to reference your partition. A more specific example of this could involve dividing the world into four squares, named a, b, c, and d. So, now we write a SQL query to, say, select a column ID where the geohash equals a. Now, Redshift will only read the data in S3 from the a quadrant of the planet. This could still be potentially a lot of data, so in a real-world scenario, you would have the planet subdivided into tens of millions of grids.

We will now explore another feature of Redshift, AQUA.

Redshift AQUA

Advanced Query Accelerator (**AQUA**) is a feature of Redshift that allows you to perform analysis with massive parallelization. It's also a good feature for our previous geohash scenario. AQUA would be a good fit if we needed to read the entire planet or basically all or most geohashes that are stored as folders in S3. AQUA works in combination with SQL `LIKE` queries. You would write a query that says `select ID where GEOHASH LIKE %A%`, and Redshift would spin up multiple smaller compute instances that would go out and pull the data in parallel, combine it, and then return it. This is a similar approach to how Hadoop clusters use parallelization on big datasets to improve speed in performance. You take a massive amount of data, split it up, set individual nodes to pull and process the data in parallel, and then aggregate the results when they are finished. Having a capability such as this is incredibly powerful when it's natively built into the data warehouse you already use for all of your analysis.

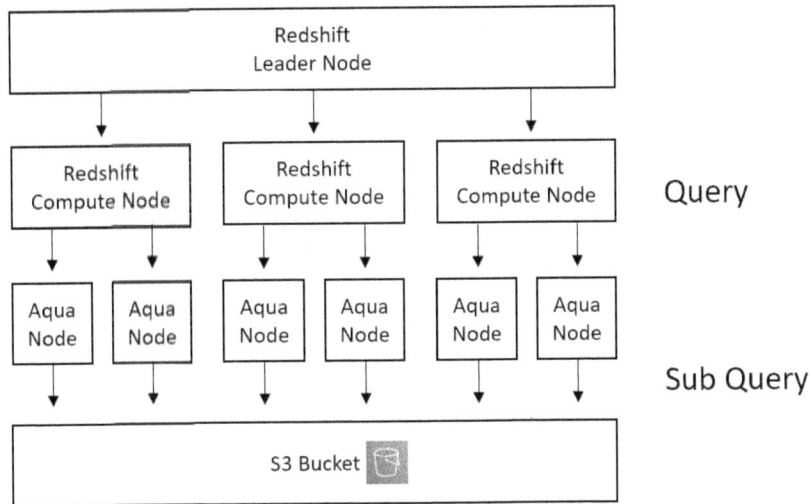

Figure 4.1 – A diagram showing how queries are split into parallelized sub-queries

Now that we saw the various features that Redshift uses for geospatial tasks, let's merge everything using a practical example in the upcoming sections.

Redshift geospatial support

Redshift continues to develop its geospatial library, and we can see increased adoption of Redshift in mainstream geospatial products, such as the recently announced Esri ArcGIS Enterprise Redshift support. At the time of writing, Redshift has 117 supported geospatial functions, with many more planned. However, the primitives really are already there, which is why we can see adoption in GIS software suites. Redshift also supports **User Defined Functions (UDFs)**, which can run snippets of Python code to run custom computations within a cluster. This works really well when a native function is missing or your workflow requires custom analysis.

Launching a Redshift cluster and running a geospatial query

Now, we will combine everything we have learned and implement a practical example, as follows:

1. Log in to the AWS Console and search for `Redshift` in the top search bar:

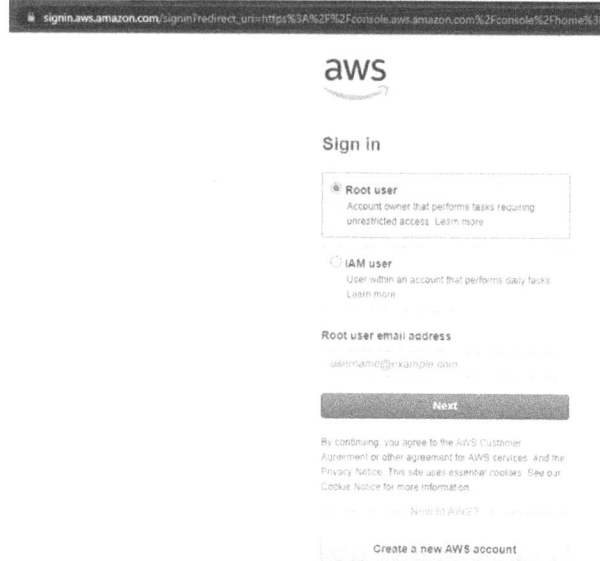

Figure 4.2 – AWS console login

When you search for `Redshift`, this should appear:

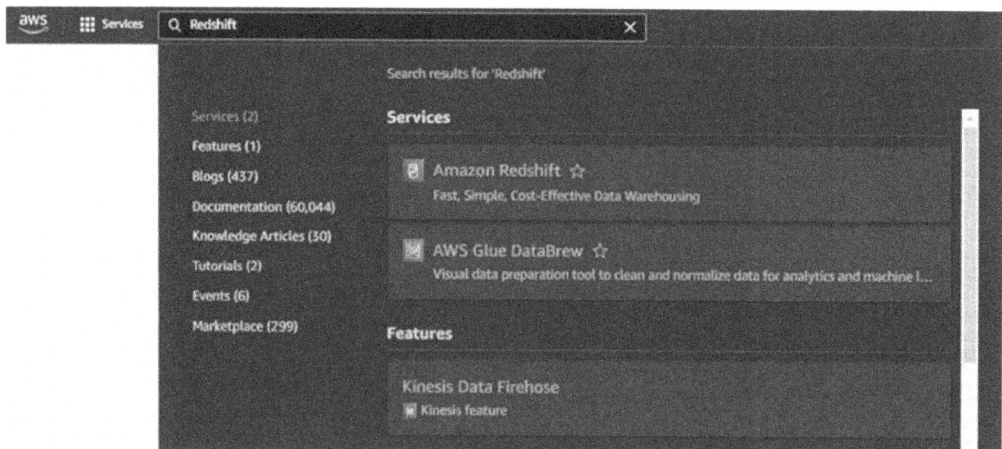

Figure 4.3 – The AWS Console showing the Redshift search results from the top navigation panel

2. Click **Create cluster** in the top-right corner:

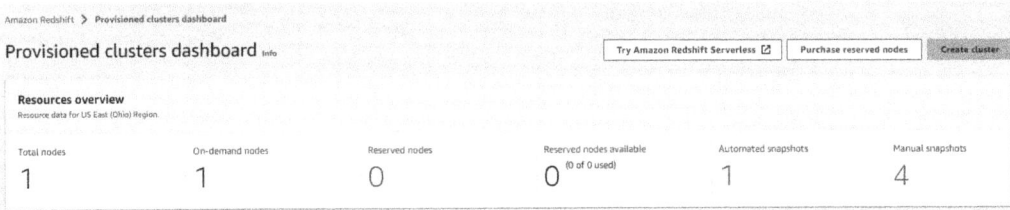

Figure 4.4 – The Redshift-provisioned cluster dashboard with an orange Create cluster button

3. Select **Free trial**:

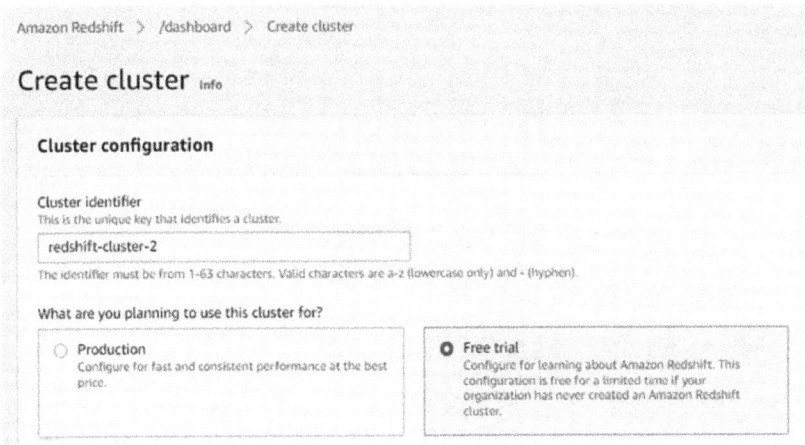

Figure 4.5 – Cluster creation

If you don't have the **Free Tier** option, alternatively you can select **dc2.large** and enter 1 as the number of nodes.

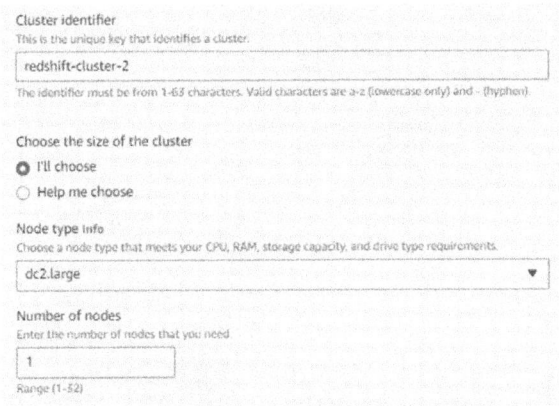

Figure 4.6 – Alternative Create cluster options

4.   Type a password and then select **Create cluster**:

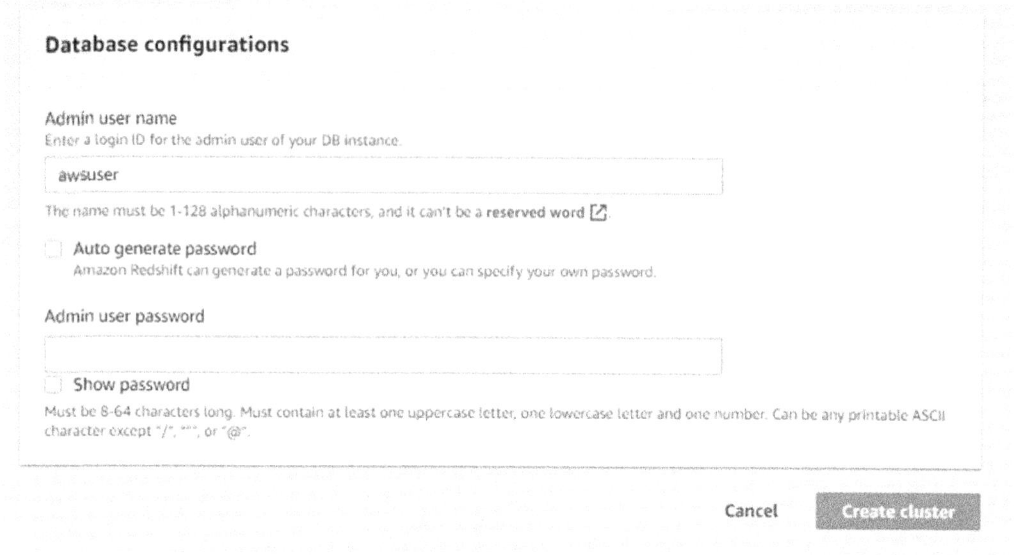

Database configurations

Admin user name
Enter a login ID for the admin user of your DB instance.

awsuser

The name must be 1-128 alphanumeric characters, and it can't be a **reserved word** [↗].

☐ Auto generate password
   Amazon Redshift can generate a password for you, or you can specify your own password.

Admin user password

☐ Show password

Must be 8-64 characters long. Must contain at least one uppercase letter, one lowercase letter and one number. Can be any printable ASCII character except "/", """, or "@".

Cancel   **Create cluster**

Figure 4.7 – Database configuration parameters

The cluster will take several minutes to start.

5.   Once the cluster is available, click on the cluster name:

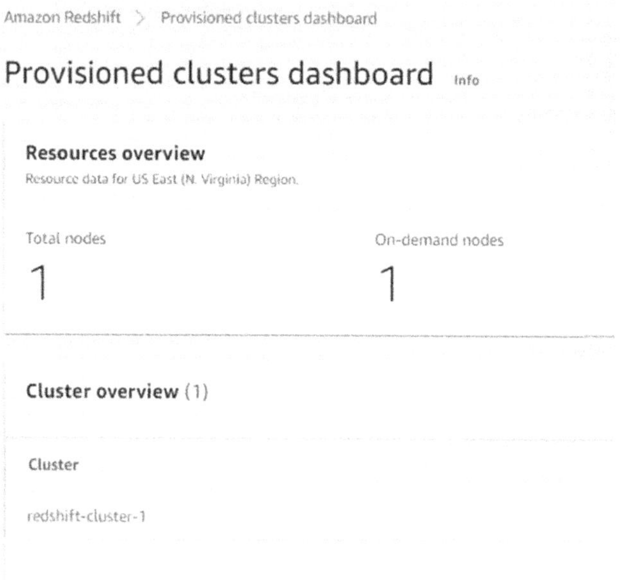

Amazon Redshift > Provisioned clusters dashboard

Provisioned clusters dashboard Info

Resources overview
Resource data for US East (N. Virginia) Region.

Total nodes

1

On-demand nodes

1

Cluster overview (1)

Cluster

redshift-cluster-1

Figure 4.8 – The Cluster overview page

6. In the top-right corner, click **Query data** and select **V2**.

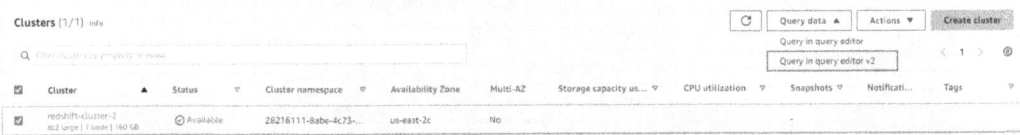

Figure 4.9 – The Cluster overview page showing the Query Editor dropdown

7. From the query editor, click on the dropdown on the left navigation panel to connect to your database and list the tables.

8. Click on **dev**, **public**, and then **Tables**.

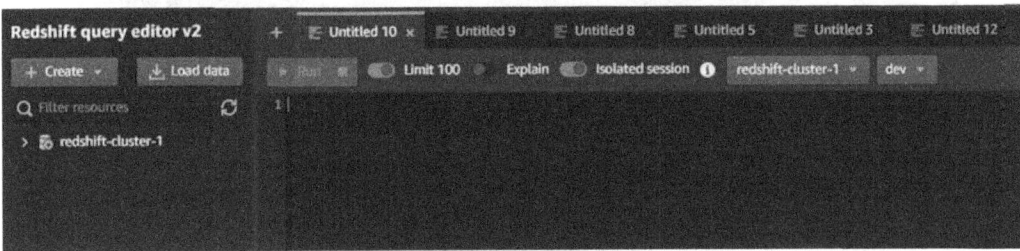

Figure 4.10 – The query editor overview page

9. At the top-left, click **Create | Table**.

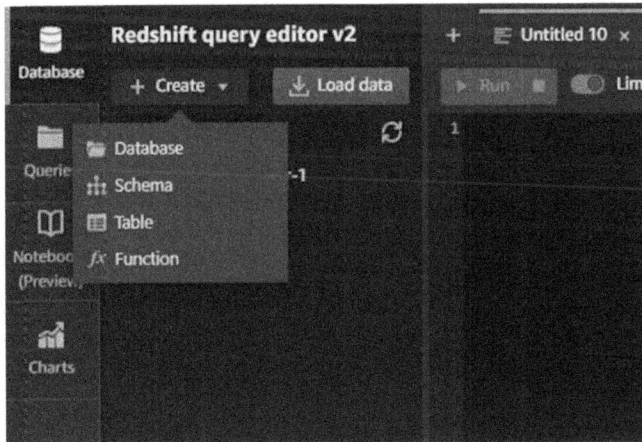

Figure 4.11 – The query editor page showing the Create dropdown

10. Under **Schema**, select **public**.

11. Under **Table**, type mygeo:

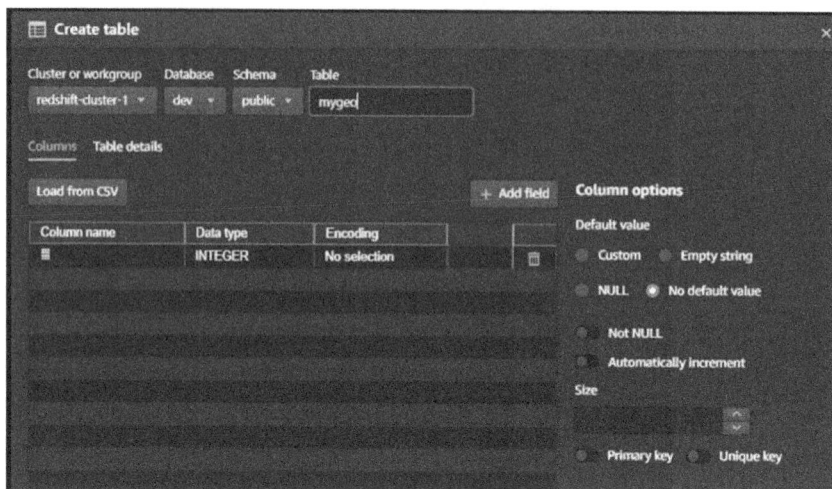

Figure 4.12 – The Create table pop-up dialog

12. Click + **Add field**.

13. Under the new field that is added, select **GEOMETRY**.

14. Give the default integer column the name ID.

15. Give the new **GEOMETRY** column we created the name GEOM.

16. Click **Create table**.

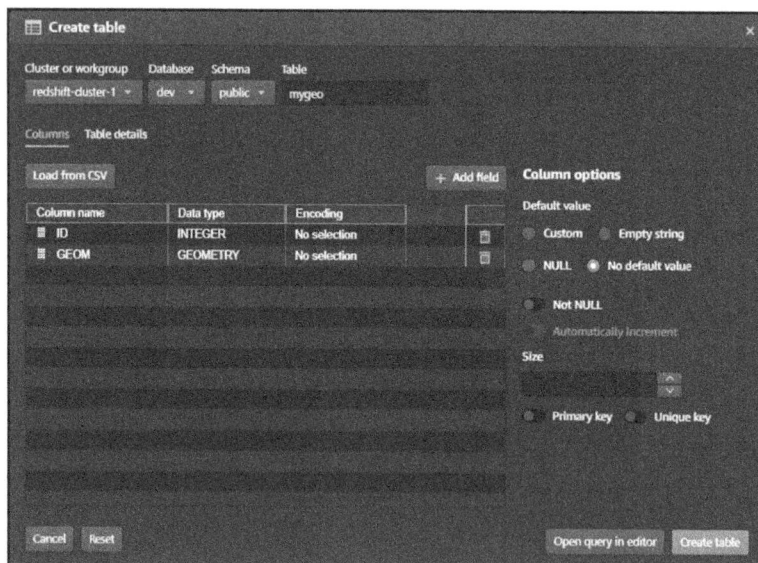

Figure 4.13 – The Create table pop-up dialog showing the ID and GEOM columns

17. After refreshing, we should see our new table listed in the navigation panel on the left.

18. Right-click on the table, click **Select table**, and then click **Run**:

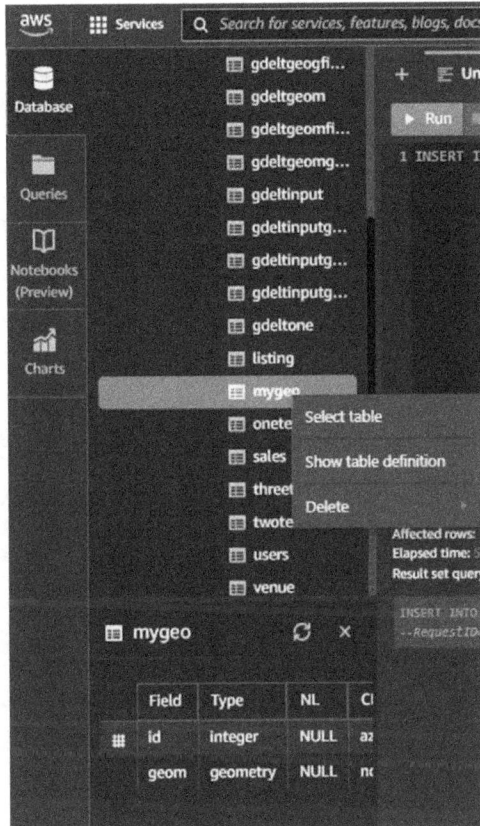

Figure 4.14 – A query editor overview with the table properties pop-up dialog box

19. You'll notice that we don't have any results yet because we haven't populated any data in our table.

20. Run the following command to convert the latitude/longitude coordinates for Austin, TX, to a geometry datatype:

```
INSERT INTO mygeo values (1, ST_SetSRID(ST_
MakePoint(-97.733330,30.266666), 4326))
```

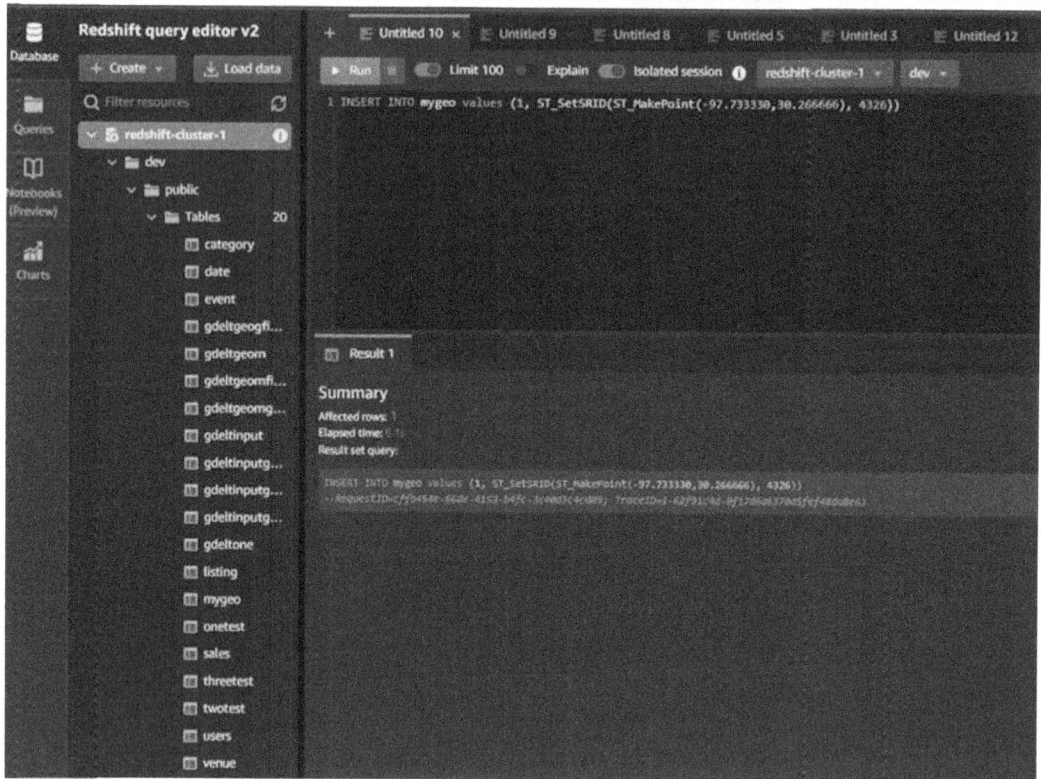

Figure 4.15 – The query editor showing the insert command to populate the table

21. Now, when we do a select on our table, we will see our results. The output should look similar to this:

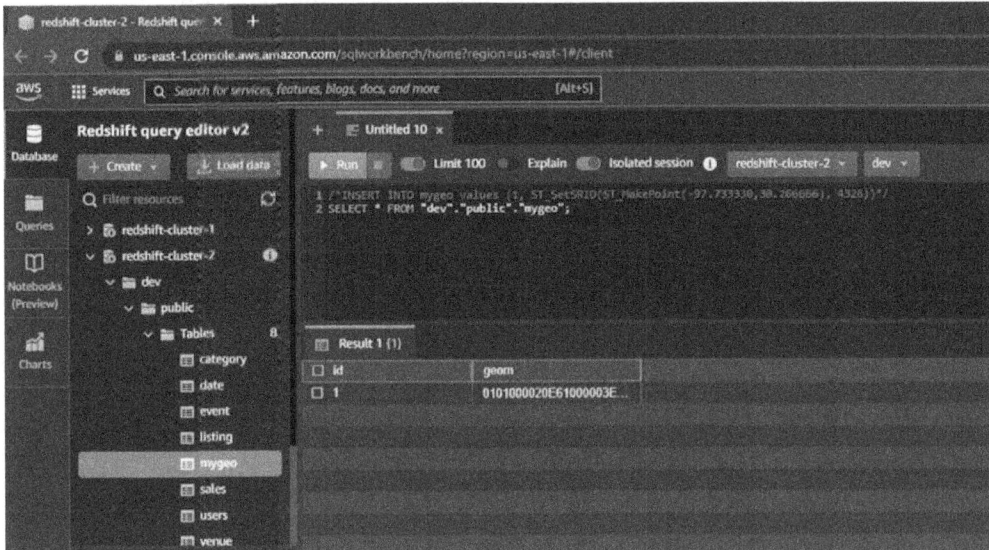

Figure 4.16 – The query editor showing the results from the SQL Select command

Congratulations! You have run your first geospatial query on Amazon Redshift. Thus, we have explored a practical example of how Redshift works with geospatial technology.

Summary

In this chapter, we covered what Redshift is and how it can be used to power geospatial workloads. We covered how Redshift partitioning works and how it applies to geospatial tables. We covered how Redshift Spectrum can be used to achieve higher efficiency and significant cost savings. Finally, we covered how AQUA can be used for significant performance increases with parallel querying and processing data.

In the next chapter, we will cover querying geospatial data using Amazon RDS and Aurora PostgreSQL for unparalleled cloud geodatabase performance.

References

- Redshift distribution keys: `https://docs.aws.amazon.com/redshift/latest/dg/c_choosing_dist_sort.html`

- Redshift distribution keys best practices: `https://docs.aws.amazon.com/redshift/latest/dg/c_best-practices-best-dist-key.html`

- Redshift geospatial functions: `https://docs.aws.amazon.com/redshift/latest/dg/geospatial-functions.html`

- ArcGIS Redshift support: `https://aws.amazon.com/blogs/apn/leveraging-the-power-of-esri-arcgis-enterprise-through-amazon-redshift/`

5

Using Geospatial Data with Amazon Aurora PostgreSQL

PostgreSQL has risen in popularity to become one of the most common geospatial platforms for storing structured relational data. Creating your own geodatabase a decade ago was reserved for the most experienced administrators. Today, we can instantly spin up a globally replicated database in the cloud using **infrastructure as code (IaC)**.

This chapter will teach you how to create, populate, use, and visualize an Amazon Aurora PostgreSQL geodatabase on **Amazon Web Services (AWS)**. Specifically, we will cover the following topics:

- Setting up the database
- Connecting to the database
- Geospatial data loading
- Queries and transformations
- Architectural considerations

Amazon Aurora is an AWS service that provides managed serverless databases on open source platforms. Aurora also provides unparalleled performance and global availability at one-tenth the cost of commercial databases.

Lab prerequisites

Included in the lab activities of this chapter, you will be creating a PostgreSQL instance. The exercises and examples will work on clusters, instances, or serverless versions of Aurora as long as you are running PostgreSQL with PostGIS installed. Before starting with the geospatial database setup, ensure you have the following:

- AWS account with administrative privileges

- Desktop software for **geographic information system** (**GIS**) data visualization (QGIS, ArcGIS Pro, and so on)

- Sample shapefile of data to load into the geodatabase

An important aspect of using geospatial data is the relationship between clusters, instances, databases, schemas, and tables. A cluster refers to one or more instances of PostgreSQL that provide both additional scale and resiliency for your geospatial database. Instances within the cluster can be designated as the primary instance supporting both read and write operations or a read-only replica instance. All of the instances share and operate on the same underlying data. Each defined database comprises schemas that own objects such as tables and views for accessing your geospatial data.

A common scenario of loading shapefiles into the database will be presented in this chapter. If you would like to use the same spatial data used here, a shapefile of US counties can be found on the *US Census* website (`https://www2.census.gov/geo/tiger/GENZ2018/shp/cb_2018_us_county_20m.zip`).

Setting up the database

Using your AWS account, you can quickly set up a database for storing geospatial data in the cloud. This section will walk you through the steps to create a serverless database using **Amazon Relational Database Service** (**Amazon RDS**). The architecture described here is not recommended for a production geospatial system but provides a simple and cost-effective way to explore geospatial data on AWS. Any business-critical systems should consider using the **Multi-Availability Zone** (**Multi-AZ**) deployment option for PostgreSQL to provide failover capabilities in the event of any infrastructure disruptions.

Many workloads have specific requirements or constraints that dictate the version of PostgreSQL or PostGIS. If your situation does not prescribe a specific operating system or version, it is often advantageous to use the AWS default recommendations.

Log in to your AWS account and navigate to the **RDS** service. You can choose whichever region is preferred based on workload requirements. Create a new database by selecting the **Create database** button, as illustrated here:

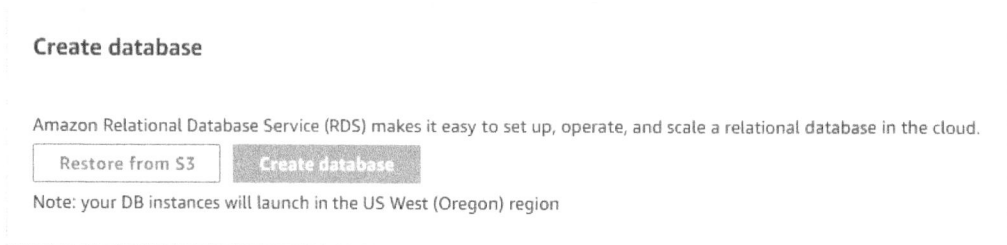

Figure 5.1: Creating a database with the click of a button

Use the standard create option to have the most control over deployment options:

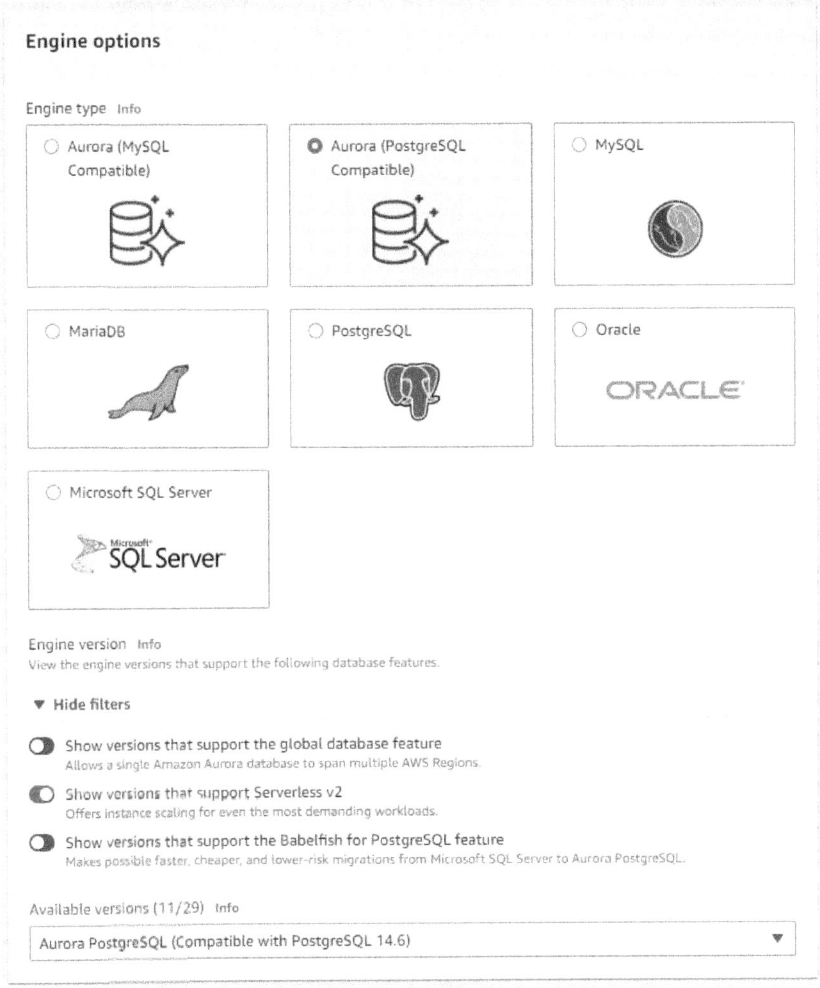

Engine options

Engine type Info

○ Aurora (MySQL
    Compatible)

● Aurora (PostgreSQL
    Compatible)

○ MySQL

○ MariaDB

○ PostgreSQL

○ Oracle

ORACLE

○ Microsoft SQL Server

Microsoft
SQL Server

Engine version Info
View the engine versions that support the following database features.

▼ Hide filters

◯● Show versions that support the global database feature
    Allows a single Amazon Aurora database to span multiple AWS Regions.

●◯ Show versions that support Serverless v2
    Offers instance scaling for even the most demanding workloads.

◯● Show versions that support the Babelfish for PostgreSQL feature
    Makes possible faster, cheaper, and lower-risk migrations from Microsoft SQL Server to Aurora PostgreSQL.

Available versions (11/29) Info

Aurora PostgreSQL (Compatible with PostgreSQL 14.6)   ▼

Figure 5.2: Selecting Amazon Aurora for simplified administration

In this example, we will be setting up an Aurora Serverless v2 PostgreSQL 14.6 version in Dev/Test mode. This configuration was chosen to leverage the latest default version as of this book's writing; however, the defaults will change over time as new versions of the platform are released.

In the **Settings** section, you'll want to choose something meaningful for the **DB cluster identifier** option. The default of database-1 has been used in this example, but something such as operations or geology may better describe the data you plan to store in the database:

Settings

DB cluster identifier Info
Enter a name for your DB cluster. The name must be unique across all DB clusters owned by your AWS account in the current AWS Region.

```
database-1
```

The DB cluster identifier is case-insensitive, but is stored as all lowercase (as in "mydbcluster"). Constraints: 1 to 60 alphanumeric characters or hyphens. First character must be a letter. Can't contain two consecutive hyphens. Can't end with a hyphen.

▼ Credentials Settings

Master username Info
Type a login ID for the master user of your DB instance.

```
postgres
```

1 to 16 alphanumeric characters. First character must be a letter.

☐ Manage master credentials in AWS Secrets Manager
Manage master user credentials in Secrets Manager. RDS can generate a password for you and manage it throughout its lifecycle.

ⓘ If you manage the master user credentials in Secrets Manager, some RDS features aren't supported.
Learn more ☑

☐ Auto generate a password
Amazon RDS can generate a password for you, or you can specify your own password.

Master password Info

```
••••••••••
```

Constraints: At least 8 printable ASCII characters. Can't contain any of the following: / (slash), '(single quote), "(double quote) and @ (at sign).

Confirm master password Info

```
••••••••••
```

Figure 5.3: Database name and authentication settings

Accept the default of **Aurora Standard** for the **Cluster storage configuration** setting, then select **Serverless v2** as the database instance class. In the **Instance configuration** window, you can specify how powerful you want the PostgreSQL instance to be. In this example, we will select **Serverless v2**.

Aurora Serverless v2 provides true on-demand autoscaling based on database usage metrics. Capacity is adjusted automatically by AWS to scale up when demand is high and scale back down automatically when the database load decreases. Database capacity is measured in **Aurora Capacity Units** (**ACUs**), and you can set the minimum and maximum values for each instance.

You may want to change the capacity range of the instance configuration to minimize cost when not in use. The **Minimum ACUs** setting was changed to 1 from the default of 2 in this example:

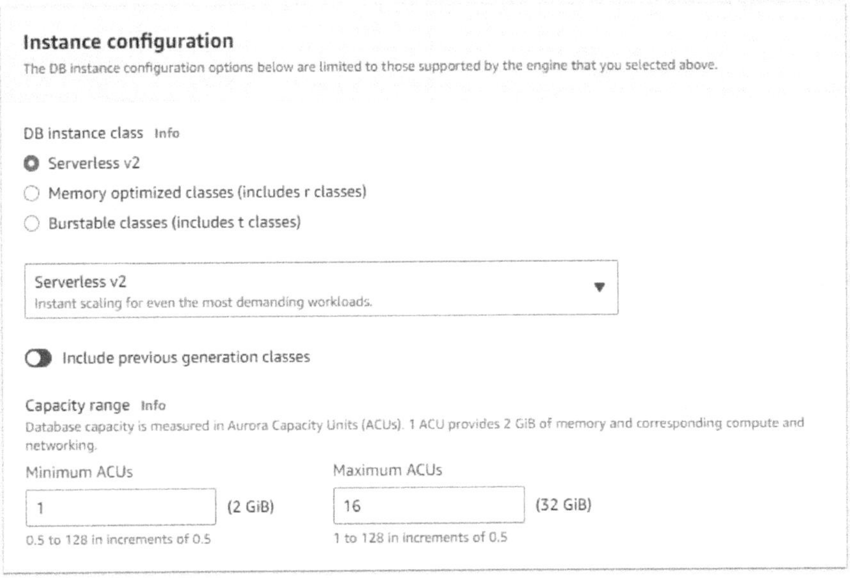

Figure 5.4: Serverless databases provide excellent cost efficiency and scalability

Accept all defaults in the **Connectivity** section, unless you would like this database to be accessible from the public internet. If your PostgreSQL database will not have any confidential data in it, you may choose the option to allow public access. This will generate and assign a public IP address for the cluster and simplify the process of connecting to your new geospatial database:

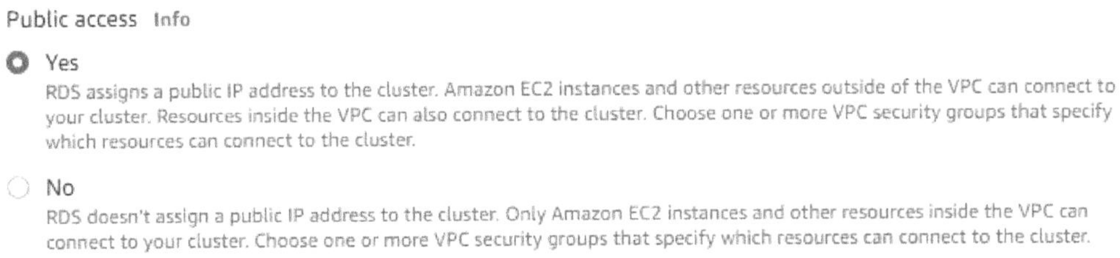

Figure 5.5: Public access should be used with extreme caution

Although the database will still be protected from unauthorized anonymous access because a login is required, public access should always be used with caution as it expands the overall attack surface that is exposed to potential hackers. We are using a publicly accessible Aurora database in this lab, but it is not recommended to store private data in a publicly accessible database. In order to connect, it will be necessary to add an inbound PostgreSQL rule to the security group with the source of your IP address. We'll cover that after the database is created. This protects the database by only allowing traffic from the IP addresses specified.

If you have existing VPC security groups you would like to have access to your data, they can be added to the default at this time. The default port of 5432 in the **Additional configuration** subsection is appropriate for most applications of PostgreSQL.

Leave the checkboxes for **Babelfish** and additional methods for **Database authentication** unchecked. The **Monitoring** and **Additional configuration** sections can be left as they are. Finally, click the **Create database** button to finish the setup. You should then see the following message:

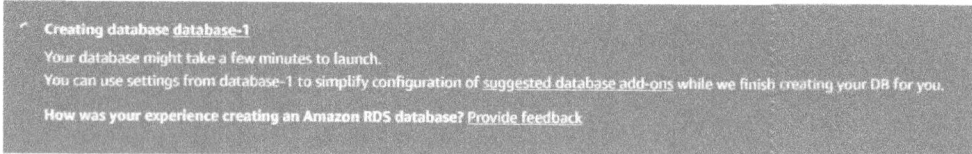

Figure 5.6: Status bar in AWS console

You can click the **View connection details** button in the notification banner to view the login information for your database.

It is critically important that you make a note of your database name, username, password, and endpoint. This is the information needed to access, configure, and load geospatial data into your Aurora instance. The password that was used to create the database can never be recovered once the **Close** button is clicked:

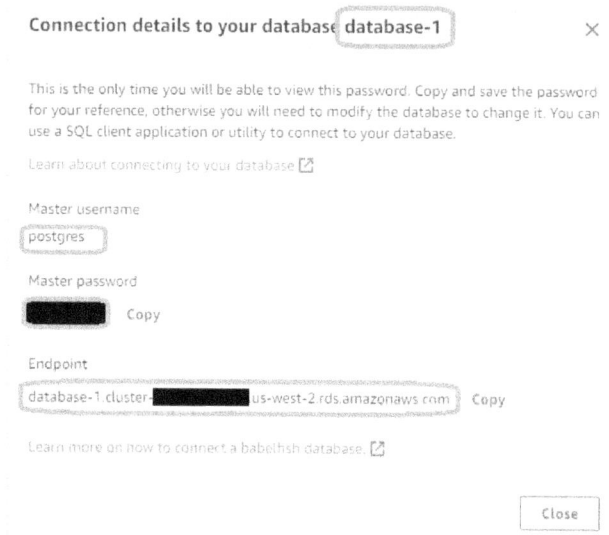

Figure 5.7: Connection details should be stored securely

For the next step in the process, you will be logging in to your newly created PostgreSQL database running on Amazon Aurora. If you are not familiar with connecting to a PostgreSQL database, click the following link at the top of the connection details popup: `https://docs.aws.amazon.com/AmazonRDS/latest/UserGuide/CHAP_CommonTasks.Connect.html`.

The AWS cloud secures by default, so if you are working from home on a laptop, you won't be able to connect to the database with your familiar geospatial tools such as Esri ArcGIS Pro or QGIS. PostgreSQL database clients from Windows or Linux machines can't connect either. This problem is simply solved by adding an inbound rule to the security group that allows your IP address to connect to the database in AWS.

In the **RDS** section of the AWS console, you will see the database and instance that were created. Also shown here is a separate Aurora Serverless v1 database called `aurora-geo` that has also been used for some of the examples in this book:

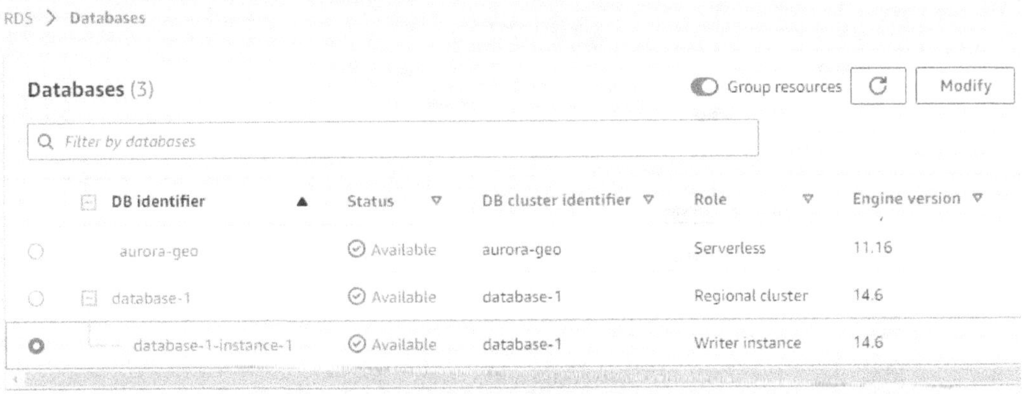

RDS 〉 Databases

	DB identifier ▲	Status ▽	DB cluster identifier ▽	Role ▽	Engine version ▽
	aurora-geo	⊘ Available	aurora-geo	Serverless	11.16
	database-1	⊘ Available	database-1	Regional cluster	14.6
	database-1-instance-1	⊘ Available	database-1	Writer instance	14.6

Databases (3)   Group resources   Modify

Figure 5.8: AWS console view of the created RDS Aurora database instance

It is helpful to familiarize yourself with the contents of each tab of your instance. The **Monitoring** tab will provide real-time metrics on the health and activity of your database. Details about versions and other technical details can be found on the **Configuration** tab. Clicking on the instance name will show important details about the connectivity and security of your database. The endpoint value at the top left was noted earlier and will be needed to connect. Always be aware as to whether you have publicly accessible data by looking in the **Connectivity & security** column of the tab. VPC security groups are the default way that resources are secured in AWS. A security group has rules that dictate what types of traffic will be allowed in and out of the database instance. By default, AWS will provide you with a default security group with outbound access to the internet. Any incoming connection is compared to these security group inbound rules to see if the traffic should be allowed. The default configuration only allows connections from other AWS resources that are in that security group.

For example, if you had a geospatial analytics server in the same security group, it would be able to connect to the PostgreSQL database. AWS AZs, VPCs, and networking subnets can also be viewed on this screen in the AWS console:

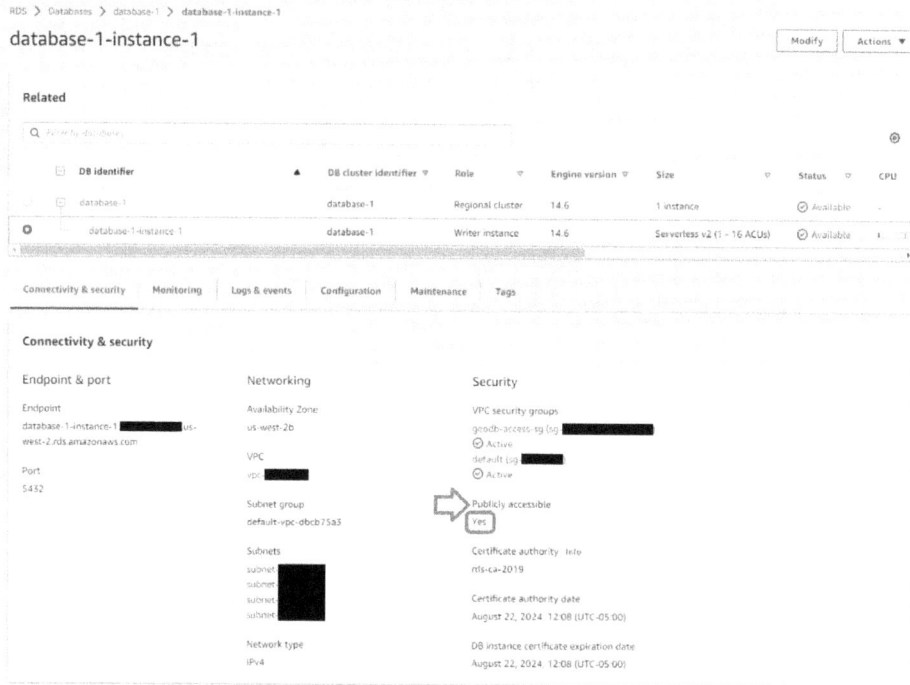

Figure 5.9: RDS database Connectivity & security tab

Below **Connectivity & security**, you can see all security group rules that are governing access to your database. Yours should look something like the orange highlighted security groups. The other entries here are not related to this lab:

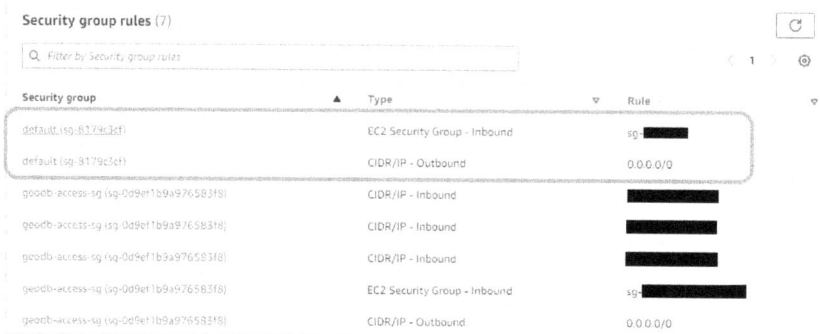

Figure 5.10: Connection details should be stored securely

Click on the hyperlinked name of your security group, then go to the **Inbound rules** tab. You should see a single rule allowing all traffic from a source that is within the same security group. Don't change anything on that inbound rule. We are going to add a new rule allowing port 5432 from your machine. Click on the **Edit inbound rules** button on the right-hand side of the screen and you should then see a screen like this:

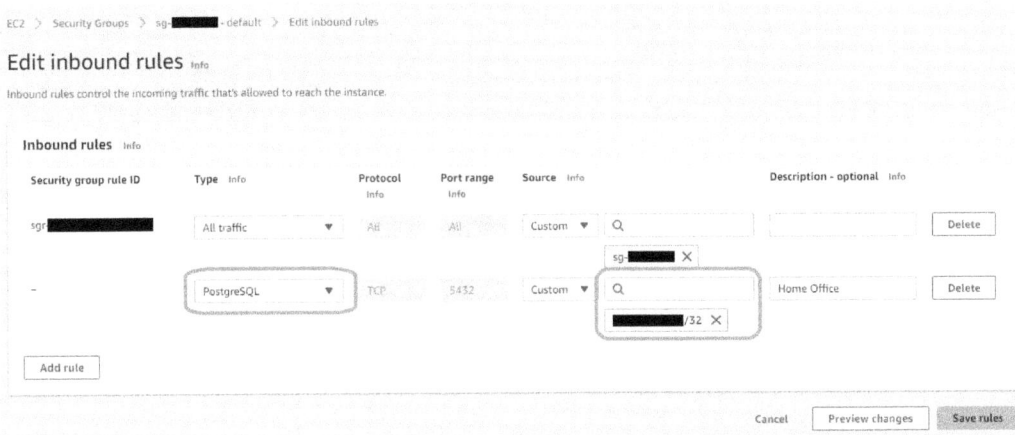

Figure 5.11: Adding a PostgreSQL inbound rule

Select **PostgreSQL** for the type of traffic, and enter the IP address of the computer you want to have access to the database. If you don't know your IP address, just point a web browser to `https://www.whatismyip.com/`. As shown in *Figure 5.11*, the /32 instance afterward is a networking designator specifying a single IP address. If you aren't familiar with **Classless Inter-Domain Routing (CIDR)**, don't worry about it as that is all you'll need to know. If you would like to know more, check the links at the end of the chapter. Once this simple configuration is in place, all of your geospatial and technical tools will have access to the database.

Connecting to the database

Before your geospatial data can be loaded into your Aurora instance, it needs to be configured as a geospatial database. The commands that you need to run will require a PostgreSQL database client, and pgAdmin is a widely used, free, and convenient tool. pgAdmin can be downloaded for Windows, macOS, or a number of other platforms from the following link: `https://www.pgadmin.org/download/`.

Using pgAdmin, or your database client of choice, create a connection by registering a new server. The database endpoint, username, and password are entered in the highlighted areas in *Figure 5.12*:

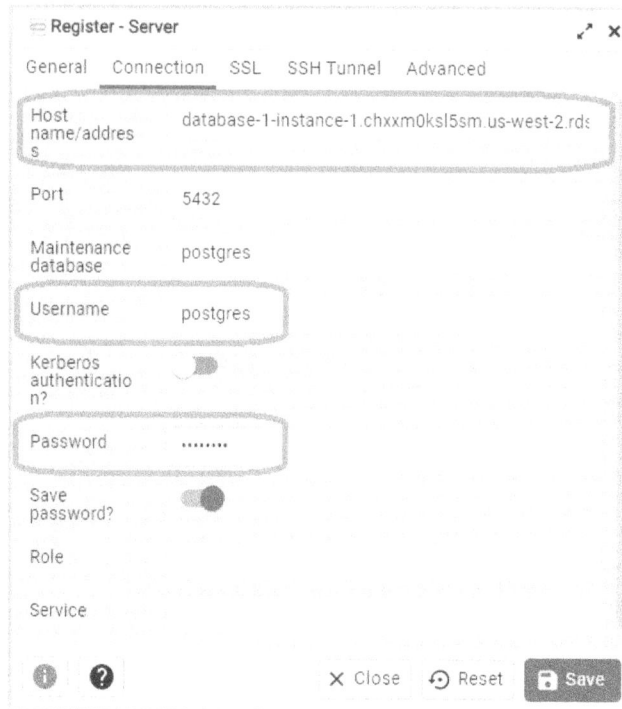

Figure 5.12: Connecting to the Amazon Aurora database instance

This completes the installation and connection to your new PostgreSQL database on Amazon Aurora. In the next section, we'll install the geospatial extensions.

Installing the PostGIS extension

Creating a PostgreSQL database does not provide the necessary support for geospatial data out of the box. To add these capabilities, you will need to install the PostGIS extension. The steps can vary slightly between versions, so the examples here can be used as a guide but may require minor changes depending on your version of PostgreSQL and PostGIS. Proceed as follows:

1. Log in using the username and password specified during database creation.

2. Expand the **Databases** section and confirm that there are two databases: `postgres` and `rdsadmin`.

3. Open a query editor window (*Alt + Shift + Q*).

4. Run the following command to verify the `postgres` system tables exist:

```
select * from information_schema.tables;
```

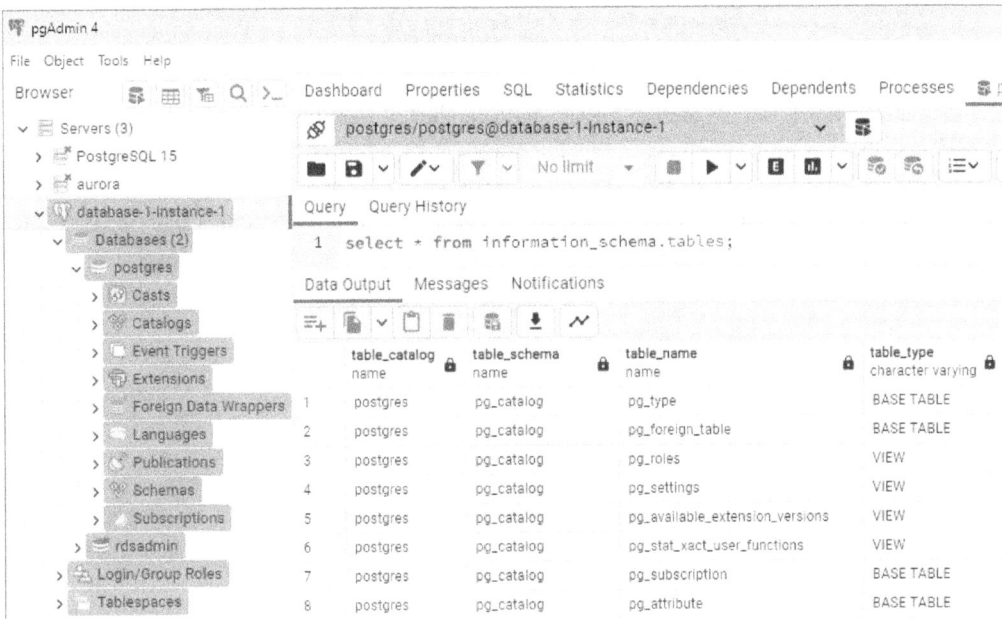

Figure 5.13: pgAdmin is a useful GUI for both administration and Structured Query Language (SQL) queries

5. Create a separate database called `geodb` for geospatial data, like so:

```
CREATE DATABASE geodb;
```

6. Establish a new role that has administrative privileges on this new database. The `'Change#M3'` password should be modified to something of your choice:

```
CREATE ROLE gis_admin LOGIN PASSWORD 'Change#M3';   -- !! CHANGE
PASSWORD !!
GRANT ALL PRIVILEGES ON DATABASE geodb TO gis_admin;
GRANT rds_superuser TO gis_admin;
```

7. We don't want to continue to use the `postgres` master user any more than is necessary, so log out and log back into the instance with the new `gis_admin` credentials. The following statements should be run after reconnecting to the database to install PostGIS in the correct location with the correct permissions:

```
-- Install geospatial extensions
CREATE EXTENSION postgis;
```

```
CREATE EXTENSION fuzzystrmatch CASCADE;
CREATE EXTENSION postgis_tiger_geocoder;
CREATE EXTENSION postgis_topology;
CREATE EXTENSION address_standardizer_data_us;
CREATE EXTENSION aws_s3 CASCADE;
```

More information on the process of installing PostGIS can be found in the *Managing spatial data with the PostGIS extension* section of the user guide for Aurora (`https://docs.aws.amazon.com/AmazonRDS/latest/AuroraUserGuide/Appendix.PostgreSQL.CommonDBATasks.PostGIS.html`). A database with the extension successfully installed will look like this with the newly created `geodb` database and associated schemas:

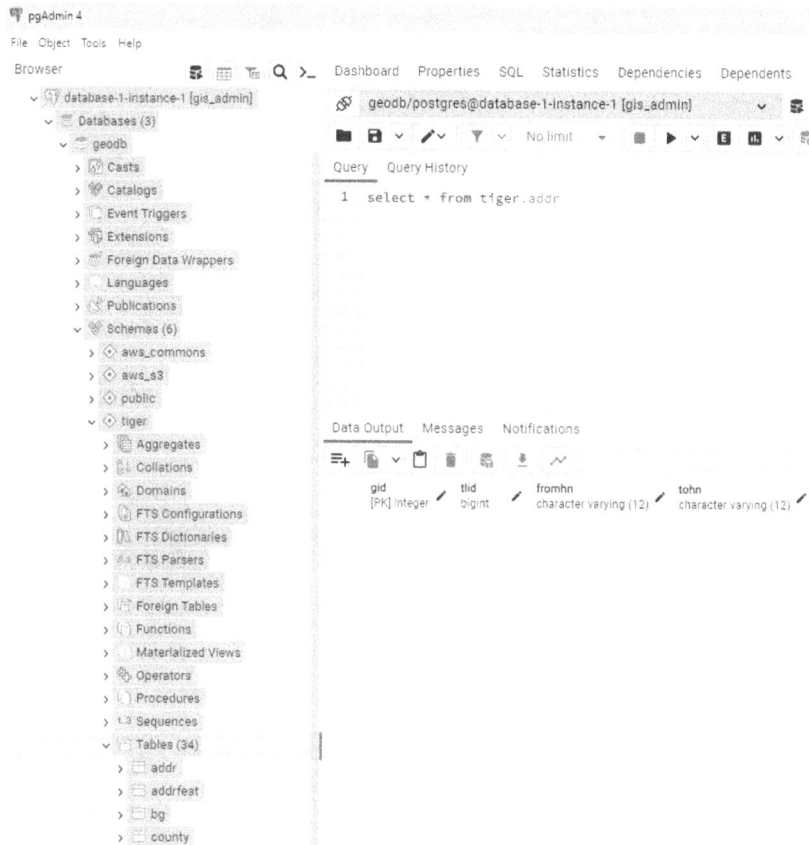

Figure 5.14: An empty PostGIS-enabled PostgreSQL geodatabase

This section provides one method to establish a PostgreSQL database with PostGIS enabled. With a geodatabase in the AWS cloud, you have a powerful and scalable platform to manage and share geospatial data. Next, we'll look at how to get geospatial data into the database instance.

Geospatial data loading

Although we now have a geodatabase, it only provides value and insights for your organization when populated with coordinates and attribute data. PostgreSQL has rich geospatial data support through the PostGIS extension. Both are open source, providing a powerful and cost-effective means to enable geospatial data storage analysis.

The most important part of establishing tables for geospatial data is to create a column that stores the geometry data type. Several different methods and tools can be used to simplify spatial data tables and indexes. One popular open source approach is to use the `shp2pgsql.exe` command-line utility. This handy tool, managed by the **Open Source Geospatial Foundation** (**OSGeo**), extracts information from the multiple files that make up a shapefile package. The contents are then converted into SQL statements that can be applied directly to your database. The content of the statements can be altered by the command-line arguments. There is also a GUI version of the tool. Both are included with the PostgreSQL installation, but when using a serverless geodatabase, you can download them directly from here: `http://download.osgeo.org/postgis/windows/`.

Another method Windows users have to load geospatial data into PostgreSQL databases is the GUI version of the PostGIS tool. You can find installation downloads and documentation for a wide range of operating systems on the PostGIS website: `https://postgis.net/install/`. This simple application is also included in the PostGIS installation in a subfolder of the `bin` folder where the other executable files are stored. For PostgreSQL 14, this folder will be called `postgisgui`, and the name of the executable file will be `shp2pgsql-gui.exe`:

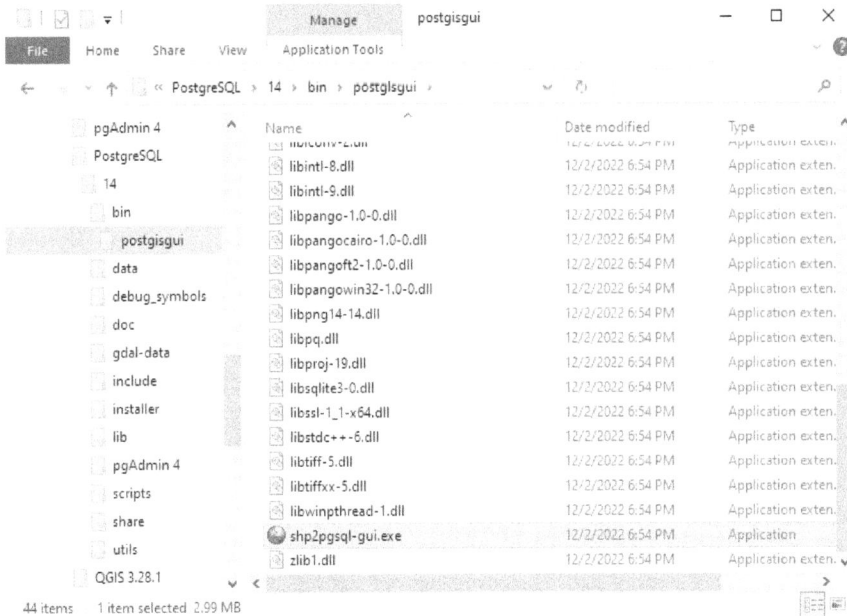

Figure 5.15: File location of GUI data loading utility

This application, titled **PostGIS Shapefile Import/Export Manager**, can be utilized as a simple way to load shapefile GIS data into your PostgreSQL database. The next steps show how to load two shapefiles using `postgisgui`.

After launching the application, the first step is to enter the database connection information. This can be specified by pressing the **View Connection details…** button at the top of the application window, which will take you to the following dialog window:

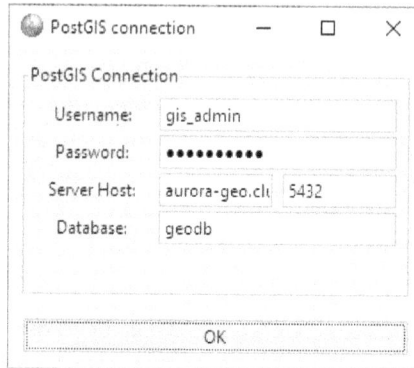

Figure 5.16: Connection details dialog window

We will select the shapefiles, as seen here:

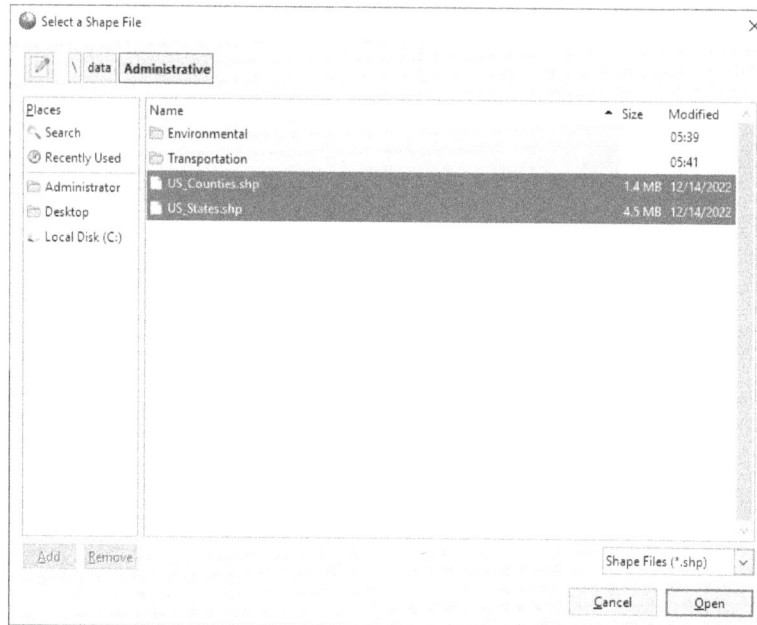

Figure 5.17: Selecting the shapefiles to import

Finally, we will review everything before using the **Import** function:

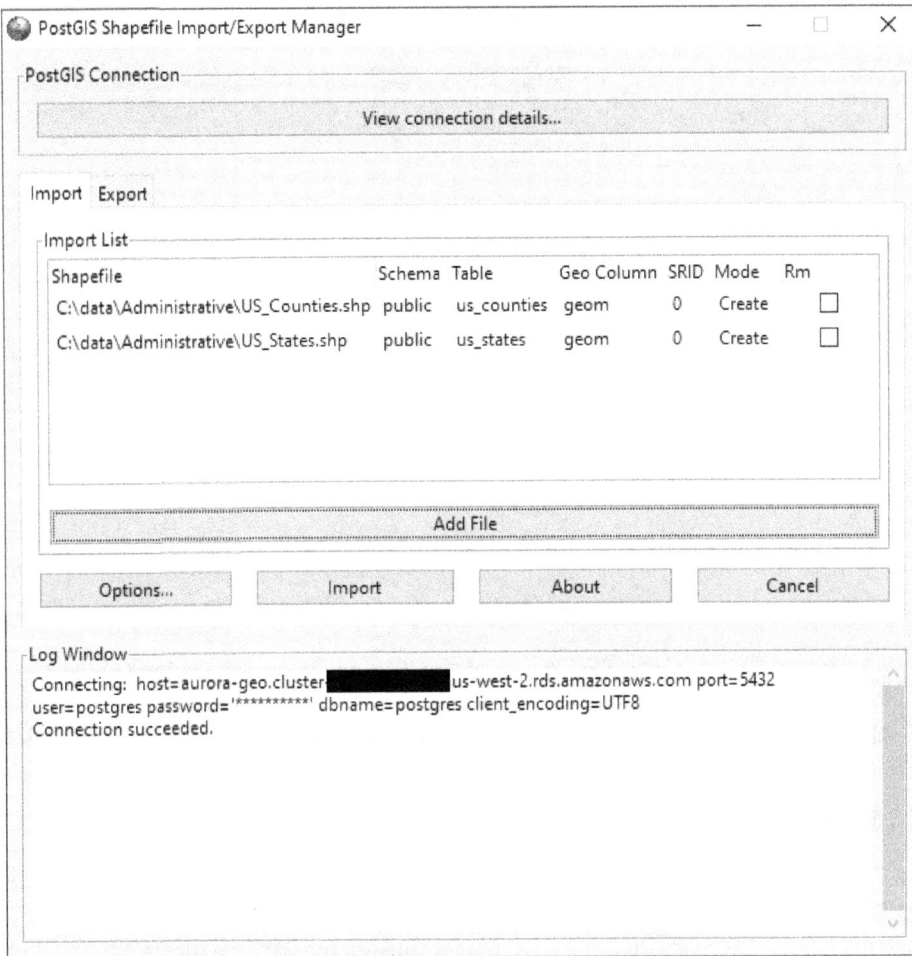

Figure 5.18: Reviewing before using the Import function

You can load multiple shapefiles at once, as shown with US states and counties in this example. After pressing the **Import** button, progress bars will indicate the status of the data loading, and the log window will show something similar to the following for all data files selected:

```
===============================
Importing with configuration: us_counties, public, geom, C:\data\
Administrative\US_Counties.shp, mode=c, dump=1, simple=0, geography=0,
index=1, shape=1, srid=0
Shapefile type: Polygon
PostGIS type: MULTIPOLYGON[2]
Shapefile import completed.
```

In addition to loading the shapefile data into a PostgreSQL table, this handy utility will also create a primary key and spatial index for you automatically, as illustrated here:

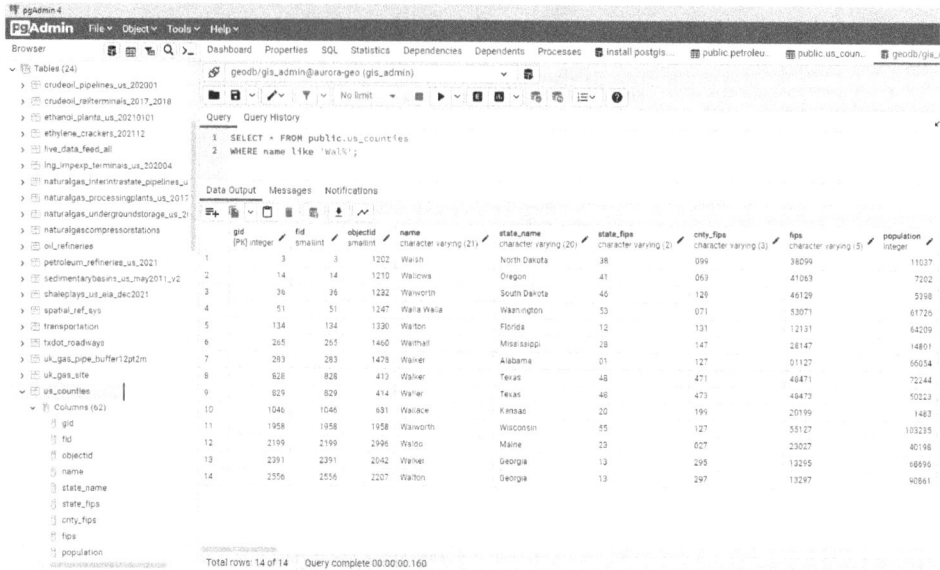

Figure 5.19: SQL query (filtered) view of the US counties geospatial dataset

Now, we will dive into some of the queries and transformations that we can do in the AWS cloud.

Queries and transformations

Geospatial data provides answers to some of our most difficult business questions, but we must know how to ask the questions. While this topic will be introduced here, additional details will be provided in the *Querying Geospatial Data with Amazon Athena* chapter. In the AWS cloud, you have the option to use traditional SQL clients to query the database directly, or one of the SQL interfaces provided in the AWS console. SQL clients that you may already be familiar with provide a familiar interface to your geospatial data. Amazon RDS and Athena offer convenient interfaces through a web browser that do not require local installation of any software.

If you have an existing Aurora Serverless v1 database with a compatible version of PostgreSQL, the **Query Editor** tool can be used in the **RDS** section of the AWS console. There are many flexible options to access your datasets based on your use case and client environment. The Aurora Serverless PostgreSQL database we loaded shapefiles into earlier in this chapter can be queried from Athena, but only v1 databases work with the RDS query editor. Within the navigation bar of Amazon RDS, the **Query Editor** tool provides a simple means to execute SQL queries against your geospatial data. The US states and counties geospatial datasets now reside in the PostgreSQL database along with the polygons making up their boundaries. We can issue SQL queries just as you would with any relational database.

If you are working with an unfamiliar database, metadata about the database objects can provide insight into the contents. PostgreSQL (and other relational database platforms such as Oracle) has a built-in information schema that can be queried to see which tables you have in your database. If you want to see which tables exist in the public schema, try this SQL query:

```
select * from information_schema.tables
where table_schema='public'
```

The results will show the following information:

- `table_catalog`: The PostgreSQL database name

- `table_schema`: Schema that contains the table

- `table_name`: Name of the table containing rows and columns of data

- `table_type`: Whether the item is a table or a view

You can see an overview of this in the following screenshot:

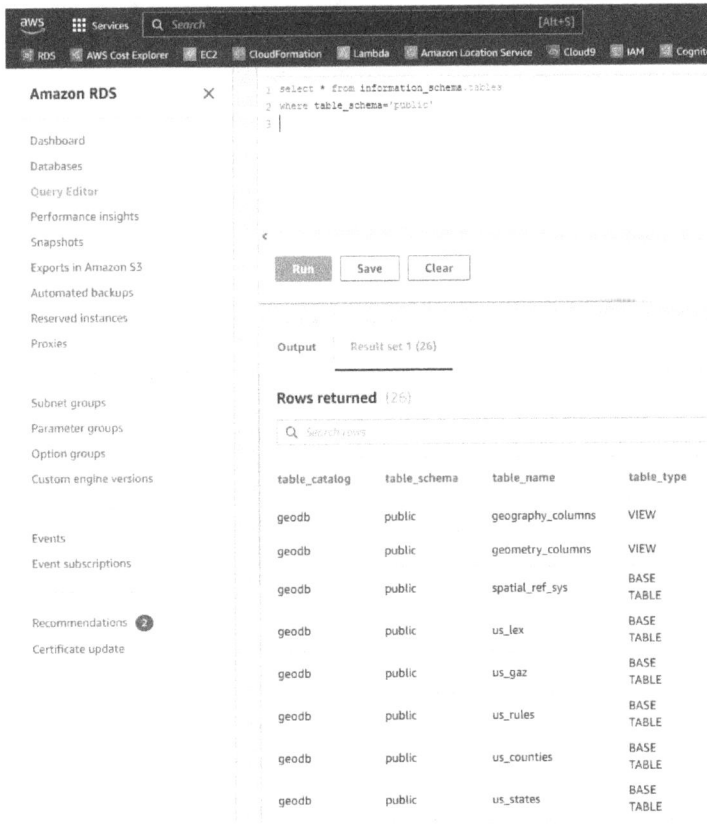

Figure 5.20: SQL query view of geospatial datasets in Amazon Aurora w/PostGIS

In addition to queries to view the catalog of your geospatial data, SQL can be used to perform simple calculations and transformations as well. In the us_counties dataset, you will find one row of data for each county in the US. You can perform queries to aggregate or filter based on the population, area, or other characteristics of each feature. Here is an example of a SQL statement that will filter to select only counties with a population greater than 2.5 million people. The results are sorted by population density within that county:

```
SELECT objectid, name, state_name, fips, population, pop_sqmi, med_
age, households, ave_hh_sz, hse_units, vacant, crop_acr12, sqmi, geom
       FROM public.us_counties
WHERE population > 2500000
ORDER BY pop_sqmi desc
```

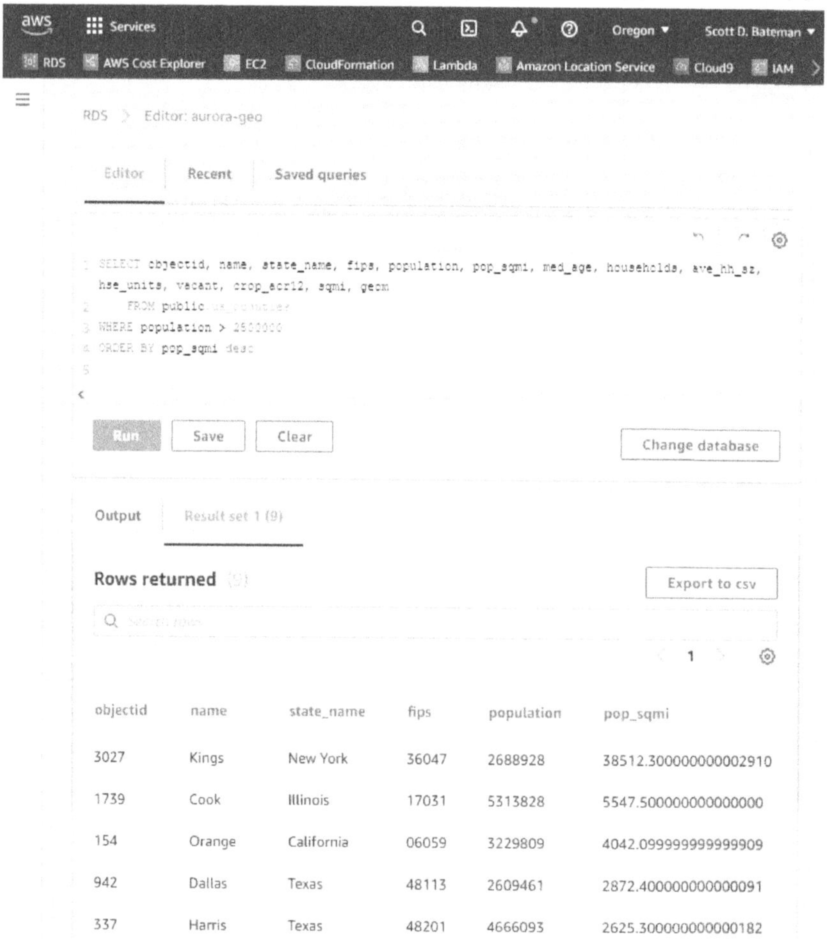

Figure 5.21: SQL query view of counties by population in AWS console

It is important to note that the geospatial feature for each row is stored in the geom column. This will be true for any geospatial data stored using PostGIS, whether the features are points, lines, or polygons.

Let's take a look at publicly available data on oil refineries in the US. For this query, we'll use pgAdmin to show additional visual cues about each column:

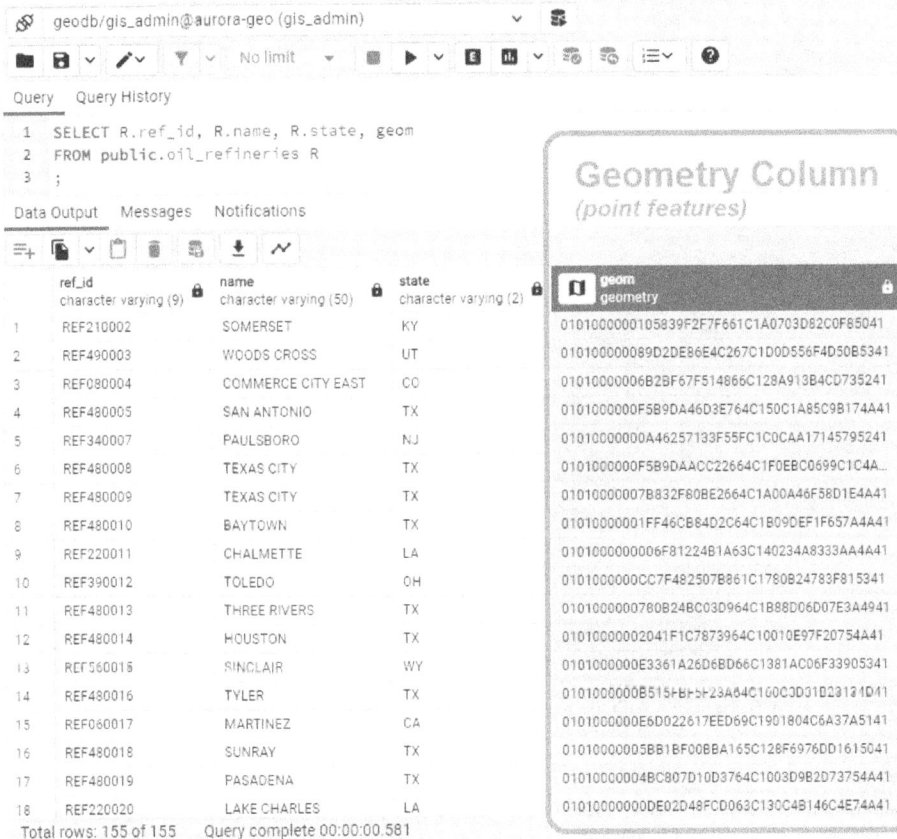

Figure 5.22: pgAdmin view of geometry-type column

Notice that the geom column is noted as a geometry type and has a small map icon as a visual cue. The contents of that column don't mean much to you and me, but PostGIS knows exactly what all of those characters mean. Conveniently, this geospatial data can be passed into PostGIS spatial functions to interrogate the location(s) within the geometry. If we want to perform a spatial comparison between point (oil refineries) and polygon (counties) data, the ST_Contains function is particularly useful. In addition to using ST spatial functions to query data, you can use them to create new data as well. Take the example of billboard signs using a GIS dataset available on the *Texas Department of Transportation* website. Overlaying billboards with road features will show where all of these roadside signs are located. After loading the data into the Aurora PostgreSQL/PostGIS database, you can visualize it in QGIS:

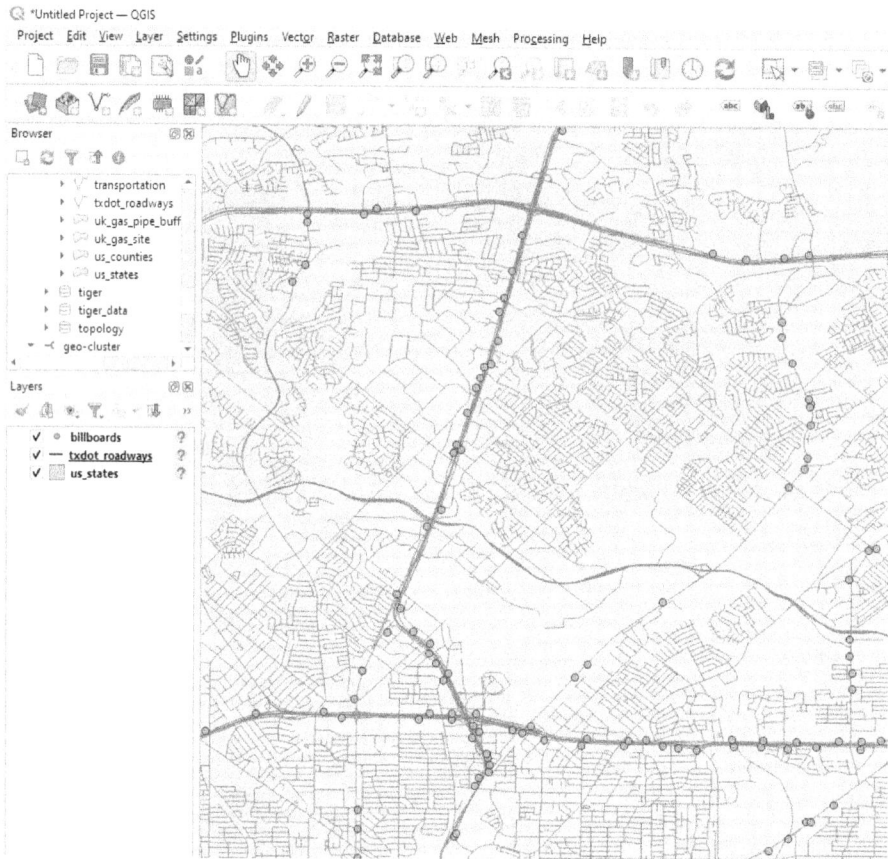

Figure 5.23: QGIS visualization of shapefiles loaded into AWS

US states are used as the background (beige), with road line features in gray and orange dots for the location of billboards along the roadways. Each orange dot has attributes that describe the billboard sign. You can see some examples of attributes here:

	rcrd_id	ownr	licns	hwy ▲	cnty	stat	addr	
29	PMT-18-00238	Lamar Advantage Outdoor Company, L.P.	6508	105	Orange	Active	1300 N Main St, Vidor, TX 77662	In
30	PMT-17-00468	Impala Outdoor Advertising	7998	114	Wise	Active	1374 E State Highway 114, Boyd, TX 76023	In
31	PMT-17-00504	Randall County Publishing, L.P.	5495	12005	Lubbock	Active	12005 S University Ave, Lubbock, TX 79423	In
32	PMT-22-00247	SignAd, Ltd.	67	146	Galveston	Application Review	4631 Hwy 146, Bacliff, TX 77518	In

Figure 5.24: Attribute table in QGIS showing details of live_data_feed_all

Using spatial functions, we can select a subset of the billboards and create a new dataset that is a geographic buffer operation from the filtered points. The original dataset name for the billboards is `live_data_feed_all`, and the new table we create is called `billboard_buffer` by selecting only features for a specific owner:

```
CREATE TABLE billboard_buffer AS
SELECT gid, rcrd_id, ownr, hwy, cnty, stat, addr, lat, lon, geom,
ST_Buffer(geom, .25)
FROM public.live_data_feed_all
WHERE ownr='Clear Channel Outdoor, Inc.'
;
```

The result is a new geospatial dataset with buffered geometries (yellow) from the filtered set of points:

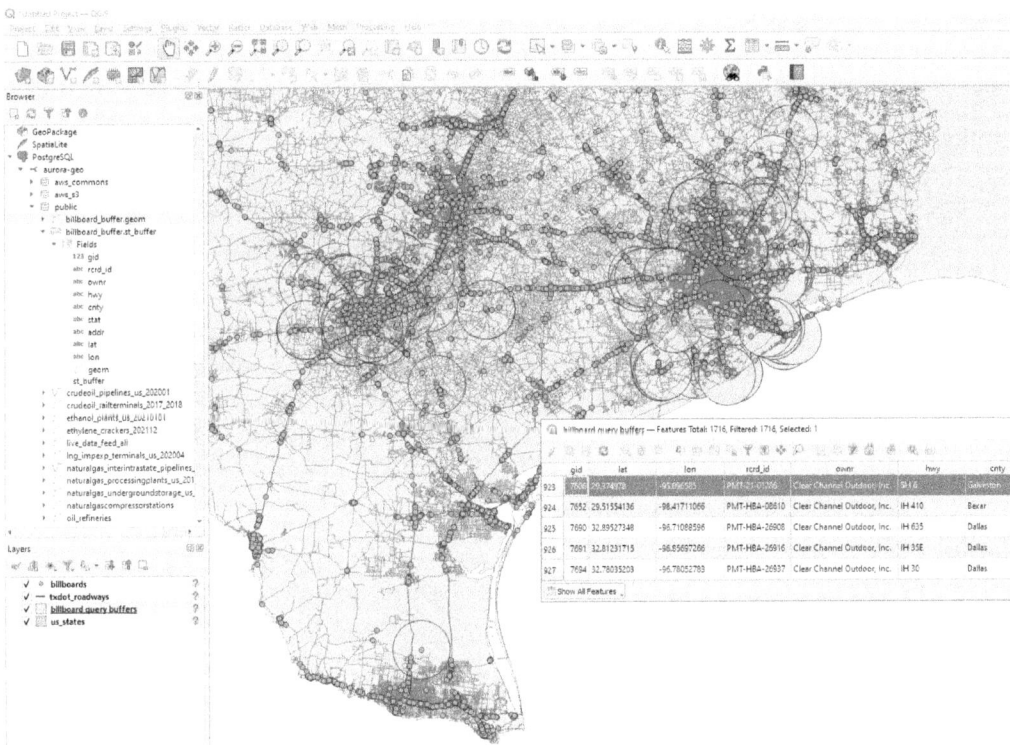

Figure 5.25: Buffered points show all billboards for a single owner in Texas

Architectural considerations

Due to the heavy use of serverless resources in this chapter's example, cost optimization elements are automatically achieved. It is always a best practice to continually evaluate usage patterns relative to projections. Significant cost savings can be realized by understanding the consumption-based cost levers available and adjusting the amount of compute you use in the cloud to align with the usage patterns of your GIS system.

Amazon Aurora provides a powerful monitoring capability that enables you to have real-time visibility into the health of your geodatabase. CPU utilization, memory, database connections, and disk I/O are just a few of the 41 health metrics that are automatically tracked for your database. Additionally, alerts can be set up on predefined thresholds to know when any conditions exist that may suggest a reevaluation of your initial sizing. Because it is possible to vertically scale your database up or down in minutes, AWS enables you to continually right-size your database to meet demand in the most cost-effective manner. Serverless options will automatically scale in response to these metrics yet stay within the minimum and maximum ACU range defined when setting up the database.

For critical production workloads, it is recommended to have at least two instances in your database cluster. These instances should be placed in separate AZs to protect against any network or hardware failures that may occur. Creating additional instances will not only provide resiliency but also improve performance by providing a larger collective set of computing power.

Aurora Serverless managed databases on AWS have continued to add features based on customer feedback. Because Aurora is the fastest-growing service in AWS's history, many customers have provided feedback and new feature requests. In fact, over 95% of the top 1,000 AWS customers use Amazon Aurora. The resulting benefit is that new features are introduced and released quickly. You can see the history of major releases in the *Document history* section of the user guide for Aurora: `https://docs.aws.amazon.com/AmazonRDS/latest/AuroraUserGuide/WhatsNew.html`.

Summary

In this chapter, we discussed the cloud-native database Amazon Aurora. This modern database technology is much easier to set up than servers in a traditional data center and provides compatibility with familiar tools and concepts to store and manage your geospatial data in a relational database. PostGIS is the most widely used extension to provide storage, functions, and management of your geospatial data. The connectivity to your database can be configured for wide or narrow access to meet the requirements of your specific use case to achieve the right combination of accessibility and security.

You have seen examples of how to quickly load shapefile data into a PostgreSQL database extended with PostGIS. Having all of this data cataloged and structured in AWS enables a wide range of processing capabilities. In the next chapter, we'll delve into geoprocessing and transforming your data at scale using the power of the cloud. Serverless processing on a secure global architecture with inexpensive storage has allowed amazing innovative ways to remold your geospatial data into insights.

References

- PostGIS documentation: `https://postgis.net/documentation/`

- Cartographic boundary files—shapefile: `https://www2.census.gov/geo/tiger/GENZ2018/shp/cb_2018_us_county_20m.zip`

- *Amazon Aurora*: `https://aws.amazon.com/rds/aurora/`

- *Performance and scaling for Aurora Serverless v2*: `https://docs.aws.amazon.com/AmazonRDS/latest/AuroraUserGuide/aurora-serverless-v2.setting-capacity.html`

- PgAdmin software download: `https://www.pgadmin.org/download/`

- Texas Department of Transportation GIS data: `https://www.txdot.gov/data-maps.html`

- Wikipedia page on CIDR: `https://en.wikipedia.org/wiki/Classless_Inter-Domain_Routing`

Serverless Options for Geospatial

In this chapter, we will talk about what serverless is, provide an overview of common services used in serverless architectures, and see how this all relates to geospatial data and service hosting. We will finish the chapter with a walk-through of deploying a serverless geospatial app as a static hosted website on Amazon **Simple Storage Service (S3)**.

This chapter covers the following topics:

- What is serverless?
- Object storage and serverless websites with S3
- Python with Lambda and API Gateway
- Deploying your first serverless geospatial application

What is serverless?

I recently bumped into someone at a conference who was wearing a funny shirt. The shirt said something along the lines of *What is the cloud?* and underneath it, *It's just someone else's servers*. The same can be said for serverless, so in the literal sense, it's not really serverless. There are still servers processing your requests somewhere, but the benefit is that they are not your servers and you don't have to worry about them. You don't have to worry about securing them, patching them, or upgrading their hardware. That is why serverless is gaining massive momentum. Write your code, hit deploy, and you are up and running. You get virtually unlimited scale with almost no infrastructure management.

Serverless services

Serverless comes in many shapes and forms on AWS. S3 is a serverless object storage and static hosting service. AWS Lambda lets you run your code in either snippets or large libraries as a service. API Gateway is a serverless REST API management service; simply define your endpoints and paths and connect them to your Lambda functions or containers. AWS Glue is a serverless ETL service; upload your Python, Spark, or ETL code and let it run for hours, days, or weeks. Lastly, SageMaker is a serverless machine learning service where you upload your algorithms and libraries and do no-code or low-code model training and inference. You could spin up all of these services in your AWS account and have working proofs of concept deployed in a few hours or less. If you tried to build out similar architectures on-premises, in the best case, you might be able to do it in a day; in the worst case, it might take you a month. Depending on how advanced your on-premises system is, you might be able to pull down some containers with similar capabilities. If you hit a single snag, you would most likely lose an entire day to debugging.

Object storage and serverless websites with S3

One service that stands out among the rest when it comes to serverless is S3. We talked about this service a bit in the intro chapters since it's the de facto standard for storing geospatial raster data and is also an up-and-coming service for vector data. In addition to its powerful capabilities for storing and serving large images, it has a feature that is absolutely critical to serverless applications: the ability to act as a web server. I'll walk you through the setup of this at the end of the chapter, but it is as easy as a few clicks, creating a bucket, uploading an HTML file, and under the bucket properties, enabling website hosting; then, you are off – you now have a website reachable from anywhere on the internet that can scale to millions of daily requests. The kicker here is the cost. Not only do you have a highly available, massively scalable website but also, if you only get a handful of visitors and users aren't downloading large artifacts, your monthly AWS bill will be a few pennies a month. I actually run my personal website, `https://www.jeffdemuth.com`, this way and have yet to get a bill larger than a few cents. In the next section, *Geospatial applications and S3 web hosting*, we will look at some popular libraries for mapping on S3.

Geospatial applications and S3 web hosting

In the previous section, I mentioned how easy it is to upload a simple HTML website to S3 to get up and running. But the real power of these sites is when you combine them with JavaScript. There are a number of geospatial JavaScript libraries that can be run straight from S3. The setup is as easy as downloading the source files from GitHub and uploading them to S3. A few of the big geospatial client libraries that you'll see deployed this way are MapLibre, Mapbox GL, ArcGIS JavaScript, and Leaflet. For the demo in this chapter, we will deploy Leaflet on S3. All of these libraries are powerful and well adopted in the industry, but Leaflet stands out a bit because of its support for both open source and OGC standards, as well as its integration with Esri ArcGIS standards. Mapbox obviously has good integration with Mapbox services, and then you have MapLibre, which is the open source fork of the Mapbox GL library. Lastly, the ArcGIS API for JavaScript is a proprietary library licensed by Esri. The ArcGIS JavaScript library is also incredibly powerful and feature-rich, and because it was developed by Esri, it is the easiest way to integrate with existing ArcGIS services. In the next section, we will look at a few security considerations for serverless applications.

Serverless hosting security and performance considerations

As amazing as serverless hosting on S3 is, it does have some limitations. A few of the limitations are around the fact that JavaScript libraries run on the client side. If you are doing any geospatial processing, that code has to run on your client's CPU resources. Also, JavaScript is single-threaded, so you won't get the same performance as running a desktop application. The users' experience of your web application will be highly dependent on the resources available on their local machine. Another limitation of client-side processing is security. Your server is dependent on storing data locally on the client, which means the client can alter any of the data before sending it back to the server. Authentication parameters are a big one and commonly, mechanisms such as **JSON Web Token (JWT)** are used to encrypt and sign the data on the client side to verify that the data is unchanged. The JWT standard is far from perfect but it's kind of the best we have at this point in time. While these may sound like significant limitations, there are workarounds I'll talk about in the next chapter that allow you to offer higher performance and security without compromising cost and scale.

Python with Lambda and API Gateway

I mentioned Lambda and API Gateway briefly previously, which give you the ability to upload and run code easily as well as create REST endpoints you can put in front of your Lambda functions. These capabilities can be used in conjunction with S3 JavaScript sites for authentication workflows as well as heavy geospatial processing workflows. For users with low-powered devices connecting to your site, you can perform some of the heavier processing inside a multicore Lambda function or even spin up power GPU instances to precompute the data before delivering it to the web client for rendering. This is actually a common architecture used in gaming on low-powered mobile devices. AWS services prerender the graphics for the mobile users and send the prerendered graphics to the mobile device, allowing for higher-quality game details that wouldn't have been possible with the handset's specifications. A geospatial example might be a hotspot analysis function with a given set of points; you could write all of that logic inside JavaScript to take all the points and calculate the quantity for given regions and run that logic on the client side. Alternatively, with API Gateway and Lambda, you could have your JavaScript site call an API Gateway endpoint and pass either the datasets or the locations of the datasets. Have the Lambda spin up and do the calculation and then return the original point data as polygons showing the hotspots.

In the first example, if you have a few million points, it would require a significant calculation for the client-side browser to loop through all of the points, make the calculations, and create its own polygons with hotspot attributes. By offloading the processing to Lambda, the only work the client is doing is a simple API call to API Gateway. API Gateway then invokes the Lambda, computes the results, and returns however many polygons are part of the analysis. If a million of the points are in a specific part of the world and only a handful in another part of the world, you might only have a few polygons returned, which would be rendered on the map instantly even on a low-powered mobile phone.

Deploying your first serverless geospatial application

For our hands-on tutorial, we will walk through deploying a popular JavaScript framework called Leaflet as a serverless application on S3. With a couple of lines of JavaScript, we will import the Leaflet libraries and draw a simple map in the browser. The finished product will be an autoscaled web browser map that can support virtually unlimited traffic:

1. Navigate to the AWS console.
2. Click on **S3**.

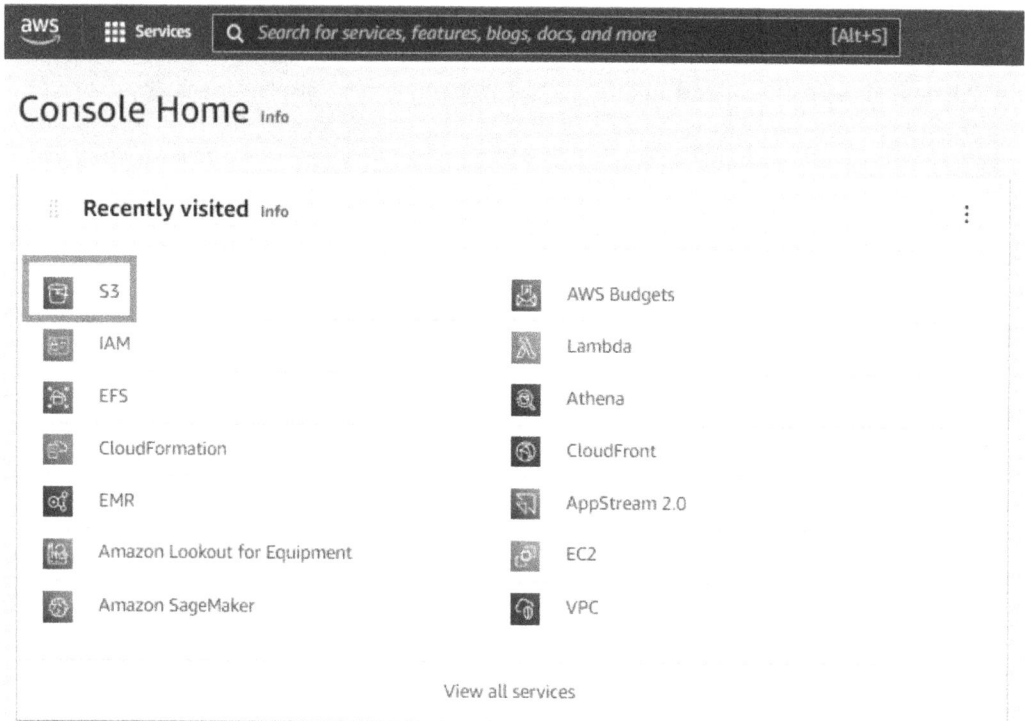

Figure 6.1: AWS console home screen

3.   Click **Create bucket**.

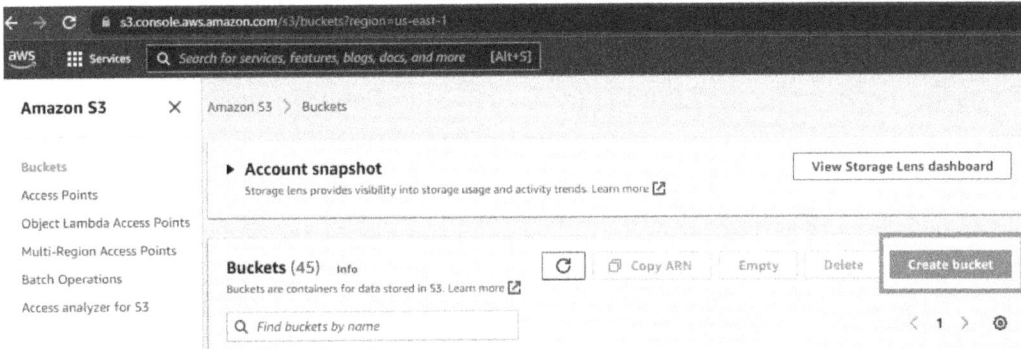

Figure 6.2: The S3 home screen

4.   Type a name for the bucket.

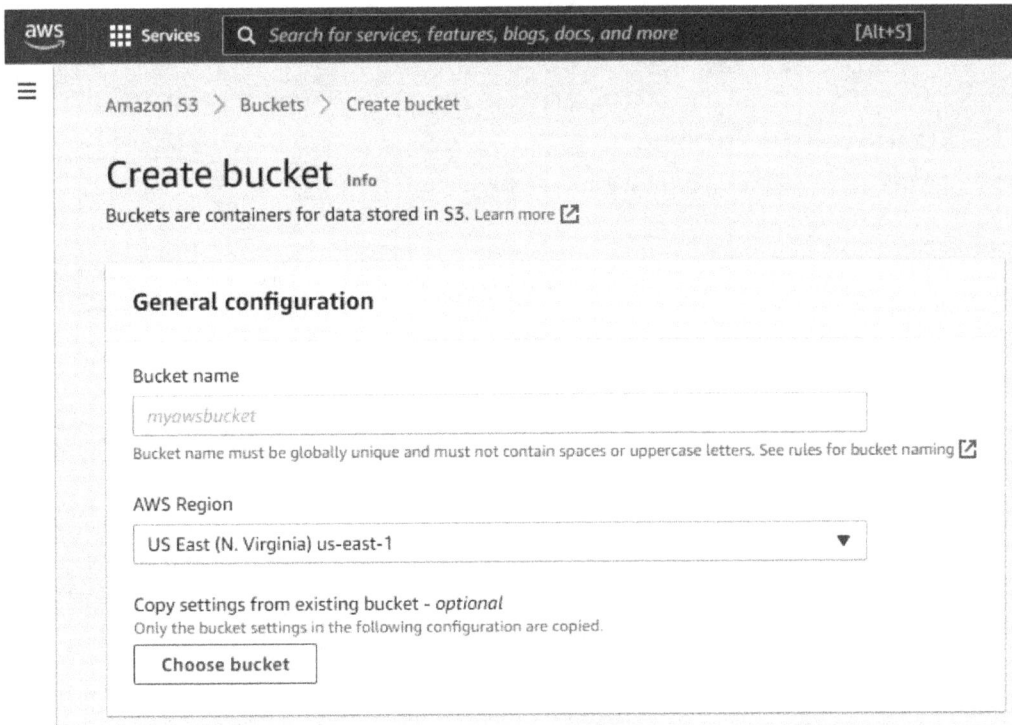

Figure 6.3: The S3 Create bucket setup page

5.   Click **Choose bucket** at the bottom of the page:

I.   Click on the bucket you just created.

II.   Click **Properties**.

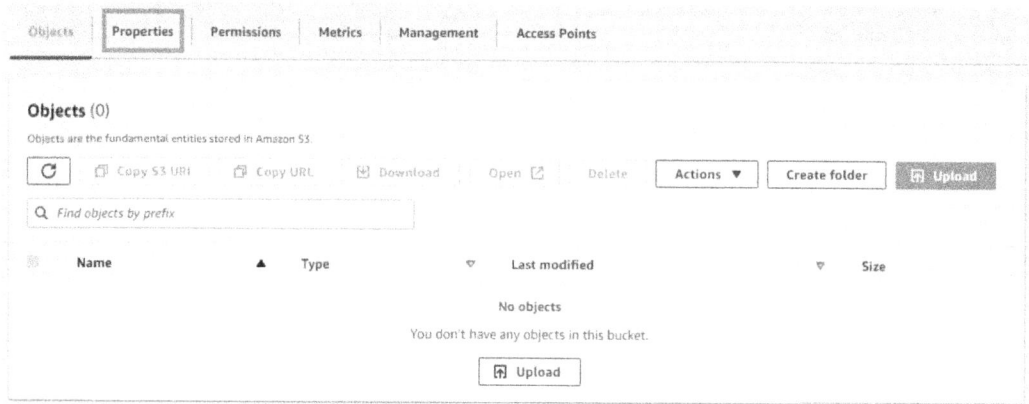

Figure 6.4: S3 bucket properties tab

6.   Scroll to the bottom and click **Edit** under **Static website hosting**.

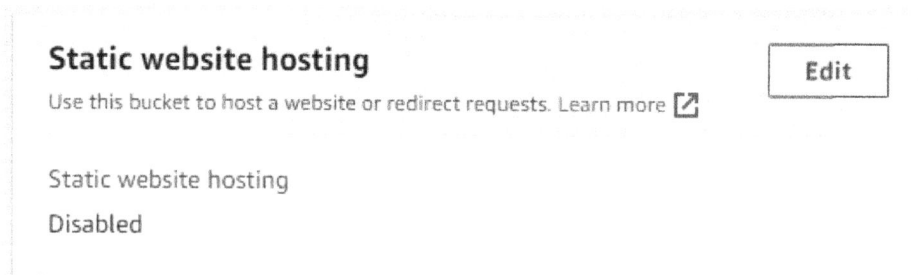

Figure 6.5: The Static website hosting option under the bucket Properties tab

7. Click the **Enable** radio button.

    Type index.html for the index document.

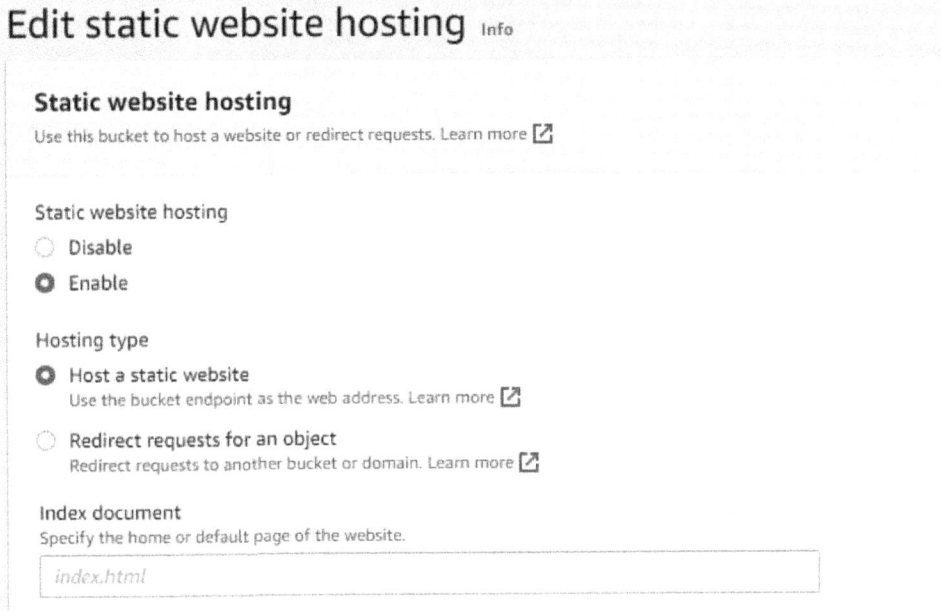

Figure 6.6: The Static website hosting configuration page

8. Scroll to the bottom and click **Save Changes**.

9. Open Notepad on your computer. Paste the following code and save it as index.html:

```
<html>
<head>
<title>Leaflet</title>
<link rel="stylesheet" href="https://unpkg.com/leaflet@1.9.1/
dist/leaflet.css"/>
<script src="https://unpkg.com/leaflet@1.9.1/dist/leaflet.js"></
script>
</head>
<body>
<div id="map" style="width: 100%; height: 100%;"></div>
<script>
var map = L.map('map').setView([30.266666, -97.733330], 13);
var tiles = L.tileLayer('https://tile.openstreetmap.org/{z}/{x}/
{y}.png').addTo(map);
</script>
</body>
</html>
```

10. Under your S3 bucket, click **Upload**.

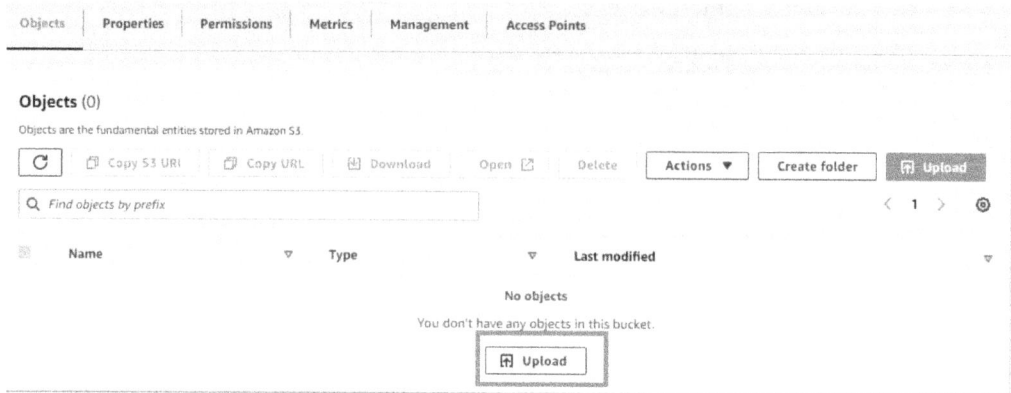

Figure 6.7: The bucket overview page showing the Upload file button

11. Click **Add Files**:

I.   Select the `index.html` file you just created and click **Open**.

II.   Scroll to the bottom and click **Upload**.

III. Check the checkbox next to the `index.html` file you just uploaded.

IV.   Click the **Actions** dropdown and select **Share with a presigned URL**.

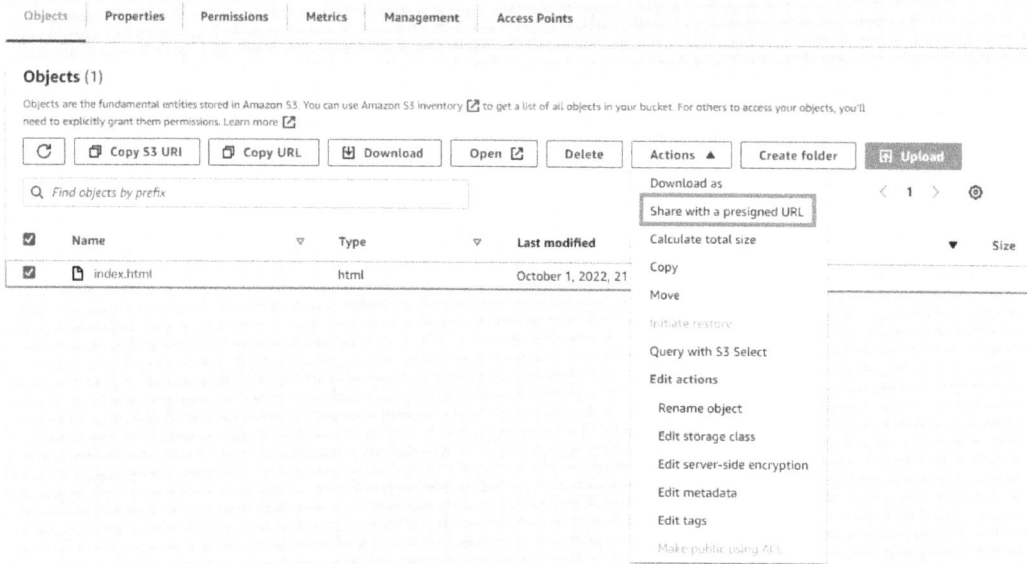

Figure 6.8: The bucket overview page showing the Actions button dropdown

12. Enter however many minutes or hours you want the URL to be valid for and click **Create presigned URL**.

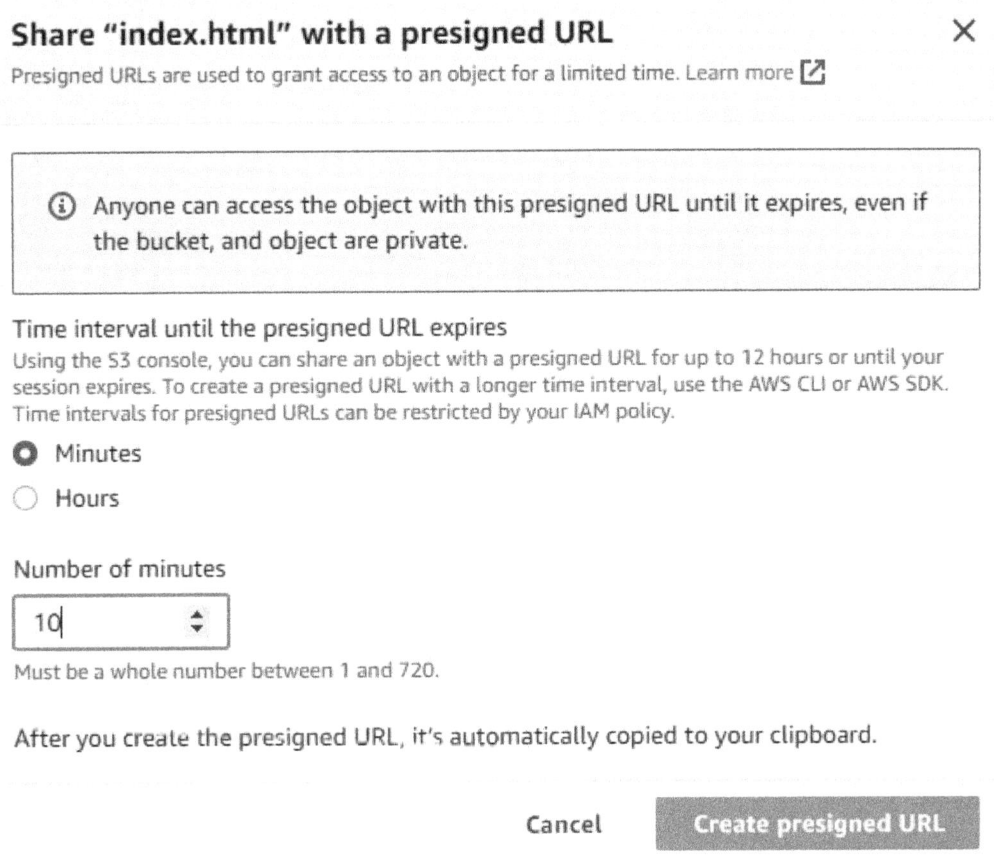

Share "index.html" with a presigned URL   ✕

Presigned URLs are used to grant access to an object for a limited time. Learn more ↗

ⓘ Anyone can access the object with this presigned URL until it expires, even if the bucket, and object are private.

Time interval until the presigned URL expires

Using the S3 console, you can share an object with a presigned URL for up to 12 hours or until your session expires. To create a presigned URL with a longer time interval, use the AWS CLI or AWS SDK. Time intervals for presigned URLs can be restricted by your IAM policy.

● Minutes

○ Hours

Number of minutes

| 10 | ⇕ |

Must be a whole number between 1 and 720.

After you create the presigned URL, it's automatically copied to your clipboard.

Cancel   **Create presigned URL**

Figure 6.9: The presigned URL configuration page

13. Enter the URL into a browser and you should see a map that looks like this:

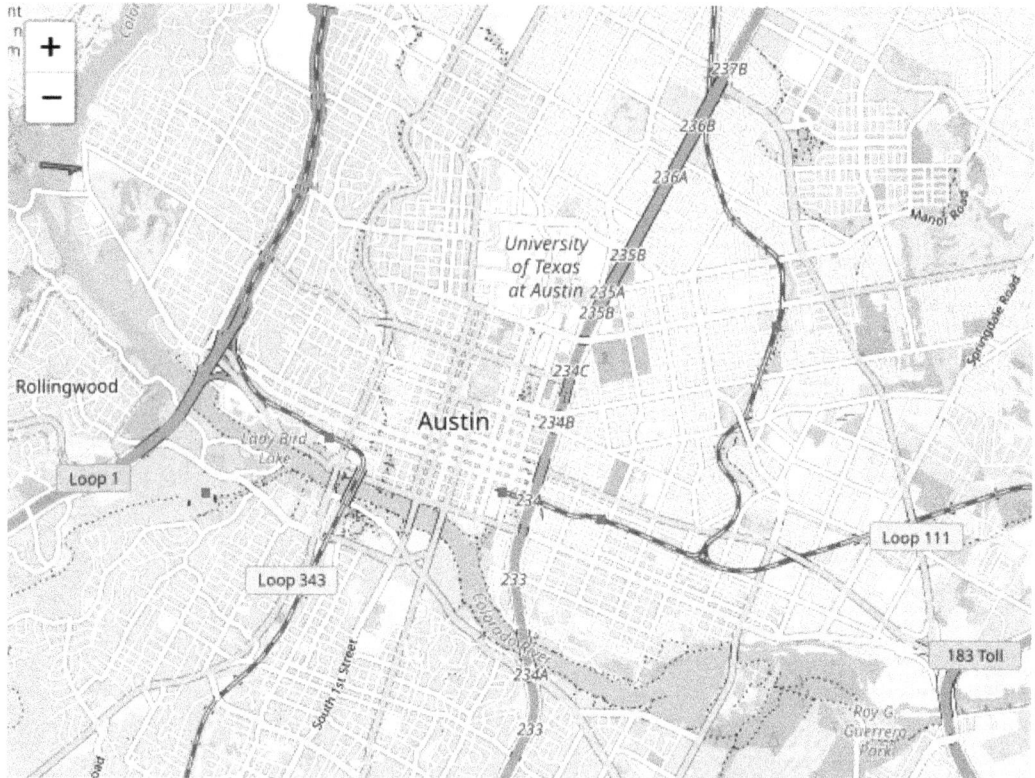

Figure 6.10: Our leaflet map centered on the city of Austin, Texas

Congrats, you have created your first geospatial website!

In this demo, we navigated to a website using a signed URL. This was for simplicity's sake as well as for security precautions as static websites require S3 buckets to be public. The best practice is to leave the S3 bucket private and grant permission to Amazon CloudFront to access the bucket. You can read more about this practice here: `https://docs.aws.amazon.com/AmazonCloudFront/ latest/ DeveloperGuide/getting-started-secure-static-website- cloudformationtemplate.html`.

Summary

In this chapter, we learned what serverless is, what some common serverless services are, and how it applies to geospatial data and applications. We also learned how to deploy Leaflet as a serverless map on S3. In the next chapter, we will learn about geospatial data lakes, which is also a great architecture powered by AWS S3.

References

- Amazon S3: `https://aws.amazon.com/s3/`
- Leaflet maps: `https://leafletjs.com/`

## 7

Querying Geospatial Data with Amazon Athena

Previously in this book, you saw how geospatial data can be stored and managed in the AWS cloud. In this chapter, we will explore the flexibility and power of using Amazon Athena to query and transform your features. Querying and performing spatial functions on geospatial datasets is typically the main reason why the geospatial data was kept in the first place. Asking questions about geospatial data can help answer your business questions with the extra dimension of location for additional insights.

This chapter will teach you how to configure and use SQL queries on AWS:

- The setup and configuration of Amazon Athena
- Geospatial data formats
- Spatial query structure
- Spatial functions
- Using Athena results as input for other AWS services

Setting up and configuring Athena

Amazon Athena provides a flexible way to access all of your geospatial data in AWS. Publicly available data sources such as Open Data in AWS provide continually updated information from authoritative sources around the globe. Using custom connectors, you are also able to access compliant databases even if they are not in AWS. Athena is a useful query tool because it can easily access geospatial data in S3, RDS, Redshift, Timestream, OpenSearch, and numerous other sources and formats.

Don't get discouraged if you find it difficult to discern the difference between AWS Glue and Amazon Athena. Both of these services work hand in hand to provide a powerful, consumption-priced analytics platform. The features of Glue depend on Athena and vice versa, so it can be difficult to know whether the objects you are using are configured in Glue or Athena. A good rule of thumb is to think of Athena as the place where you create SQL views, and Glue as the place that catalogs and understands the structure of the underlying geospatial data.

For the examples in this chapter, we will leverages sample data that is provided in the *Examples: Geospatial queries* section of the Amazon Athena user guide. You can find the link in the *References* section of this chapter, and it has additional information and helpful considerations. The datasets used are simple and familiar to a wide range of audiences as they depict earthquakes as point data and a subset of the county polygons for California. By using these two datasets together, we can see how geospatial operations can be performed in Amazon Athena:

- `Earthquakes.csv`: Comma-separated values listing of earthquakes in the Western United States: `https://github.com/Esri/gis-tools-for-hadoop/blob/master/samples/data/earthquake-data/earthquakes.csv`

- `California-counties.json`: Esri-compliant GeoJSON providing the municipal boundary outline of California counties that are prone to earthquakes: `https://github.com/Esri/gis-tools-for-hadoop/blob/master/samples/data/counties-data/california-counties.json`

The following figure shows the earthquake points as red dots and the counties of interest as yellow polygons:

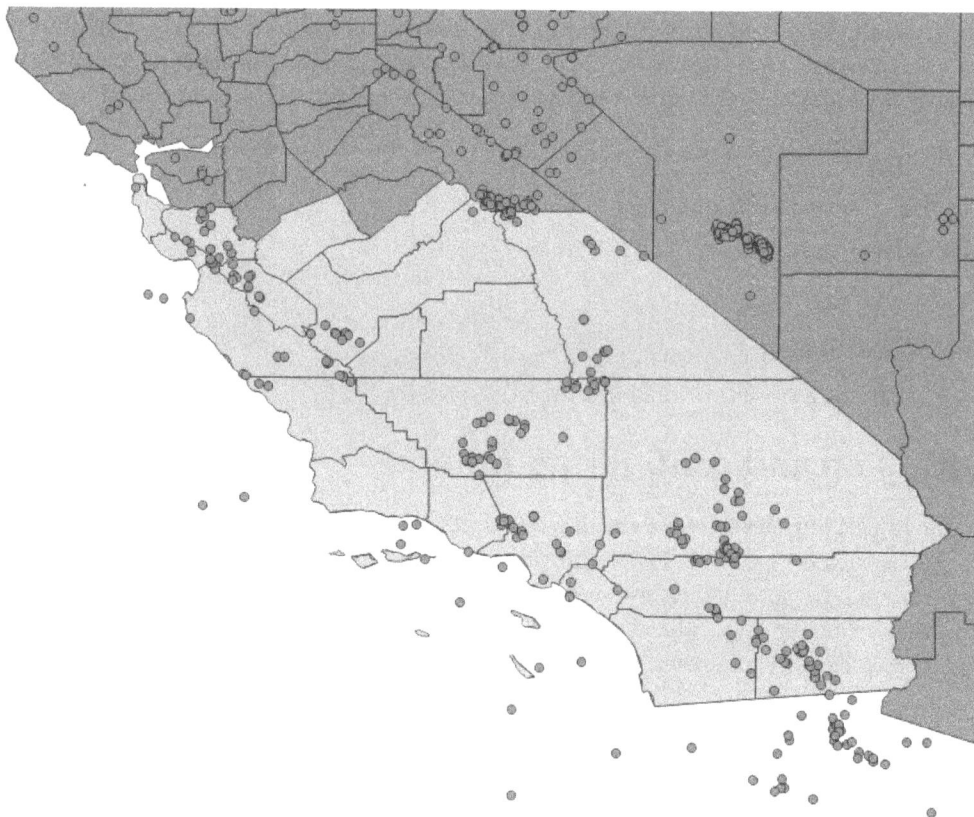

Figure 7.1: Example data of earthquakes on the United States' west coast

Using the power of the serverless, managed service Amazon Athena, you will be able to perform geospatial analytics on this data without provisioning or configuring any servers. All of your geospatial data is securely stored within the AWS cloud and enjoys the benefit of a consumption-based pricing model for nearly limitless capacity.

If this is your first time using Athena, you'll need to select an S3 bucket in which to store your query results and create a database. The *Getting started* section of the Amazon Athena user guide walks through this process step by step. This section has a link to the .csv file containing the earthquake data, which can be found here:

```
https://github.com/Esri/gis-tools-for-hadoop/blob/master/samples/
data/earthquake-data/earthquakes.csv
```

Once you're in the query editor, you can create an external table to access the .csv files stored in S3. This Athena table can be thought of as a view into the data sitting in the S3 bucket. In this case, we are using the earthquakes.csv file, which has a column for latitude and a column for longitude. Additional attribute fields describe the date, time, and magnitude, among other characteristics of the earth-shaking event.

The view can be created using a statement that shows what we would like to call the table, how the columns are structured, and where the data is stored. We give the table the name earthquakes, specify the column data types, and provide the format and path to the data using this Athena query:

```
CREATE external TABLE earthquakes
(
    earthquake_date string,
    latitude double,
    longitude double,
    depth double,
    magnitude double,
    magtype string,
    mbstations string,
    gap string,
    distance string,
    rms string,
    source string,
    eventid string
)
ROW FORMAT DELIMITED FIELDS TERMINATED BY ','
STORED AS TEXTFILE LOCATION 's3://<bucket>/<folder>/';
```

Replace the `<bucket>` and `<folder>` placeholders with the name of the S3 bucket and the folder location where you have uploaded the `.csv` file to S3.

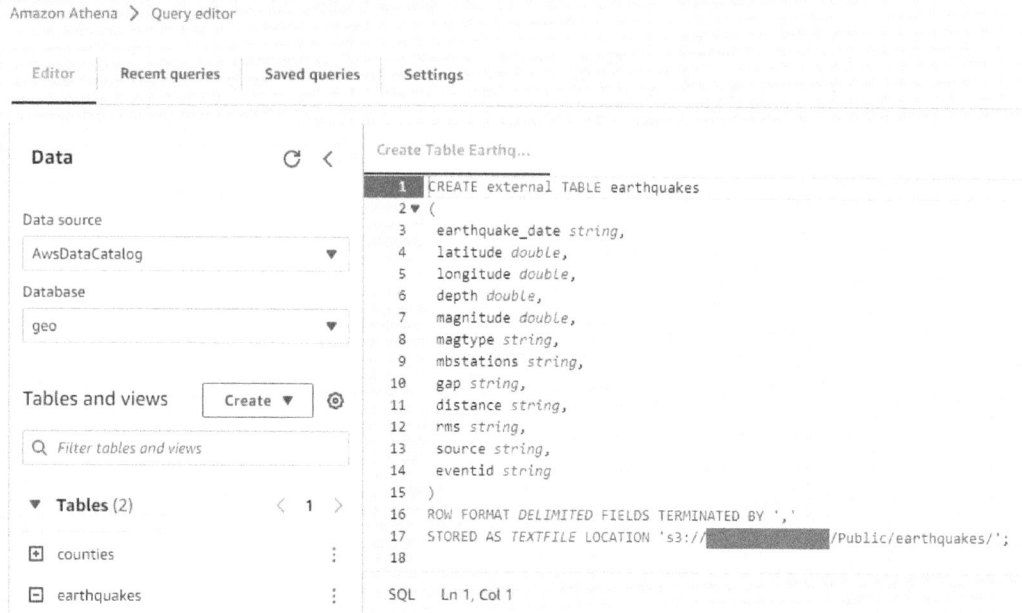

Amazon Athena > Query editor

Editor   Recent queries   Saved queries   Settings

Data   C   <

Data source

AwsDataCatalog   ▼

Database

geo   ▼

Tables and views   [Create ▼]   ◎

Q *Filter tables and views*

▼ **Tables** (2)   < 1 >

⊞ counties   ⋮

⊟ earthquakes   ⋮

```
Create Table Earthq...
 1  CREATE external TABLE earthquakes
 2▼ (
 3      earthquake_date string,
 4      latitude double,
 5      longitude double,
 6      depth double,
 7      magnitude double,
 8      magtype string,
 9      mbstations string,
10      gap string,
11      distance string,
12      rms string,
13      source string,
14      eventid string
15  )
16  ROW FORMAT DELIMITED FIELDS TERMINATED BY ','
17  STORED AS TEXTFILE LOCATION 's3://          /Public/earthquakes/';
18
```
SQL   Ln 1, Col 1

Figure 7.2: Creation of Athena table from text file on S3

Running the example here (in query provided in the user guide) creates an Athena table that supports serverless queries at scale on a comma-separated values file. If you want to find the most recent earthquake that was greater than 8.0 magnitude, a query like this would do the trick:

```
SELECT * FROM earthquakes WHERE magnitude > 8
ORDER BY earthquake_date desc;
```

But wait, isn't this a chapter about *geospatial* queries? Many people may not categorize the list of earthquakes as geospatial data, even though it contains latitude and longitude information. Where might you have untapped geospatial data within your organization? Any data with coordinates, addresses, tax parcels, zip codes, or even just the name of a county is data about the location. Using Amazon Athena, geospatial query capabilities can be pointed directly to where your file-based data exists today. Many companies already store much of their data in Amazon S3, which has 11 9s of data durability to ensure the data is safe. Before we get into the really cool stuff, let's look at the format and structure of geospatial queries using Amazon Athena.

Geospatial data formats

It is important to point out that there are two main geospatial data formats used by geospatial functions in Athena. We'll dive a bit deeper into the **Well-Known Text (WKT)** and JSON formats, along with a simple example you can try in your AWS account.

WKT

This common format, defined by the **Open Geospatial Consortium (OGC)**, is universally digestible to represent points, lines, and geometries. Coordinates are listed out individually in plain ASCII text using a standardized format. Points, lines, and polygons can all be represented by providing the coordinates of the points that make up that geometry.

The format is very simple, most easily introduced with the POINT term:

```
POINT (-111.5531807 40.6099522)
```

It should be noted that the latitude value is specified first in the numbered pair. The format for lines is very similar but provides a list of points that comprise the geometry:

```
LINESTRING (-111.5531807 40.6099522, -111.5506534 40.6139341,
-111.548126 40.617916)
```

Polygons are constructed similarly to lines with an extra set of parentheses to facilitate multi-ring polygons. Close the polygon by matching the first and last points:

```
POLYGON ((-111.597066 40.696168, -111.463993 40.696168, -111.463993
40.608, -111.597066 40.608,  111.597066 40.696168))
```

JSON-encoded geospatial data

The JSON text-based format for complex data structures provides the location and metadata of geospatial features. Athena leverages the Esri GeoJSON format standard, which provides a rich set of metadata in addition to the location data. Amazon Athena uses the Hive JSON **serialization/deserialization (SerDe)** to parse the contents.

The following is a portion of the county's GeoJSON file with county boundary polygons from Esri's GitHub repository, as referenced earlier:

```
{
  "displayFieldName" : "",
  "fieldAliases" : {
    "OBJECTID" : "OBJECTID",
    "AREA" : "AREA",
    "PERIMETER" : "PERIMETER",
    "STATE" : "STATE",
```

```
      "COUNTY" : "COUNTY",
      "NAME" : "NAME",
  ...
    },
    "geometryType" : "esriGeometryPolygon",
    "spatialReference" : {
      "wkid" : null
    },
    "fields" : [
      {
        "name" : "OBJECTID",
        "type" : "esriFieldTypeOID",
        "alias" : "OBJECTID"
      },
      {
        "name" : "AREA",
        "type" : "esriFieldTypeDouble",
        "alias" : "AREA"
      },
    ...
```

The top section of the file defines the fields and metadata. A bit further down in the file, you can find the individual geometry features:

```
        "geometry" : {
          "rings" : [
            [
              [
                -122.5024267151224,
                37.708132349276738
              ],
              [
                -122.506483,
                37.723731000000001
              ],
              [
                -122.50782901995821,
                37.735330999999753
              ],
```

You can try this by uploading the GeoJSON file here to an S3 bucket in your account:

`https://github.com/Esri/gis-tools-for-hadoop/blob/master/samples/`
`data/counties-data/california-counties.json`

Once the file exists in S3, the following statement in Athena will create a table for issuing queries on the data:

```
CREATE EXTERNAL TABLE `counties_ca`(
  `name` string COMMENT 'from deserializer',
  `boundaryshape` binary COMMENT 'from deserializer')
ROW FORMAT SERDE
  'com.esri.hadoop.hive.serde.JsonSerde'
STORED AS INPUTFORMAT
  'com.esri.json.hadoop.EnclosedJsonInputFormat'
OUTPUTFORMAT
  'org.apache.hadoop.hive.ql.io.HiveIgnoreKeyTextOutputFormat'
LOCATION
  's3://<bucket>/<folder>/json'
```

Either of these input formats can be used to operate on point, line, polygon, multiline, and multipolygon geometries. The spatial functions used by Athena are implemented as a Presto plugin, which uses the Esri Java Geometry library and operates under the Apache 2 license. It should also be noted that Athena engine versions 1 and 2 have slightly different implementations, so be sure to check the documentation for your specific environment. In the next section, we'll look into how to construct geospatial queries that interrogate the locational aspects of your data.

Spatial query structure

Performing any kind of query on geospatial data that interrogates the location information of the geometry can be referred to as a spatial query. Spatial queries unlock new opportunities and threats by adding the context of where the data exists. Not only can you determine where a particular feature sits on Earth but you can also find out what that feature is close to, contained within, or related to.

Spatial queries follow the similar SQL format of attribute queries but gain location awareness. When working with geospatial data, it is important to always know the coordinate reference system of your data. The coordinate system can be specified as an argument when converting latitude and longitude into a point geometry. Knowing the correct reference system will ensure that your location accuracy is maintained throughout conversions and transformations.

A common example of where spatial queries can provide unique insights can be seen with the `ST_Contains` spatial function. This built-in function allows you to find out whether or not one geometry is contained within the boundaries of another. This function will return `true` if the second argument is completely contained within the boundary of the first argument. This functionality can be combined with a join of two spatial datasets, as shown here, to determine which earthquakes occurred in Kern County, California:

```
SELECT counties.name, earthquakes.earthquake_date, earthquakes.
magnitude, earthquakes.latitude, earthquakes.longitude
FROM counties
CROSS JOIN earthquakes
WHERE ST_CONTAINS (ST_GeomFromLegacyBinary(counties.boundaryshape),
ST_POINT(earthquakes.longitude, earthquakes.latitude))
AND counties.name = 'Kern'
```

This results in the following output:

Results (36)

#	name	earthquake_date	magnitude	latitude	longitude
1	Kern	1946/03/18 15:50:42.81	5.24	35.7787	-117.7775
2	Kern	1995/08/17 22:39:58.99	5.36	35.776	-117.662
3	Kern	1982/10/01 14:29:01.70	5.12	35.743	-117.756
4	Kern	1946/03/15 14:00:36.68	5.19	35.6913	-117.7497

Figure 7.3: Results from a spatial join of points and polygons

Spatial functions

The previous section explained how we can combine multiple geospatial datasets in Amazon Athena, but you may be asking, "What does ST_ mean?" The abbreviation **ST** stands for **Spatial Type**, and it designates that the data function performs some kind of geospatial processing. Spatial functions can be used to convert from text to geometry and back again to meet the specific usage needs of each query.

The complete list of geospatial functions available in Amazon Athena can be found here: https://docs.aws.amazon.com/athena/latest/ug/geospatial-functions-list-v2.html. The list is extensive and is broken down into the following categories:

- **Constructor functions**: Used to get binary formats of geometries or convert binary into text

- **Geospatial relationship functions**: Used to determine location relationships by returning a Boolean value indicating whether the tested condition was satisfied

- **Operation functions**: Used to interrogate the geometry data type or create new features based on the geometric characteristics of a feature

- **Accessor functions**: Used to get quantitative aspects of a geometry, such as area, length, or bounded area

- **Aggregation functions**: Used to create new geometries based on aggregated points of input geometries

- **Bing tile functions**: Used to convert between geometries and a Microsoft Bing maps tile system

To show a simple example, we can take some coordinates obtained from OpenStreetMap. In order to represent each of the three main geometry types, I've selected a ski lodge for a point, a ski lift for a line, and a ski area for a polygon that contains both the line and the polygon (which do not intersect).

You can take the text here and save it as a `.csv` file if you would like to try this in your AWS account:

```
Feature,WKT
Jupiter Lift, "LINESTRING(-111.548126 40.617916, -111.5506534
40.6139341, -111.5531807 40.6099522)"
Miners Camp, "POINT (-111.528363 40.641716)"
Park City, "POLYGON ((-111.597066 40.696168, -111.463993 40.696168,
-111.463993 40.608, -111.597066 40.608, -111.597066 40.696168))"
```

Upload the saved `.csv` file to an S3 bucket, then create a table in Athena:

```
CREATE EXTERNAL TABLE IF NOT EXISTS wkt_sample
( Feature string
,   WKT  string
)
ROW FORMAT SERDE 'org.apache.hadoop.hive.serde2.OpenCSVSerde'
WITH SERDEPROPERTIES ( 'escapeChar'='\\', 'quoteChar'='\"',
'seperatorChar'=',')
LOCATION 's3://<your-bucket>/<your-folder>/'
TBLPROPERTIES ( "skip.header.line.count"="1")
```

After you create the Athena table pointing to S3 data, the raw WKT data can be queried and filtered. The spatial functions you have learned about in this section can describe the location relationships between features. An example is shown here to pick a point and see which features intersect that point with `ST_Intersects`.

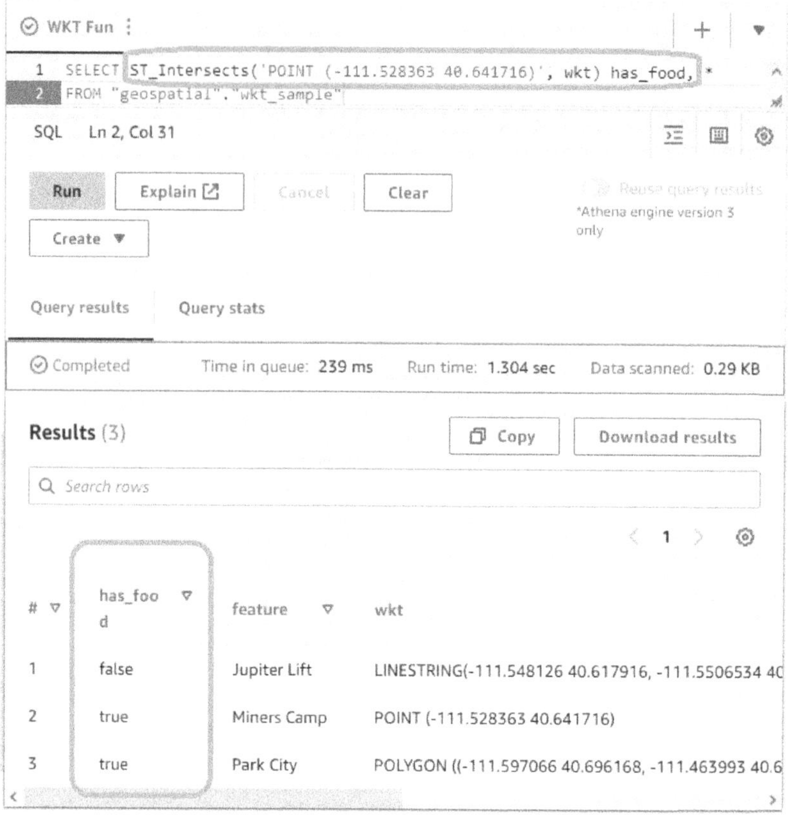

Figure 7.4: Using spatial functions in Athena

The tremendous power contained in these spatial functions cannot be understated. To amplify your insights even further, Amazon Athena integrates natively with most core AWS services. In the next section, we'll look at some of the ways Athena can drive solutions in your organization.

AWS service integration

Creating geospatial tables and views that can be queried by Amazon Athena opens up a wide range of possible ways to extend access. Because Athena is inherently integrated across AWS, you can use these data sources for analysis and visualization in Amazon QuickSight, check logs and metrics in Amazon CloudWatch, or coordinate orchestrated workflows using AWS Lambda and Step Functions. The possibilities of what you can build are only limited by your imagination, and the native integration options provide a powerful platform for geospatial intelligence.

Each individual and organization will have different needs for geospatial data, but when you consider leveraging both public and proprietary data, here are some possibilities:

- Sending an email using Amazon Simple Notification Service (SNS) to your leadership when a competitor opens a location within a certain distance of any of your stores

- Tracking assets using GPS tracker pings and geofences using Amazon Location Service

- Creating and sharing dashboards with maps in Amazon QuickSight

- Hosting microservice geospatial functions using AWS Lambda

- Transforming geospatial data formats and storing them for distribution on Amazon S3

Architectural considerations

Cost optimization opportunities are realized automatically with AWS built-in features such as S3 Intelligent-Tiering, and the Amazon Aurora Serverless v2 auto-scaling improvements made in April 2022. As cloud technology and hardware improve, the compute cost of a given workload continues to go down. When coupled with AWS Lambda to modernize from traditional virtual servers, the cost of a well-architected enterprise GIS environment is a fraction of what it was a decade ago.

During the Athena setup and configuration topic, it was noted that Amazon Athena has the capability to connect to non-AWS databases – even those on-premises. While technically possible, it should be noted that latency can be the enemy of a highly distributed GIS environment. Access between two endpoints on a low-latency, high-bandwidth network is always going to outperform the alternative. To mitigate performance surprises, a network landscape architecture should be reviewed during the selection of geospatial data storage. Looking at where data is stored, where it is used, and how it gets from one place to another is the best way to optimize your storage capacity, performance, security, and cost. The geographical location of end users and compute nodes is also critical when designing where and how to store your geospatial data.

Monitoring should be established to identify any spiky patterns in usage to ensure that the response time is not impacted. Become familiar with baselines of production workloads and use Amazon CloudWatch KPIs to set alerts for desired thresholds. The creation of an Amazon **SNS** topic can be helpful for administrative or business alerts through email or SMS text messages. Once your monitoring and alerts have been in place for a month or two, it is always a good idea to stress-test your environment. Generate or simulate more traffic and usage than the system is designed to handle. Try to break it. Ensure that the correct alerts are triggering communications. You can do all of these things in a secure and inexpensive controlled environment to be better prepared for production changes. If you are familiar with the cost and effort of maintaining your own data center, you will be amazed at the way AWS serverless auto-scaling performs across the technology stack. Peak usage times are handled by the automatic allocation of AWS resources, which are scaled back down afterward to reduce cost.

Summary

In this chapter, you explored how Amazon Athena can serve as a powerful platform for gathering, classifying, validating, and transforming geospatial data. You learned how to configure Athena and point it to geospatial datasets in various formats. We also saw how spatial functions and aggregations provide lightning-fast insights into our location-based data. Through understanding the geospatial data types supported, the information in this chapter will also provide you with insight into data transformations to meet your organization's requirements.

The AWS cloud provides numerous scalability and efficiency benefits that save money and demand fewer energy resources when compared to legacy on-premises enterprise GIS environments. In the next chapter, we'll combine the power of containerized computing in the cloud with your geospatial workloads for maximum agility and performance.

References

- Amazon Athena user guide – Getting started: `https://docs.aws.amazon.com/athena/latest/ug/getting-started.html`

- Amazon Athena user guide – Querying geospatial data: `https://docs.aws.amazon.com/athena/latest/ug/geospatial-example-queries.html`

- Well-known text representation of geometry: `https://en.wikipedia.org/wiki/Well-known_text_representation_of_geometry`

- Open Data on AWS: `https://registry.opendata.aws/`

- Esri GeoJSON specification: `https://doc.arcgis.com/en/arcgis-online/reference/geojson.htm`

- Creating tables in Athena: `https://docs.aws.amazon.com/athena/latest/ug/creating-tables.html`

Part 3: Analyzing and Visualizing Geospatial Data in AWS

We will learn to harness the benefits of managing geospatial data in the cloud by performing analysis and creating visualizations to share insights derived from the data.

This part has the following chapters:

- *Chapter 8, Geospatial Containers on AWS*, covers what containers are and how they benefit geospatial workloads on the cloud.

- *Chapter 9, Using Geospatial Data with Amazon EMR*, explores Elastic MapReduce (EMR). We will walk through a demo of Hadoop, EMR and visualize geospatial data using them.

- *Chapter 10, Geospatial Data Analysis using R on AWS*, explores the use of the R programming language to construct commands and procedures for geospatial analysis on AWS

- *Chapter 11, Geospatial Machine Learning with SageMaker*, SageMaker is the cornerstone AWS service for statistical and machine learning computing. This chapter provides us with step by step guidance to import, analyze, and visualize geospatial data on AWS using SageMaker

- *Chapter 12, Using Amazon QuickSight to Visualize Geospatial Data*, delves into how geospatial data on AWS can be converted into visualizations that can be shared with others and combined with web maps and other geospatial visualizations.

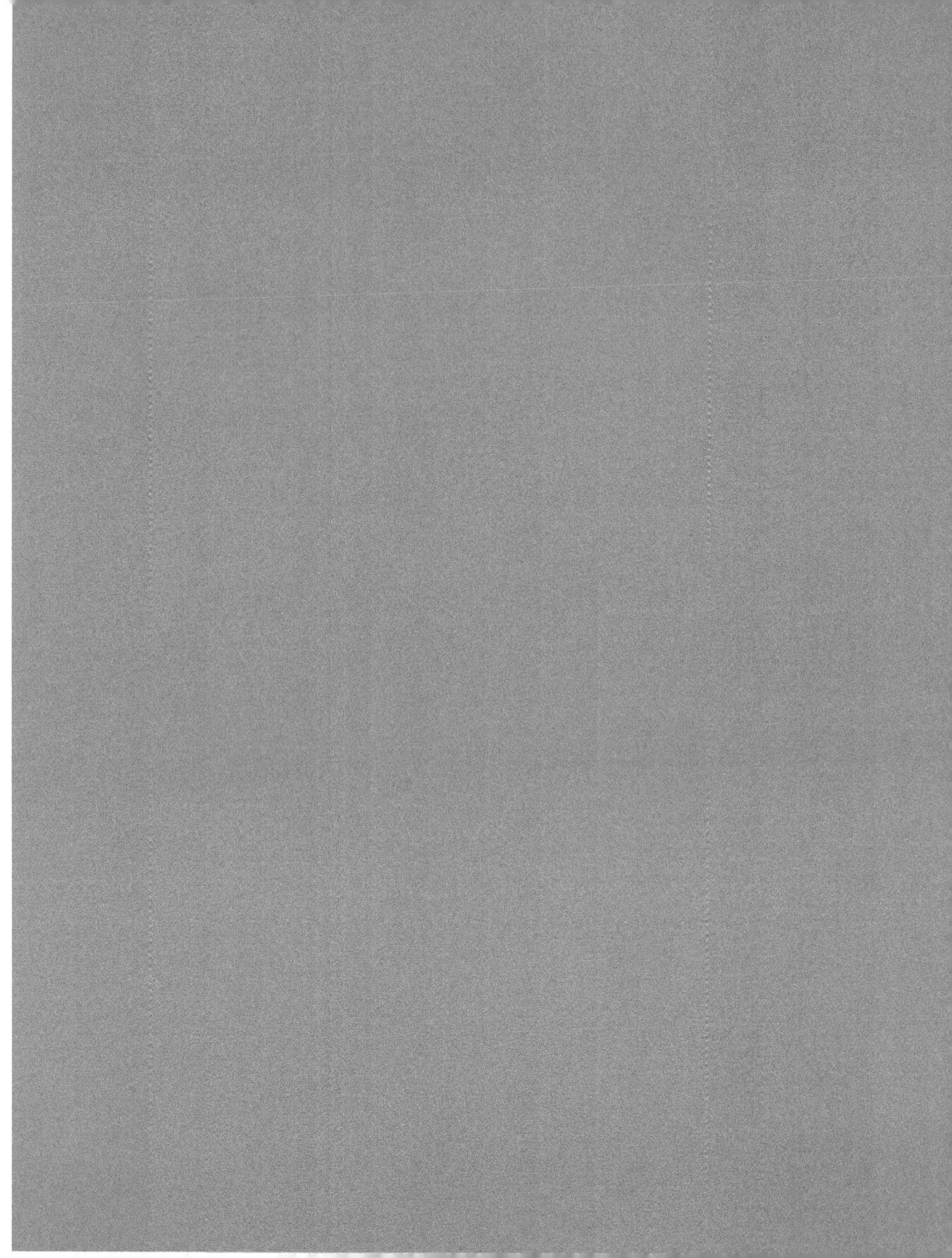

## 8

Geospatial Containers on AWS

Many people believe containers are the future of technology and the next generation of virtual machine images, which is the traditional approach where the entire OS and application are stored as a **virtual hard disk (vHD)** file. Containers have revolutionized the way we develop, manage, and deploy applications while maintaining control of scalability and availability. In this chapter, we will cover what containers are and how they benefit geospatial workloads on the cloud.

In this chapter, we will cover the following topics:

- Understanding containers
- The ECS and EKS AWS services
- Deploying a container to ECR and EC2

Understanding containers

So, to kick off this chapter, let's provide a quick overview of what a container is and why they are all the rage. In this chapter, I don't want to get into the specifics of the inner workings of containers, but in short, you can think of them as very lightweight and portable virtual machines or machine images but only in the sense of starting multiple instances of an application. From an inner-workings standpoint, containers more closely resemble a single server with multiple processes running. A typical virtual machine with all the OS components can easily be a couple of gigabytes – and in the case of Windows images, upward of 10, 20, 30, or more gigabytes. A container's size can usually be measured in megabytes. Most containers share the resources of their host OS and only contain the libraries they need to run their application. Another notable benefit is how quickly they can launch. When you boot a full computer image, you usually wait for a few minutes for it to come online. If the image has been significantly optimized, you might be able to get it down to a minute or two, but it's not uncommon for an image to take several minutes or longer to boot and initialize. Containers can spin up in single-digit seconds. This allows applications to horizontally scale remarkably fast, but it also allows developers to be agile and test changes quickly.

Here is a quick example of what a simple geospatial application for data manipulation would look like on AWS. You would load your geospatial libraries, such as Shapely or Rasterio, into a container. Shapely is a popular library for vector transformations and, alternatively, Rasterio is a popular library for raster data transformations. You could then frontend those libraries with a web server to handle REST-based API calls or some sort of web interface to interact with the libraries.

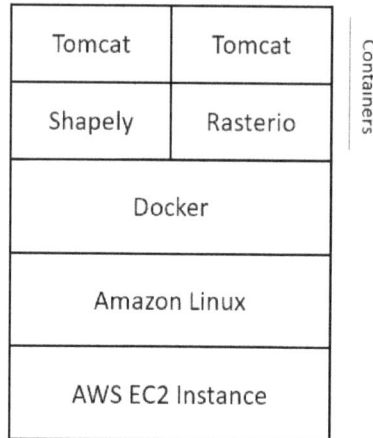

Tomcat	Tomcat
Shapely	Rasterio
Docker	
Amazon Linux	
AWS EC2 Instance	

Containers

Figure 8.1: GDAL output

Scaling containers

In the cloud, we like to scale services horizontally, and we do this by spinning up virtual machines such as EC2 when they start to come under load. Traditionally, on-premises or older applications scaled vertically by adding compute and memory to an existing instance. In the cloud, we scale horizontally by adding multiple instances to a load balancer and fanning the traffic across the instances. When we see a significant increase in load, we initialize the autoscaling group, but depending on how many instances we spin up, it could be 10 or 20 minutes until the instances come online and start serving traffic. Now, in the last section, we mentioned how quickly these containers can spin up and spin down. You can see how this would be beneficial for autoscaling events as you could easily add hundreds of containers in seconds to address load and more closely fit your supply/demand curve.

A common example of this is when content on the internet goes viral. This is a massive challenge for administrators and has commonly taken on-premises data centers down completely. Being in the cloud and having the ability to access virtually unlimited network bandwidth and compute, memory, and storage allows you to scale every component in your architecture to respond to these events in seconds.

Container portability

While containers are lightweight and initialize very quickly, a couple of the main reasons containers gained so much popularity are their portability and ease of management. With a few lines of code in a Dockerfile, you can have a container download its needed libraries and initialize. You can then either share this Docker file through a container repository or even just share the text file with Docker commands. Now, any user with this capability can run your application and not have to worry about library dependencies. The application just works. Any developer can relate to sharing their code with another developer only to have the developer receive an error that they are missing a library or that one of their libraries is an incompatible version. Being able to share these Docker images or files and having everything the library needed to run the application is an incredible experience.

GDAL

No geospatial book is complete without mentioning GDAL several times. GDAL is a collection of geospatial libraries to do just about every transformation imaginable. You can think of it as a raster and vector data translator. It is worth mentioning that while GDAL has some vector capabilities, it has a companion library called OGR that is really the standard for working with vector data. These two libraries are very similar, though, in their operation and syntax as well as their dependency challenges. As mentioned in the previous section, dependency hell, as we like to call it, is a big problem with many open source applications, and GDAL has a long history of dependency issues. A quick search of how to install GDAL on Windows will return many frustrated posts from developers. Running GDAL in a container is as easy as issuing two or three Docker commands and then initializing and connecting to the container. This works 100% of the time and without error; this is the power of containers. A developer could easily lose a week debugging dependency issues trying to get GDAL running. You can now have GDAL running in a matter of seconds in a container. Also, because it's a container and you can run it on AWS, you can easily script and automate your tasks using it. Have GDAL in a container as part of a data conversion pipeline that automatically spins up when new data is detected in your AWS object storage bucket.

I have a recent example using OGR. I tend to do more work with vector data than raster, but I was trying to get some hands-on practice with the new Overture Maps release (`https://overturemaps.org/`), which is a combined effort between Amazon, Meta, Microsoft, and TomTom to make data more accessible but also sanitized and to help fight map vandalism. The current release is only available in `osm.pbf`, which isn't a great format for performance or analytics. Luckily, OGR supports `osm.pbf` as a target and `postgres` as a destination. With a single command such as `ogr2ogr -f PostgreSQL file.osm.pbf` with the database login information, I can copy the `osm.pbf` file into an AWS RDS Postgres database! Other common transformations are `shapefile` to `postgres`, or alternatively, pulling data out of `postgres` for offline sharing.

GeoServer

Another popular geospatial application that is run in a container is GeoServer. This is a popular application for hosting OGC-compliant geospatial services, such as **Web Feature Service (WFS)** or **Web Map Service (WMS)**. There is no better way to run a GeoServer than to run it in a container, which we will walk through later in this chapter. As mentioned earlier, you can download a Docker file or pull the Docker image from a container repository and launch it locally on your computer or on an AWS service such as Fargate, ECS, or Kubernetes, which we'll talk about later in this chapter. GeoServer is a great example of leveraging the power of containers. These feature services and map services can get hit with a lot of traffic very quickly during certain world events. A few common scenarios are COVID dashboards; there were a few variations of these for contact tracing as well as tracking open hospital beds. You also see quick-load events during power outages if you have ever used your phone to view your power company's outage map while sitting in the dark. Lastly, another common scenario is natural disasters, such as fires. When a fire breaks out, you might have a large population near the fire hitting your map service to get the most updated information on how the fire is spreading. Because, when there is no fire, you may have a single instance running, it's easy for this to get overwhelmed when a fire breaks out and you now have tens of thousands of users hitting your service. Running GeoServer in a container would allow you to quickly scale your service up to a dozen containers to meet the demand in a situation like this.

Updating containers

Lastly, another big benefit is the upgrade and maintenance process with containers. Typically, what you would see with a GeoServer software upgrade is users would just download the new container with the updated software in it and deploy it to their fleet. Once the containers were up and running, again in just a few seconds, an administrator would start to cut over DNS or their load balancer rules to start serving the traffic to the containers with the new version of the software. This is a very common approach to software upgrades when containers are used and it makes the experience seamless for both the users and the administrators.

Now that we have learned what containers do, let's start deploying them on AWS.

AWS services

Let's talk about the methods of deploying and storing containers on AWS. First, for storage, AWS has a service called **Elastic Container Registry (ECR)**. There isn't much to this service; it's just a way to store and version your containers. As mentioned earlier, the upgrade process allows you to upload your containers to AWS so they can be easily referenced, but it also allows you to store multiple versions of your container, either different software configurations or completely different versions of the software. Then, when you reference the container in your configuration scripts, you can simply pass in a variable for which version you want to launch.

Deployment options

There are several deployment options on AWS for containers. There is a bit of a running joke about just how many options there are for deploying containers. In this chapter, I'll talk about the main two options, which are **Elastic Container Service (ECS)** and **Elastic Kubernetes Service (EKS)**.

ECS

ECS is where most customers start on their container journey on AWS. It's easy to get started with. You create a cluster, define several virtual machine hosts for the containers to run in, and then deploy your containers to them. AWS has two mechanisms to deploy containers: one is a service and the other is a task. You can think of a task as a one-time operation or a scheduled job that runs periodically or against a trigger or event. A service is used for a web service that you want to always keep running. With a service, ECS will monitor your containers and automatically replace or restart them if something happens to them, such as a kernel panic or a restart. ECS is a great service to get started with containers, but there can be considerations that need to be taken into account if you have a service that needs to scale significantly or a large number of applications that will be running on the cluster. Service discovery, host resource management, and host maintenance have to be considered for your cluster. This is where a service such as Kubernetes or AWS EKS shines.

EKS

There are a lot of mixed feelings toward EKS in the developer community; some worship it and others think it led to the demise of many start-ups because of its high cost and complexity. EKS is a proven technology when it comes to containers and one of the most scalable container frameworks in existence, as proven by Google, which runs one of the largest Kubernetes clusters in the world. But the criticism is justified; there are numerous books written about managing Kubernetes and well-paid salaries for administrators. It's an advanced and complex system of sub-services that all work together to solve some of the complexities I mentioned about containers in ECS. Kubernetes will easily let you declare an application and enter the number of instances and Pods you want to deploy, and you are off. The challenges come into play when things don't work as expected or things break. Kubernetes can be somewhat of a black box, and when the system breaks, there is a significant level of expertise required to get it back up and running. We'll now dive into actually deploying a container in the following section.

Deploying containers

Launch a t3a.medium EC2 instance with Amazon, Linux, and either SSH connectivity or a systems manager role for connectivity.

Use the following commands to install Docker:

```
sudo yum install docker -y
sudo usermod -a -G docker ec2-user
newgrp docker
```

This command is used to enable the Docker service so that we can start it with the next command:

```
sudo systemctl enable docker.service
```

This command is used to start the Docker service:

```
sudo systemctl start docker.service
```

This command will search the public Docker repository for any containers named or labeled GDAL:

```
sudo docker search gdal
```

This results in the following output:

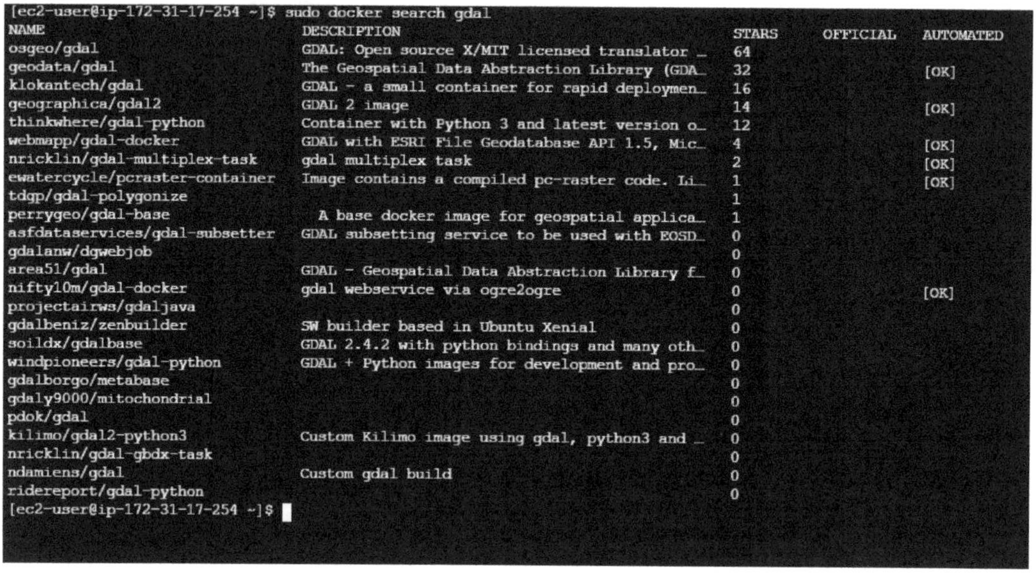

```
[ec2-user@ip-172-31-17-254 ~]$ sudo docker search gdal
NAME                              DESCRIPTION                                       STARS   OFFICIAL   AUTOMATED
osgeo/gdal                        GDAL: Open source X/MIT licensed translator …     64
geodata/gdal                      The Geospatial Data Abstraction Library (GDA…     32                 [OK]
klokantech/gdal                   GDAL - a small container for rapid deploymen…     16
geographica/gdal2                 GDAL 2 image                                      14                 [OK]
thinkwhere/gdal-python            Container with Python 3 and latest version o…     12
webmapp/gdal-docker               GDAL with ESRI File Geodatabase API 1.5, Mic…     4                  [OK]
nricklin/gdal-multiplex-task      gdal multiplex task                               2                  [OK]
ewatercycle/pcraster-container    Image contains a compiled pc-raster code. Li…     1                  [OK]
tdgp/gdal-polygonize                                                                1
perrygeo/gdal-base                  A base docker image for geospatial applica…     1
asfdataservices/gdal-subsetter    GDAL subsetting service to be used with EOSD…     0
gdalanw/dgwebjob                                                                    0
area51/gdal                       GDAL - Geospatial Data Abstraction Library f…     0
nifty10m/gdal-docker              gdal webservice via ogre2ogre                     0                  [OK]
projectairws/gdaljava                                                               0
gdalbeniz/zenbuilder              SW builder based in Ubuntu Xenial                 0
soildx/gdalbase                   GDAL 2.4.2 with python bindings and many oth…     0
windpioneers/gdal-python          GDAL + Python images for development and pro…     0
gdalborgo/metabase                                                                  0
gdaly9000/mitochondrial                                                             0
pdok/gdal                                                                           0
kilimo/gdal2-python3              Custom Kilimo image using gdal, python3 and …     0
nricklin/gdal-gbdx-task                                                             0
ndamiens/gdal                     Custom gdal build                                 0
ridereport/gdal-python                                                              0
[ec2-user@ip-172-31-17-254 ~]$
```

Figure 8.2: GDAL output

This command will pull down the GDAL container from the Docker public container registry so we can run it locally on our machine:

```
Sudo docker pull osgeo/gdal
```

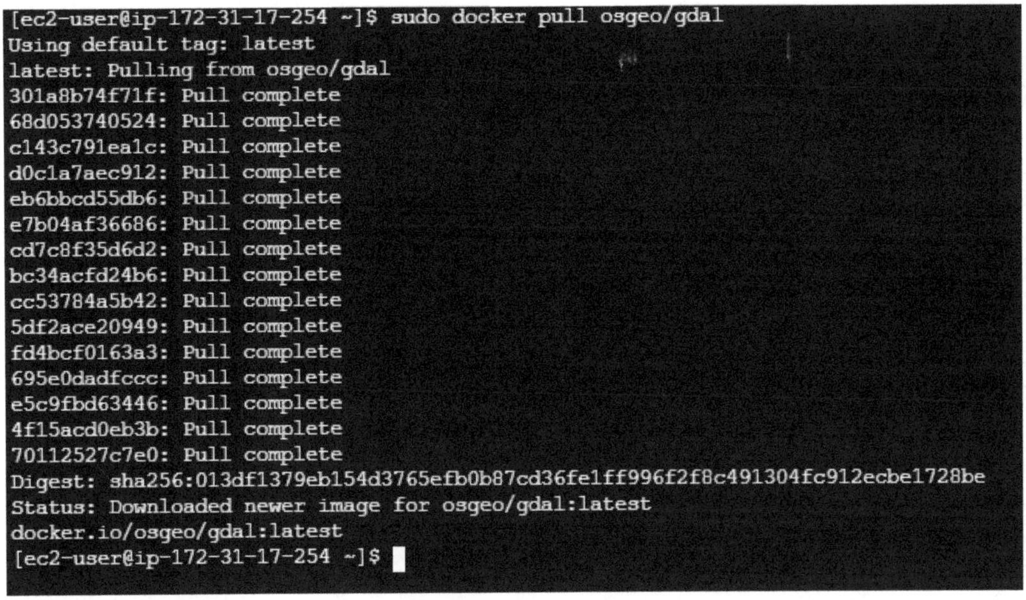

```
[ec2-user@ip-172-31-17-254 ~]$ sudo docker pull osgeo/gdal
Using default tag: latest
latest: Pulling from osgeo/gdal
301a8b74f71f: Pull complete
68d053740524: Pull complete
c143c791ea1c: Pull complete
d0c1a7aec912: Pull complete
eb6bbcd55db6: Pull complete
e7b04af36686: Pull complete
cd7c8f35d6d2: Pull complete
bc34acfd24b6: Pull complete
cc53784a5b42: Pull complete
5df2ace20949: Pull complete
fd4bcf0163a3: Pull complete
695e0dadfccc: Pull complete
e5c9fbd63446: Pull complete
4f15acd0eb3b: Pull complete
70112527c7e0: Pull complete
Digest: sha256:013df1379eb154d3765efb0b87cd36fe1ff996f2f8c491304fc912ecbe1728be
Status: Downloaded newer image for osgeo/gdal:latest
docker.io/osgeo/gdal:latest
[ec2-user@ip-172-31-17-254 ~]$
```

Figure 8.3: Installing GDAL

This command will show the Docker container images that we have downloaded. We can see our gdal container image here:

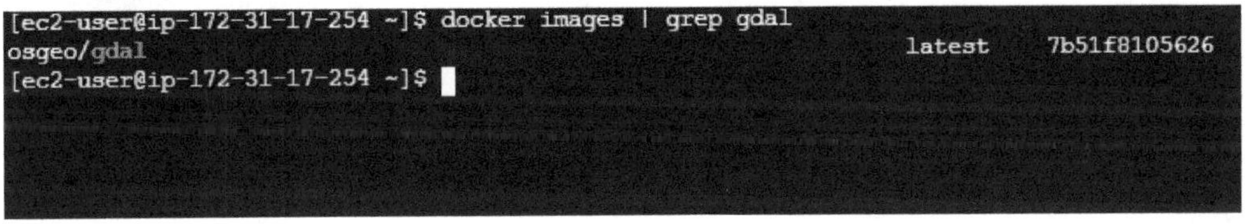

```
[ec2-user@ip-172-31-17-254 ~]$ docker images | grep gdal
osgeo/gdal                                           latest      7b51f8105626
[ec2-user@ip-172-31-17-254 ~]$
```

Figure 8.4: Pulling GDAL using Docker

This command will start our container and drop us into the container in a Bash shell so we can run commands.

Start our container in interactive mode with docker run -it osgeo/gdal /bin/bash.

Then, run `ogr2ogr` to confirm the environment is working:

```
[ec2-user@ip-172-31-17-254 ~]$ docker run -it osgeo/gdal /bin/bash
root@a1b2cfb463bb:/# ogr2ogr
Usage: ogr2ogr [--help-general] [-skipfailures] [-append | -upsert] [-update]
               [-select field_list] [-where restricted_where|@filename]
               [-progress] [-sql <sql statement>|@filename] [-dialect dialect]
               [-preserve_fid] [-fid FID] [-limit nb_features]
               [-spat xmin ymin xmax ymax] [-spat_srs srs_def] [-geomfield field]
               [-a_srs srs_def] [-t_srs srs_def] [-s_srs srs_def] [-ct string]
               [-f format_name] [-overwrite] [[-dsco NAME=VALUE] ...]
               dst_datasource_name src_datasource_name
               [-lco NAME=VALUE] [-nln name]
               [-nlt type|PROMOTE_TO_MULTI|CONVERT_TO_LINEAR|CONVERT_TO_CURVE]
               [-dim XY|XYZ|XYM|XYZM|layer_dim] [layer [layer ...]]
```

Figure 8.5: Working container output

Congratulations, you have launched a GDAL container on AWS! In *Chapter 15*, we will expand on this demo by pulling down a GeoServer container, publishing to ECR, and hosting our container with ECS Fargate.

Summary

In this chapter, we had an overview of containers and how they are being adopted for GIS workflows. We covered a few container services on AWS, and we deployed a quick demo showing how to launch a GDAL container on an EC2 instance. In the next chapter, we will learn how to work with geospatial data on Hadoop and EMR.

References

- GDAL: https://gdal.org/

- GeoServer: https://geoserver.org/

- ECS: https://aws.amazon.com/ecs/

- EKS: https://aws.amazon.com/eks/

- Fargate: https://aws.amazon.com/fargate/

- Geohash: https://en.wikipedia.org/wiki/Geohash

- Overture: https://overturemaps.org/

9

Using Geospatial Data with Amazon EMR

In the previous chapter, we learned about machine learning with Amazon SageMaker, a powerful service for creating, testing, and tuning machine learning algorithms. In this chapter, we will learn about **Elastic Map Reduce** (**EMR**), which is essentially a managed Hadoop cluster. Hadoop is a powerful framework for the massively parallel processing of data. This ability is unique to the Hadoop architecture and is the only way to efficiently query petabytes of data using commodity hardware. Hadoop is an interesting community project that is really made up of hundreds of plug-and-play widgets. There is also a service on Hadoop to do machine learning called Mahout, as well as Spark ML. In this chapter, we will walk through a quick overview of Hadoop, EMR, and a demo for launching EMR and visualizing geospatial data.

This chapter covers the following topics:

- Introducing Hadoop
- Common frameworks
- Geospatial with EMR

Introducing Hadoop

Hadoop was released in 2006 and was a revolutionary concept of using hundreds, thousands, or even more compute nodes to solve and crunch big datasets. This framework was a great fit to apply to commodity resources such as old aging servers; companies that may have had a fleet of aging hardware could repurpose them with this framework to be powerful data processing clusters. This is also a great fit for AWS as there are massive amounts of unused capacity that have to be available for demand spikes. Thus, EMR was born and is commonly used with EC2 Spot Instances, which is discounted compute resources that are older and less used capacity. Spot instances can have savings of up to 90% off their on-demand prices but can be revoked by Amazon at any time, whereby you are given a 1-hour notification. This makes them a great option for Hadoop, which can restart tasks if a node is removed.

Introduction to EMR

Let's dive into EMR and why it is such a powerful service. Anyone who has managed a Hadoop cluster will tell you it's a dependency nightmare. Hadoop is kind of a perfect storm for dependency issues because you have hundreds of projects being built on top of it that all depend on each other. When one of these high-level services adds capabilities, those capabilities must also be present in certain frameworks underneath. You have to play package version musical chairs until a build completes successfully. This entails building a cluster with a set of libraries until an error is thrown stating that you have incompatible libraries; you repeat the process of changing libraries until you finally have a successful build. In addition to services such as EMR being popular, we are also seeing containers play a large part in this system. They play a large part because it's easy for a single user to solve these dependency issues and publish a container that others in the community can use instead of everyone trying to figure them out on their own.

Installing and setting up Hadoop is only part of the challenge though; scheduling and automating workflows and having access to specialists who can look at a cluster and troubleshoot when things go awry are a few of the big benefits of EMR. Maintaining a mission-critical production Hadoop cluster is not for the faint-hearted. Aside from supporting a cluster though, being able to write a PySpark, Spark, Apache Pig, or any other processing job and simply upload your `pyspark.py` file to kick off a workflow is powerful. You can schedule your job to run at certain increments or use an event-based architecture, where, if a file is uploaded to AWS S3 object storage, your cluster automatically spins up, runs your job, and then shuts off. For example, some sensors upload their last hour of data as a CSV file to an S3 bucket; this would automatically kick off the EMR cluster to pick up that file and perform some computations on it such as enriching it with geospatial calculations. You could use a geospatial library to convert the lat/long of the device to a more efficient geospatial format such as **Well-Known Text** (**WKT**), which is easily convertible to a database geometry.

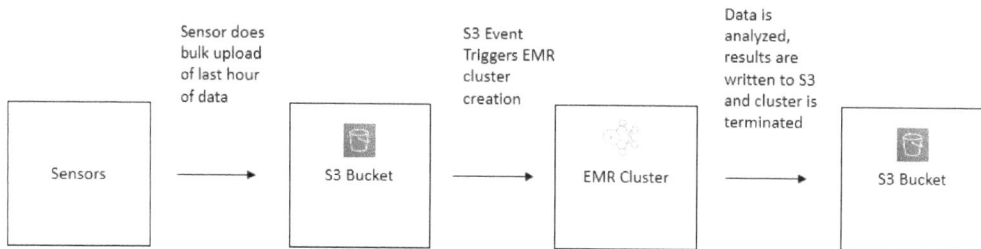

Figure 9.1: An event-based EMR architecture

Now that we have an understanding of Hadoop and EMR, let's look at some common frameworks.

Common Hadoop frameworks

I've mentioned a few frameworks already such as PySpark, Spark, and Apache Pig, but there are hundreds more that do just about everything under the sun. You have data storage and database frameworks such as **Hadoop Distributed File System (HDFS)**, NoSQL and SQL capabilities such as HBase and Hive, and machine learning with Mahout, to name a few. I have a good example of how these services came to be when I was first learning Hadoop. Over a decade ago, I got frustrated trying to run a **Map Reduce** job and stumbled across Apache Pig. Apache Pig (which was named after Pig Latin) was built to be a simple analytics language syntax for Hadoop and was an attempt to make it easier for users who didn't know Java. This is also similar to what happened with PySpark, where the Hadoop users wanted a familiar language to work with Spark, so PySpark was born.

These frameworks are somewhat in the process of being disrupted with the release of Spark. Traditionally, Hadoop would read and write to disk between states such as mapping and reducing, which was fine when the frameworks were being developed. At the time, RAM was still expensive and many large datasets couldn't fit in memory. However, lately, RAM has gotten much cheaper. Spark was built to be able to run these jobs all in memory, leading to massive speed improvements. We are now seeing Spark dominate the Hadoop ecosystem with services such as Spark ML, Spark Streaming, and PySpark. Older services such as Apache Pig are now supporting Spark as well.

EMRFS

The last architecture point I want to hit on is the storage tier. Hadoop was originally used with HDFS on top of cheap commodity storage. You didn't need ultra-fast disks because you could have millions of disk IOPS spread across tens of thousands of disks and nodes. This is similar to what you see with AWS S3 Object Storage; you can put your data in S3 and S3 can optimize the partitions on the backend for parallel reads from a Hadoop cluster. EMR built a connector to make S3 look like a filesystem to make it easy to pull data in and out, as well as to optimize the requests. This lets you run a command such as `spark.read().text(s3://myfile)` and Hadoop can natively read that file as if it was local.

Now that we have discussed a few common frameworks, let's see how they apply to geospatial and EMR.

Geospatial with EMR

Alright, now let's get to the good part: Geospatial with EMR! Out of the box, EMR has pretty limited geospatial support. I've seen a few projects with Hive to support SQL geospatial functions that have seen some success. Two big initiatives are Apache Sedona and Esri GeoAnalytics. These products have launched and are both currently running production workloads. In our previous example, we talked about using EMR with the default Python frameworks loaded to work with data, but to take advantage of parallel processing on the cluster, you would want to use something built on Spark. Both Sedona and GeoAnalytics do exactly that: they allow you to run PySpark with Python or SQL syntax against your data and they are able to parallelize the processing.

With PySpark, the syntax is pretty trivial, as in the following example, where we load `geojson` into a pandas DataFrame. We could easily create a Spark dataframe with a command like this: `SparkDataFrame=spark.createDataFrame(Pandas  DataFrame)` or, in our example, change `PandaDataFrame` to our `countries` dataset. As of writing this, Sedona has support for over 70 SQL spatial functions. You can use Spark SQL syntax to run a command like this to create a temp table: `spark.read.json("s3://myfile").registerTempTable("countries")`. You could then use a Sedona spatial function like this: `results = spark.sql("SELECT ST_Centroid(countries.geometry)  FROM countries")`. This command would create a new variable named `results` that has the central point of all of the country polygons in our dataset.

> **Note**
>
> Setting up a Sedona cluster or a GeoAnalytics cluster is outside the scope of this book but Sedona has an excellent user community and ArcGIS GeoAnalytics has specific EMR documentation on their website.

Launching EMR

In this example, we will launch an EMR cluster and work with some geospatial JSON data. We will load in a library called **Geopanda** that was designed to be able to work with geometry and geography datatypes. It's required to read the spatial data from various sources and create a geometry or geography index on the fly. It also works with matplotlib to help us visualize things such as polygons, as we will see in our example:

1. Navigate to EMR in the console. You can search through the list of services by typing EMR into the search bar in the top navigation panel. You can also connect directly to the EMR service after logging in with the following link (make a note to update the Region as this is using us-east-1): `https://us-east-1.console.aws.amazon.com/emr/home`.

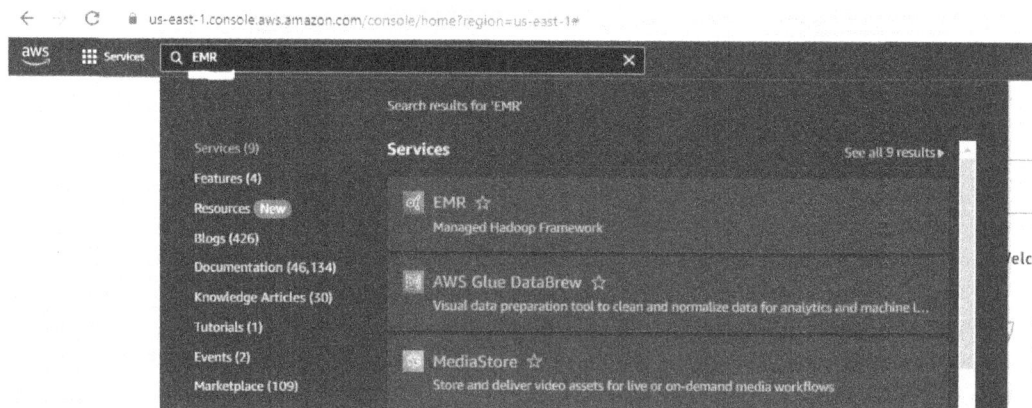

Figure 9.2: The search bar in the AWS console

2. Click **Clusters** on the left navigation panel.

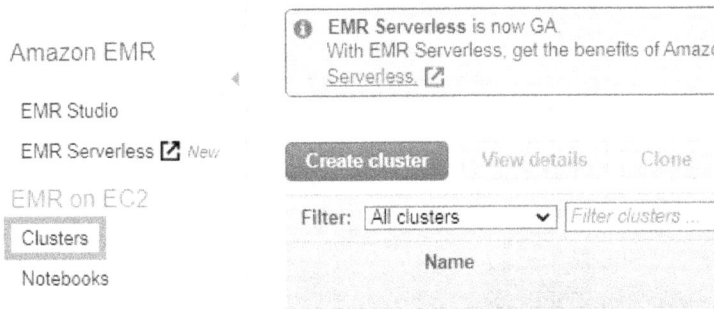

Figure 9.3: The EMR console navigation panel highlighting Clusters

3. Click the blue **Go to advanced options** link.

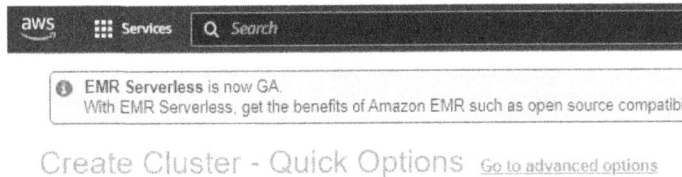

Figure 9.4: The EMR cluster creation page, highlighting the Go to advanced options link

4. Now we can begin selecting the software packages and configurations for our cluster:

    A. Select the latest release.

    B. Unselect **Hue** and **Pig.**

    C. Select **Spark.**

Software Configuration

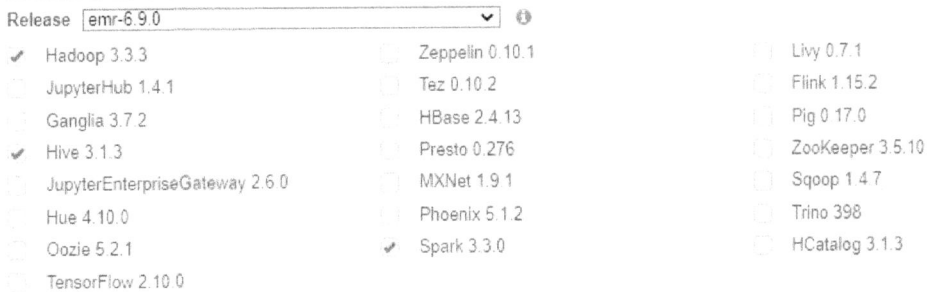

Release emr-6.9.0

✔ Hadoop 3.3.3	Zeppelin 0.10.1	Livy 0.7.1
JupyterHub 1.4.1	Tez 0.10.2	Flink 1.15.2
Ganglia 3.7.2	HBase 2.4.13	Pig 0.17.0
✔ Hive 3.1.3	Presto 0.276	ZooKeeper 3.5.10
JupyterEnterpriseGateway 2.6.0	MXNet 1.9.1	Sqoop 1.4.7
Hue 4.10.0	Phoenix 5.1.2	Trino 398
Oozie 5.2.1	✔ Spark 3.3.0	HCatalog 3.1.3
TensorFlow 2.10.0		

Figure 9.5: The available software packages for the EMR cluster

5. I've written an example configuration script that we can use to bootstrap our cluster. Save this as a .sh file and upload it to an S3 bucket:

```
#!/bin/bash
sudo python3 -m pip install jupyter
mkdir /home/hadoop/.jupyter
touch /home/hadoop/.jupyter/jupyter_notebook_config.py
echo "c = get_config()" >> /home/hadoop/.jupyter/jupyter_
notebook_config.py
echo "c.IPKernelApp.pylab = 'inline'" >> /home/hadoop/.jupyter/
jupyter_notebook_config.py
echo "c.NotebookApp.ip = '0.0.0.0'" >> /home/hadoop/.jupyter/
jupyter_notebook_config.py
echo "c.NotebookApp.open_browser = False" >> /home/hadoop/.
jupyter/jupyter_notebook_config.py
echo "c.NotebookApp.password =
u'sha1:84b8ea1999e8:ddccd1e17b8139b0759ff9d207081561cd613564'"
>> /home/hadoop/.jupyter/jupyter_notebook_config.py
echo "c.NotebookApp.port = 8887" >> /home/hadoop/.jupyter/
jupyter_notebook_config.py
/usr/local/bin/jupyter notebook --config /home/hadoop/.jupyter/
jupyter_notebook_config.py
```

6. Scroll down and under the **Steps** section, change **Step type** to **Custom JAR**. The JAR location will be a built-in AWS JAR to execute .sh files. You can navigate to the previous .sh file in your bucket and select it.

Step type	Custom JAR		Add step	
Name	Action on failure	JAR location	Arguments	
Custom JAR	Continue	s3://us-east-1.elasticmapreduce/libs/script-runner/script-runner.jar	s3://jeffdm-emr-studio/emr-jupyter-step-v2.sh	✎ ✖

Cancel   Next

Figure 9.6: The EMR cluster step configuration page

Note that this config is not secure and is meant for demonstration purposes. You should be generating an SSL certificate to enable HTTPS connectivity as well as locking down 0.0.0.0 to only the subnets that should have access.

7. Click **Next**.

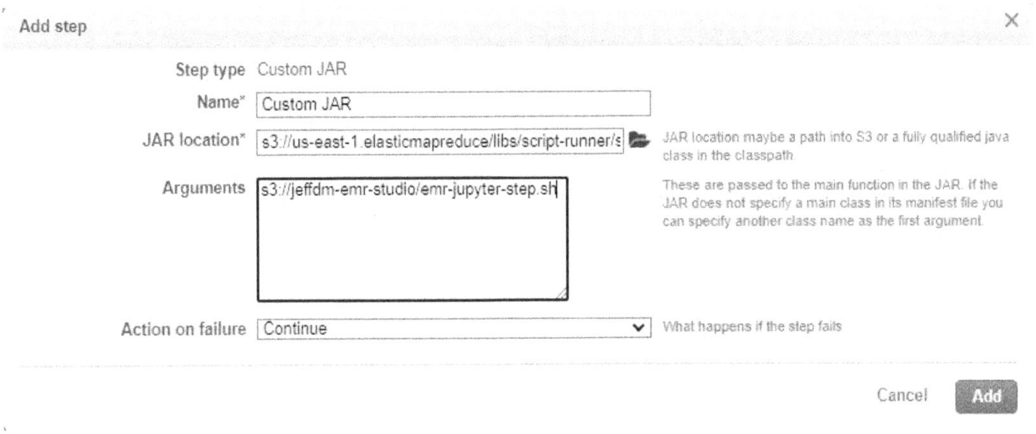

Figure 9.7: The Add step pop-up box

8. Click **Add**.

9. On the next page, increase the EBS size to 3 0; this isn't required but will give our cluster a little extra breathing room with additional storage. Click **Next**.

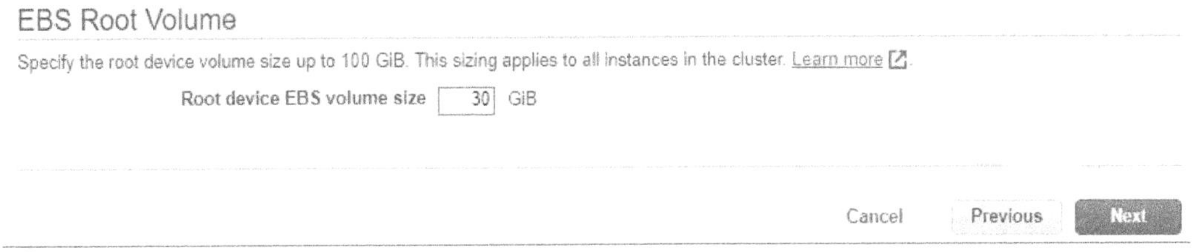

Figure 9.8: The EMR cluster EBS volume configuration

10. Click **Next** again to accept the defaults.

11. We now reach the last page, as shown in the following screenshot, so go ahead and click **Create cluster**:

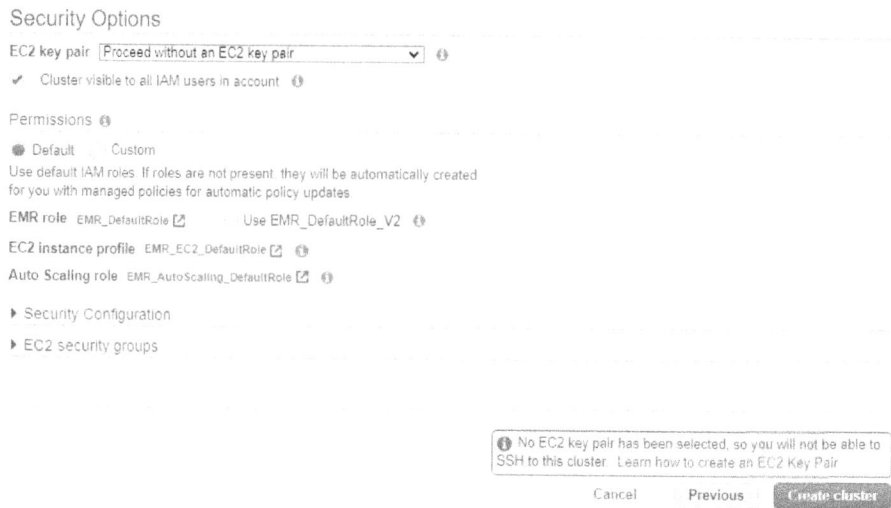

Security Options

EC2 key pair   Proceed without an EC2 key pair

✓   Cluster visible to all IAM users in account

Permissions

● Default   Custom
Use default IAM roles. If roles are not present, they will be automatically created
for you with managed policies for automatic policy updates

EMR role   EMR_DefaultRole   Use EMR_DefaultRole_V2

EC2 instance profile   EMR_EC2_DefaultRole

Auto Scaling role   EMR_AutoScaling_DefaultRole

▶ Security Configuration

▶ EC2 security groups

ⓘ No EC2 key pair has been selected, so you will not be able to
SSH to this cluster. Learn how to create an EC2 Key Pair

Cancel   Previous   Create cluster

Figure 9.9: The EMR cluster security configuration page

12. On the cluster creation page, you'll see your security groups. Click on the **Security group for Master** node.

13. Add a rule to allow port 8887 from your IP address or 0.0.0.0/0 to be reachable from anywhere on the internet.

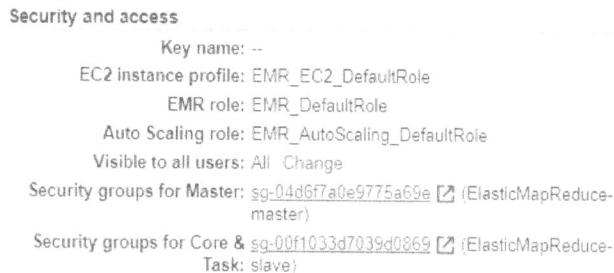

Security and access

Key name: --
EC2 instance profile: EMR_EC2_DefaultRole
EMR role: EMR_DefaultRole
Auto Scaling role: EMR_AutoScaling_DefaultRole
Visible to all users: All Change
Security groups for Master: sg-04d6f7a0e9775a69e [(ElasticMapReduce-master)
Security groups for Core & sg-00f1033d7039d0869 [(ElasticMapReduce-
Task: slave)

Figure 9.10: The security group configuration

14. After about 5 minutes, click on the **Steps** tab and confirm your custom JAR step is in a running state. The cluster will take around 8 minutes to fully initialize. The first few minutes will be AWS provisioning hardware and loading the EMR machine image. Then, EMR will pull down our shell file and start processing the commands from our file.

Cluster: My cluster   Running Running step

Summary   Application user interfaces   Monitoring   Hardware   Configurations   Events   Steps   Bootstrap actions

Concurrency: 1 Change
After last step completes: Cluster waits

Add step   Clone step   Cancel step

Filter: [All steps ▾] [Filter steps]   2 steps (all loaded) ⟳

	ID	Name		Status	Start time (UTC-6) ▾	Elapsed time
▸ ⊕	s-216PEAQ1D4JTX	Custom JAR		Running	2022-12-03 16:41 (UTC-6)	2 minutes
▸	s-2TIEM0WFCDEX	Setup hadoop debugging		Completed	2022-12-03 16:41 (UTC-6)	18 seconds

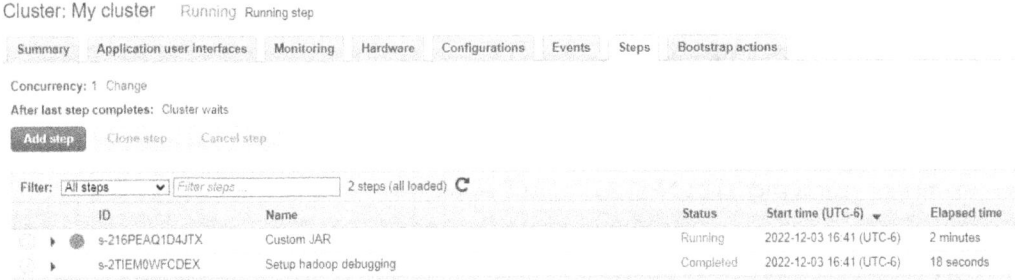

Figure 9.11: The Steps tab on the EMR cluster page

15. Click on the **Hardware** tab and grab the public DNS name of your master instance.

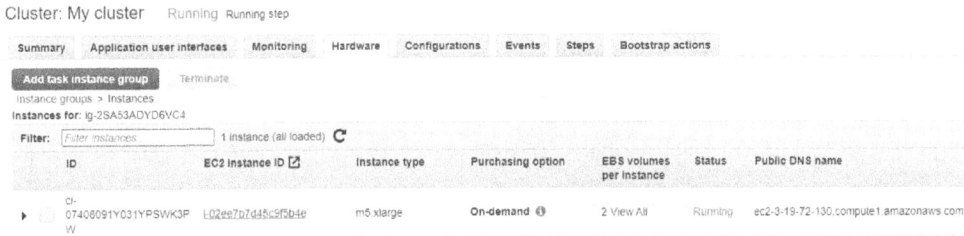

Cluster: My cluster   Running Running step

Summary   Application user interfaces   Monitoring   Hardware   Configurations   Events   Steps   Bootstrap actions

Add task instance group   Terminate
Instance groups > Instances
Instances for: ig-2SA53ADYD6VC4

Filter: [Filter instances]   1 instance (all loaded) ⟳

	ID	EC2 Instance ID ↗	Instance type	Purchasing option	EBS volumes per instance	Status	Public DNS name
▸	ci-07408091Y031YPSWK3PW	i-02ee7b7d45c9f5b4e	m5.xlarge	On-demand ⓘ	2 View All	Running	ec2-3-19-72-130.compute1.amazonaws.com

Figure 9.12: The Hardware tab on the EMR cluster page

16. Enter the public DNS name into your browser with the `http://<dnsname>:8887` format to connect to Jupyter Notebook. Note that `8887` is a non-standard port and some firewalls will block non-standard outbound ports. You can adjust the custom JAR we run to use a different port number. This is the `.sh` script we saved to our S3 bucket earlier. Jupyter commonly runs on port `8888` but EMR clusters occasionally use `8888`, which is why I decremented to `8887`. Modify the following line to change the port in the `.sh` file: `echo "c.NotebookApp.port = 8887"`.

⟳ ec2-54-164-176-167.compute-1.amazonaws.com:8887/

⟳ Jupyter

Password: [   ]   [Log in]

Figure 9.13: The Jupyter Notebook login page

17. Log in with the password `Packt123`, which was set with the following configuration hash in the `.sh` file we created:

```
c.NotebookApp.password =
u'sha1:84b8ea1999e8:ddccd1e17b8139b0759ff9d207081561cd613564'"
```

18. In the top-right corner, click **New** and select **Python 3**.

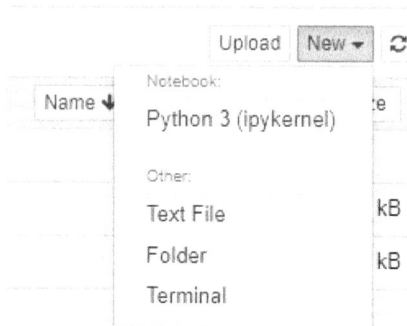

Figure 9.14: The Jupyter Notebook main page with the New dropdown selected

19. Run the following commands in your Jupyter notebook. I'm using a simple `geojson` dataset that has country polygons in it. You can use this link to download it: `https://d2ad6b4ur7yvpq.cloudfront.net/naturalearth-3.3.0/ne_50m_admin_0_countries.geojson`. There are many other `geojson` open datasets available to test with at `http://geojson.xyz/`:

```
!sudo pip3 install geopandas
import geopandas
!sudo pip3 install boto3
from boto3 import client
client = client('s3')
result = client.get_object(Bucket='<yourbucketname>',
    Key='low.geo.json')
mygeojsonfile = result["Body"].read().decode()
countries = geopandas.read_file(mygeojsonfile)
countries['geometry'][17]
```

Once you have entered the commands, your Jupyter notebook will look like the following figure. There is a **Run** button in the middle navigation panel that you can use to run each line of Python.

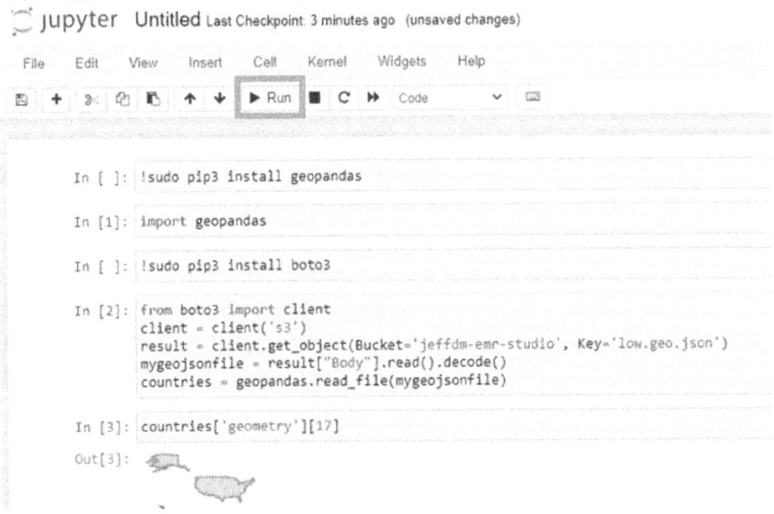

Figure 9.15: The Jupyter application depicting a new notebook with our commands and output

Congratulations, you have completed this example! We have loaded a geojson file from S3 and have printed a polygon of the United States to the screen. The built-in visualizations are basic but there are many advanced visualization libraries available such as rasterio, ipyleaflet, and arcgis. EMR is mostly used for crunching highly complex calculations and massive amounts of data so while the visualizations are nice, from this point, you would want to start using libraries such as shapely to project different coordinate systems or sedona to run st_distance-like functions to calculate the nearest neighbor of other polygons or any of the hundreds of other spatial functions available.

Data preparation and visualization like this on EMR is fine, but to maximize parallel processing, you'll want to use Spark or PySpark, which are designed to be split across multiple EMR nodes. The Apache Sedona project has built-in geospatial functions that were developed in Spark, which has a SQL or Python syntax. You can work with the data just like we did in this chapter but using Sedona libraries instead and still achieve parallel processing. For the example in this chapter, we used the geopandas.read_file(mygeojsonfile) command, but if you installed Sedona, you would use a command such as countries = spark.read.csv("countries.csv"). The purpose of this demonstration is to get you more familiar with working with EMR. Now that you have some geospatial data loaded, you can explore additional geospatial libraries, such as rasterio, shapely, sedona, and geoanalytics.

Summary

In this chapter, we learned about the power of Hadoop and distributed processing and how EMR makes it easy to manage, deploy, and automate these clusters. We also learned how to create a cluster in EMR, load a simple geospatial library, and import some geospatially enriched JSON data. You would never be able to load every building on the planet into a SQL query in a database but it is theoretically possible to do it in Hadoop. It is still early days for geospatial analytics with Hadoop. GeoAnalytics by Esri was only recently released and Sedona is also in its early days with its v1.0 release. Luckily, your timing is perfect as both solutions have been industry-proven and are ready for production workloads on EMR. A good rule of thumb with big data processing is if you start having issues storing all of your data in your database, it's probably a good idea to start looking into building a data lake. Once the data is outside the database, you can still query it as if it was in a database using tools such as EMR.

In the next chapter, we will explore geospatial analysis using Python on AWS Cloud9.

References

- Apache Hadoop Wiki: https://en.wikipedia.org/wiki/Apache_Hadoop

- Apache Pig: https://pig.apache.org/

- ArcGIS GeoAnalytics for EMR Setup: https://developers.arcgis.com/geoanalytics/install/aws_emr/

- Getting Started with Sedona: https://sedona.apache.org/1.3.1-incubating/tutorial/sql-python/

## 10

Geospatial Data Analysis Using R on AWS

R is a popular open source programming language widely used for statistical computing and visualization[1]. Its active community, extensive libraries, and flexibility make it a popular choice for data analytics, machine learning, and graphics. It provides a rich ecosystem of packages for handling, analyzing, and visualizing geospatial data. This chapter will explore the power of using AWS and R programming languages for geospatial data analysis. Diving deep into every geospatial R library is beyond the scope of this chapter, but we will cover the following topics:

- Introduction to the R geospatial data analysis ecosystem
- Setting up R on EC2
- RStudio on Amazon SageMaker
- Loading, analyzing, and visualizing geospatial data using R on AWS

Introduction to the R geospatial data analysis ecosystem

R is an open source software ecosystem designed for statistical computing and graphics. It can be executed on various operating systems, including Unix platforms, Windows, and macOS. The ability of R to analyze and visualize data makes it a favorable option for spatial data analysis. In specific spatial analysis projects, R alone may be satisfactory. However, in many instances, R is utilized in combination with GIS.

Comprehensive R Archive Network (CRAN)[2] is a central repository that collects R packages, documentation, and resources. It provides a platform for R users to access and download various packages that extend the functionality of the R language. The CRAN repository hosts thousands of R packages developed and contributed by the R community. These packages cover various domains, including data analysis, statistical modeling, machine learning, visualization, spatial analysis, and more. Dedicated developers maintain the packages and undergo rigorous quality checks to ensure their reliability and compatibility with different versions of R. R users can easily install packages from

CRAN using the `install.packages()` function in R. Additionally, CRAN serves as a platform for communication and collaboration within the R community. It hosts mailing lists, forums, and bug-tracking systems, allowing users to seek help, report issues, and contribute to package development. In this chapter, we will cover the basics of setting up an R environment on AWS and geospatial data handling in R, including importing and exporting data, manipulating spatial objects, conducting spatial operations, and creating thematic maps. CRAN Task Views have curated collections of R packages grouped based on specific domains or tasks. Go to `https://cran.r-project.org/web/views/Spatial.html` to find Task Views designed to assist R users in discovering and selecting geospatial packages that align with their needs.

Let us quickly learn about a few critical R libraries helpful in handling spatial data. Simple Features, also known as Simple Feature Access, is a recognized and formal standard (ISO 19125-1:2004) that outlines the representation of real-world objects within computer systems, with a specific focus on their spatial geometry. This standard encompasses guidelines for storing, retrieving, and processing these objects within databases and defining the geometric operations applicable to them. The Simple Features standard has gained widespread adoption and implementation across various domains. It serves as the foundation for spatial databases such as PostGIS and commercial **Geographic Information System** (**GIS**) software such as Esri's ArcGIS and acts as the underlying structure for vector data in libraries such as GDAL. GeoJSON, a widely used format for geospatial data, is based on a subset of the Simple Features standard. This highlights the standard's significance and impact on the interchange and representation of spatial data across different systems and applications. The `sp`[3] R package enhances R's capabilities by incorporating specialized classes and methods for handling spatial data. These classes establish a structured framework for organizing and storing spatial data, while methods are customized functions designed for specific data classes. However, R has previously faced challenges in comprehensively implementingsimple features, leading to complex, inefficient, or incomplete conversions. The `sf` package[4] has emerged to address this gap, aiming to bridge these limitations and, ultimately, supersede the `sp` package in the long run. The `sf` package strives to provide a more complete and streamlined approach to working with spatial data in R. It focuses on implementing the simple features standard, ensuring seamless integration and compatibility with other tools and systems that adhere to this widely adopted standard. By adopting `sf`, R users can expect improved efficiency, greater functionality, and enhanced interoperability when handling and analyzing spatial data.

Another R package, `terra`[5], offers methods for manipulating geographic (spatial) data in raster and vector formats. This package implements two primary classes or data types: `SpatRaster` and `SpatVector`. `SpatRaster` provides functionality for efficiently handling large raster files that may exceed available memory. It supports various raster operations such as local, focal, zonal, and global. It also enables conversion between polygons, lines, points, and raster data. Additionally, `SpatRaster` integrates well with modeling methods, allowing for spatial predictions and more advanced analyses. `SpatVector`, on the other hand, supports a wide range of geometric operations such as intersections between vector objects. `terra` is very similar to the `raster` package, a widely popular package for reading, writing, manipulating, analyzing, and modeling spatial data, but `terra` has superseded `raster` because it is more straightforward, better, and faster.

RStudio[6] is a versatile **integrated development environment (IDE)** for R and Python programming languages. It offers a range of powerful features and tools to streamline the coding process and enhance productivity. The core components of RStudio include a console, a syntax-highlighting editor that supports real-time code execution, and various tools for tasks such as plotting, history tracking, debugging, and workspace management. These features enable developers and data scientists to write, test, and debug their code efficiently within a single environment. RStudio is available in two editions: open source and commercial. The open source version provides all the essential features and can be installed on desktop systems running Windows, macOS, or Linux operating systems. The commercial edition offers advanced features and is suitable for professional use cases. By leveraging RStudio, users can benefit from a user-friendly interface, a code editor with syntax highlighting, seamless execution of code, and tools for managing and analyzing data. It simplifies development and provides a comprehensive environment for working with R and Python code on desktop platforms.

Shiny[7] is an R package that simplifies the creation of interactive web applications directly from the R programming language. With Shiny, developers can build web-based applications and dashboards without extensive web development knowledge. Shiny leverages the power of R and allows users to utilize their existing R code and data analysis skills to create dynamic and interactive applications. It provides a framework for building user interfaces that incorporate various interactive elements such as sliders, input fields, buttons, and plots. Shiny abstracts away the complexities of web development, enabling R users to focus on creating the application's logic and functionality. It utilizes reactive programming principles, meaning that changes to the user interface automatically trigger corresponding updates in the underlying data and outputs. This ensures that the application remains responsive and reflects real-time changes. Shiny also allows direct integration with R code, functions, and data. R scripts can be embedded within the application to perform complex calculations and generate dynamic output. It provides a wide range of user interface components that allow users to interact with the application. These components can include input fields, sliders, checkboxes, and more. Shiny applications can be easily deployed on various platforms, including Shiny Server, Shinyapps.io, or integrated into other web frameworks.

Setting up R and RStudio on EC2

Setting up R and RStudio on an Amazon EC2 instance allows you to harness the power of cloud computing for R-based geospatial data analysis. It provides scalable computing resources, and with R installed on an EC2 instance, you can leverage its capabilities to handle large geospatial datasets, perform complex calculations, and deploy R applications. One of the significant benefits of using Amazon EC2 is the freedom to choose different operating systems and configurations based on your needs. Changing the instance type is a seamless process that takes just a few minutes. By stopping the instance, modifying the instance type, and starting it again, you can quickly increase or decrease the computing power according to your requirements. This capability aligns perfectly with R and RStudio's in-memory architecture, enabling you to process and analyze data efficiently. With EC2, you can adapt your computing resources and leverage the full potential of R and RStudio for your data-intensive workloads.

This section provides a few simple steps for you to quickly configure an EC2 instance with R and RStudio, enabling you to utilize the vast ecosystem of R packages and tools for your geospatial data analysis needs, empowering you to take advantage of the flexibility and computational resources offered by the AWS cloud:

1.   Log in to your AWS console, click on **Services**, go to the **Compute** section, and choose **EC2**.

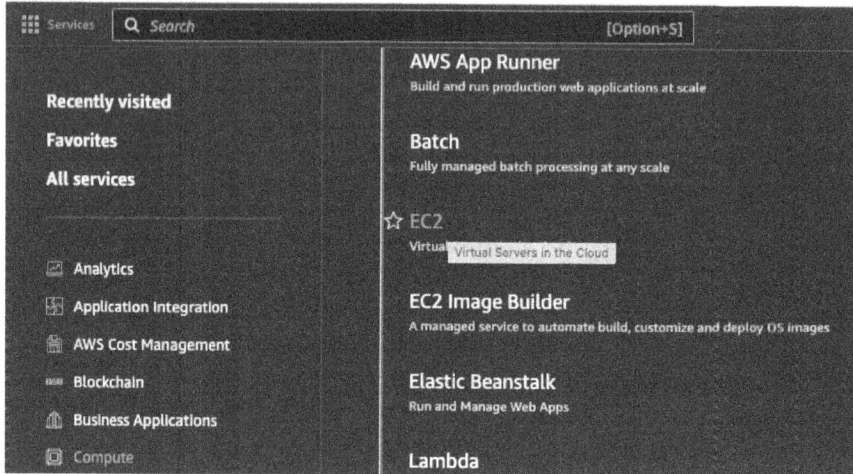

Figure 10.1: Searching for EC2

2.   On the EC2 console, click on **Launch instance** and then on **Launch instance**.

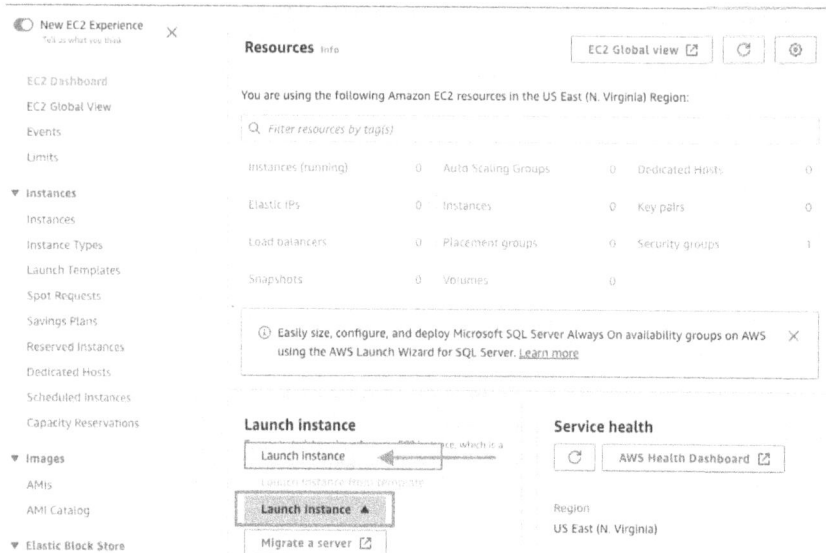

Figure 10.2: Launching the instance

3. In the **Launch an instance** screen, provide a name for your instance and choose **Amazon Linux 2 AMI**. Make sure not to choose **Amazon Linux 2023 (AL2023)** because AL2023 doesn't support EPEL or EPEL-like repositories. Also, Amazon Linux 2 features a high level of compatibility with CentOS 7. Select **t2.micro** as the instance type (free-tier eligible), and then under **Key pair**, click on **Create new key pair**. You could also use an existing key pair if you have one.

Name

| my-rstudio | | Add additional tags |

▼ **Application and OS Images (Amazon Machine Image)** Info

An AMI is a template that contains the software configuration (operating system, application server, and applications) required to launch your instance. Search or Browse for AMIs if you don't see what you are looking for below

Q *Search our full catalog including 1000s of application and OS images*

Recents   Quick Start

| Amazon Linux | macOS | Ubuntu | Windows | Red Hat | S |
| aws | Mac | ubuntu® | Microsoft | RedHat | |

Q
Browse more AMIs

Including AMIs from AWS, Marketplace and the Community

Amazon Machine Image (AMI)

Amazon Linux 2 AMI (HVM) - Kernel 5.10, SSD Volume Type   Free tier eligible
ami-0bef6cc322bfff646 (64-bit (x86)) / ami-09212035c6444f37a (64-bit (Arm))
Virtualization: hvm   ENA enabled: true   Root device type: ebs

▼ **Instance type** Info

Instance type

| t2.micro   Free tier eligible |
| Family: t2   1 vCPU   1 GiB Memory   Current generation: true |
| On-Demand Windows pricing: 0.0162 USD per Hour |
| On-Demand SUSE pricing: 0.0116 USD per Hour |
| On-Demand RHEL pricing: 0.0716 USD per Hour |
| On-Demand Linux pricing: 0.0116 USD per Hour |

⬤ All generations

Compare instance types

▼ **Key pair (login)** Info

You can use a key pair to securely connect to your instance. Ensure that you have access to the selected key pair before you launch the instance.

Key pair name - *required*

| Select | | C Create new key pair |

Figure 10.3: Selecting the parameters for the AMI

4. Provide a name for your key pair and click on **Create key pair**.

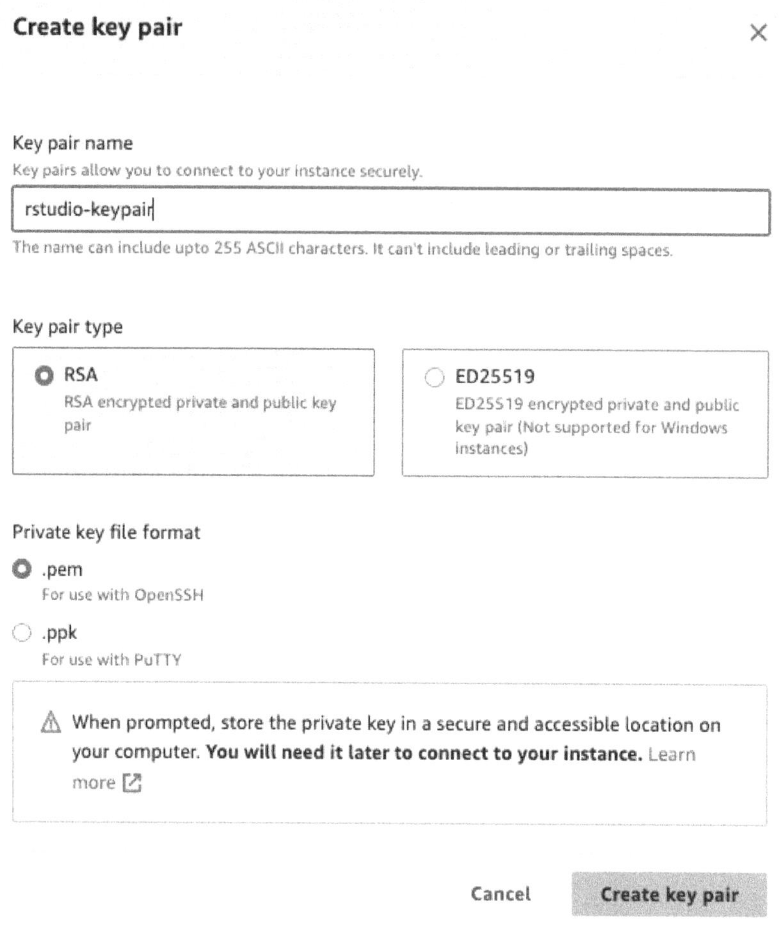

Figure 10.4: Creating the key pair

5. Under **Network Settings**, create a security group to allow SSH and HTTPS traffic from anywhere. Configure your storage (you could keep **8** GB for this exercise) and click on the **Launch instance** button on the right.

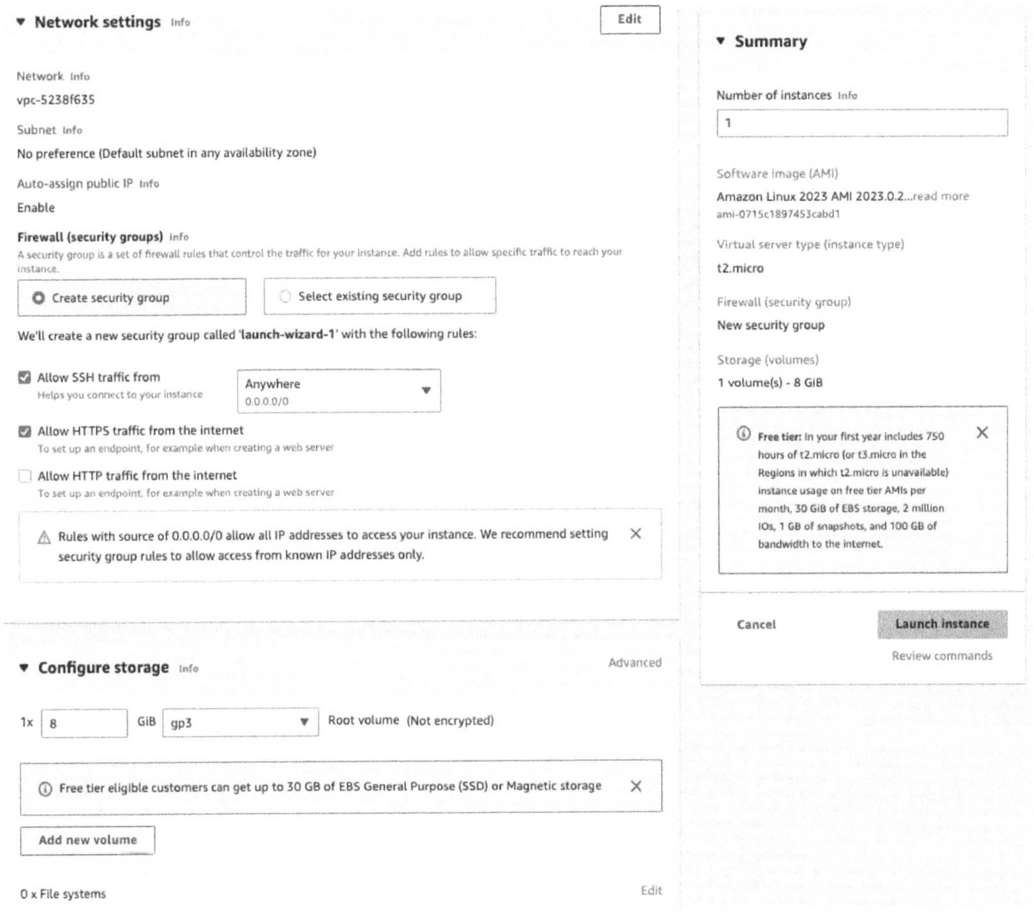

▼ Network settings Info   Edit

Network Info
vpc-5238f635

Subnet Info
No preference (Default subnet in any availability zone)

Auto-assign public IP Info
Enable

Firewall (security groups) Info
A security group is a set of firewall rules that control the traffic for your instance. Add rules to allow specific traffic to reach your instance.

- ◉ Create security group
- ○ Select existing security group

We'll create a new security group called '**launch-wizard-1**' with the following rules:

☑ Allow SSH traffic from   Anywhere   ▼
    Helps you connect to your instance   0.0.0.0/0

☑ Allow HTTPS traffic from the internet
    To set up an endpoint, for example when creating a web server

☐ Allow HTTP traffic from the internet
    To set up an endpoint, for example when creating a web server

⚠ Rules with source of 0.0.0.0/0 allow all IP addresses to access your instance. We recommend setting   ✕
security group rules to allow access from known IP addresses only.

▼ Configure storage Info   Advanced

1x   8   GiB   gp3   ▼   Root volume (Not encrypted)

ⓘ Free tier eligible customers can get up to 30 GB of EBS General Purpose (SSD) or Magnetic storage   ✕

Add new volume

0 x File systems   Edit

▼ Summary

Number of instances Info

1

Software Image (AMI)
Amazon Linux 2023 AMI 2023.0.2...read more
ami-0715c1897453cabd1

Virtual server type (instance type)
t2.micro

Firewall (security group)
New security group

Storage (volumes)
1 volume(s) - 8 GiB

ⓘ **Free tier:** In your first year includes 750   ✕
hours of t2.micro (or t3.micro in the
Regions in which t2.micro is unavailable)
instance usage on free tier AMIs per
month, 30 GiB of EBS storage, 2 million
IOs, 1 GB of snapshots, and 100 GB of
bandwidth to the internet.

Cancel   **Launch instance**

Review commands

Figure 10.5: Updating the network settings

6. In our security group, we need to allow ports 3838 for Shiny apps and 8787 for RStudio to be accessed from the public internet. Go back to the EC2 dashboard, choose **Security Groups** under the **Network & Security** section on the left panel, check the box of the security group you created in the previous step, go to the **Inbound rules** tab, and click on **Edit inbound rules**.

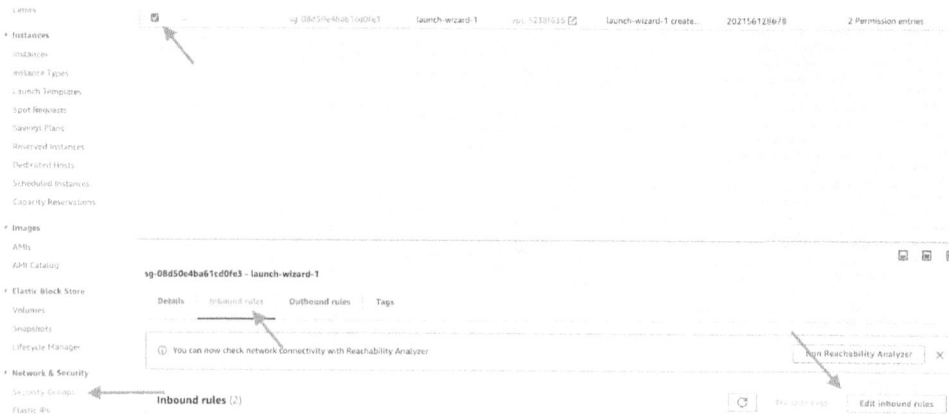

Figure 10.6: Updating networking rules to allow parts

In the **Edit inbound rules** window, click on **Add rule** and add both 3838 and 8787 custom TCP ports, select **Anywhere** for the **Source** type, and click on **Save rules**.

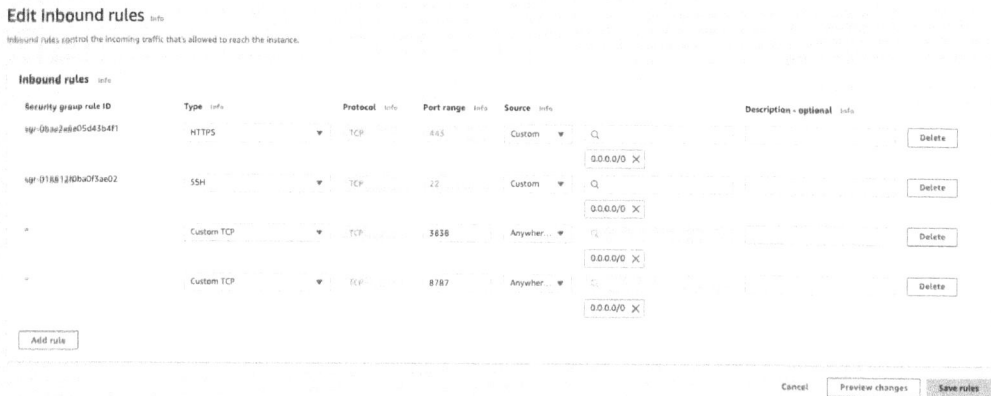

Figure 10.7: Editing the inbound rules

7. Now that our EC2 instance is created with proper firewall configurations, return to the EC2 dashboard and click **Instance (running)**. Click the checkbox of the appropriate EC2 instance and then click on **Connect**. You will see all the EC2 instances that are part of your AWS account running in a chosen AWS Region.

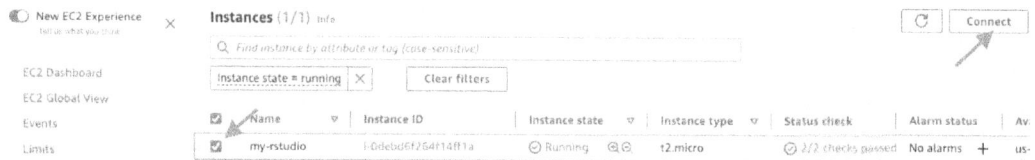

Figure 10.8: Checking the EC2 instances

8. You could SSH into your EC2 instance in a few different ways. For this exercise, select the **EC2 Instance Connect** tab and click on the **Connect** button.

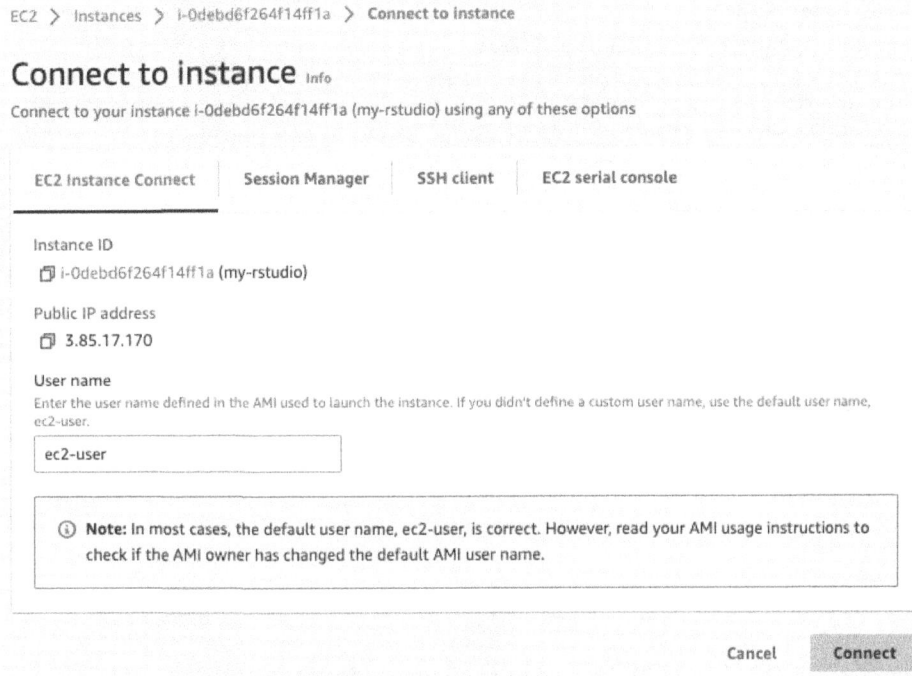

EC2 > Instances > i-0debd6f264f14ff1a > Connect to instance

Connect to instance Info

Connect to your instance i-0debd6f264f14ff1a (my-rstudio) using any of these options

| EC2 Instance Connect | Session Manager | SSH client | EC2 serial console |

Instance ID

🗐 i-0debd6f264f14ff1a (my-rstudio)

Public IP address

🗐 3.85.17.170

User name

Enter the user name defined in the AMI used to launch the instance. If you didn't define a custom user name, use the default user name, ec2-user.

```
ec2-user
```

ⓘ **Note:** In most cases, the default user name, ec2-user, is correct. However, read your AMI usage instructions to check if the AMI owner has changed the default AMI user name.

Cancel   Connect

Figure 10.9: Connecting to the instance

9. On the EC2 **Instance Connect** console, run the following commands to set up R and RStudio servers on the EC2 cloud server:

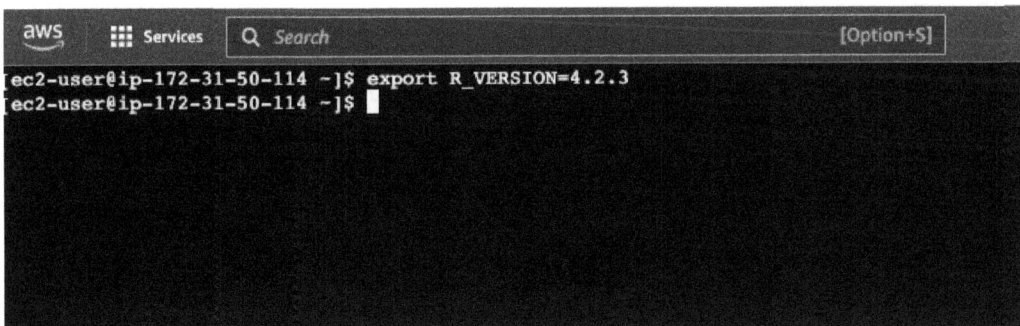

```
[ec2-user@ip-172-31-50-114 ~]$ export R_VERSION=4.2.3
[ec2-user@ip-172-31-50-114 ~]$ 
```

Figure 10.10: The EC2 instance connect console

I.   We begin by installing the dependencies and libraries:

```
#Install dependencies
sudo yum update -y
sudo amazon-linux-extras install epel
sudo yum install openssl-devel fontconfig-devel libxml2-devel
harfbuzz-devel fribidi-devel freetype-devel libpng-devel libtiff-devel
libjpeg-turbo-devel udunits2-devel geos geos-devel
sudo yum install gcc-c++.x86_64 cpp.x86_64 sqlite-devel.x86_64
libtiff.x86_64 cmake3.x86_64 -y
#We need gdal > 2.x version for using sf package
sudo yum install gcc-c++.x86_64 cpp.x86_64 sqlite-devel.x86_64
libtiff.x86_64 cmake3.x86_64 -y

#Installation of PROJ
cd /tmp
wget https://download.osgeo.org/proj/proj-6.1.1.tar.gz
tar -xvf proj-6.1.1.tar.gz
cd proj-6.1.1
./configure
sudo make
sudo make install
#Installation of GDAL
cd /tmp
wget https://github.com/OSGeo/gdal/releases/download/v3.2.1/gdal-
3.2.1.tar.gz
tar -xvf gdal-3.2.1.tar.gz
cd gdal-3.2.1
./configure --with-proj=/usr/local --with-python
sudo make
sudo make install
#Testing your installation
which gdalinfo; gdalinfo --version
```

II.   Choose the desired R version, download it, and install it on EC2. Learn more at `https://docs.posit.co/resources/install-r/`:

```
#Amazon Linux 2 features a high level of compatibility with CentOS 7.
export R_VERSION=4.2.3
curl -O https://cdn.rstudio.com/r/centos-7/pkgs/R-${R_VERSION}-1-1.
x86_64.rpm
sudo yum install R-${R_VERSION}-1-1.x86_64.rpm
#Test the successful installation of R
/opt/R/${R_VERSION}/bin/R --version
```

III.   To ensure that R is available on the default system PATH variable, create symbolic links to the version of R that you installed:

```
sudo ln -s /opt/R/${R_VERSION}/bin/R /usr/local/bin/R
sudo ln -s /opt/R/${R_VERSION}/bin/Rscript /usr/local/bin/Rscript
#Install RStudio Server.
#Find the latest release at https://posit.co/download/rstudio-server/
#Amazon Linux 2 features a high level of compatibility with CentOS 7.
sudo wget https://download2.rstudio.org/server/centos7/x86_64/rstudio-server-rhel-2023.03.1-446-x86_64.rpm
sudo yum install rstudio-server-rhel-2023.03.1-446-x86_64.rpm
#Optional step: The port that RStudio Server listens on can be changed by adding www-port=80 to this file: /etc/rstudio/rserver.conf
#Add a username and password for the RStudio user
sudo useradd rstudio
sudo passwd rstudio
#Start the RStudio server.
#Learn more about RStudio server management at https://support.posit.co/hc/en-us/articles/200532327-Managing-RStudio-Workbench-RStudio-Server
sudo rstudio-server start
```

10. Once you successfully installed the RStudio server on EC2, go to the EC2 dashboard and find the public IP of your EC2 instance. In your local browser, type that address with port 8787 (e.g., XXXX.XXXXXXXX.XXXXXX:878). This will take you to the RStudio login page. Enter a username and password to log in.

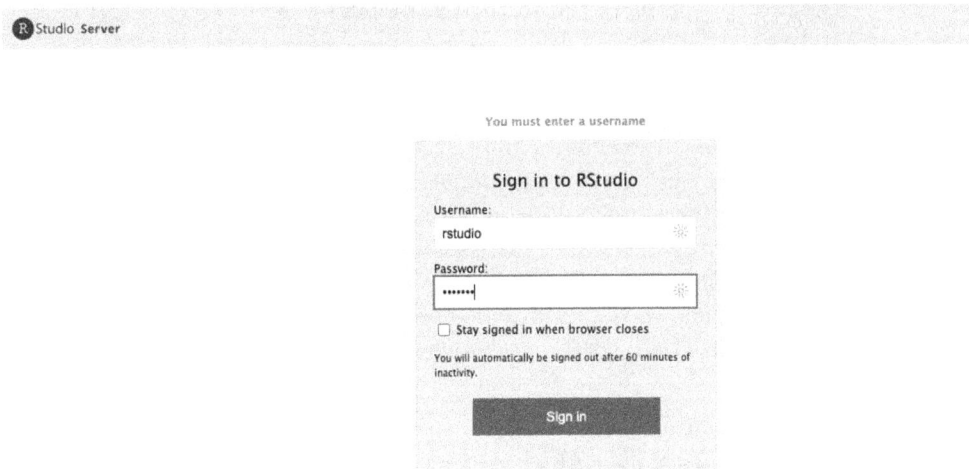

Figure 10.11: Signing into RStudio

11. Once logged in, you will be taken to the RStudio IDE console. Let us test a sample R script to install and load the `RCurl` library and then read the data from the CCAFS-Climate Data's CGIAR S3 bucket[8], publicly accessible as part of our Registry of Open Data on AWS[9]:

```
install.packages("RCurl")
library("RCurl")
data <- read.table(textConnection(getURL("https://cgiardata.s3-us-
west-2.amazonaws.com/ccafs/amzn.csv")), sep=",", header=FALSE)

head(data)
```

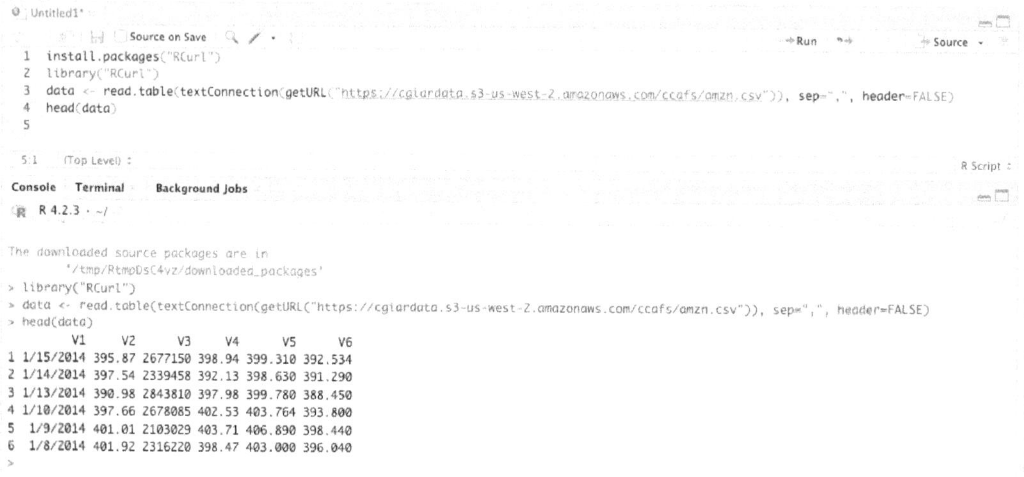

Figure 10.12: The final data output

This section explored the process of setting up R and RStudio on Amazon EC2, providing a comprehensive guide for users looking to leverage the power of RStudio in a cloud environment. Following the step-by-step instructions and best practices outlined in this section, you can easily configure an RStudio environment on an Amazon EC2 instance, enabling seamless collaboration, scalability, and enhanced data analysis capabilities. With Amazon EC2, users gain access to flexible computing resources, allowing them to scale up or down based on their needs. This elasticity ensures optimal performance and cost efficiency. Additionally, the ability to choose from a wide range of instance types and configurations allows users to tailor their RStudio environment to meet specific requirements. You could also select an appropriate **Amazon Machine Image** (**AMI**) that includes R and RStudio pre-installed, simplifying the setup process.

RStudio on Amazon SageMaker

RStudio is widely cherished among R developers for its data science, statistical analysis, and machine learning prowess. However, the complexities of building, securing, scaling, and maintaining RStudio environments on your own can be laborious. Amazon SageMaker revolutionizes the RStudio experience by providing the industry's first fully-managed RStudio IDE in the cloud. Amazon SageMaker integrates the power of RStudio by offering the first fully managed cloud-based Posit Workbench[10] (formerly known as RStudio Workbench). Migrating your self-managed RStudio environments to Amazon SageMaker is now a seamless process that can be accomplished in a few straightforward steps. With RStudio on Amazon SageMaker, the burden of managing the underlying Posit Workbench infrastructure is lifted, allowing your teams to focus on delivering value to your business. You can effortlessly transition your existing RStudio licenses to the cloud. Utilizing AWS License Manager, you can seamlessly bring your current licenses to SageMaker. Security is paramount, and SageMaker offers robust features to fortify your RStudio environment. Through AWS **Identity and Access Management (IAM)**, you can establish fine-grained access controls, ensuring that only authorized users have appropriate permissions. Network traffic can be restricted to your **Virtual Private Cloud (VPC)**, shielding your environment from external threats. Additionally, data encryption at rest is automatically applied, enhancing data protection. Monitoring logs via Amazon CloudWatch and managing billing through AWS Billing further simplify operations. Working within the familiar RStudio interface, you can confidently write R code. The elastic compute capabilities of SageMaker enable you to dynamically scale compute resources, adjusting them to match your requirements without interrupting your workflow. This seamless scalability allows you to build robust machine learning and analytics solutions in R at any desired scale. This elasticity accelerates model development, enhances productivity, and amplifies the overall efficiency of your RStudio experience on SageMaker.

Acquiring a new Posit Workbench license or requesting a trial has been made convenient through direct access from AWS Marketplace. You can now obtain your license or initiate a trial for Posit Workbench directly within the AWS Marketplace platform. Once you have acquired the license or trial, setting up your environment with the intuitive AWS Management Console is a breeze. This section provides a few simple steps to configure RStudio on Amazon SageMaker quickly:

1. First, we create an IAM role for SageMaker domain execution with access to the AWS Marketplace, License Manager, logs, and others. In the AWS console, search and go to the IAM console. On the left panel, click **Roles** and then select **Create role**.

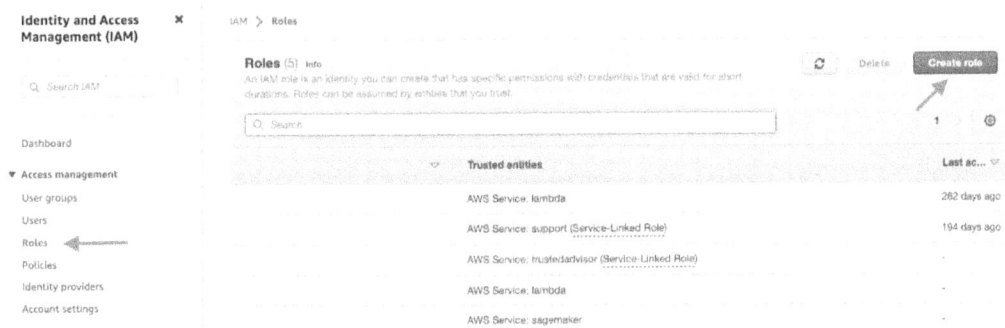

Figure 10.13: Creating the role

2. For the first step of the role creation, choose **AWS service** under **Trusted entity type**, and under **Use case**, use the dropdown to select **SageMaker**, and click **Next**.

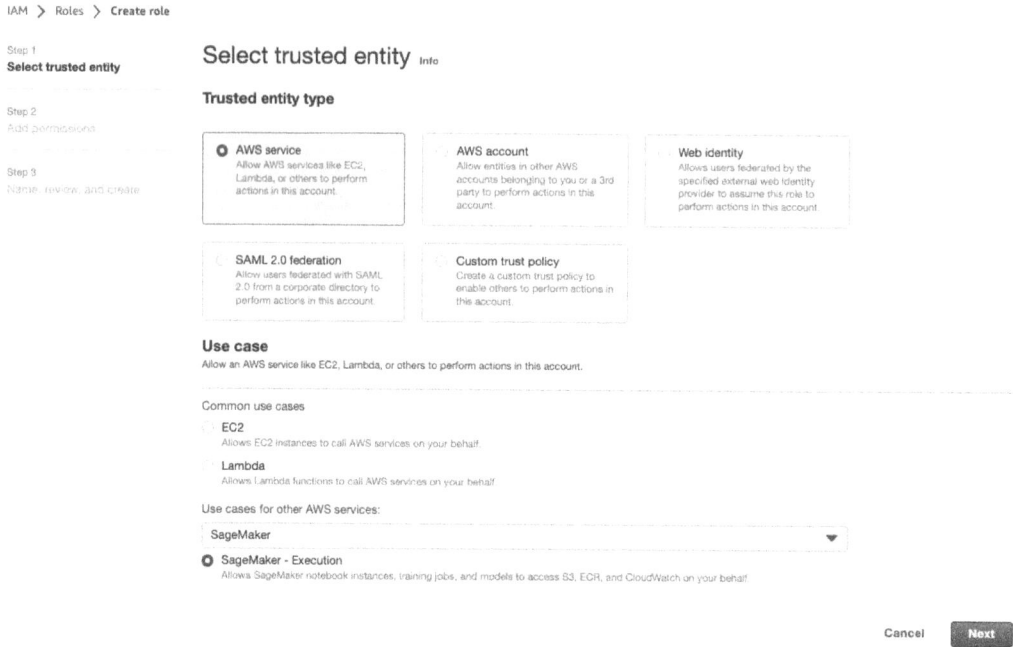

Figure 10.14: Selecting the trusted entity

3. In the next step, leave everything as default and click on **Next**.

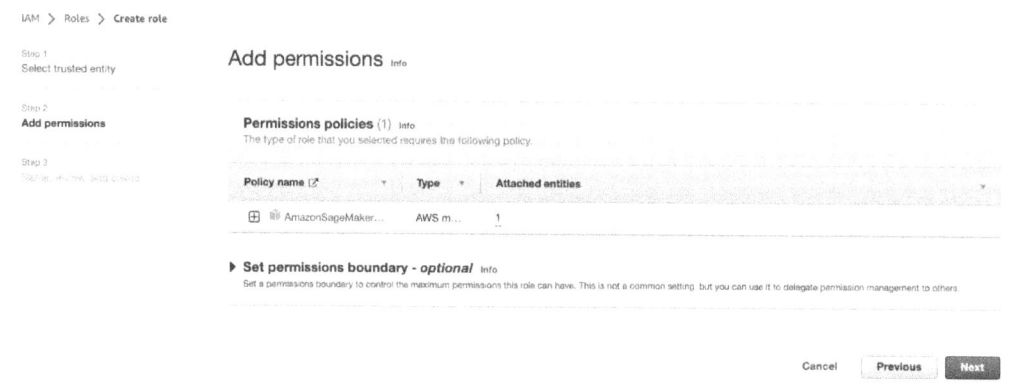

Figure 10.15: Adding permissions to the role

4.   Provide a name for your role and choose **Create role**.

Figure 10.16: Finalizing the role

5.   Go back to the IAM console and choose the role you just created, then under the **Permission policies** section, select **Add permissions**, and click on **Create inline policy**.

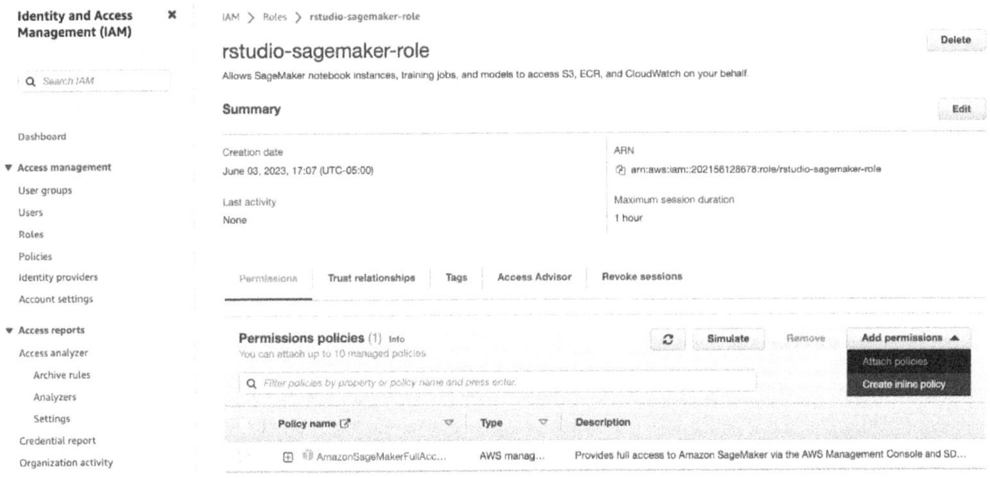

Figure 10.17: Creating an inline policy

6. On the **Create policy** page, select the **JSON** tab, clear the existing policy template, copy and paste the following inline policy that will allow this role to access AWS License Manager and have access to both SageMaker and CloudWatch, and click on **Review policy**:

```
{
    "Version": "2012-10-17",
    "Statement": [
        {
            "Sid": "VisualEditor0",
            "Effect": "Allow",
            "Action": [
                "license-manager:ExtendLicenseConsumption",
                "license-manager:ListReceivedLicenses",
                "license-manager:GetLicense",
                "license-manager:CheckoutLicense",
                "license-manager:CheckInLicense",
                "logs:CreateLogDelivery",
                "logs:CreateLogGroup",
                "logs:CreateLogStream",
                "logs:DeleteLogDelivery",
                "logs:Describe*",
                "logs:GetLogDelivery",
                "logs:GetLogEvents",
                "logs:ListLogDeliveries",
                "logs:PutLogEvents",
                "logs:PutResourcePolicy",
                "logs:UpdateLogDelivery",
                "sagemaker:CreateApp"
            ],
            "Resource": "*"
        }
    ]
}
```

Create policy

A policy defines the AWS permissions that you can assign to a user, group, or role. You can create and edit a policy in the visual editor and using JSON. Learn more

Visual editor   JSON   Impor

```
 1 {
 2     "Version": "2012-10-17",
 3     "Statement": [
 4         {
 5             "Sid": "VisualEditor0",
 6             "Effect": "Allow",
 7             "Action": [
 8                 "license-manager:ExtendLicenseConsumption",
 9                 "license-manager:ListReceivedLicenses",
10                 "license-manager:GetLicense",
11                 "license-manager:CheckoutLicense",
12                 "license-manager:CheckInLicense",
```

Security: 0   Errors: 0   Warnings: 0   Suggestions: 0

Figure 10.18: Updating the JSON

7.   On the next **Review policy** page, provide your inline policy name, and click **Create policy**.

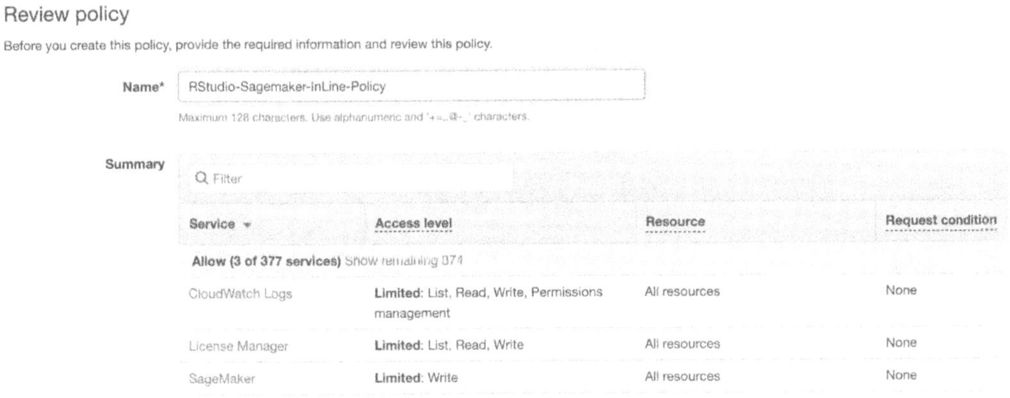

Review policy

Before you create this policy, provide the required information and review this policy.

Name*   RStudio-Sagemaker-InLine-Policy

Maximum 128 characters. Use alphanumeric and '+=,.@-_' characters.

Summary   Q Filter

Service ▼	Access level	Resource	Request condition
Allow (3 of 377 services) Show remaining 374			
CloudWatch Logs	Limited: List, Read, Write, Permissions management	All resources	None
License Manager	Limited: List, Read, Write	All resources	None
SageMaker	Limited: Write	All resources	None

Figure 10:19: Creating the policy

Posit Workbench is a commercially licensed IDE for monthly and annual subscribers on Marketplace.

> **Note**
>
> When authoring this book, a standard named user RStudio Workbench would cost $125 monthly. You could either pay for the license or evaluate it for a month using a trial license.

8. The next step is to request a trial Posit Workbench license to evaluate the product using Amazon SageMaker. Please use the contact form[11] from the Posit website to request a trial license. You can also locate the evaluation request under the **Overview** tab of Posit Workbench in the AWS Marketplace. Fill out the contact form and make sure you include your AWS account ID in the **Let us know how we can help** section. Once your trial request is accepted, you will receive an email with a unique link to the trial offer. Make sure to open this link while logged in to your AWS account. After you accept the offer, you can follow the next steps to activate your license grant.

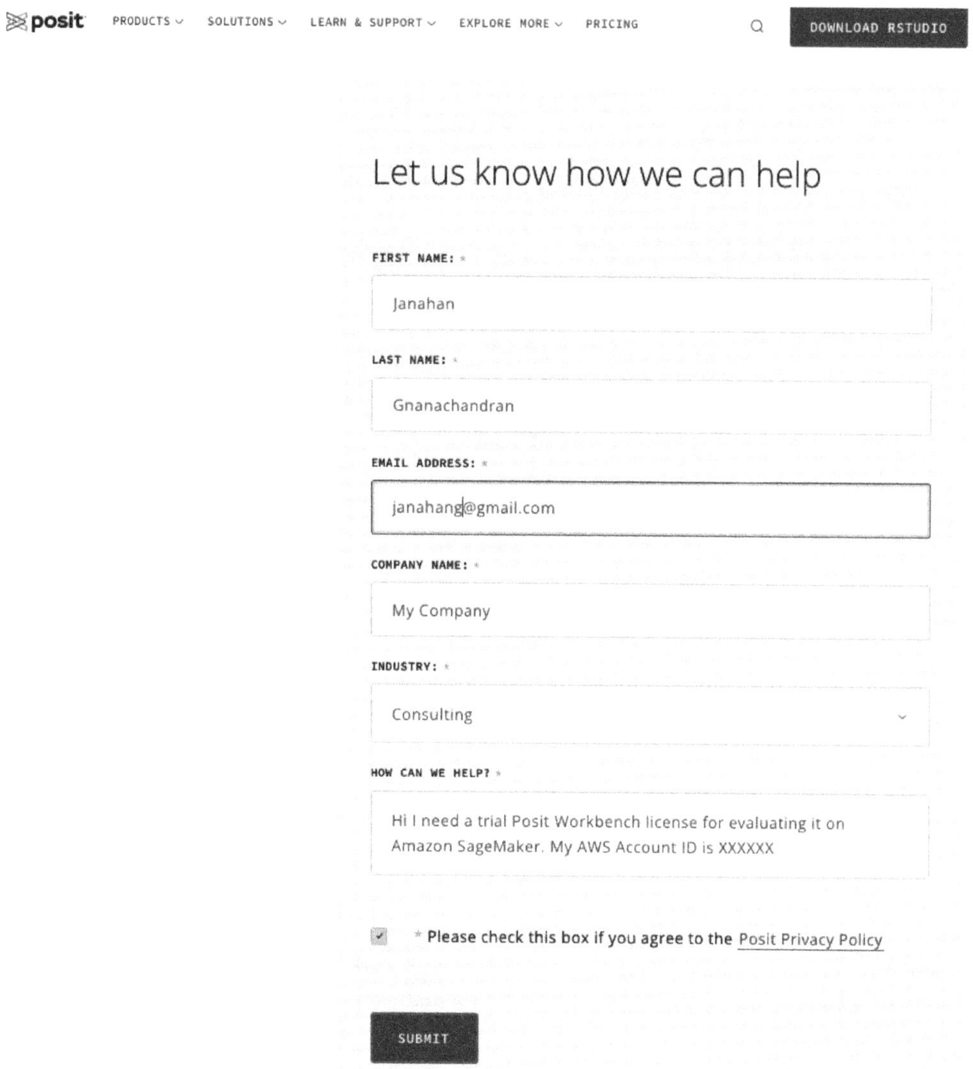

Figure 10.20: Signing up on the Posit website

9. Next, we should manage the license grant in AWS License Manager. Search and navigate to the AWS License Manager console to view the Posit Workbench trial license you received. If this is the first time you are using the AWS License Manager, you have to grant permission to use the License Manager. On the **AWS License Manager** console, click on **Start using AWS License Manager**, check the box for **I grant AWS License Manager the required permissions**, and click on **Grant permissions**.

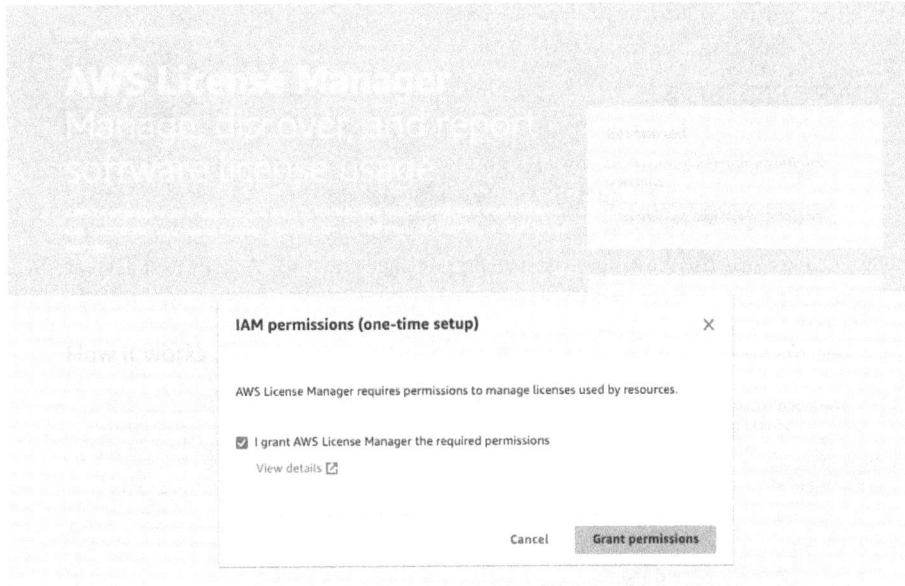

Figure 10.21: Granting permissions

10. Click **Granted licenses** on the left panel. In the **Granted license entitlements** section, you would see two entitlements related to Posit Workbench: AWS Marketplace usage and named users.

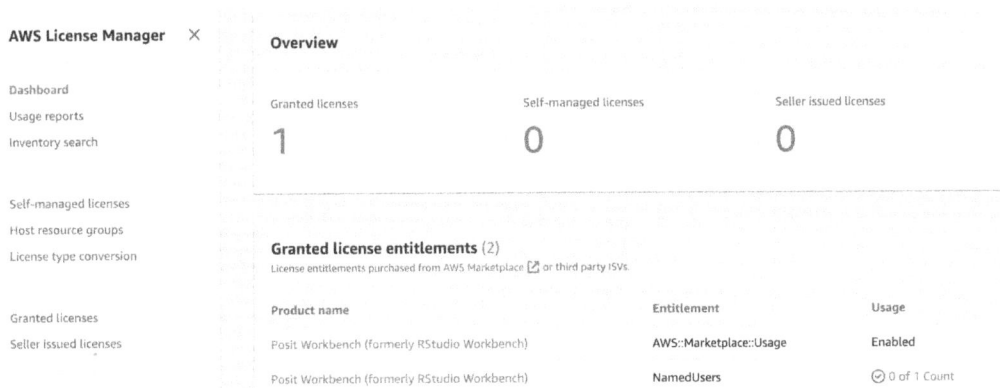

Figure 10.22: Checking the license

11. Select the license grant with RStudio Workbench as the product name and click **View**.

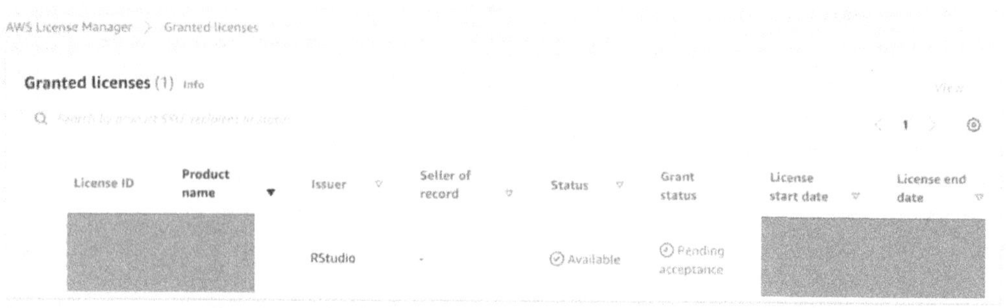

Figure 10.23: The license details

12. Review the licensing details on the License details page and click **Accept and activate license**. The status will change to **Active** after you accept the grant. Choose the license ID to see the details of the license. Click **Accept & activate license**. Once you accept your Posit Workbench license, you can create your RStudio on the Amazon SageMaker domain. RStudio can consume your license on Amazon SageMaker in any AWS Region that supports the feature.

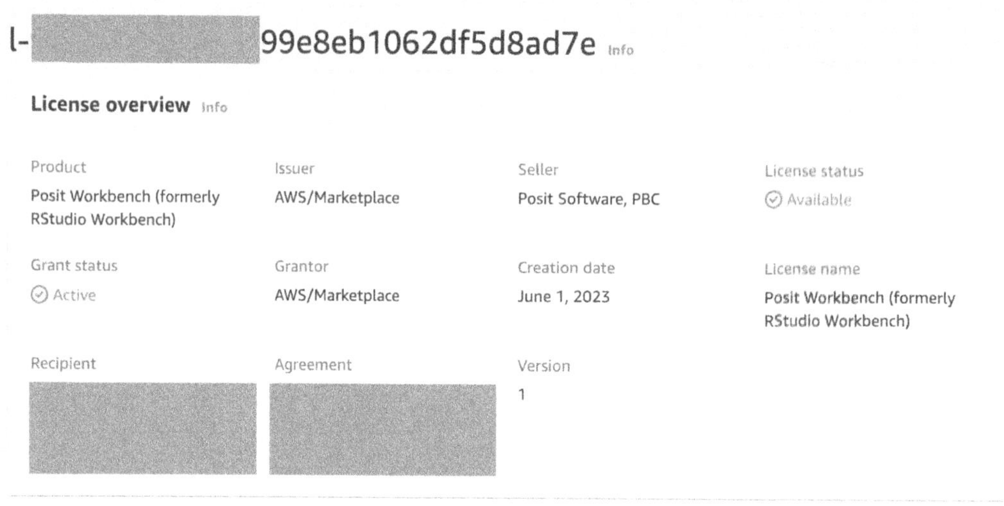

Figure 10.24: Overview of the license with the creation date and place

13. The next step is creating a SageMaker domain. Go to the **AWS SageMaker** console, select **RStudio**, and click **Create a SageMaker domain**. You could also create an Amazon SageMaker domain with RStudio using the AWS CLI[12].

Figure 10.25: Setting up an RStudio SageMaker domain

14. On the **Setup SageMaker Domain** page, choose **Standard setup** and click **Configure**.

Figure 10.26: Setup options for SageMaker domain

15. Provide a name for your SageMaker domain in the **General settings** section. For this exercise, choose the AWS IAM authentication method. The SageMaker domain could be authenticated using IAM Identity Center (successor to AWS Single Sign-On) or AWS IAM. For this exercise, choose the AWS IAM authentication method.

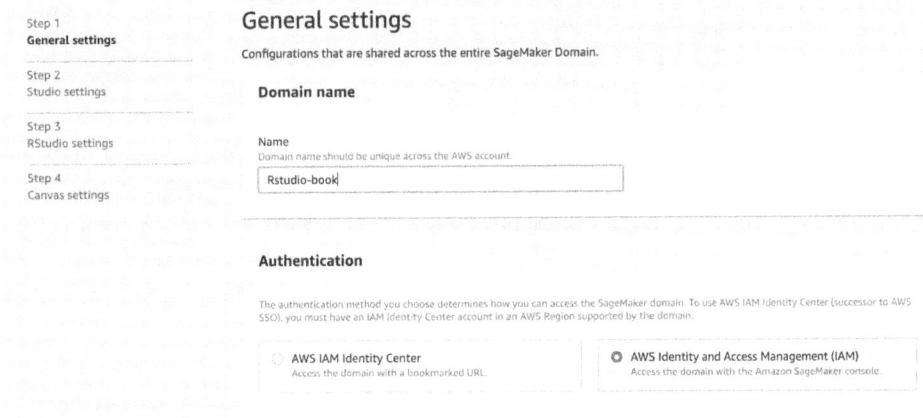

Figure 10.27: Authentication options

16. Under the **Permission** section, choose the IAM execution role we created in *step 4* for both **Default execution role** and **Space default execution role**. Ensure these roles can access AWS License Manager, AWS Marketplace, and Amazon S3. Under **Network and Storage Section**, choose the right VPC, subnet(s), and security group(s). Select **Public Internet Only**, and select **Next**.

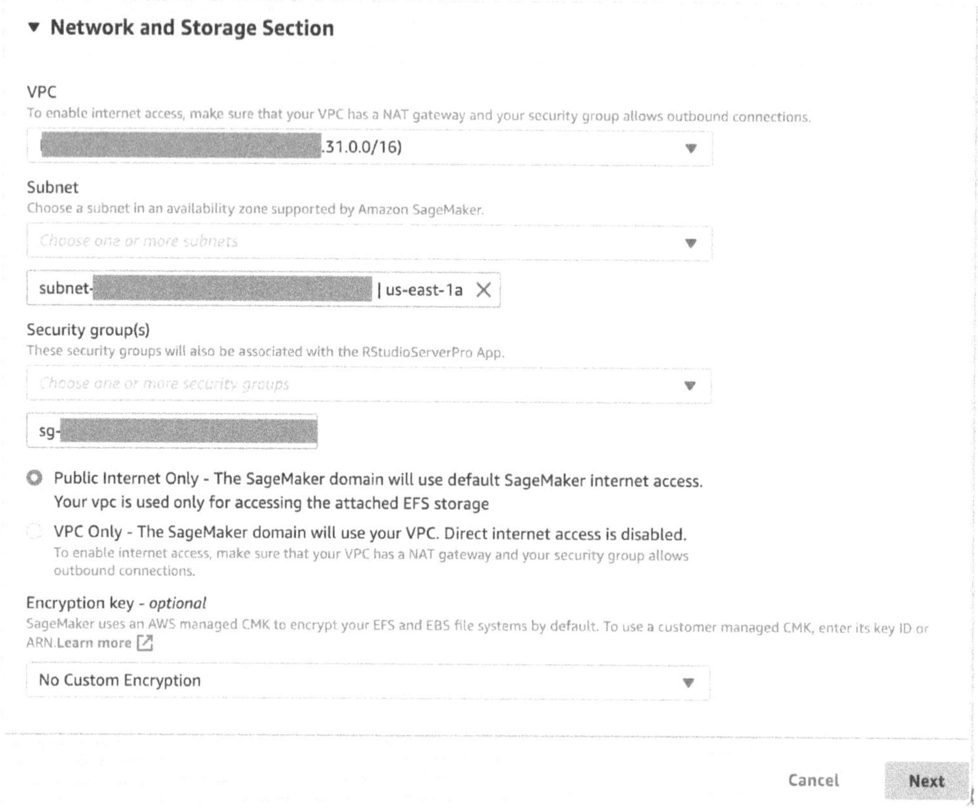

▼ **Network and Storage Section**

VPC
To enable internet access, make sure that your VPC has a NAT gateway and your security group allows outbound connections.

| .31.0.0/16) | ▼ |

Subnet
Choose a subnet in an availability zone supported by Amazon SageMaker.

| Choose one or more subnets | ▼ |

| subnet- | us-east-1a ✕ |

Security group(s)
These security groups will also be associated with the RStudioServerPro App.

| Choose one or more security groups | ▼ |

| sg- | |

◉ Public Internet Only - The SageMaker domain will use default SageMaker internet access. Your vpc is used only for accessing the attached EFS storage

○ VPC Only - The SageMaker domain will use your VPC. Direct internet access is disabled. To enable internet access, make sure that your VPC has a NAT gateway and your security group allows outbound connections.

Encryption key - *optional*
SageMaker uses an AWS managed CMK to encrypt your EFS and EBS file systems by default. To use a customer managed CMK, enter its key ID or ARN. Learn more 🗗

| No Custom Encryption | ▼ |

Cancel   **Next**

Figure 10.28: Network settings

17. In the **Studio settings** section, leave everything as default, and click **Next** to move to the next section. Under **RStudio settings**, the saved RStudio license from AWS License Manager will be automatically detected once a license has been added. You will have the option to change the instance type as you like. Choose the same IAM execution role we created in *step 4* and click **Next**. Leave everything as default under **Canvas settings** and click the **Submit** button.

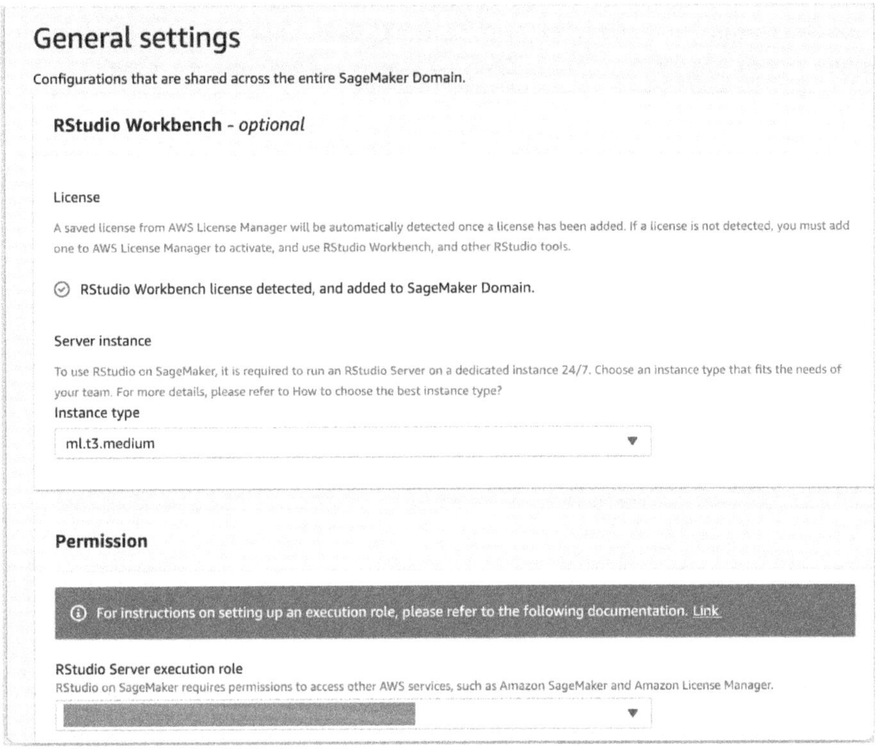

Figure 10.29: General settings for the domain

18. The next step is to add users. On the **Domain details** page, choose **Add user** and provide a username.

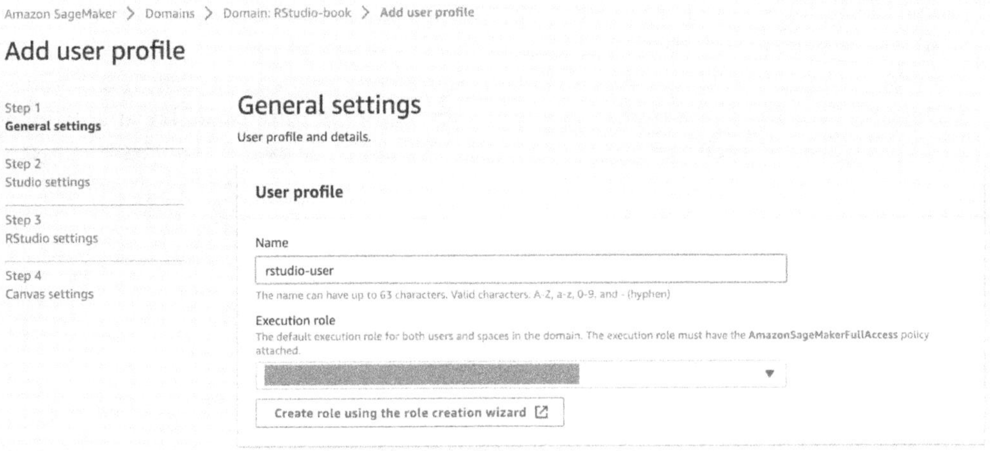

Figure 10.30: Creating a new user

19. For **Execution role**, from the dropdown, choose **Create a new role**, pick the appropriate S3 settings, click on **Create role**, and select **Next**. You could also manage RStudio users via the AWS CLI[13].

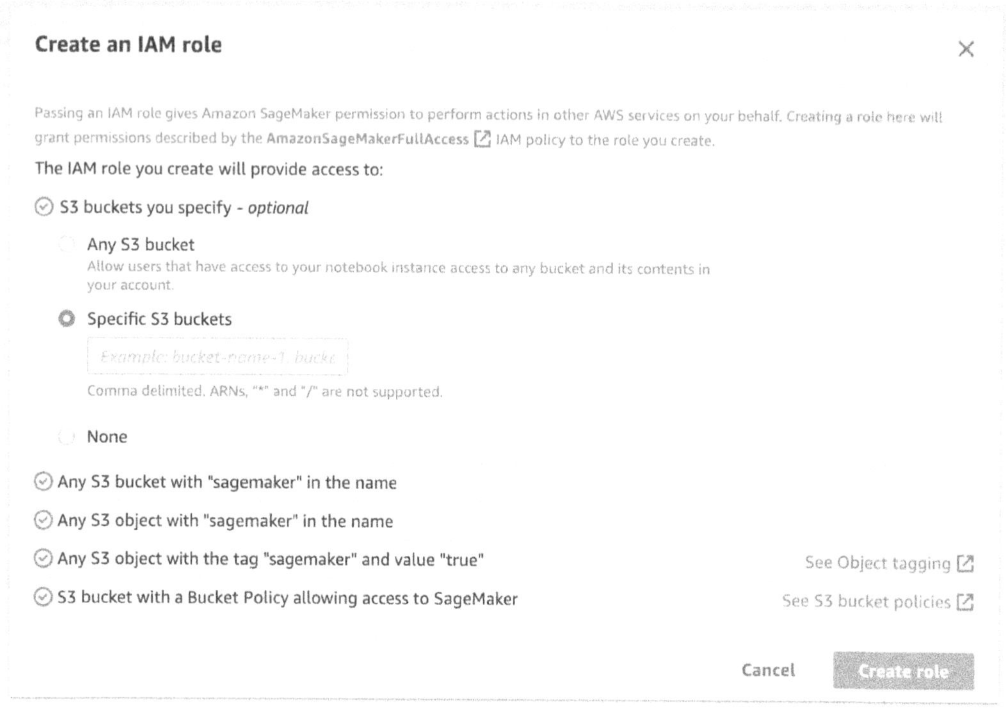

Figure 10.31: Creating an IAM role

Studio automatically detects and adds RStudio Workbench licenses to the domain for the **License Authorization** to choose. Leave everything as default in **Studio settings** and click **Next**. Under **RStudio settings**, pick the appropriate RStudio license authorization and click **Next**. RStudio admins will have access to the RStudio IDE and RStudio administrative dashboard, RStudio users will only have access to the RStudio IDE, and unauthorized users will not have access to the RStudio IDE. All three options grant access to the Studio. Leave everything as default in **Canvas settings** and click **Submit**.

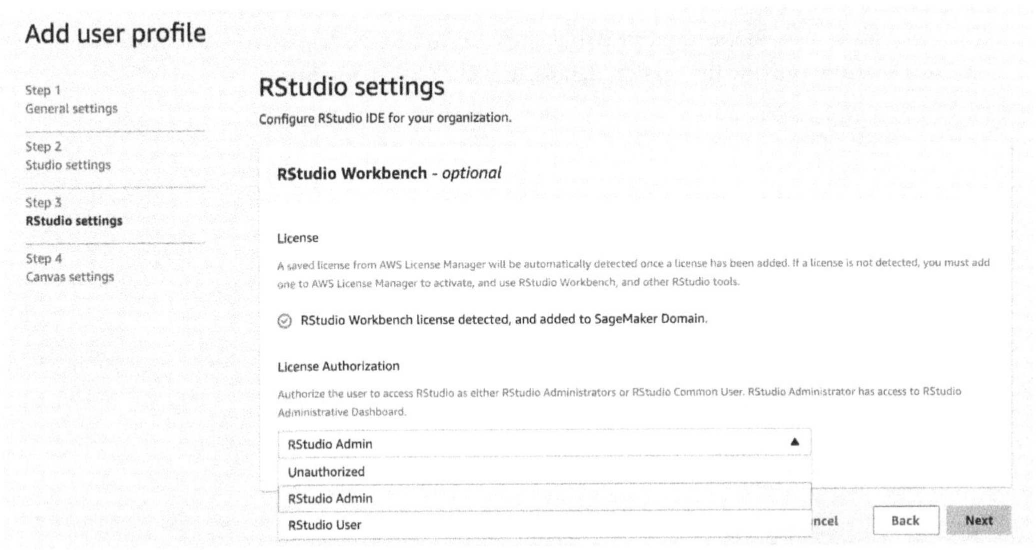

Add user profile

Step 1
General settings

Step 2
Studio settings

Step 3
RStudio settings

Step 4
Canvas settings

RStudio settings

Configure RStudio IDE for your organization.

RStudio Workbench - *optional*

License

A saved license from AWS License Manager will be automatically detected once a license has been added. If a license is not detected, you must add one to AWS License Manager to activate, and use RStudio Workbench, and other RStudio tools.

⊘ RStudio Workbench license detected, and added to SageMaker Domain.

License Authorization

Authorize the user to access RStudio as either RStudio Administrators or RStudio Common User. RStudio Administrator has access to RStudio Administrative Dashboard.

RStudio Admin ▲
Unauthorized
RStudio Admin
RStudio User

ncel   Back   **Next**

Figure 10.32: Choosing the license

20. After the user profile is created, go to the **Domain** section, click on the domain you created, and click on **RStudio** from the **Launch** button selection in the user list.

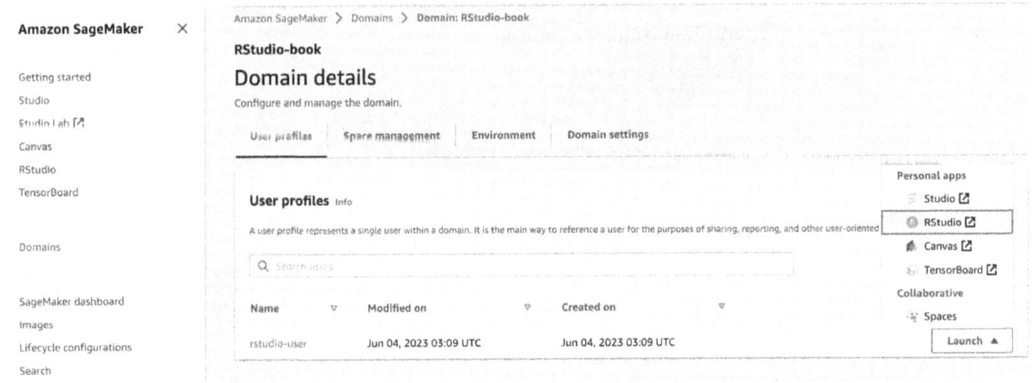

Figure 10.33: Launching the domain

21. This will redirect you to the RStudio Workbench on Amazon SageMaker. Under **Sessions**, click on **New Session**, provide the session details, and click **Start Session**.

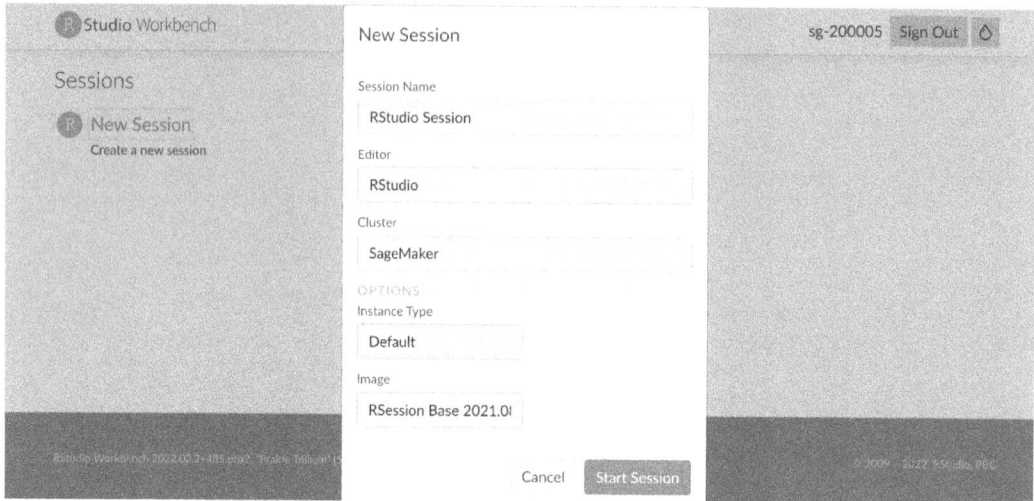

Figure 10.34: Creating a session

22. The new RStudio console will be available shortly. Let's run the same sample code to verify that it can load the AWS Open Data Registry data.

Figure 10.35: Running the sample data in this setup

RStudio on Amazon SageMaker differs significantly from RStudio Workbench in several aspects. Firstly, users do not have direct access to the RStudio configuration files. The configuration is managed by Amazon SageMaker, which sets predefined defaults. However, users can customize the RStudio Connect and RStudio Package Manager URLs while creating their RStudio-enabled Amazon

SageMaker domain. It is important to note that while authoring this book, specific features such as project sharing, real-time collaboration, and Job Launcher are currently not supported when using RStudio on Amazon SageMaker. These features may be available in RStudio Workbench but not in the SageMaker version. Regarding infrastructure, when utilizing RStudio on SageMaker, the RStudio IDE operates on Amazon SageMaker instances, which offer on-demand containerized compute resources. This ensures that users can leverage scalable and flexible computing power as needed. Additionally, it is crucial to highlight that RStudio on SageMaker exclusively supports the RStudio IDE and does not support other IDEs that may be compatible with an RStudio Workbench installation. Lastly, it is worth mentioning that RStudio on SageMaker is designed to support a specific version of RStudio, as specified in the *Upgrade the RStudio Version* documentation. Users should ensure they are using the supported RStudio version to maintain compatibility and take advantage of the features and optimizations provided by the SageMaker integration. By understanding these distinctions between RStudio on Amazon SageMaker and RStudio Workbench, users can make informed decisions about utilizing the appropriate platform for their specific needs and leverage the advantages offered by each environment.

In this section, we delved into the capabilities of leveraging Amazon SageMaker for geospatial data analysis using the R programming language. It's important to note that using R on Amazon SageMaker requires a commercial license. R offers a comprehensive ecosystem of packages designed specifically for handling, analyzing, and visualizing geospatial data. With RStudio as the IDE for R, you gain access to a feature-rich toolkit that includes a console, a syntax-highlighting editor for seamless code execution, and a range of tools for plotting, version history management, debugging, and workspace organization. Amazon SageMaker fully supports RStudio as an IDE seamlessly integrated within the Amazon SageMaker Domain. This integration empowers R developers with the ability to effortlessly scale the underlying compute resources, enabling the execution of large-scale geospatial data processing and analysis. With the flexibility and scalability offered by Amazon SageMaker, R developers can easily tackle complex geospatial tasks, unlocking new possibilities for geospatial data exploration and insights.

Analyzing and visualizing geospatial data using RStudio

Geospatial data is crucial in various domains, such as environmental analysis, urban planning, and location-based services. In this section, we will explore the process of importing and exporting geospatial data using R on AWS. We can efficiently handle large-scale geospatial datasets and perform advanced spatial analysis by leveraging the power of R and AWS storage and analytics services. We will cover the steps involved in importing different geospatial data formats, manipulating the data, and exporting the results back to various file formats.

For this example, let's continue to use the RStudio that was installed on EC2 from the *Setting up R and RStudio on EC2* section of this chapter. We will be importing a sample shapefile from NYC OpenData[1] and visualizing it:

```
Install.packages( "tidyverse","sf")
library(tidyverse)
```

```
library(sf)
# Specify URL where NYC OpenData shape file is stored
url <- "https://data.cityofnewyork.us/api/geospatial/tqmj-j8zm?method=
export&format=Shapefile"
# Specify local destination where file should be saved
destfile <- "/home/rstudio/myfile.zip"
# Download and unzip the folder locally
download.file(url,destfile)
unzip(destfile)
```

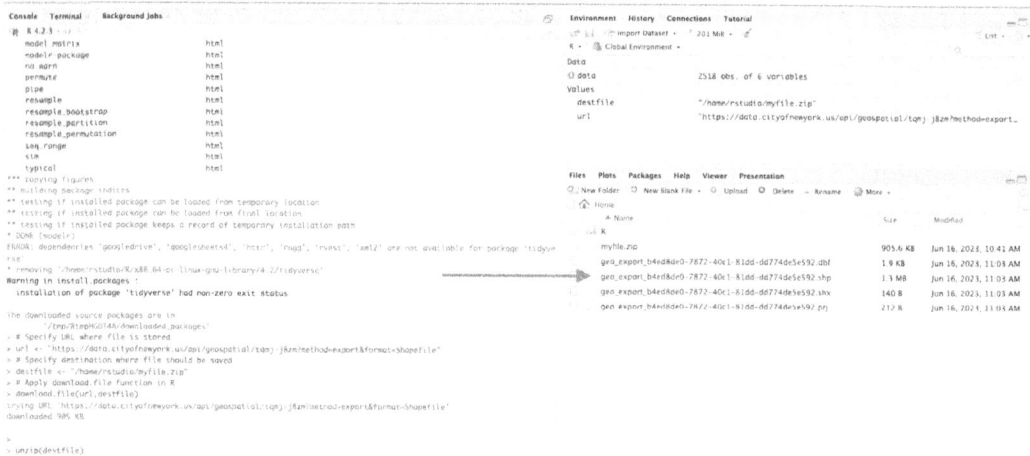

Figure 10.36: Importing the data

Once the file is unzipped, get the shape filename from the file browser section of the right panel:

```
#Read the unzipped shapefile from your local instance
shape_file <- st_read("geo_export_b4ed8de0-7872-40c1-81dd-
dd774de5e592.shp")
# Visualize it
hape_file %>% ggplot() + geom_sf()
# You could also export the shapefile
st_write(shape_file, "output_shapefile.shp")
```

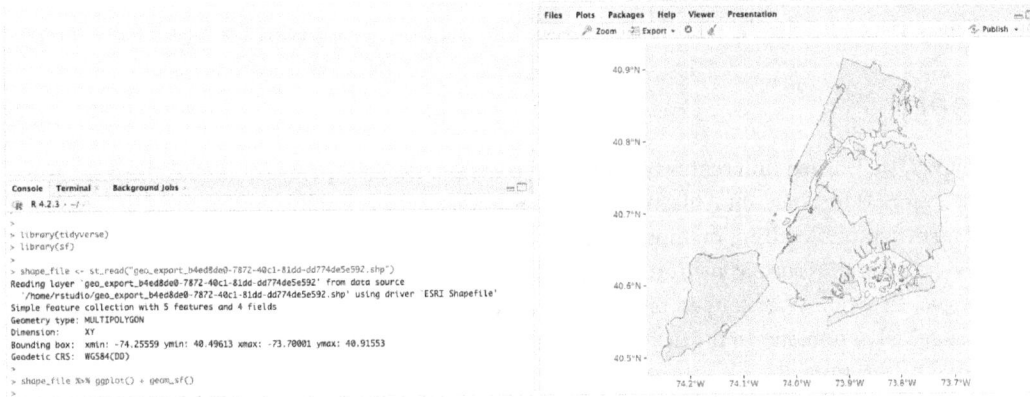

Figure 10.37: Visualizing the data

Once imported, we often need to manipulate spatial objects to extract meaningful information or perform spatial operations. Let's look at an example of creating a subset of the `"Queens"` city and visualize it:

```
# Create a subset from the shapefile
subset = shape_file %>%
    filter(boro_name == "Queens") %>%
    dplyr::select(boro_code, boro_name, shape_area) %>%
    slice(1:5)
#Visualize it
subset %>% ggplot() + geom_sf()
```

This results in the following output:

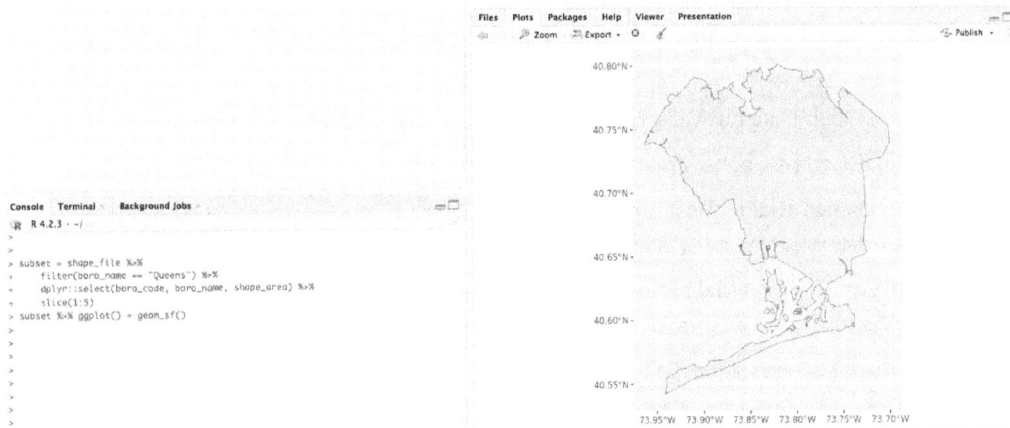

Figure 10.38: Visualizing the data for Queens

Thus, we have visualized the data for the country as a whole as well as specifically for Queens here.

Summary

In this chapter, we learned different ways of setting up R on AWS. As part of this walk-through, we provisioned an EC2 instance, an Amazon SageMaker domain, user profiles, and an RStudio session. We also learned about loading, manipulating, and visualizing geospatial data using RStudio. You could also use R libraries such as `aws.s3`, `aws.lambda`, and others to integrate RStudio with other AWS services. To avoid AWS charges, please make sure to terminate the EC2 instance and delete the Amazon SageMaker domain. In the next chapter, we will explore how machine learning can be used in geospatial applications.

References

1. *The R Project for Statistical Computing*: `https://www.r-project.org/`

2. *The Comprehensive R Archive Network*: `https://cran.r-project.org/index.html`

3. Pebesma E, Bivand R (2005). "Classes and methods for spatial data in R." R News, 5(2), 9–13: `https://CRAN.R-project.org/doc/Rnews/`

4. *Simple Features for R*: `https://cran.r-project.org/web/packages/sf/vignettes/sf1.html`

5. *terra: Spatial Data Analysis*: `https://cran.r-project.org/web/packages/terra/terra.pdf`

6. *RStudio*: `https://posit.co/products/open-source/rstudio/`

7. Shiny for R: `https://shiny.posit.co/r/getstarted/shiny-basics/lesson1/index.html`

8. *CCAFS-Climate Data*: `https://aws.amazon.com/datasets/ccafs-climate-data/`

9. Registry of Open Data on AWS: `https://registry.opendata.aws/`

10. *Posit Workbench*: `https://posit.co/products/enterprise/workbench/`

11. Posit Workbench trial request form: `https://posit.co/about/contact/?utm_source=amzn&utm_campaign=aws_partner_ref&utm_content=Eval_AWS`

12. Create an Amazon SageMaker domain with RStudio using the AWS CLI: `https://docs.aws.amazon.com/sagemaker/latest/dg/rstudio-create-cli.html`

13. RStudio manage users via the AWS CLI: `https://docs.aws.amazon.com/sagemaker/latest/dg/rstudio-create-user.html`

14. *NYC OpenData Borough Boundaries*: `https://data.cityofnewyork.us/City-Government/Borough-Boundaries/tqmj-j8zm`

15. Installing GDAL 3.2.1 on Amazon Linux 2: `https://gist.github.com/abelcallejo/e75eb93d73db6f163b076d0232fc7d7e`

16. *NYC OpenData*: `https://opendata.cityofnewyork.us/`

## 11

Geospatial Machine Learning with SageMaker

Amazon Web Services (**AWS**) provides a wide range of services and applications that can be used for **machine learning** (**ML**). ML can generally be thought of as using computers to make predictions based on probabilities and correlations between data. This chapter will outline some common ways geospatial data is used to feed ML models to make predictions.

This chapter will teach you how to recognize opportunities to use ML for geospatial workloads and understand some of the options available to implement. In this chapter, we will talk about using Python with SageMaker for **extract, transform, and load** (**ETL**), analytics, and ML, as well as SageMaker's native geospatial capabilities. We will cover some popular Python libraries for these tasks as well as an overview of a few of SageMaker's native ETL and ML capabilities.

We will cover the following topics in this chapter:

- AWS ML background
- Common libraries and algorithms
- Introducing Geospatial ML with SageMakerDeploying a SageMaker Geospatial example
- Architecture considerations

AWS ML background

SageMaker was launched in November 2017 as an advanced ML service that could natively take advantage of cloud elasticity and scale. Analytics and ML are very challenging workloads because of how resource intensive they are. Analytics is a bit different because it focuses on drawing insights out of data from the past, whereas ML focuses on the future. Today, some ML platforms are either completely low code or, at least, easy to use. However, simplicity is often a trade-off for a low level of flexibility if your use cases do not fit into the existing patterns or algorithms.

SageMaker provides low-code features as well as a full-featured ML platform. SageMaker has **automated ML (AutoML)** low-code capabilities and it also provides the ability for you to package up your own custom models in a container and import them. Once the model is created, you can fine-tune it where necessary to meet your needs. One of the most impactful benefits is the ability to train models using virtually unlimited CPU/GPU resources from EC2.

Many analysts are familiar with running their query in the background and walking away from their environment for days while it runs. The best case is when they leave the office and come back the next day and they will find their query complete, but the worst case is they come back to discover an error and have to start over or, in my case recently, my laptop had an update and rebooted. Lesson learned on my part – always use the cloud no matter how small the task! On AWS, you can run multiple queries in parallel with different parameters and have them all complete in minutes. Many of these queries have linear performance in that if you run it with one CPU and it takes one day, if you change the server to two CPUs, it takes half a day. With that, pricing is also linear so the cost to run one CPU for a day is the same as running two CPUs for half a day. Take that and apply it to your query and provision 1,000 CPU cores for 10 minutes. Virtually unlimited scale and elasticity are key benefits of analytics and ML on AWS. In the next section, we will talk about a few service integrations.

AWS service integration

One of the convenient features of AWS cloud services is that they are built to work together. The output of one service workload often feeds as the input to another workflow or data stream. Because the services have defined use patterns and interfaces, this provides a great way to integrate ML into your geospatial workloads. The source data for your geospatial analysis can be accessed directly from Amazon S3, and this can be in your account or a publicly accessible account to which you have access. You can display the results of your ML analysis on a map, and use geospatial data as input for ML workloads. Using CloudWatch is a useful tip to view additional logging for running notebooks. While your job is running, SageMaker is adding log messages to the `/aws/sagemaker/studio` CloudWatch log group.

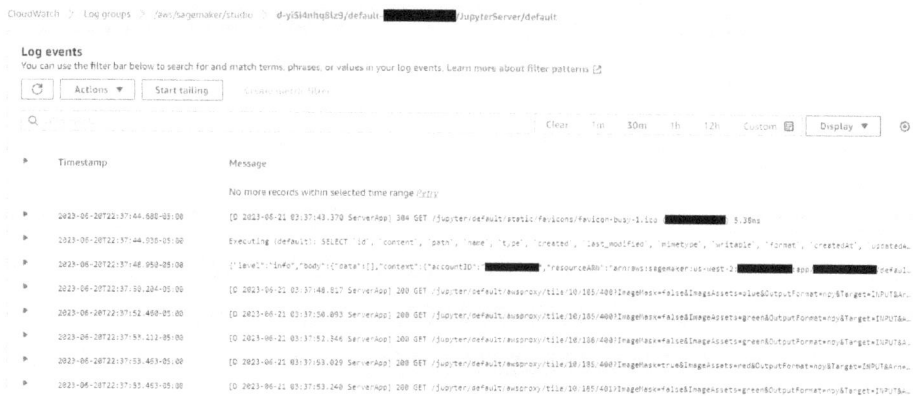

Figure 11.1: CloudWatch logs from SageMaker Studio

Amazon S3 is a favorite place for data scientists to collaborate and share data. It is a durable, convenient, and cost-effective location for input files as well as the results of SageMaker jobs.

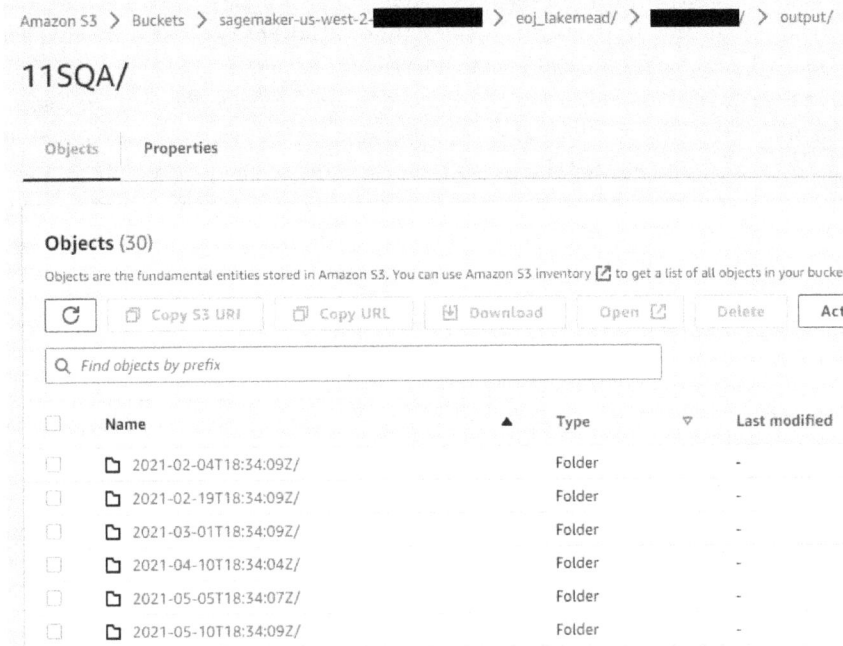

Figure 11.2: Earth Observation job outputs in Amazon S3

The ability to access this level of integrated information helps to fine-tune and provide contextual information for your SageMaker jobs. Because your jobs are running on Amazon-managed hardware, you can scale your workloads up or down in order to meet your geospatial processing demand. In the next section, we will talk about a few common libraries and algorithms used in geospatial ML.

Common libraries and algorithms

SageMaker originally launched mostly as a notebook service called SageMaker Notebooks. Most data scientists are intimately familiar with Jupyter Notebook environments and it's a fantastic environment for analysis as well as collaboration. In the following demo, we will launch a SageMaker notebook and pull in a few common Python libraries to work with a dataset. Probably one of the most common libraries is called pandas, and there is also GeoPandas, which is more common with geospatial datasets. The pandas framework has fantastic support for reading in and writing out CSV datasets as well as binary formats such as Parquet, Avro, and ORC.

There is also a plethora of functions to do just about any kind of data manipulation you could think of – pivots, resampling, dropping columns, renaming columns, trimming, and regex filters. pandas is the de facto standard for ETL in the data science community. Another library we will load in is a built-in Python ML library that Amazon maintains called **Random Cut Forest** (**RCF**). This is a derivative of the traditional ML random forest algorithm that has native support and has been tuned for better performance in SageMaker. "*An implementation of the Random Cut Forest data structure for sketching streaming data, with support for anomaly detection, density estimation, imputation, and more*" is a brief description from the AWS-maintained GitHub repo for RCF. The in-depth details of these algorithms are out of the scope of this book, but we will include a simple demo using this algorithm. In the next section, we will explore SageMaker Geospatial, a new geospatial ML capability developed by AWS.

Introducing Geospatial ML with SageMaker

At re:Invent 2022, the Amazon SageMaker Team made a major announcement, the launch of a native geospatial-focused capability. AWS is continuing to invest in its geospatial capabilities adding to its current offerings in Amazon Location Service, S3, Aurora, and now SageMaker Geospatial. The ability to access geospatial datasets and capabilities from within SageMaker democratizes and simplifies the analysis of large publicly available satellite datasets in S3. You now have access to readily available geospatial data sources to include in your projects. Map visualizations and other convenience features make this a useful tool for any data scientists looking to leverage location in their models. There is a built-in map visualization that can provide immediate value to any data analytics project:

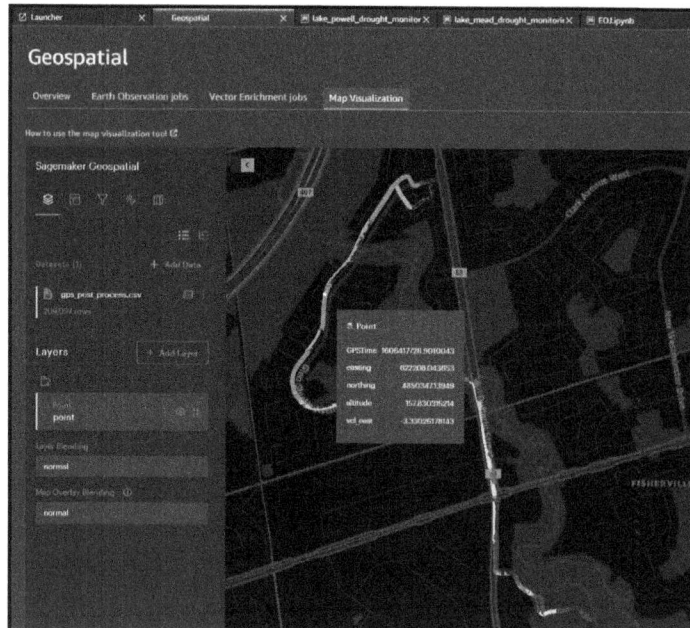

Figure 11.3: Over 200,000 GPS data points visualized in SageMaker Geospatial

ML is difficult; ML on geospatial data is extremely difficult. There are very limited tools to work with geometry and geography data types, and the tools that do exist are rarely optimized for parallel and in-memory performance. SageMaker is innovating a unique new way to help in a much-needed vertical. SageMaker is launching a handful of models with the plan to add capabilities to the roadmap. The initial launch included services for Cloud Removal, Temporal Statistics, Zonal Statistics, Resampling, Geomosaic, Band Stacking, Band Math, Land Cover for Raster Data and Reverse Geocoding, and Map Matching for Vector Data.

As explored elsewhere in this book, geospatial data can manifest itself as raster or vector data. Both of these geospatial data types can be used for geospatial ML in SageMaker. Raster data is commonly satellite imagery but could also be land use classification, climate patterns, or a number of other earth surface measurement datasets. Vector data can be created from raster data by performing image analysis to identify rooftop polygons from satellite imagery, for example. Each of the sample notebooks provided relies on geospatial data based on the type of processing performed, and the samples are built into the notebooks.

Deploying a SageMaker Geospatial example

In this section, we will stand up a SageMaker Geospatial ML environment and perform a simple **Earth Observation job (EOJ)** to monitor the amount of water present in satellite imagery of water bodies. EOJs are useful when the desired outcome is to acquire and transform data from the surface of our planet to make predictions – in this case, regarding water presence in a given area.

There is a one-time environment setup for SageMaker that can be accomplished with the following steps. However, if you already have a SageMaker domain configured, you can leverage the geospatial capabilities from there.

> **Note**
> At the time of this book's writing, geospatial capabilities are only released for SageMaker in the Oregon (**us-west-2**) Region.

First-time use steps

We will use the following steps:

1. Navigate to SageMaker from the AWS Console:

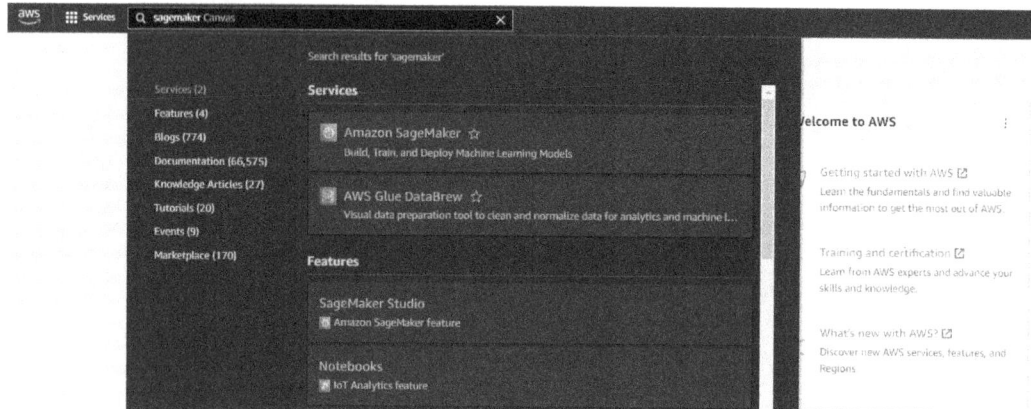

Figure 11.4: AWS Console with SageMaker typed into the top navigation panel

2. Click **Create a SageMaker domain**:

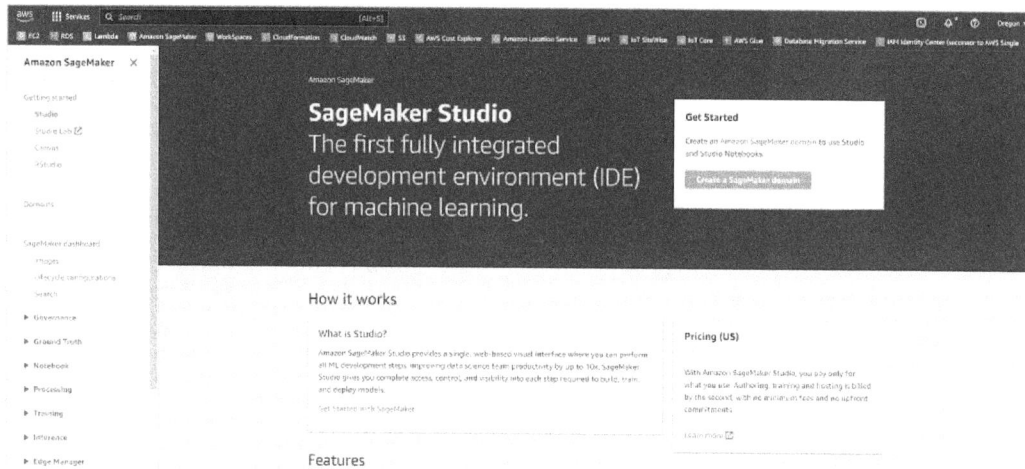

Figure 11.5: SageMaker service screen in the AWS Console

3.   Enter a name for your domain. Anything you choose is fine.

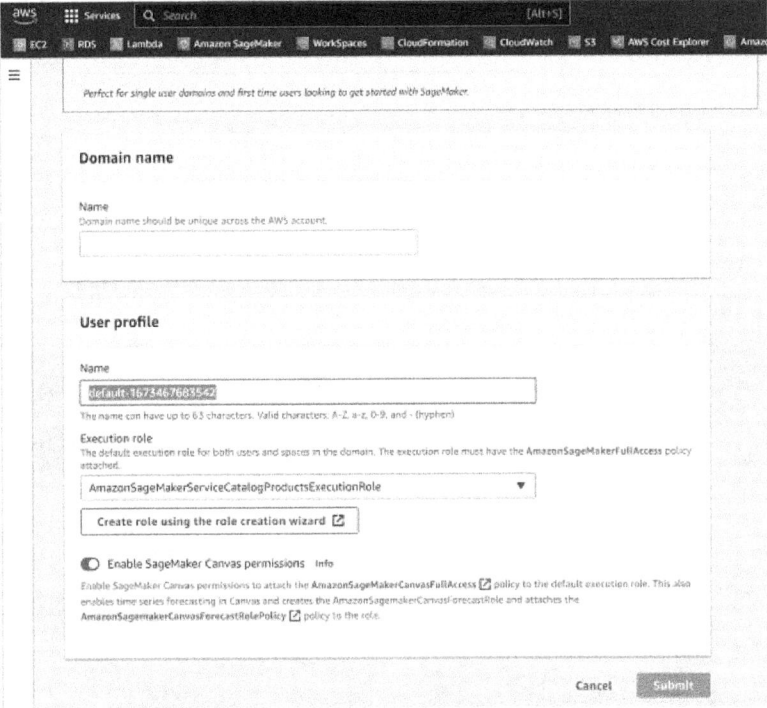

Figure 11.6: SageMaker domain setup

4.   Click on the domain you just created to see the details, including user profiles. The **User profiles** row contains a button on the right that allows you to launch SageMaker tools for that user profile. For this example, click the **Launch** button and select the **Studio** option.

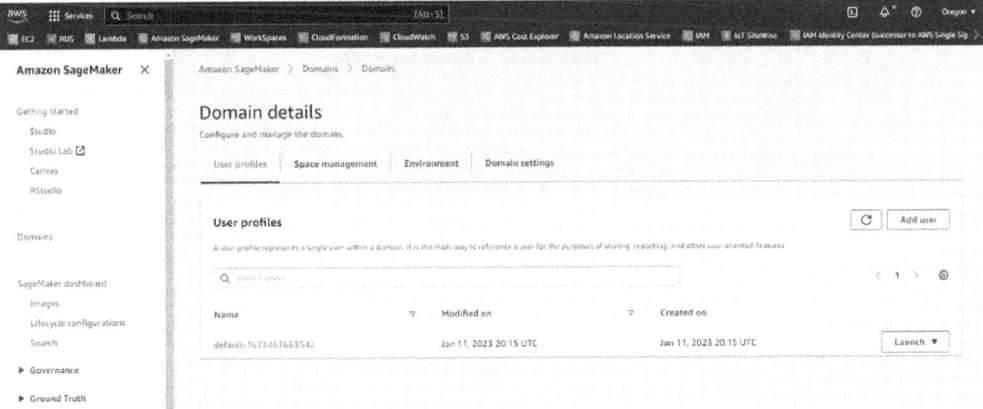

Figure 11.7: Domain details on the SageMaker console

Your SageMaker domain is your workspace for ML workloads and a platform for collaboration with others. Now that you have an active domain, the next step is to leverage the pretrained ML models to perform analysis and predictions on earth observation geospatial data.

Geospatial data processing

From the **Home** section of the SageMaker navigation bar on the left, click the **Data** dropdown and select **Geospatial**. This area within SageMaker Studio provides access to a focused set of tools for geospatial data analysis, ML, and visualization. Transforming and enriching the wide range of geospatial data available in the AWS cloud allows your organization to ask big questions and, more importantly, to be able to find the answers quickly through the efficient use of geospatial ML.

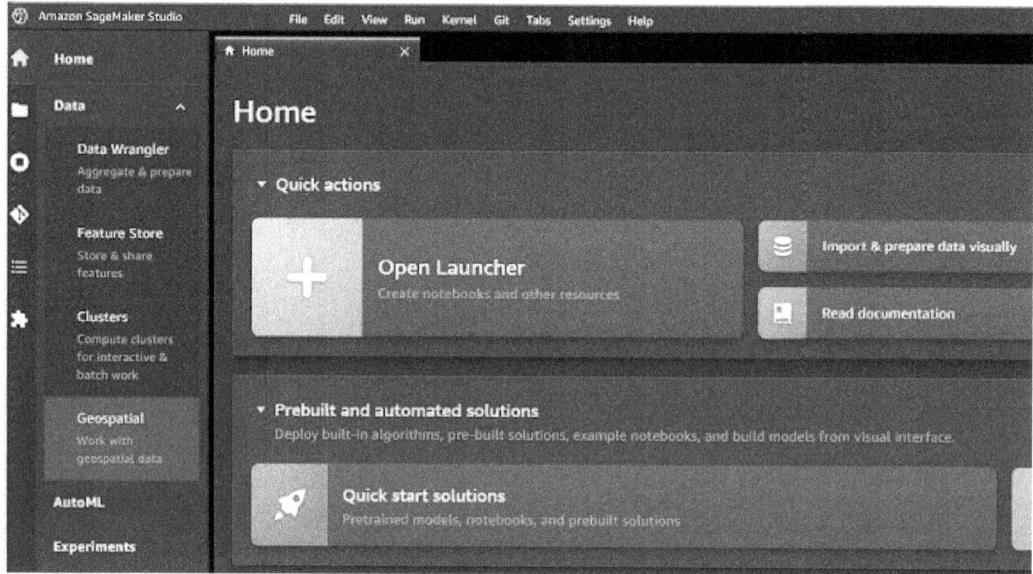

Figure 11.8: SageMaker Geospatial console

The feature that we will be using in this example is Earth Observation jobs, and to prevent permissions errors, now is a good time to verify that your SageMaker execution roles have the necessary permissions. As shown in *Figure 11.6*, an IAM role is specified that SageMaker uses to execute processes. Make sure that the role's trust policy allows the SageMaker Geospatial service to assume the role in addition to SageMaker itself. You can use the following trusted entities entry to add `sagemaker-geospatial.amazonaws.com` to the default:

```
{
    "Version": "2012-10-17",
    "Statement": [
        {
```

```
        "Effect": "Allow",
        "Principal": {
            "Service": [
                "sagemaker.amazonaws.com",
                "sagemaker-geospatial.amazonaws.com"
            ]
        },
        "Action": "sts:AssumeRole"
    }
    ]
}
```

Now back to SageMaker, where you can click the Git icon on the left to clone a GitHub repository. This will provide you with access to the code for this example, as well as other AWS-provided examples of geospatial analytics and ML using Amazon SageMaker. To download these code samples into your SageMaker Studio environment, click the **Clone a Repository** button.

Figure 11.9: GitHub integration is built into SageMaker

Enter this URL for the location of the repository:

```
https://github.com/aws/amazon-sagemaker-examples.git
```

You will notice that the publicly available `amazon-sagemaker-examples` GitHub repository has many more resources than we'll be using for this example. Navigate in the folder tree to `/sagemaker-geospatial/lake-mead-drought-monitoring/` and you will find a Jupyter Notebook `.ipynb` file of the same name.

Double-click on the `lake_mead_drought_monitoring.ipynb` file in the folder tree to launch the notebook. Upon first use, it will prompt you to select the notebook environment image to use. Scroll down in the list of images until you see **Geospatial 1.0**.

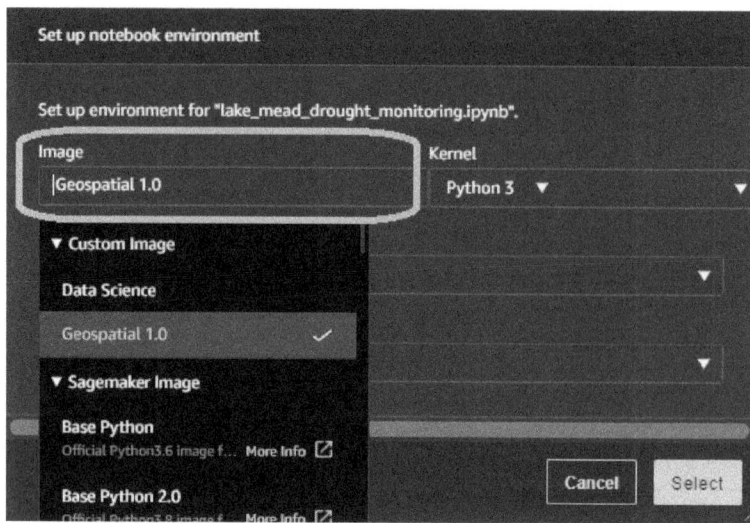

Figure 11.10: SageMaker notebook environment image, Geospatial 1.0

After clicking **Select**, give your notebook a moment to initialize, and you are ready to begin gathering and analyzing satellite imagery data. Your SageMaker Studio workspace should show that the Geospatial 1.0 kernel is active.

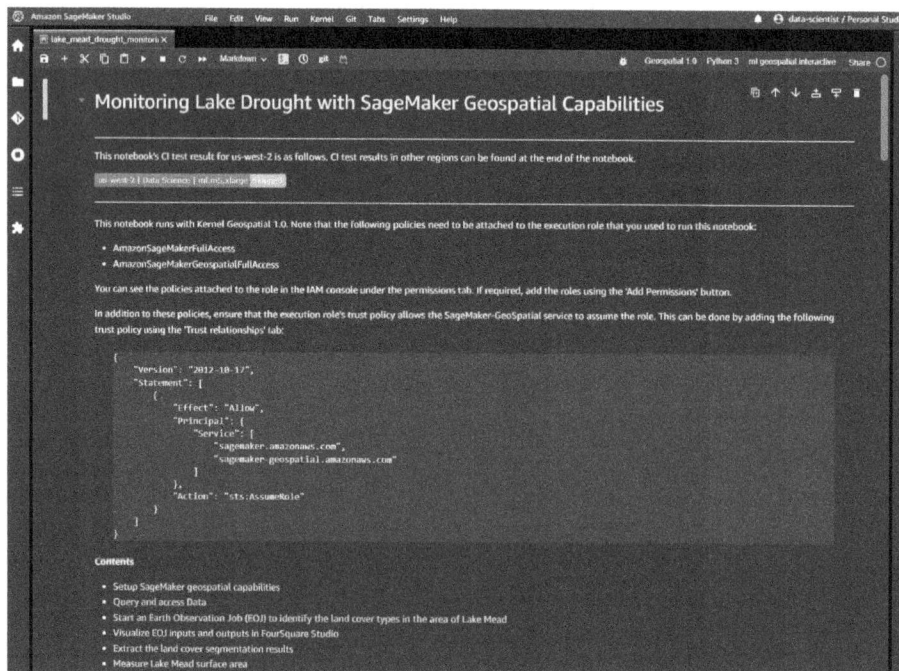

Figure 11.11: Lake Mead drought-monitoring notebook with active Geospatial 1.0 kernel

The provided commentary within the notebook explains the examples well and is easy to follow. If you encounter permissions errors, remember to check the SageMaker execution role trust relationships.

This Jupyter notebook can be executed one step at a time as interim results are analyzed, or you can process the entire notebook by pressing the button with two arrows on the notebook toolbar.

Figure 11.12: Process the entire notebook by clicking the double arrow button

While the job is running, it will show a status of **IN_PROGRESS** on the **Earth Observation jobs** monitoring tab.

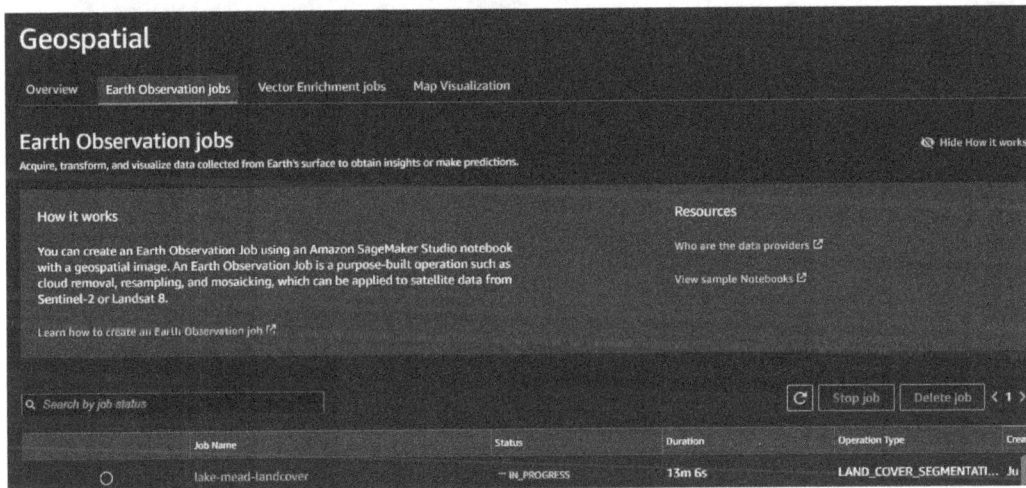

Figure 11.13: View currently running and historical EOJs

The job should take around 30 minutes to complete.

> **Note**
>
> If you want to take this time to read more on using the geospatial image in SageMaker, browse the Developer Guide (titled *Create an Earth Observation Job Using a Amazon SageMaker Studio Notebook with a SageMaker geospatial Image*) here:
>
> `https://docs.aws.amazon.com/sagemaker/latest/dg/geospatial-eoj-ntb.html`

Once the status on the **Earth Observation job** screen is **COMPLETED**, click on the job name to see the details of the job and the results.

Figure 11.14: Job details showing blue results button

Clicking on the **Visualize job output** button will open a map display of Lake Mead with ML-generated land cover changes over a period of 18 months from the beginning of 2021 through mid-July 2022. The resulting geospatial data is stored on S3 and can be easily accessed from within SageMaker as a map visualization, or passed along as input to another geospatial processing job.

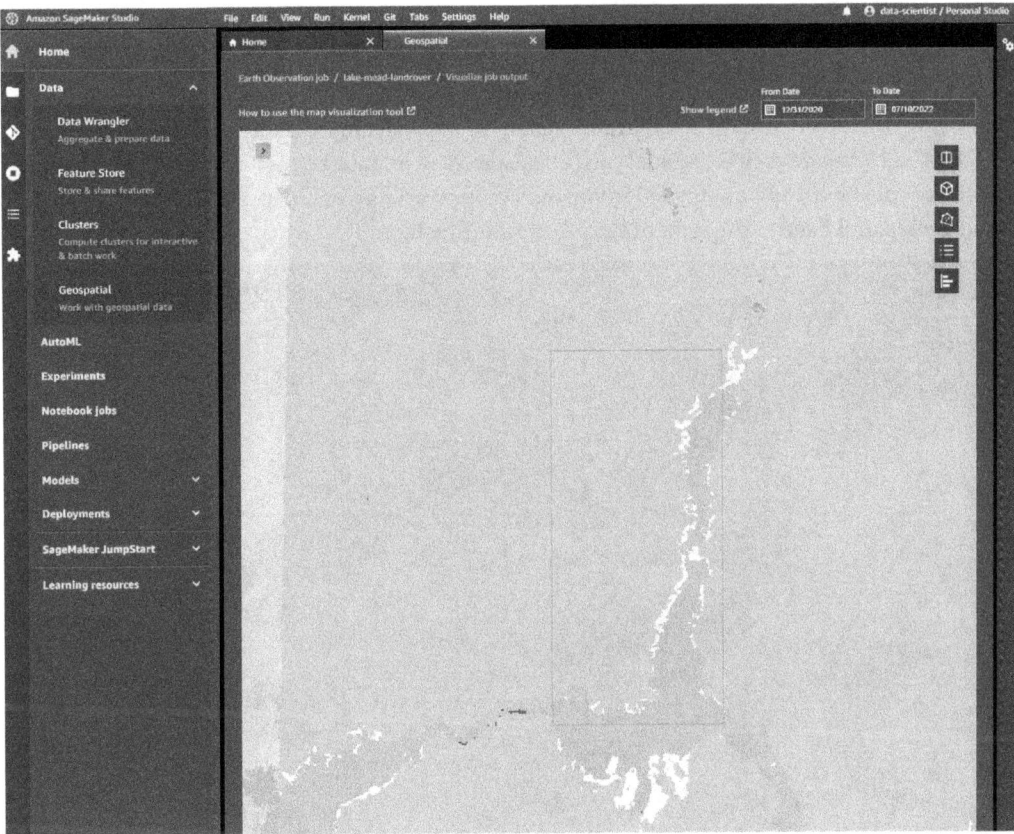

Figure 11.15: EOJ output for Lake Mead land cover

Notebook step details

I would recommend taking some time to step through the notebook and review the Python code that executes the geospatial processing steps. Once you understand how this example works, you can experiment with the area of interest, date range, and other aspects of the model.

In the section titled **Query and access data**, modify the latitude and longitude values for the bounding box to change the area of interest. These coordinates specify the four corners for which the model will download the corresponding satellite imagery.

There are other useful sections of the notebook that demonstrate how to extract water body areas to measure their surface area. Seeing these examples will generate ideas of how you and your organization can use this powerful geospatial data processing platform to get greater insights, in less time, and with less effort.

Geospatial data visualization

The **Map Visualization** tab is more than just a convenient geospatial data viewer. Each layer has grouping and symbology options that allow rapid experimentation with data representations. The default color scheme applied by SageMaker Geospatial can be visualized on an interactive map by simply selecting a file with coordinates in S3 or uploaded from your computer. To access **Map Visualization**, look on the main **Geospatial** page to the right of the job monitoring tabs.

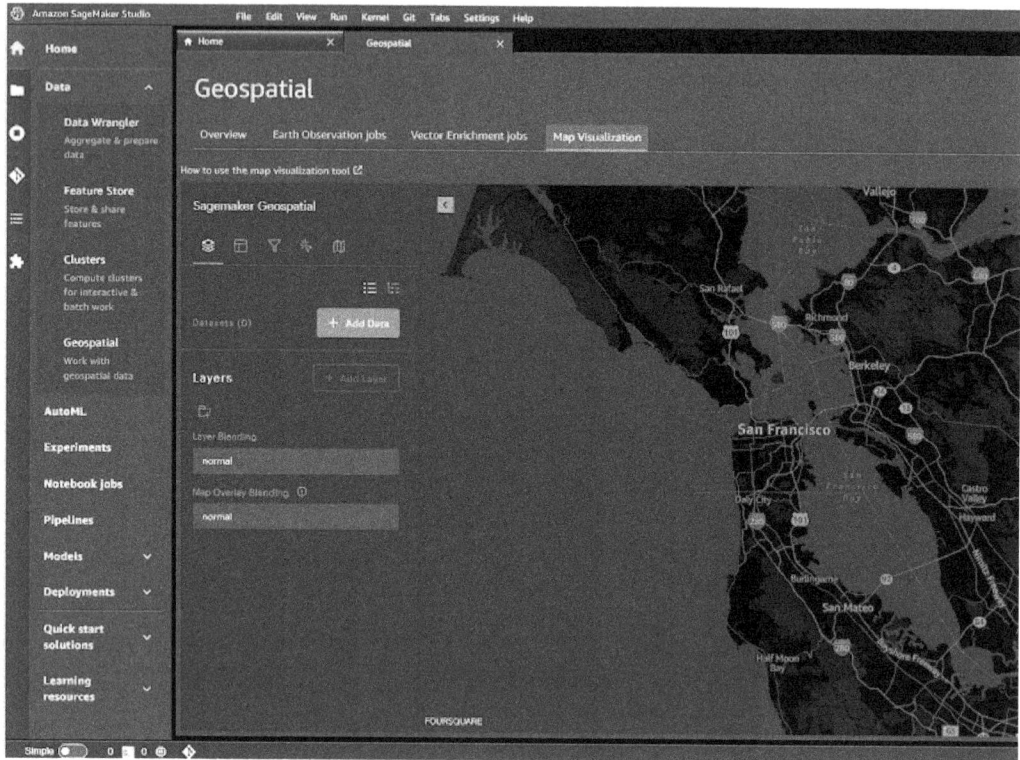

Figure 11.16: SageMaker Geospatial console Map Visualization tab

Click **Add Data** and select a dataset with geometries. In this example, we will load a CSV with point geometries.

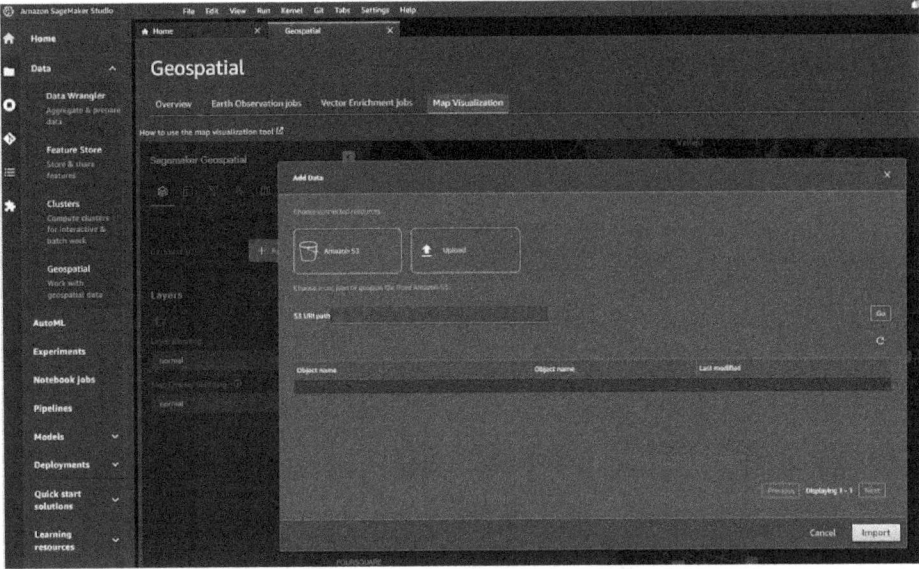

Figure 11.17: The Add Files dialog box under SageMaker Geospatial Map Visualization

Click **Import**:

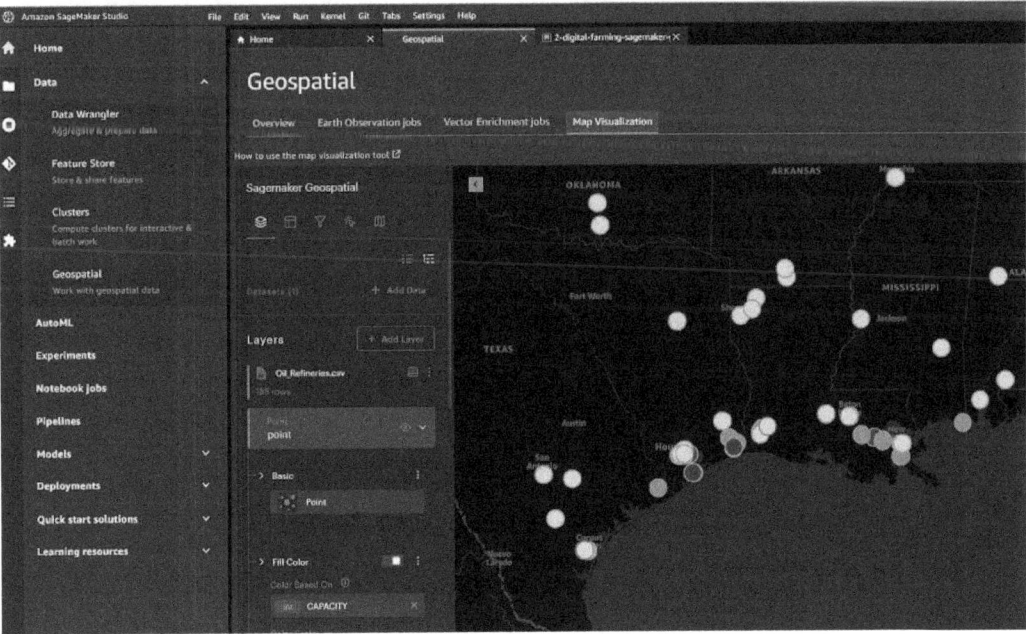

Figure 11.18: Our points plotted on the map inside SageMaker Geospatial

Congratulations, you have loaded your own data into SageMaker Geospatial and are now ready to begin exploring your dataset!

As you can see in the preceding example, SageMaker handles much of the undifferentiated heavy lifting required to set up a robust ML environment, but there are still ways your environment can be configured, or misconfigured. In the next section, let's look at some architectural considerations.

Architectural considerations

Before you can do any real analysis or prediction, it is critical to find the right data and determine the quality. There is an old rule of thumb for data prep. Any analysis will tell you that, with analysis, 80% of the work is in the normalization of the data. You will also want to try and use binary formats such as Parquet and GeoParquet, which are optimized for parallel reads, columnar storage, and compression. Selecting a data partitioning structure is also crucial to performance, such as partitioning by time, location (such as country, state, zip), or Geohash. Lastly, you may want to consider storing data in a database that can create a true geospatial index in memory. Geospatial partitioning in a data lake can only be optimized so much; at some point, you may need a database such as RDS or Redshift that has native index support for geometry and geography datatypes.

Summary

In this chapter, we learned about some ML concepts and how they apply in the geospatial field. We learned about a few AWS ML capabilities as well as a few common libraries used for geospatial ML. Lastly, we walked through a demo visualizing some points inside SageMaker Geospatial. In the next chapter, we will learn how to use Amazon QuickSight to analyze and visualize geospatial data.

References

- AWS SageMaker Geospatial overview: `https://aws.amazon.com/sagemaker/geospatial/`

- Wikipedia – Random Forest: `https://en.wikipedia.org/wiki/Random_forest`

- GitHub – Random Cut Forest by AWS: `https://github.com/aws/random-cut-forest-by-aws`

- SageMaker Geospatial user guide: `https://docs.aws.amazon.com/sagemaker/latest/dg/geospatial.html`

- SageMaker Geospatial examples: `https://github.com/aws/amazon-sagemaker-examples/tree/main/sagemaker-geospatial`

- Geospatial Analysis on SageMaker Studio article: `https://towardsdatascience.com/getting-started-with-geospatial-analysis-b2116c50308b`

- AWS GitHub Lake Drought Monitoring example: `https://github.com/aws/amazon-sagemaker-examples/tree/main/sagemaker-geospatial/lake-mead-drought-monitoring`

12

Using Amazon QuickSight to Visualize Geospatial Data

There are more options available today than ever before for you to visualize your geospatial data. In this chapter, we will explore Amazon QuickSight to see the features and capabilities the **business intelligence (BI)** platform has for working with geospatial data.

This chapter will teach you everything you need to know to present geospatial data in AWS. The concepts will focus on QuickSight but can be applied to other BI tools as well. By the end of this chapter, you will be familiar with the following concepts:

- Making geospatial data available in QuickSight
- Creating analyses and dashboards
- Accessing visualizations from the web and mobile devices
- Automating and sending reports

Geospatial visualization background

As you are aware of from previous chapters, geospatial data is made up of not only the geometry of the feature but also often a wealth of attribute data that describes the point, line, or polygon that is represented by the record. When visualizing geospatial data, sometimes it is helpful to analyze the attribute data independently of the feature. A good dashboard or analysis of a dataset will generally include both location-based and attribute-based elements to provide a complete picture of what the data can reveal:

Unique Key	Attribute 1	Attribute 2	...	Attribute N	Geometry Data

Table 12.1: Table showcasing the identifiers of data

The **Unique Key** value specifies an identifier for the record or feature of geospatial data. This value must not exist in any other records to maintain the fidelity of your dataset. Using a relational geodatabase allows you to apply this unique constraint automatically, but if your storage mechanism doesn't enforce uniqueness for the row, you may end up with duplicated data in your visualizations. This may be difficult to detect by looking at the data on a map as it will result in multiple features stacked on top of each other appearing to be a single geospatial feature. The **Attribute** values provide context and additional information about the feature, and **Geometry Data** describes the characteristics of the location on Earth where this feature exists.

Previously in this book, we showed an example of **JavaScript Object Notation** (**JSON**)-formatted county data for some of the counties in California. The source data used can be difficult to understand when looking at the raw data since it is designed primarily to reflect the geospatial nature of the features. For example, the first section of the file defines the dataset and columns:

```
{
  "displayFieldName" : "",
  "fieldAliases" : {
    "OBJECTID" : "OBJECTID",
    "AREA" : "AREA",
    "PERIMETER" : "PERIMETER",
    "CO06_D00_" : "CO06_D00_",
    "CO06_D00_I" : "CO06_D00_I",
    "STATE" : "STATE",
    "COUNTY" : "COUNTY",
    "NAME" : "NAME",
    "LSAD" : "LSAD",
    "LSAD_TRANS" : "LSAD_TRANS",
    "Shape_Length" : "Shape_Length",
    "Shape_Area" : "Shape_Area"
  },
  "geometryType" : "esriGeometryPolygon",
  "spatialReference" : {
    "wkid" : null
  },
  "fields" : [
    {
      "name" : "OBJECTID",
      "type" : "esriFieldTypeOID",
      "alias" : "OBJECTID"
    },
    {
      "name" : "AREA",
      "type" : "esriFieldTypeDouble",
      "alias" : "AREA"
```

```
    },
    {
      "name" : "PERIMETER",
      "type" : "esriFieldTypeDouble",
      "alias" : "PERIMETER"
    }...
```

Even more perplexing is the geospatial data section, which shows the specific latitude and longitude coordinates that make up the rings of the polygon:

```
"features" : [
    {
        "attributes" : {
          "OBJECTID" : 39,
          "AREA" : 0.0125060450672465,
          "PERIMETER" : 0.46770550097881602,
          "CO06_D00_" : 40,
          "CO06_D00_I" : 39,
          "STATE" : "06",
          "COUNTY" : "075",
          "NAME" : "San Francisco",
          "LSAD" : "06",
          "LSAD_TRANS" : "County",
          "Shape_Length" : 0.46770550097881591,
          "Shape_Area" : 0.012506045067245427
        },
        "geometry" : {
          "rings" : [
            [
              [
                -122.5024267151224,
                37.708132349276738
              ],
              [
                -122.506483,
                37.723731000000001
              ],
              [
                -122.50782901995821,
                37.735330999999753
              ],
              [
                -122.50939539266651,
```

```
            37.74882999999992
        ],
        [
            -122.50939990408358,
            37.748868879392219
        ]
    ...
```

When working with QuickSight, it is important to explore the convenience features that have been built in for working with location data. This is tremendously helpful when your data does not already have **Well-Known Text (WKT)**- or JSON-formatted geospatial data. As long as your dataset contains latitude, longitude, or geographic indicators, such as city, state, or country, you'll be able to visualize the data in QuickSight.

Amazon QuickSight overview

Using the built-in AWS-managed service QuickSight, you are able to leverage a powerful BI platform with no servers to manage. The service is priced so that you pay by usage with the option to pay per session. This flexible capability is perfect for organizations that have unpredictable user activity that may ebb and flow over time. QuickSight has an in-memory feature called SPICE that allows you to cache data for lightning-fast response times. Data is encrypted from end to end to ensure that your information is safe, and the platform supports row- and column-level security on your datasets. Authorization of who can see created visualizations can be done at the user or group level using AWS's native **Identity and Access Management (IAM)** service.

Connecting to your data source

To provide an example of a free, public dataset that can be used to create a map in QuickSight, you can leverage the Kaggle dataset of major league sports stadiums in the United States.

	A	B	C	D	E
1	Team	League	Division	Lat	Long
2	Dallas Mavericks	NBA	West	32.790556	-96.810278
3	Orlando Magic	NBA	East	28.539167	-81.383611
4	San Antonio Spurs	NBA	West	29.426944	-98.4375
5	Denver Nuggets	NBA	West	39.74892	-105.0084
6	Brooklyn Nets	NBA	East	40.682661	-73.975225
7	Washington Wizards	NBA	East	38.8982	-77.0209
8	Golden State Warriors	NBA	West	37.768056	-122.3875
9	Los Angeles Clippers	NBA	West	34.043056	-118.267222
10	Los Angeles Lakers	NBA	West	34.043056	-118.267222
11	Memphis Grizzlies	NBA	West	35.138333	-90.050556

Figure 12.1: Sports stadium data .csv file contents

This data can be downloaded in tabular format and uploaded to Amazon **Simple Storage Service (S3)** as a **comma-separated values (CSV)** file:

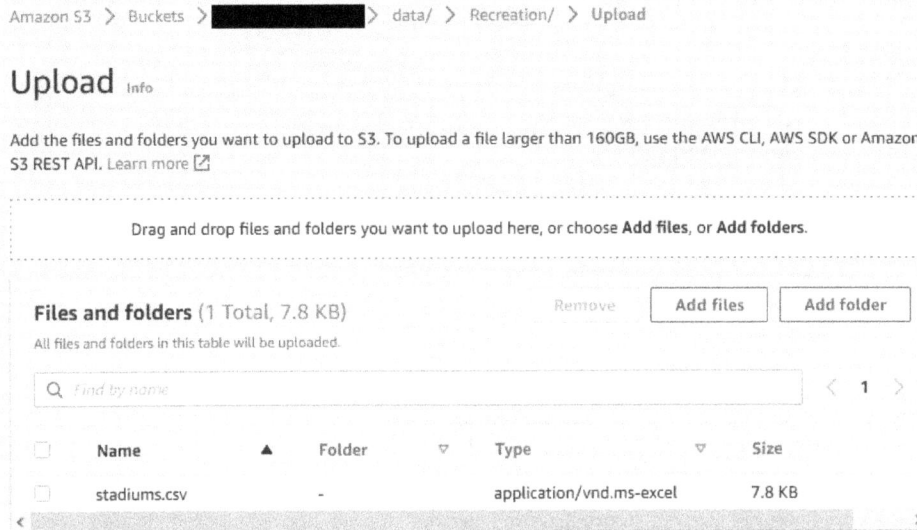

Figure 12.2: Sports stadium data .csv file in an S3 bucket

Configuring Athena

You will now have a static dataset in S3 that we will expose to Amazon Athena in order to make the dataset accessible to **Structured Query Language (SQL)** queries. This approach is recommended for data that may change over time. Any changes made to the source data in S3 will automatically update the AWS Glue and Amazon Athena constructs that represent the data to QuickSight and other AWS services. The following query can be used in the Amazon Athena query editor to create the table pointing to the S3 data source. If your data has a header row (which most data will), be sure to include the `skip.header.line.count` table property. Otherwise, your column headers will appear as a row of data as well.

The following statement can be run in Amazon Athena to create the `stadiums` table with the S3 location updated to match your environment:

```
:
CREATE external TABLE stadiums
(
    team string,
    league string,
    division string,
    lat double,
```

```
    long double
)
ROW FORMAT DELIMITED FIELDS TERMINATED BY ','
STORED AS TEXTFILE LOCATION 's3://<bucket>/<folder>/'
TBLPROPERTIES (
  "skip.header.line.count"="1");
```

This results in the following output:

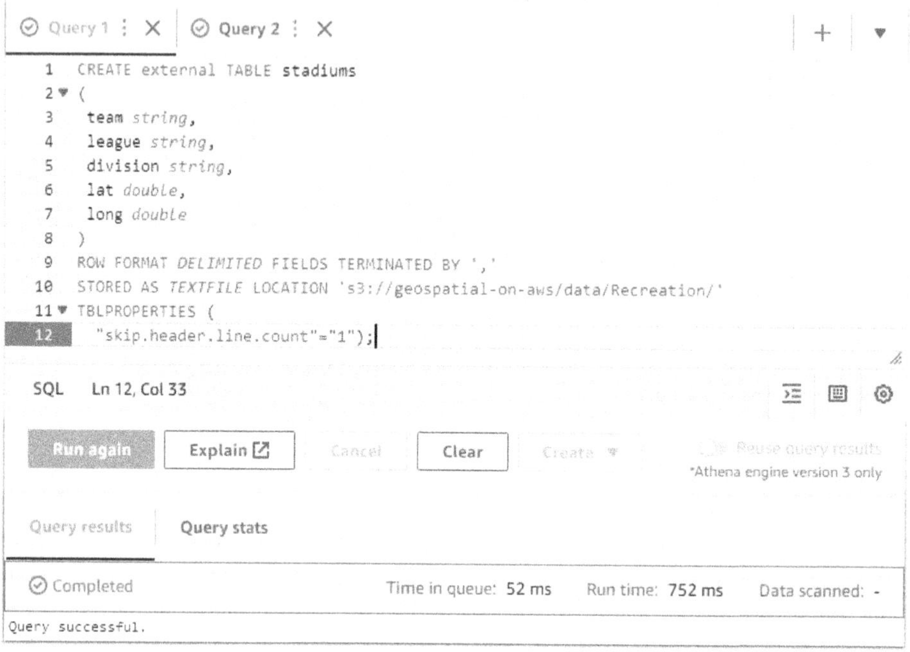

Figure 12.3: Athena creation of stadiums table from .csv file in S3 bucket

Once you have established the table in Athena, it will show up in the data navigation pane to the left and queries can be issued on the source data. You can now use standard SQL queries to filter and view your data, including the lat and long columns, which represent the decimal degree coordinates of each stadium.

Figure 12.4: Results of a simple filter query in Athena

Configuring QuickSight

Amazon QuickSight can be set up in just a few minutes, providing you with a BI platform that can be used to visualize and analyze your geospatial data. Step-by-step instructions can be found in the QuickSight user guide (`https://docs.aws.amazon.com/quicksight/latest/user/signing-up.html`).

In order for QuickSight to have access to data provided by Athena, you will need to enable it in the management settings. To modify the settings, first click on the user icon at the top right of your web browser, then select the **Manage QuickSight** option.

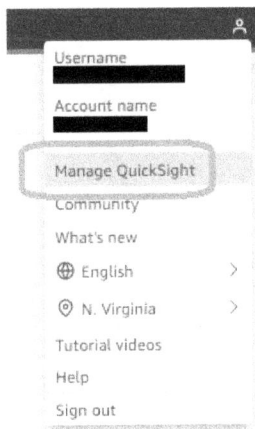

Figure 12.5: Manage QuickSight option in the user menu

We then select the **Manage** button in the **Security & permissions** section:

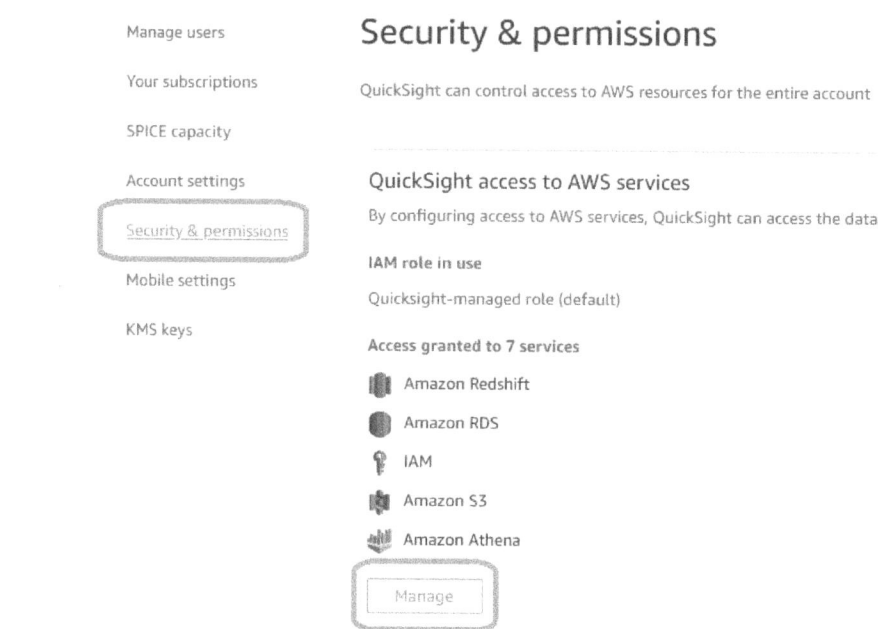

Figure 12.6: QuickSight access to AWS services as data sources

To connect to your Athena dataset, navigate to the **Datasets** section and click the button to create a new dataset. Choose **Athena** as the source type.

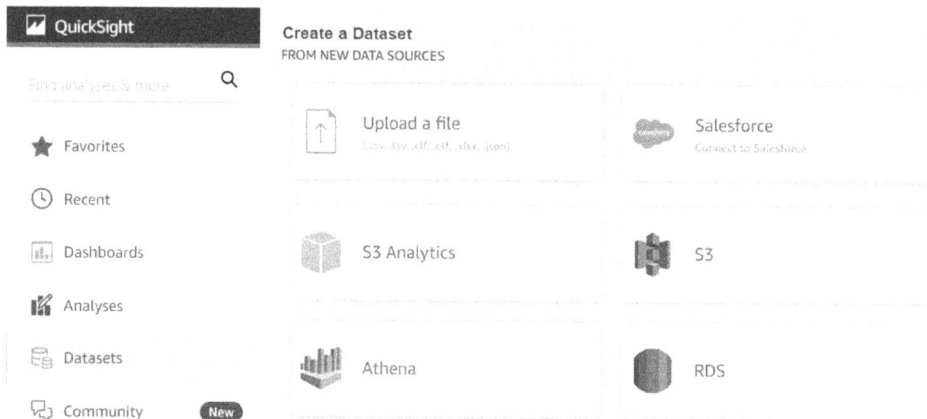

Figure 12.7: Creating a new Athena dataset in QuickSight

Give your data source a name, and QuickSight will validate that Athena is accessible. As long as there are no applied security constraints, you will see the catalog, database, and table in Athena to select for your QuickSight dataset. You must explicitly grant QuickSight access to your S3 bucket in the **Manage QuickSight** option under the user menu on the top right of the screen:

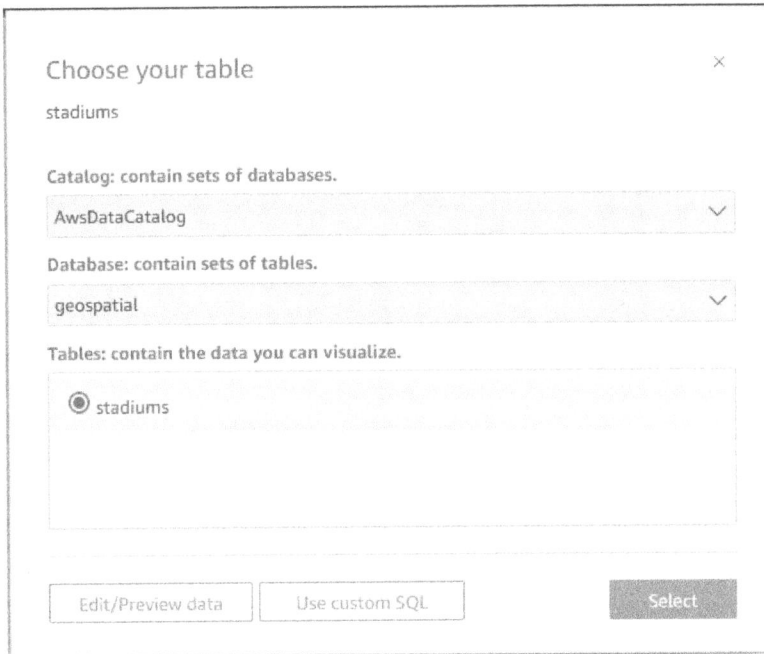

Figure 12.8: Selecting the stadiums data as the source for QuickSight

Selecting the **Edit/Preview data** option will allow you to preview the data. This is not only helpful to ensure that QuickSight has the proper permissions to view the S3 data through Athena but also allows verification of the data types. In this example, the column named `lat` was automatically identified as a latitude value, but `long` is represented as a decimal data type.

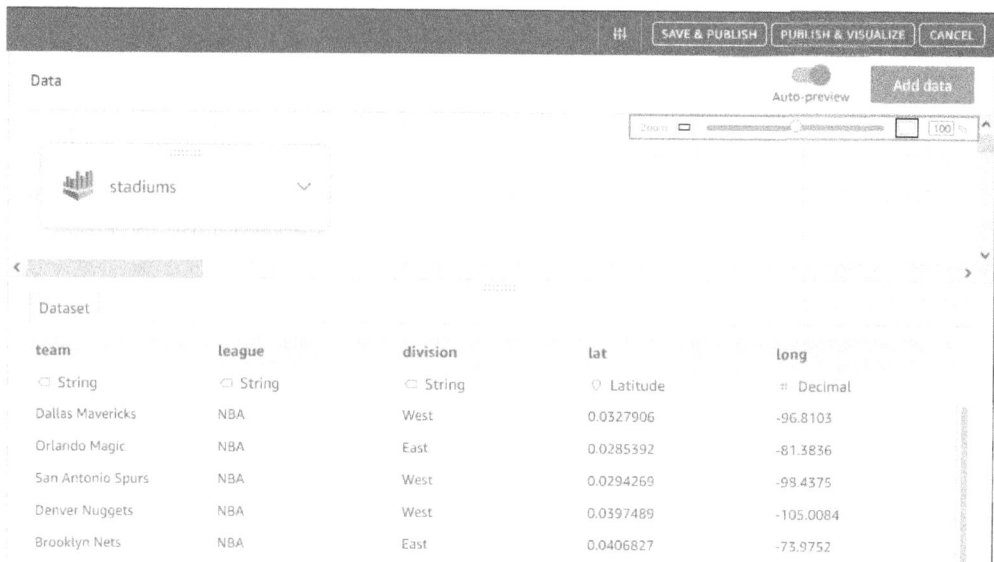

Figure 12.9: Dataset editor in QuickSight

Any issues like this in your data can be simply rectified by clicking on the data type and choosing the desired classification.

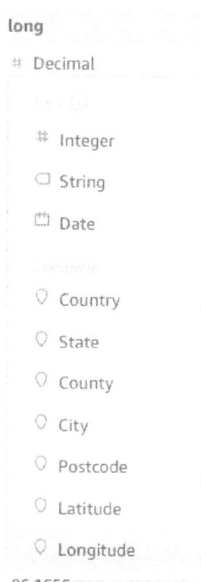

Figure 12.10: Geospatial data types in QuickSight

It should be noted that latitude and longitude values must be in decimal degrees for QuickSight to properly map the location. Degrees, minutes, seconds is not a valid format to use for latitude and longitude values.

When changing the data type, you can see that there are several specialized geospatial data types available in addition to the string, date, integer, and decimal data types:

- **Country**
- **State**
- **County**
- **City**
- **Postcode**
- **Latitude**
- **Longitude**

These data classifications are extremely useful if you have geographic areas represented by commonly accepted polygons. QuickSight will match your data to the known polygon and allow you to display it on a map in your analyses and visualizations.

Visualization layout

Connecting to your data and configuring the dataset is often a one-time activity, and you can modify and duplicate datasets as necessary to meet your reporting needs. Once you have prepared your data, create a new QuickSight analysis based on the data. The layout to design your visualizations is intuitive and has detailed documentation in the QuickSight user guide. You have the ability to set filters on your data and define parameters that allow your analysis to behave differently under different contexts. For example, you can specify date parameters to show current or historical data values. Actions, themes, and settings control the overall look and feel of the analysis and provide the capability to define what happens when the user interacts with the visualization.

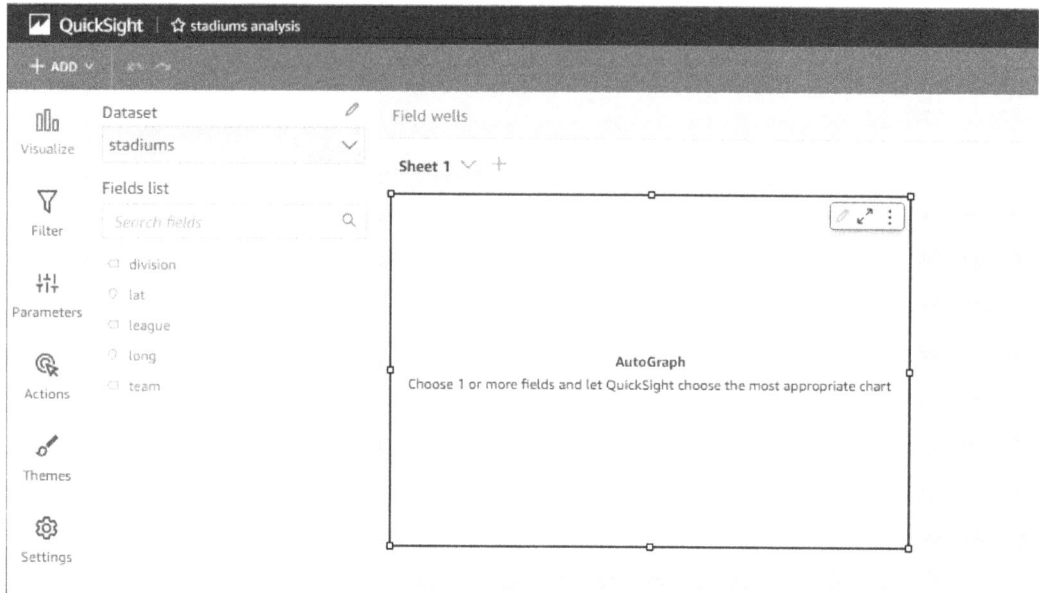

Figure 12.11: Creating a new analysis in Amazon QuickSight

Features and controls

On the bottom left of the QuickSight layout, you will see the various visual types that can be added to represent your data in the most compelling way.

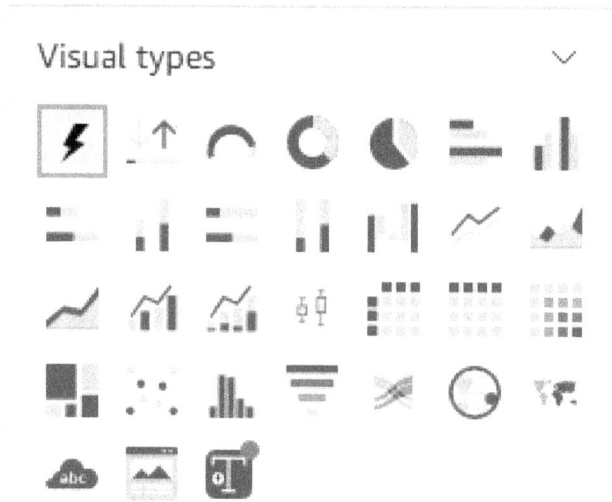

Figure 12.12: QuickSight visual types visualize geospatial data

Most datasets can be represented by more than one of the visual types to achieve a specific effect or unveil particular insights. It is important to think about who will consume your visualizations to pick the best visual type. Although it is natural to gravitate toward the map types for geospatial data, many useful visuals can be created based on the attribute data associated with your features. QuickSight has many non-spatial visual types that can be helpful to add context to your map visual. Since you are reading this book to learn about geospatial visualization, let's take a look at the options for representing your features on a map. The stadiums dataset only has latitude and longitude coordinate values to describe the location, so the point map will be the right visual type to use.

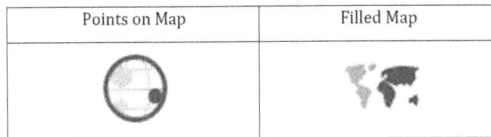

Points on Map	Filled Map

Figure 12.13: Map visual types in QuickSight

Let's consider another dataset of electric charging and alternative fuel stations, which can also be found on Kaggle. This rich set of information includes coordinates but also has street address, city, state, US zip code, and country attribute columns. QuickSight will automatically detect columns it thinks may relate to municipal boundaries and suggests the appropriate location based on pre-existing features QuickSight already knows about. Following the same steps to import this data, you will see something similar to the following:

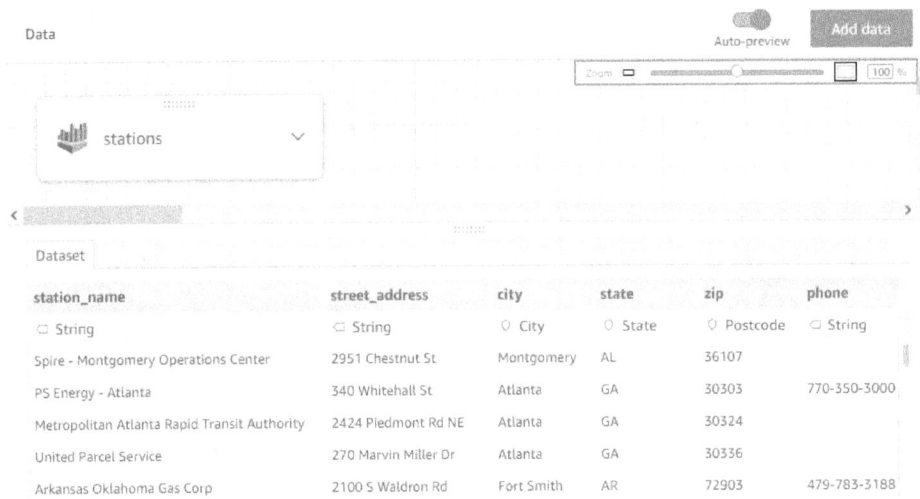

Figure 12.14: QuickSight dataset editor

Notice how most string columns are unaltered; city, state, zip, and country (not pictured in the screenshot) are suggested. Latitude and longitude columns are also easily identified as the column name matches exactly.

Point maps

The first geospatial visual type we'll review in Amazon QuickSight is called a point map. As you probably guessed, this visual type is only applicable to features that have latitude and longitude coordinate values. As long as one of the datasets in your analysis has coordinates, then you are able to use this visual type to quickly create a map and plot points for each of your records.

Figure 12.15: Points on map visual type

Using this visual type, simply dragging both of your coordinate columns into the **Geospatial** box will render a map image with your data:

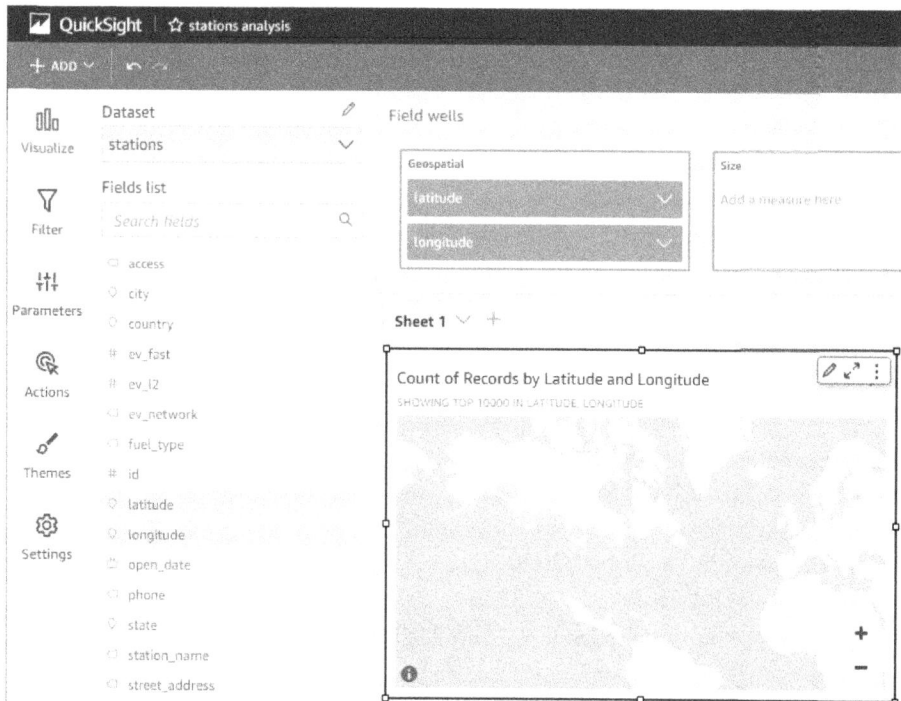

Figure 12.16: Points on map example

This particular dataset has over 70,000 rows that cover the US, so the default styling and scale seem to just be a poorly colored map of the US, but this is actually all of the overlapping points with no styling or configuration. The top area of the QuickSight workspace is referred to as the **Field wells** section. This is where you specify not only the latitude and longitude but also any fields you want to use for the size or color of your points. By dragging two additional fields up and zooming into your area of interest, the visualization quickly becomes more useful.

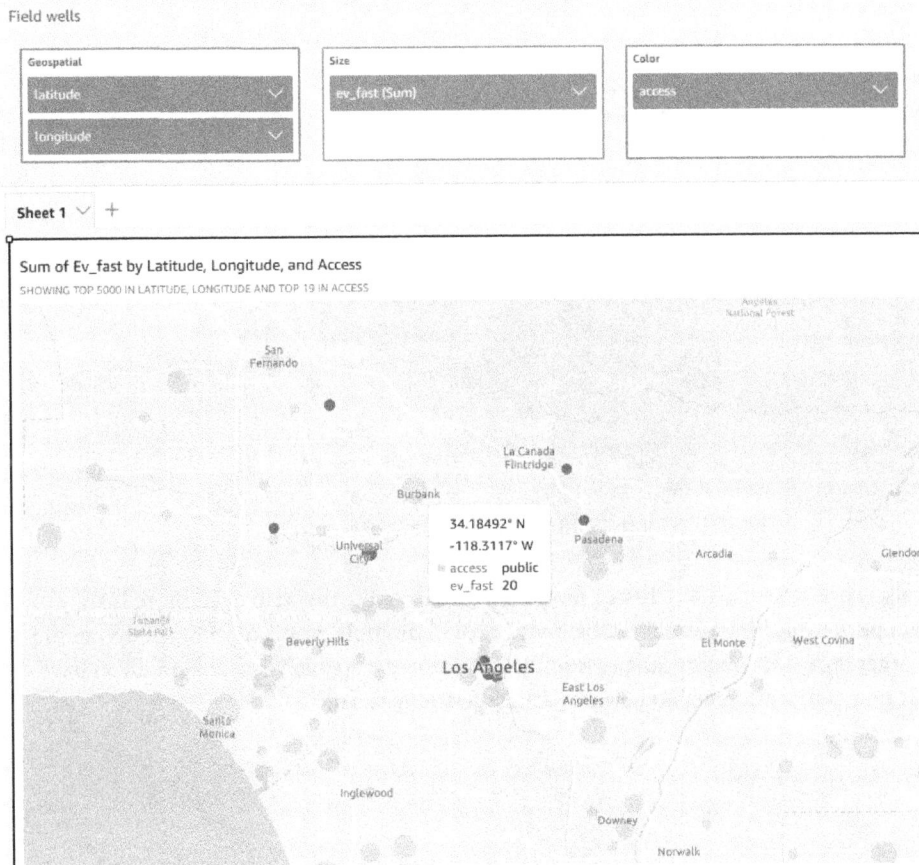

Figure 12.17: Improved symbology using Field wells

Now, instead of just having a rough idea of the data coverage area, I can find the nearest publicly available fast electric vehicle charger in Los Angeles. Filtering the data can focus on a particular electric vehicle charging network to further refine the visual.

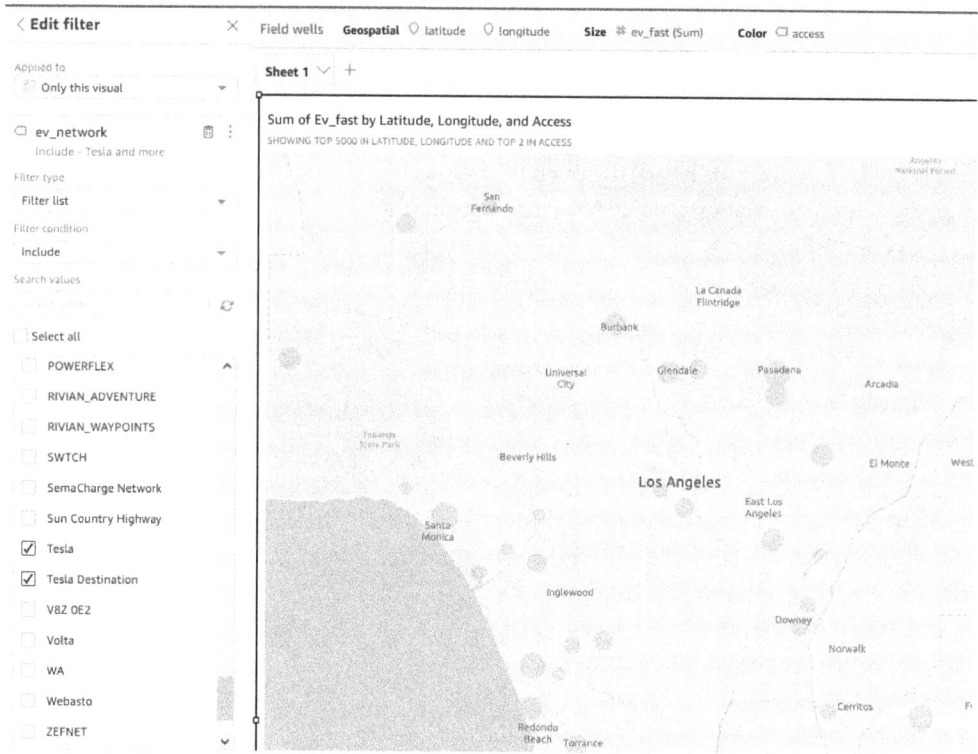

Figure 12.18: QuickSight dataset editor

You can also choose to use the **Cluster points** feature to make the map even more insightful. The clustering option will show a larger bubble in the area of multiple points to show groupings of points across a larger area. This option can provide a much better geospatial visualization if you have dense clusters of points that also need to be viewed at large zoom scales.

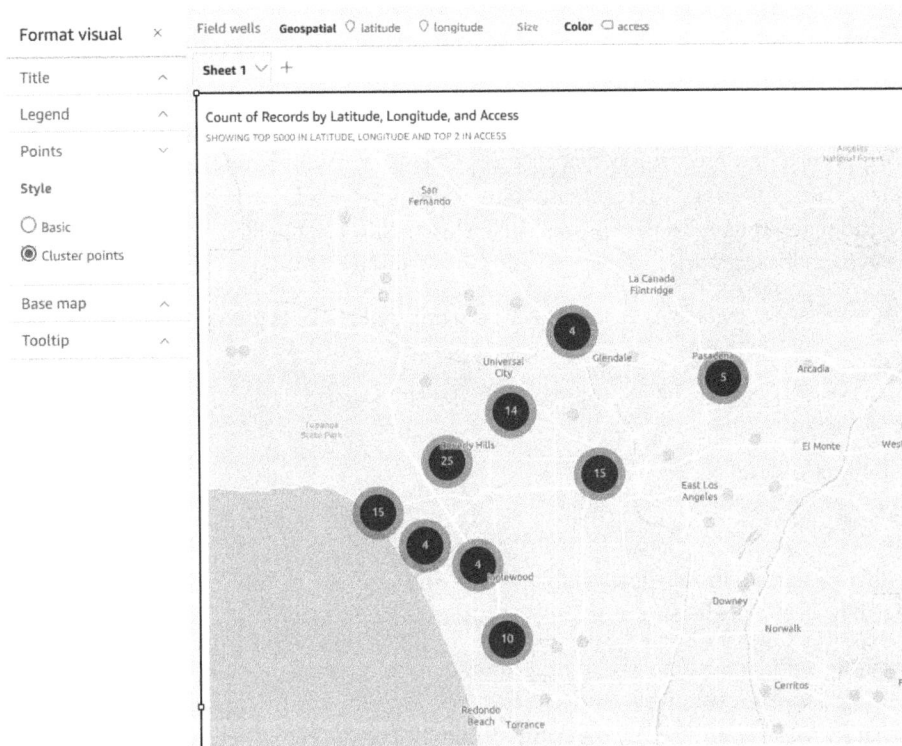

Figure 12.19: Cluster points option for points on map visual type

Base map selection can also be a useful way to present your map in a way that augments your data while adhering to your styling and use case criteria. The exact same map can be made to look very different by simply changing the base map in the visual type.

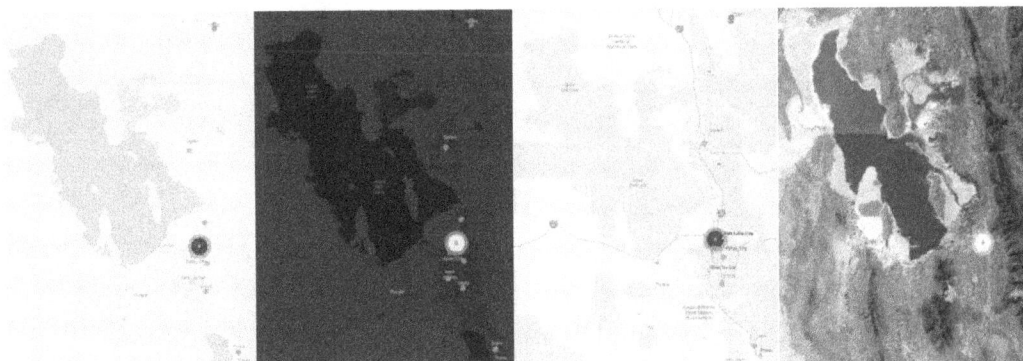

Figure 12.20: QuickSight base map options

Filled maps

Creating point maps is something that most geospatial practitioners do on a **regular** basis. Creating maps with filled-in polygon areas is also a common map request. Amazon **QuickSight** has limited capabilities to incorporate proprietary shape data but has dramatically simplified the creation of filled maps. Typically, this involves geoprocessing to intersect points and polygons, followed by attribute wrangling and many manual, error-prone steps. QuickSight has taken the most commonly used polygons, such as cities, counties, and states, and provided them for you in Amazon QuickSight.

The fields in your dataset that have been identified or configured as one of these geospatial data elements:

- Country
- State or region
- Country or district
- ZIP or postal code

This field will be specified in your **Location** field well, and you have the option to specify a color field well also. Luckily, all of these fields of data are present and correctly identified in our stations dataset.

To show what the simplest form of a filled map looks like, we can drag the state from the fields list and drop it onto the **Location** field well. By doing this, you are telling QuickSight that you want to have a map of states with different colors or shading based on the values of the associated attributes. By default, QuickSight will use the number of records in the dataset that have each state in the designated column. States with more stations show up as a darker shade, while states that have fewer stations show up as a lighter shade of the color. The following map tells a different story about where Tesla charging stations can be found. Filled maps present a visualization to support different questions about the municipalities that contain stations but do not provide the same level of individual data on where exactly they are located.

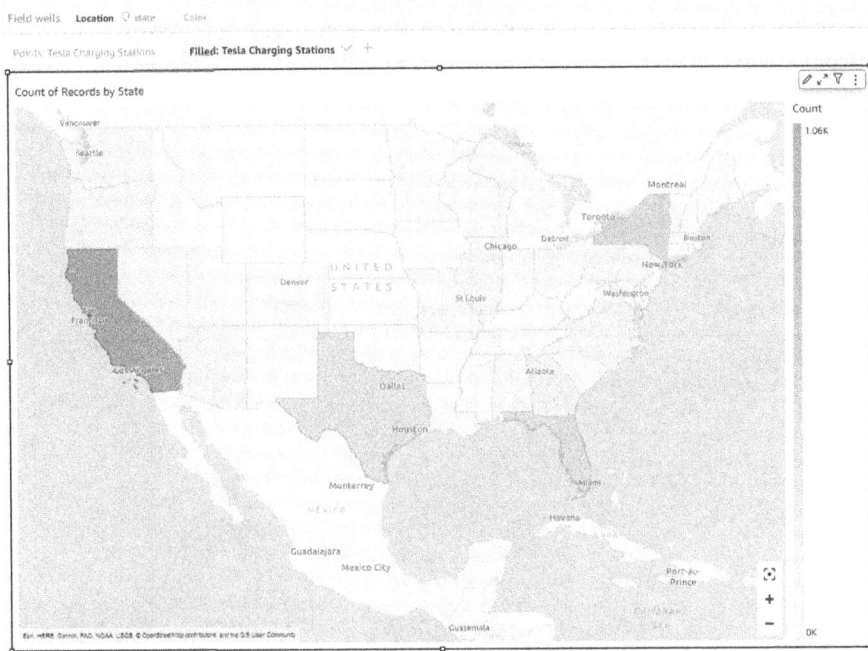

Figure 12.21: Instant geospatial insights from any dataset with the US state attribute

Depending on your use case, seeing the data by zip code may be what you need.

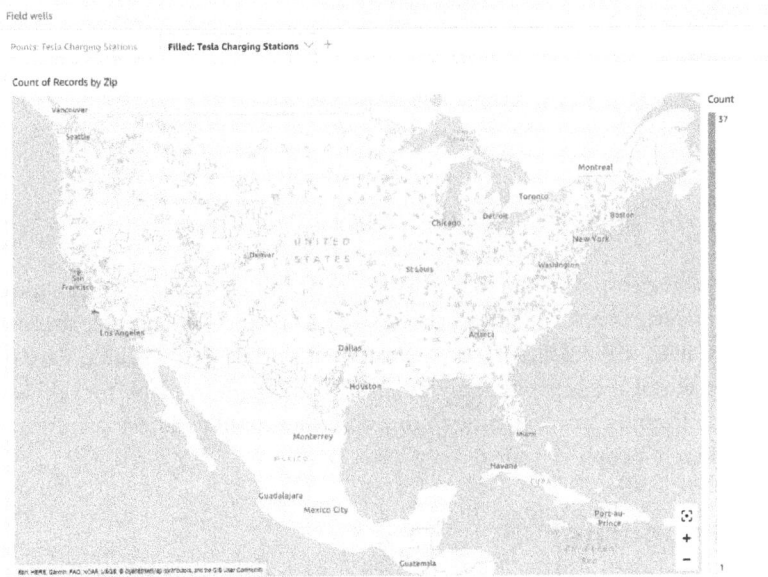

Figure 12.22: Location of Tesla charging stations visualized by zip code

At local and regional levels, postal code mapping can be very useful. Adding the geospatial visualization of data that contains zip codes provides a simple way to view organizational data alongside freely available public data.

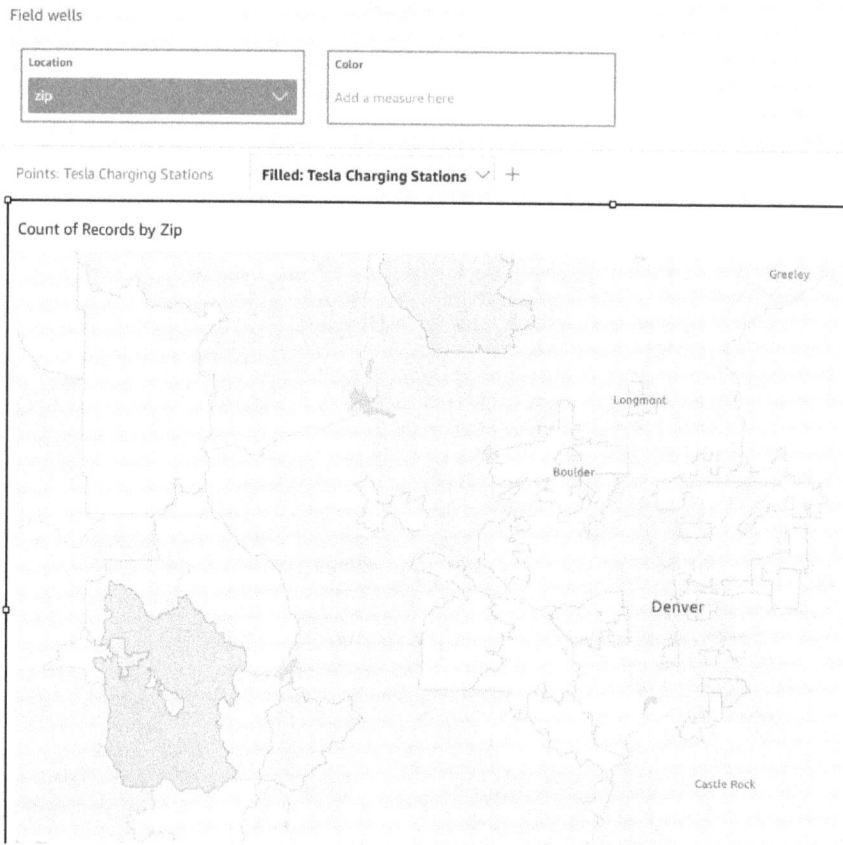

Figure 12.23: Postal code mapping in QuickSight

It is common for the same geospatial data to be used for many different maps. With QuickSight, you don't have to choose or switch back and forth between different views. You are able to create as many flavors of a map as you need without altering or duplicating the original data source. Each of the maps can be placed on separate tabs or separate analyses entirely and made available for self-service using a web browser or mobile app. Using the same source CSV file stored in S3, we can create dozens of different maps for different people or teams.

Putting it all together

There are too many controls and options to cover all of them in detail here, but the following published dashboard shows how you can display the default map with points symbolized by league. Even with a simple dataset that has only a unique key (team name) and two **attributes** (league and division), QuickSight can help to provide a rich, insightful visualization far more useful than the simple CSV list we started with.

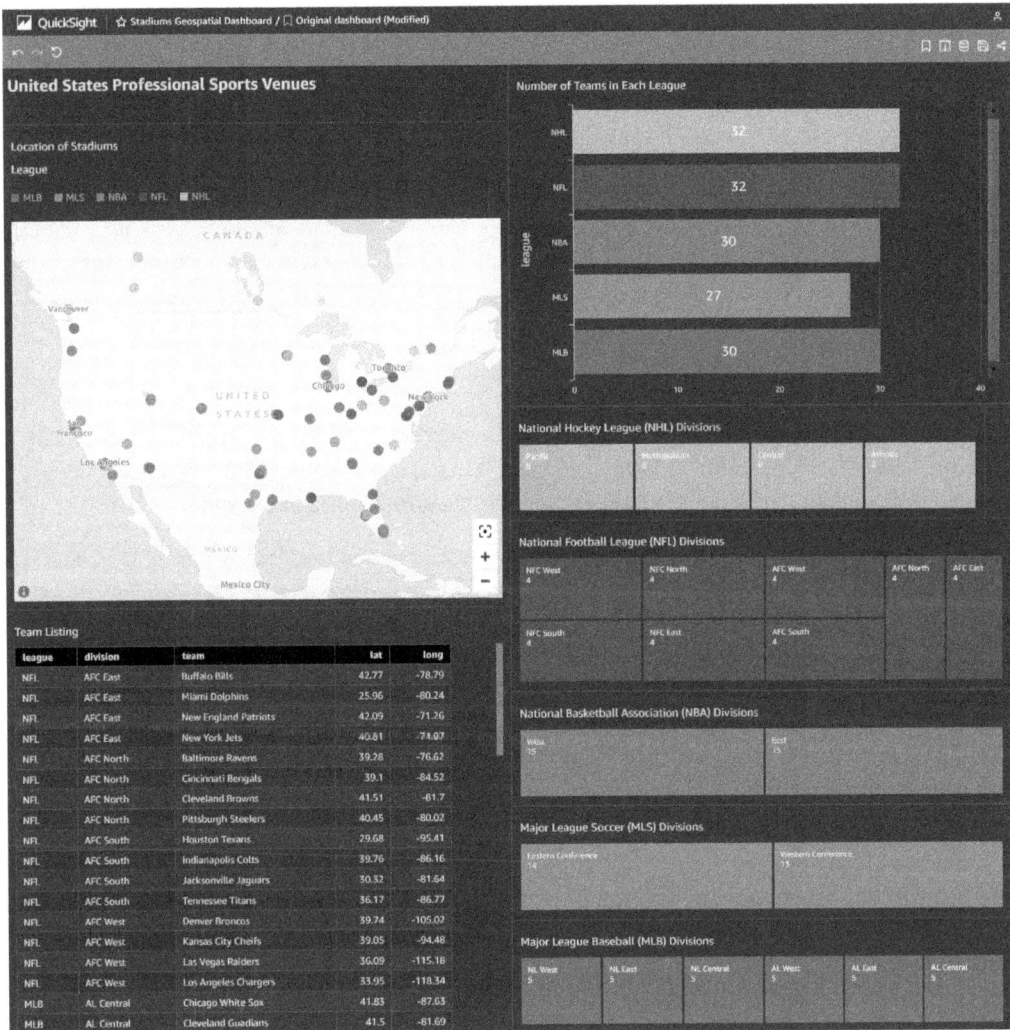

Figure 12.24: Example QuickSight dashboard with map

Once you have created dashboards to share with others, QuickSight provides a secure capability for web and mobile app connections. This will allow you and your organization to have access to your geospatial data whether at home, at work, or on the go. Next, we'll cover a few points on team collaboration in QuickSight, then wrap up the chapter with a summary.

Reports and collaboration

Visualizations of geospatial data, or any data for that matter, are only useful if they are accessible to the people that need them. Because QuickSight is a web-based tool with a mobile app, there are many ways to grant access to others inside or outside of your organization. For an even easier way to disseminate your geospatial data, you can send the dashboard in email form on-demand or based on a set schedule. The attached PDF documents can be shared or archived for a historical account of how your geospatial data has changed over time.

QuickSight was built from the ground up to be a collaborative platform. Any users with access to AWS and QuickSight can work together on analyses and dashboards to facilitate real-time working sessions and provide a simple way to share your completed work simply by saving it. Of course, there are permission controls to ensure that data is only available to those who are intended to have access to it.

Summary

Amazon QuickSight is an easy-to-use BI platform that provides some great out-of-the-box functionality. While geospatial data visualization in QuickSight is still maturing in feature richness, the ease of use and ability to share data across the AWS platform make it a good choice in many situations.

You have seen how to take simple data that represents locations and upload it to Amazon S3. Amazon Athena, with the help of AWS Glue, structures your data and classifies the geospatial elements for you automatically. With just a few clicks, your data will be securely available to share with your team, who can access your maps on the go from their mobile devices. Because it is a full-featured BI platform, Amazon QuickSight provides a robust set of non-spatial visual types to help you tell the story of your map in a consolidated and easy-to-use interface.

References

- Amazon QuickSight user guide: `https://docs.aws.amazon.com/quicksight/latest/user/welcome.html`

- Kaggle Sports Stadium Locations: `https://www.kaggle.com/datasets/logandonaldson/sports-stadium-locations`

- Kaggle Electric & Alternative Fuel Charging Stations 2022: `https://www.kaggle.com/datasets/saketpradhan/electric-and-alternative-fuel-charging-stations?select=Electric+and+Alternative+Fuel+Charging+Stations.csv`

- AWS documentation – *Signing up for an Amazon QuickSight subscription*: `https://docs.aws.amazon.com/quicksight/latest/user/signing-up.html`

Part 4: Accessing Open Source and Commercial Platforms and Services

In this final part of the book, we will gain context of commonly used platforms and organizations that can optimize efficiency and provide a broad community for continued learning.

This part has the following chapters:

- *Chapter 13, Open Data on AWS*, Open Data on AWS offers public data made available through AWS services from across the globe. This chapter highlights public datasets on demographics, public health, industry, and environment that are ready to use.

- *Chapter 14, Leveraging OpenStreetMap*, From roads and buildings to businesses and parks, millions of places can be found on OpenStreetMap. This chapter will show what data can be leveraged using Amazon Athena queries directly against the latest updates.

- *Chapter 15, Map and Feature Services on AWS*, looks at tools and services available on AWS to create a durable, scalable platform optimized for the cloud.

- *Chapter 16, Satellite Imagery on AWS*, talks about how to find and use this data and use Amazon SageMaker for incorporating near real-time machine learning into your applications.

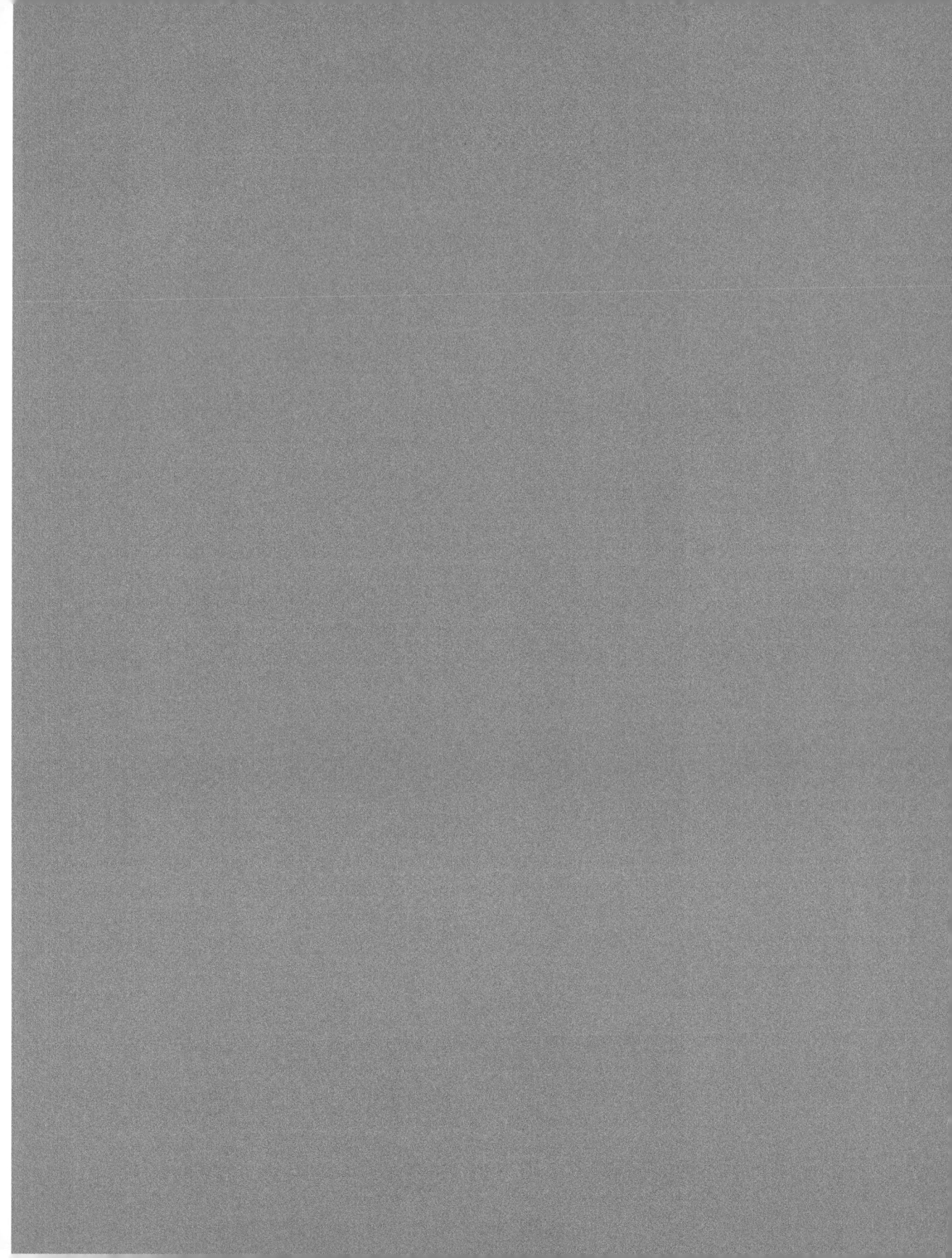

13
Open Data on AWS

Geospatial data provides powerful capabilities to individuals and organizations looking to better understand our planet. The insights that can be derived from location intelligence are even further amplified when collaboration occurs across diverse teams and specialist organizations. Open data is free and available for anyone to use, and in this chapter, we will explore the following topics:

- Open data overview and sources
- Accessing the Registry of Open Data on AWS
- Common use case examples
- Analysis using AWS services
- Benefits of cloud collaboration

What is open data?

The cost of remote sensing data acquisition has decreased exponentially over time with the expansion of connected and airborne sensors. As with most industrial and technical domains, price decreases follow innovation and scale. When humanity's need for something is driven by both innovation and scale at the same time, it is possible to have a dramatic step-change in the cost and capability available to end users. We have seen this in the ability of individuals to get access to high-quality weather forecasts, aerial imagery, and other insights that can be derived from pointing flying cameras at our floating rock.

Bird's-eye view

Most of the early advances in aerial photography were achieved by, and belonged to, military organizations. During World War II, planes in the air provided the opportunity to put cameras in the air. Recently captured photographs helped armies figure out what the enemy troops were doing. In the United States, the concept of taking a color photograph from the air to see a larger portion of the Earth was already established by 1935. While beautiful and interesting, this type of photograph didn't have enough value to justify the cost until wartime. In 20th-century combat, superior reconnaissance has been noted as one of the strongest links to a victorious outcome. Aerial photographs were a tool for elite military forces to obtain a commanding advantage over their opponent.

These photos, taken at the Italian Military Geographical Institute in 2022, show one of the camera rigs used inside the aircraft and the resulting image. When compared to the resolution of today, these images seem low-quality. However, given the fact that aerial surveillance was not previously able to be captured and shared with those on the ground, these early data capture missions represented a huge step forward in our ability to record details about our planet from the sky.

Figure 13.1: Early aerial surveillance camera, Istituto Geografico Militare, 2022

Figure 13.2: Example of collected imagery, Istituto Geografico Militare, Firenze, 2022

In addition to aerial photographs, contour lines of elevation data could be captured over unfamiliar territory with this ingenious sight line tracing device:

Figure 13.3: Topographical aerial map-making tools on display
at the Istituto Geografico Militare, Firenze, 2022

Militaries are not known for their tendency to share data, and this prevented the proliferation of the images and knowledge that they contained. It also took many years of research and development to overcome the optical and physical challenges of taking photographs from the air or from space. Of course, there are more than just light sensors (cameras) mounted on drones, helicopters, airplanes, satellites, and spaceships. Modern satellites have a host of sensors and capabilities, including the ability to stay in one place or travel around the Earth collecting fresh images and data measurements from our changing planet. All of this costs a lot of money, so ongoing data collection needs to be shared since it is cost-prohibitive for individuals to ever attempt this themselves.

Modern applications

Open data can generally be defined as data that is made available for use by anyone, at any time, for any reason, without any explanation or individualized approval. Open data is free for everyone to access and use; you don't even need to have an AWS account. In the summer of 2022, AWS announced that it would provide cloud hosting for open data that organizations wished to share free of charge. Despite the wide range of "open data" that governments and organizations have collected over the decades, it is really not truly open if on film or tape locked in a basement. Through collaboration with the agencies that own the data, AWS has provided a powerful mechanism to deliver rich datasets with absolutely no cost to the producer or the consumer, which we will explore in the next section.

The Registry of Open Data on AWS

Announced on June 21, 2022, the catalog of open data that is available on AWS was added to AWS Marketplace. AWS Marketplace is an online repository of data sources, software, and other resources that integrate directly with AWS. At the time of writing of this book, a search for "geospatial data" on the marketplace (`https://aws.amazon.com/marketplace/search?searchTerms=Geospatial+data`) returns around 100 data products, dozens of which can be used free of charge as open data. When data products are provided with associated costs, there is often a free trial that will let you explore the data to determine whether it is appropriate for your needs before you purchase. There are also useful packages of geospatial software and tools in AWS Marketplace that may be useful in working with the data.

Here is an example of one of the free LiDAR geospatial datasets available on AWS:

Figure 13.4: Example of AWS Marketplace geospatial dataset

Requester Pays model

There is one caveat that may be present in some of the geospatial datasets that are open data and hosted on S3. It should be noted that some of the data is available with the Requester Pays model. This means that the charge for data egress from the AWS cloud is paid by the entity requesting the data (you). When ingesting data into S3, there is no charge for bringing the data into the cloud. When that data leaves the cloud, there is a charge incurred called an egress charge. The first 100 GB per month transferred out of S3 to the internet does not incur any charge. In any month that 100 GB is exceeded, the rate starts at 9 cents per GB, decreasing with use to 5 cents per GB above an incremental 150 GB beyond the allocated monthly free amount. In order to use any of the Requester Pays datasets, an AWS account is required, although there is no charge for the use of the open data itself.

Each dataset has a description of the contents, source, and usage considerations. Instructions and sample commands for accessing the data directly are often included to simplify access and get you visibility into the data quickly.

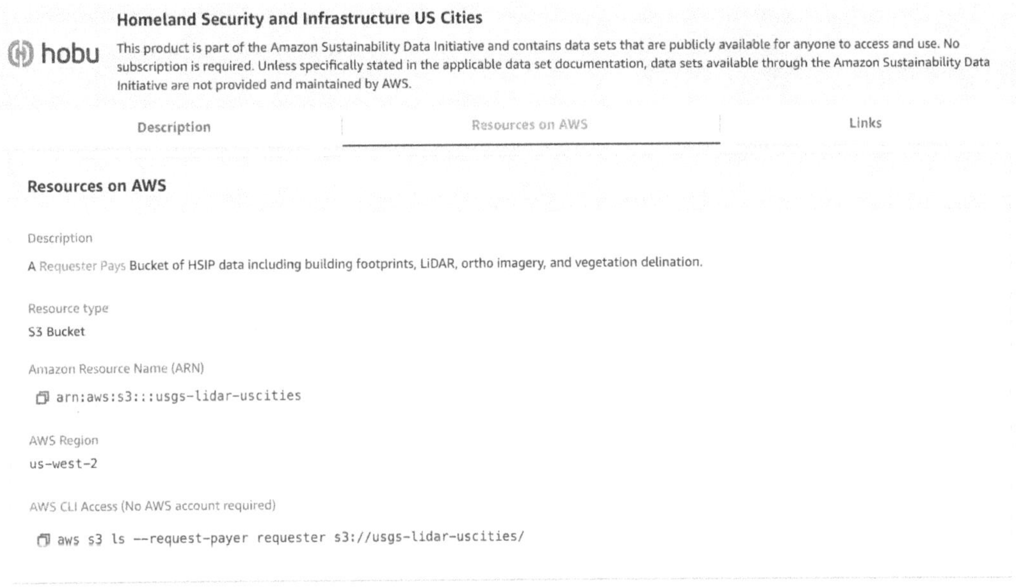

Figure 13.5: Subscription and access details

The following are some **Open Data on AWS** examples that may be useful in a broad range of geospatial workloads:

- **Homeland Security and Infrastructure US Cities**:

  - https://aws.amazon.com/marketplace/pp/prodview-likphwmfv3gyi?sr=0-6&ref_=beagle&applicationId=AWSMPContessa

- **CoreLogic Bulk Property Dataset Samples**:

  - https://aws.amazon.com/marketplace/pp/prodview-qmtygvhtwpibc?sr=0-12&ref_=beagle&applicationId=AWSMPContessa

- **Land Surface Temperature Maps - High Resolution**:

  - `https://aws.amazon.com/marketplace/pp/prodview-5r4vd3mxk5esc?sr=0-40&ref_=beagle&applicationId=AWSMPContessa`

- **Spatial Features (USA, H3 Resolution 8)**:

  - `https://aws.amazon.com/marketplace/pp/prodview-tvhejhmfvbopg?sr=0-19&ref_=beagle`

This broad availability of open geospatial data is fascinating, but even more exciting is what you can do with it. Long gone are the days of long overnight jobs downloading data from public and subscription-based sites. With Open Data on AWS, you can run high-volume analytics in place because your compute resource is already next to the data. In the next section, we'll look at ways you can use the AWS cloud to analyze the data that is freely available and open to the public.

Analyzing open data

Previously in this book, you have learned about several different ways geospatial data can be stored, accessed, and analyzed. Most organizations perform analysis of their proprietary GIS datasets and keep the results of those analyses proprietary. The open data concept extends to all use cases and is encouraged to be used in conjunction with internal organizational data to maximize the value of the result. Leveraging the publicly available Earth observation datasets is not only simple with Open Data on AWS but it also performs better because everything is in the cloud. You can layer your own proprietary data on top of the open geospatial data and perform analysis directly in the cloud where both of the data sources live. This saves processing time, supports unpredictable workloads, and minimizes cost using the AWS consumption-based pricing on all cloud resources.

Using your AWS account

If you are new to using AWS to access and analyze geospatial data, you might find AWS CloudShell useful. CloudShell provides a preconfigured **command-line interface** (**CLI**) for interacting with your account. Browsing a dataset on the command line simplifies initial data discovery so it can be done quickly from a variety of devices. I find it particularly useful in Requester Pays scenarios as the CLI is preconfigured with your account credentials. CloudShell is browser-based and included free in all AWS accounts. The green arrow in the following diagram shows the inconspicuous button to activate this useful service:

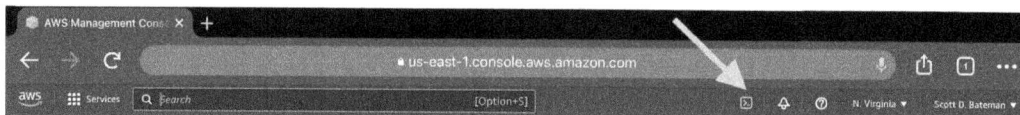

Figure 13.6: Icon for AWS CloudShell

First-time users will see a one-time initialization that takes about a minute, and this will happen in each AWS Region. Subsequent uses launch CloudShell much faster. In just a few seconds, you'll have a current version of the CLI to interact with your account, or other AWS accounts that have shared resources.

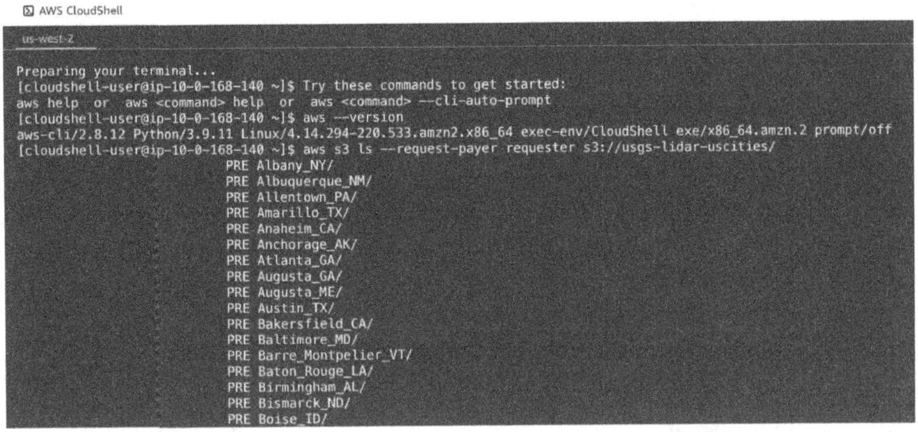

Figure 13.7: Catalog of free LiDAR data by geographical area

Analyzing multiple data classes

An example of performing analysis that combines proprietary and open data is the use of H3 hexagon grid features or other publicly available survey land grid data. These polygon features describe the Earth in universally agreed-upon formats and conventions. Well-described and documented geospatial datasets such as the Resolution 8 features referenced earlier can be subscribed to for a convenient catalog of interesting data.

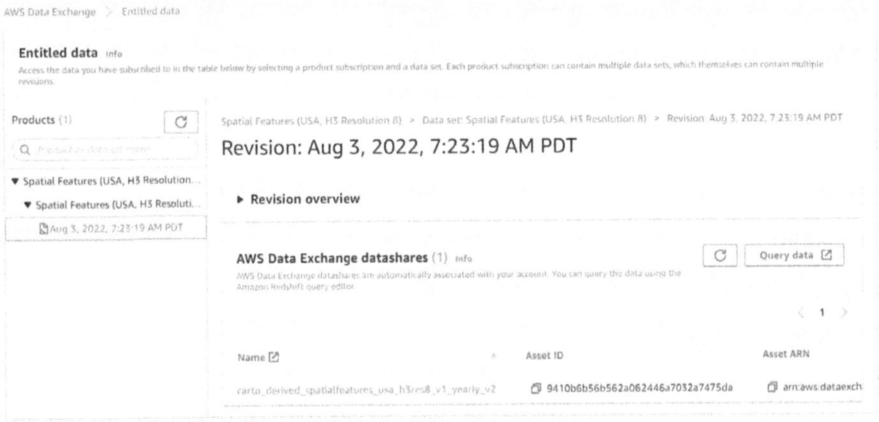

Figure 13.8: Reviewing Entitled data in the AWS console

Sometimes, the most powerful geospatial analytics are done by combining public and proprietary datasets. Storing your proprietary enterprise geodatabases on AWS is secure, cost-effective, and flexible, as we showed in the chapter on Amazon Athena. A possibility-expanding feature exists within Athena to submit federated queries that leverage data in multiple purpose-built data stores.

Federated queries with Athena

As you become more familiar with the types and locations of spatial data in AWS, a feature that you may find particularly useful is Athena Federated Query. Whether your geospatial data lives in S3 or one of the relational or NoSQL databases, federated queries give you the ability to query across data sources and formats without moving your data. Athena Federated Query uses Lambda functions to provide connectivity between Athena and other data source services in your AWS account. This can incorporate known AWS source formats as well as custom formats due to the nature of the connector architecture. Having the ability to define how the connection is made and the parameters that are used provides the flexibility to connect to virtually any data source.

Federated queries in Athena allow you to connect to data sources and fetch records back to Athena. These results can be joined with data from other sources using the familiar SQL-like syntax. This capability provides extreme flexibility in selecting and prioritizing multiple sources of data for rationalization and data quality checks. As of May 2023, Athena provides data source connectors for the following providers:

- Azure Data Lake Storage
- Azure Synapse
- Cloudera Hive
- Cloudera Impala
- CloudWatch
- CloudWatch metrics
- CMDB
- Db2
- DocumentDB
- DynamoDB
- Google BigQuery
- Google Cloud Storage
- HBase
- Hortonworks

- Kafka
- MSK
- MySQL
- Neptune
- OpenSearch
- Oracle
- PostgreSQL
- Redis
- Redshift
- SAP HANA
- Snowflake
- SQL Server
- Teradata
- Timestream
- TPC-DS
- Vertica

A common example of industrial use cases is to interface **Enterprise Resource Planning (ERP)** or **Computerized Maintenance Management System (CMMS)** databases to cloud storage on AWS. Companies that globally replicate their asset and work management data enjoy fast operational access from the field and the office. What work processes could your organization streamline by combining the power of Open Data on AWS with the insights contained in your proprietary data? Amazon Athena provides a fast, flexible, and cost-optimized serverless platform for analyzing petabyte-scale data where it lives.

Open Data on AWS benefits

Hopefully, this chapter has provided you with some tangible examples of how Open Data on AWS can enrich your GIS ecosphere. **Store once, use many** is a pattern that works well in the cloud and results in dramatic reductions in cost and wait times for large geoprocessing workflows.

Using Amazon Workspaces, you can launch a virtual desktop in the same AWS Region as your data for a low-latency geospatial workstation. The chatty network nature of many popular GIS desktop tools is latency-sensitive and performs best when the software is close to the data. Less time watching screen refreshes means more time drawing insights out of your geospatial data.

You can run those massive compute transformations during small windows, knowing that the scale and elasticity of AWS will ensure your process completes. Replications to other Regions can be added where global latency constraints arise. The scale and functionality of the AWS global infrastructure grows as does the amount and value of Open Data on AWS.

Summary

More data is being collected today than ever before, and right now, you have access to continually updated free geospatial data that is truly open. While there are still premium data offers in the marketplace, the amount of data in Open Data on AWS is truly remarkable. Most geospatial use cases can benefit from incorporating this publicly available data into proprietary location-based data. You have seen how this can be accomplished on AWS, providing simple access that is cost-efficient. For your production geospatial workloads, cloud-based geospatial data provides the fastest possible way to move and transform large datasets.

Others around the world are constantly creating and maintaining highly accurate point-of-interest datasets. This open source community has created an entity called **OpenStreetMap, which** has raised the bar in global crowd-sourced geospatial data. In the next chapter, we will explore the world through an OpenStreetMap lens by leveraging cloud resources on AWS.

References

- *Aerial reconnaissance in World War II*: https://en.wikipedia.org/wiki/Aerial_ reconnaissance_in_World_War_II

- *Italian Military Geographic Institute*: https://www.igmi.org/en

- *Announcing Open Data on AWS Data Exchange*: https://aws.amazon.com/about- aws/whats-new/2022/06/announcing-open-data-aws-data-exchange/

- *AWS Marketplace*: https://aws.amazon.com/mp/marketplace-service/ overview/

- *Athena RedShift Query Extension App*: https://us-west-2.console.aws.amazon. com/lambda/home?region=us-west-2#/create/app?applicationId= arn:aws:serverlessrepo:us-east-1:292517598671:applications/ AthenaRedshiftConnector

- *Using Amazon Athena Federated Query*: https://docs.aws.amazon.com/athena/ latest/ug/connect-to-a-data-source.html

14

Leveraging OpenStreetMap on AWS

We use geospatial data every day to guide our driving experience. Whether getting directions to an unfamiliar destination or making sure that our journey is efficient by monitoring current traffic conditions, navigational applications save us time and headaches on the road. In this chapter, you'll learn that **OpenStreetMap (OSM)** has a wealth of data and services for streamlining your analytics and navigational needs. In this chapter, we'll explore the following topics:

- The OSM platform
- Accessing OSM from AWS
- Practical applications
- Community projects and organizations
- Architectural considerations

What is OpenStreetMap?

OSM is the most widely known and well-maintained free collection of geospatial data on the planet. It consists of an online portal that can be used to browse and search for data, a search engine for geospatial data, and a massive repository of accessible data that can be used outside of the platform. The online map website has geospatial editing features in a web map enabling the digitization of points, lines, and polygons. The data in OSM is contributed by a volunteer community via open collaboration and geospatial practitioners that are passionate about open data.

OSM's data structure

You may be wondering what geospatial data schema supports the representation of any physical object on the surface of the entire planet. Roads are lines, buildings are polygons, and fire hydrants are latitude and longitude coordinates. How does one technology organize all of the data that represents our world?

OSM designates three data types, referred to as elements:

- **Nodes**: Data structures that define a point on Earth using WGS84

- **Ways**: Line metadata created by a sequenced list of nodes

- **Relations**: Definition of how elements work together for complex geometry representations

Using only these three mechanisms, OSM is able to describe any of the features on the Earth's surface. The critical attributes associated with each of these data types are OSM **tags**. Nodes, ways, and relations can all have tags that depict the meaning of the geospatial data. Each data point can have multiple unique tags that take the format of a key-value pair of up to 255 characters. OSM provides conventions and standards for tagging to promote consistency.

The schema and metadata of an element can be easily viewed on the OSM web map. If we consider the example of a restaurant, it may be represented as a node if only the latitude and longitude are known. In populated areas, restaurants are often represented as ways to depict the building outline. The following is the OSM representation of the historical and entertaining Casa Bonita cliff-diving performance restaurant in Lakewood, Colorado.

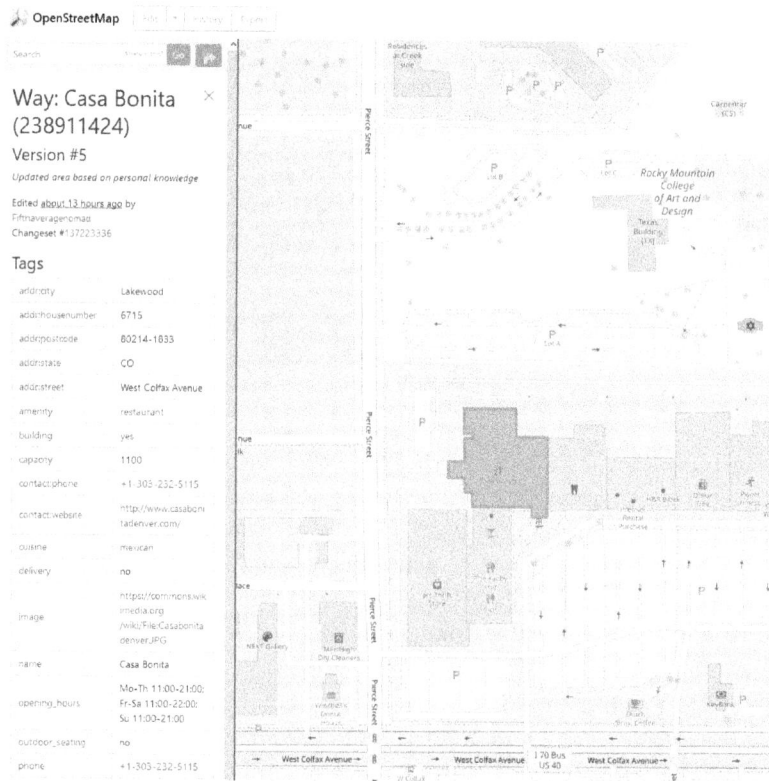

Figure 14.1: OSM representation of a restaurant

The tags associated with this way element are displayed along the left navigation pane of the web map. You may notice that the phone number for the business is duplicated in two different tags. Tags exist for both of these pieces of metadata:

- `contact:phone` = +1-303-232-5155

- `phone` = +1-303-232-5155

This may be intended to support specific community usage, or it could be that two different contributors provided tag updates without being aware of the other. This brings us to the last key feature provided by the OSM data structure, which is the editing history of the data. Each node, way, or relation will have a common attribute called a changeset. This number represents a group of changes applied to the geospatial dataset. By using the changeset information, you can see how the geometry and attributes have changed over time, and who was responsible for those changes. Using this OSM feature, we can see that both attributes have existed since version 1 of the way created by a user named `Mr_Brown` in September 2013.

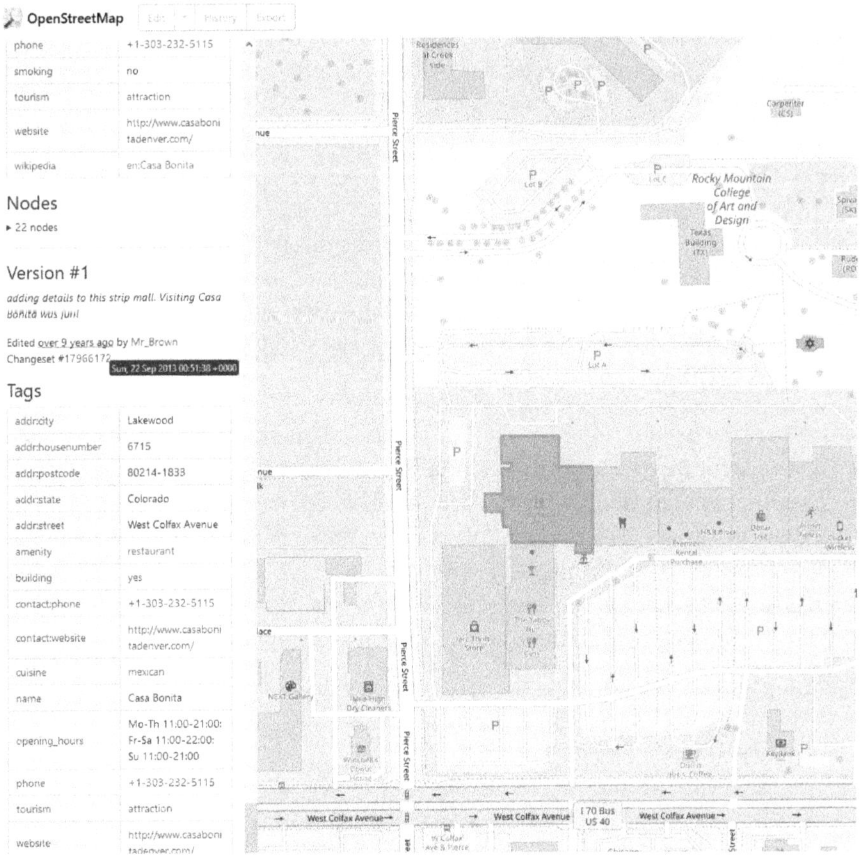

Figure 14.2: Viewing OSM history for a way element

OSM benefits

The following are the benefits of using OSM:

- **License cost**: OSM is free under the **Open Database License (ODbl)**
- **Adoption**: Companies such as Amazon, Apple, Facebook, and Garmin all use OSM
- **Up to date**: Data is continuously updated globally
- **Customizable**: You can create your own maps and cartography

Geospatial data is intellectual property and there are license types and restrictions that are important to understand for proper use. OSM is licensed under the Open Data Commons ODbL. This license affords you the ability to freely share, create, or adapt the data as long as you attribute it in the manner specified by the ODbL. Any adapted versions of the data must also be licensed under the ODbL to promote continuity of openness. In other words, you can use OSM for personal, commercial, or educational purposes as long as OSM and its contributors are credited.

While the power of OSM by itself is compelling, leveraging the AWS cloud to incorporate OSM data into your workflows is a secure and powerful way to leverage open source geospatial data. In the next section, we'll dive deep into how you can access OSM from your AWS account.

Accessing OSM from AWS

There are several ways that the AWS platform can integrate nicely with OSM. Current planet data can be accessed and filtered, while changesets showing historical modifications provide additional insight into how geospatial data has changed over time. Thanks to numerous white papers and blog posts on the topic since the AWS Public Datasets program released access in 2017, accessing OSM from within AWS is surprisingly simple.

As with many other data exploration examples in this book, Amazon Athena will be used. Athena is a great AWS service for exploring geospatial data since it can access a wide range of source data. Unstructured, semi-structured, and structured data stored in S3 or other formats can be structured into tables and views that query the data from the source location. Because OSM data is hosted on S3, Athena integrates well with OSM. If you plan to follow along with these examples, make sure Athena is configured with an S3 bucket for the results. Once inside the Athena console, accessing the most current OSM data usually begins with the `planet` table.

Choose a data source and database in Athena, then run the following query:

```
CREATE EXTERNAL TABLE planet (
    id BIGINT,
    type STRING,
    tags MAP<STRING,STRING>,
    lat DECIMAL(9,7)
```

```
    lon DECIMAL(10,7),
    nds ARRAY<STRUCT<ref: BIGINT>>,
    members ARRAY<STRUCT<type: STRING, ref: BIGINT, role: STRING>>,
    changeset BIGINT,
    timestamp TIMESTAMP,
    uid BIGINT,
    user STRING,
    version BIGINT
)
STORED AS ORCFILE
LOCATION 's3://osm-pds/planet/';
```

The resulting Athena table created will provide instant access to query the broadest and most widely adopted open geospatial dataset, OSM. You can see the individual IDs for each data element in the planet table, and the type, which tells you whether the data represents a node or a way.

Tags provide descriptive metadata on each record, and of course, the location can be found using the **lat** and **lon** fields. The **changeset** field contains information that can be related back to details of changes in the data. Change frequency over the life of the feature can be inferred from the **version** field:

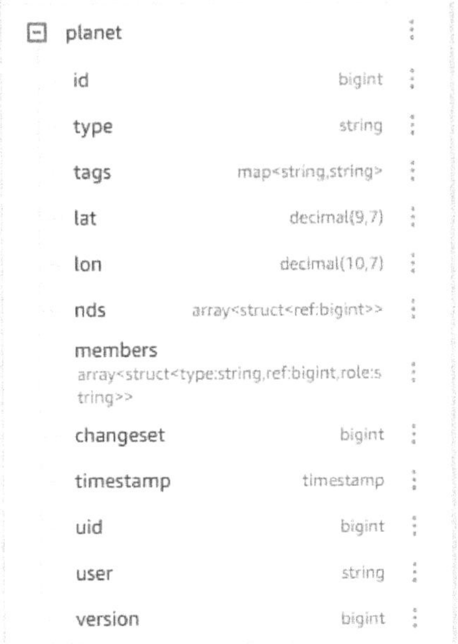

planet	
id	bigint
type	string
tags	map<string,string>
lat	decimal(9,7)
lon	decimal(10,7)
nds	array<struct<ref:bigint>>
members	array<struct<type:string,ref:bigint,role:string>>
changeset	bigint
timestamp	timestamp
uid	bigint
user	string
version	bigint

Figure 14.3: OSM planet columns

Once you have the table created, it should appear in your navigation panel to the left. Take some time to familiarize yourself with the schema and start to think about useful data that can augment your geospatial intelligence. For our first example, I'll turn to mountain peaks as I have always loved the outdoors. OSM has a specific node type tag designation for mountain peaks.

You can read more details on usage considerations on the OSM *Tag:natural=peak* page: `https://wiki.openstreetmap.org/wiki/Tag%3Anatural%3Dpeak`.

Understanding the tags for the type of data you are interested in can unlock some hidden gems. In the documentation on the tags for peaks, you'll notice that there is a `Wikipedia.org` link ID that can be used to generate URL links directly from web maps or other applications. In this chapter, we are not interested in wiki pages, so we'll leave that tag out of the specific fields we extract from the tags:

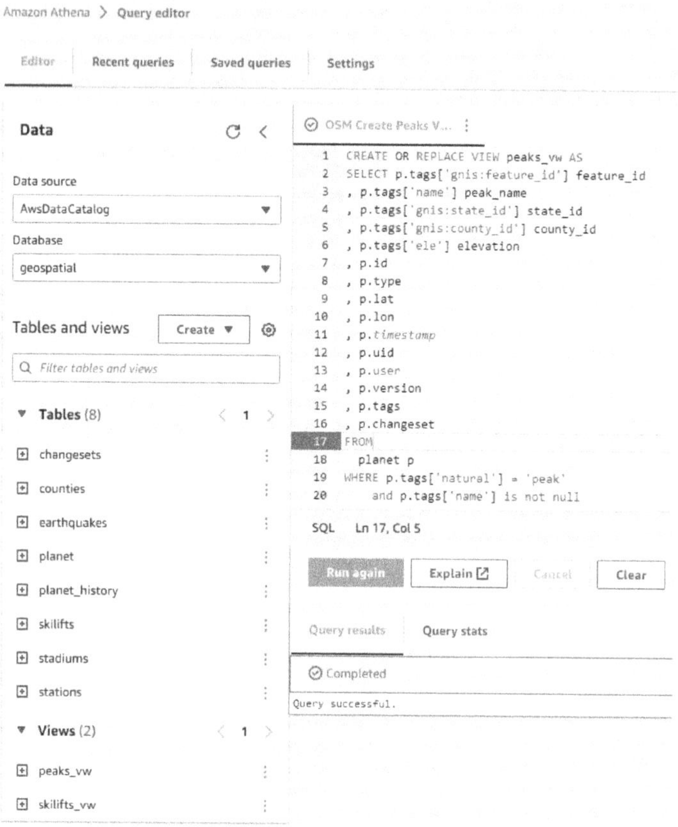

Figure 14.4: Example of Athena view on OSM data

The first part of the script denotes that the command will create or replace a view to make the SQL code easily re-runnable. This approach should be used with caution in case consumers of your view are sensitive to the presented schema. Each of the tags that you find interesting for your dataset can be called out and aliased. The first instance of this can be seen in the `gnis:feature_id` tag:

- `p.tags['gnis:feature_id'] feature_id`

This alias in this case simply removes the `gnis:` prefix to make the resulting dataset more usable. You can also add some text as done with the name to clarify the type of thing we are looking at the name of. County and state information is of limited utility in the current state as it is represented as an ID number instead of a human-readable name. We'll show how that can be fixed later. The elevation is a nice tag to highlight as it can be used to perform statistical calculations and aggregations on the mountain peak results.

- `p.tags['name'] peak_name`
- `p.tags['gnis:state_id'] state_id`
- `p.tags['gnis:county_id'] county_id`
- `p.tags['ele'] elevation`

Following the specific tag extractions, we also grab the **lat/lon** coordinates and other information about the age of the record. Before making any significant decisions about how you'll use the data, be sure to validate the quality of the contents. Because the OSM community draws from a wide range of contributors, sometimes there can be unresolved errors or strange contents in the data. Sometimes, the unit of measure (feet versus meters) is not specified and is therefore up to interpretation. Using the try-and-cast constructs of the Amazon Athena query language can safeguard you from unwanted data in your results. By adding a filter clause such as `WHERE try(CAST(elevation AS int))` `IS NOT NULL` to SQL applied to the `peaks_vw` created earlier, we can determine whether the value of the elevation tag is a valid integer number or not.

Putting it all together, we can see which peaks have the highest reported numeric elevation with the following query based on the view we created earlier:

```
select * from peaks_vw
WHERE try(CAST(elevation AS int)) IS NOT NULL
order by CAST(elevation AS int) desc
```

Because this data is returned in descending order by elevation, we would expect to see Mount Everest as the first item on the list. The results of this query demonstrate a few things we should be aware of about globally contributed open data:

- Data may not specify units of measure
- Data may be in other languages
- Data may not be correct

Looking for Mount Everest, we don't actually see it in the list anywhere. The 14th returned item and the `peak_name` value are not in English. Based on the location and elevation, we can deduce this record signifies Mount Everest; however, the elevation does not match generally accepted measurements for the monolith.

```
1  select * from peaks_vw
2  WHERE try(CAST(elevation AS int)) IS NOT NULL
3  order by CAST(elevation AS int) desc
```

SQL   Ln 1, Col 1

| Run again | Explain 🔗 | Cancel | Clear | Create ▾ |

Query results   Query stats

⊘ Completed   Time in queue: **185 ms**

Results (100+)

🔍 Search rows

# ▽	feature_i ▽ d	peak_name ▽	state_i ▽ d	county_id ▽	elevatio ▽ n	id ▽	type ▽
1		Chumbar sar 1			15925	6461716962	node
2		Chumbar sar 2			15820	6461706818	node
3		Chumbar sar 3			15575	6461726163	node
4		Chumbar sar 4			15575	6461710898	node
5		Chumbar 5			15470	6497515037	node

Figure 14.5: Tallest mountain peaks from OSM planet

Whatever it is your organization needs to expand the inputs for analysis, OSM is likely to have quality geospatial data that can enrich your transformations at virtually no cost. Using serverless consumption-based services, it is possible to create a simple application using OSM with AWS. The next section will depict a potential application that could be built for vacation skiers and ski bums alike to keep tabs on the slope conditions.

Application – ski lift scout

To show the ability to assess current data and use notifications to learn of changes, we'll present a scenario related to the ski lifts used at ski resorts to transport passengers. Yes, in the wide array of data updated in the OSM platform, you'll find most major ski areas are mapped out with the exact location of loading stations as well as the cable lines themselves.

To understand how this data can be accessed, it is first important to look at how it is stored. You have been introduced to the concept of tags in OSM nodes and way data. Let's take a look at the data tagged with `aerialway=station`:

```
CREATE OR REPLACE VIEW "skilifts_vw" AS
SELECT
  p.tags['name'] lift_name
, p.tags['operator'] operator
```

```
, p.tags['state'] state
, p.id
, p.type
, p.lat
, p.lon
, p.timestamp
, p.uid
, p.user
, p.version
, p.tags
FROM
  planet p
WHERE ((p.tags['aerialway'] = 'station') AND (p.tags['name'] IS NOT
NULL))
```

To limit the results to potentially higher-quality nodes, any nodes that don't have a name are excluded. The operator and state data may be sparse, but we'll leave those columns in as they provide an additional dimension to the data.

We now have a view that shows us the location, name, and related information about every node in OSM marked as an aerial waystation. Creating a changesets table similarly to how we created the planet table provides a way to see who changed the data last, when it was changed, and the tags associated with the change:

```
CREATE EXTERNAL TABLE changesets (
    id BIGINT,
    tags MAP<STRING,STRING>,
    created_at TIMESTAMP,
    open BOOLEAN,
    closed_at TIMESTAMP,
    comments_count BIGINT,
    min_lat DECIMAL(9,7),
    max_lat DECIMAL(9,7),
    min_lon DECIMAL(10,7),
    max_lon DECIMAL(10,7),
    num_changes BIGINT,
    uid BIGINT,
    user STRING
)
STORED AS ORCFILE
LOCATION 's3://osm-pds/changesets/';
```

Since we have defined an area of interest with the bounding box for ski lifts within a range of latitude and longitude values, it is now easy to see when the last data update was made to any of the ski lifts:

```sql
1  SELECT slw.id, slw.lift_name, slw.lat, slw.lon, slw.timestamp, slw.user, slw.version, slw.changeset, c.tags, c.num_changes
2  FROM changesets c
3  JOIN skilifts_wasatch slw on c.id = slw.changeset
4  ORDER BY timestamp desc;
```

SQL   Ln 1, Col 1

[Run again] [Explain ↗] Cancel   [Clear]   [Create ▼]

Query results   Query stats

⊙ Completed

Results (100+)

Q Search rows

#	id	lift_name	lat	lon	timestamp	user	version	changeset
1	1509814217	Sugarloaf	40.5672150	-111.6283720	2022-08-14 17:02:39.000	tcarlisle	5	124895998
2	9925723532	Midway Station	40.3844880	-111.5875494	2022-08-01 22:32:12.000	tcarlisle	1	124366688
3	355682329	Dreamscape	40.6488407	-111.5643850	2022-07-19 19:46:51.000	tcarlisle	5	123822368
4	355682247	Dreamcatcher	40.6488376	-111.5640660	2022-07-19 19:46:51.000	tcarlisle	4	123822368
5	2632798338	Flatiron	40.6546949	-111.5479310	2022-07-13 21:02:14.000	tcarlisle	3	123581160
6	2632754008	Alta Lodge Tow	40.5886217	-111.6378680	2022-06-23 20:01:07.000	tcarlisle	4	122774062
7	83867385	Super Condor Express	40.6896737	-111.5931090	2022-06-21 20:53:52.000	tcarlisle	6	122685511
8	1510139506	Crest Express	40.5834539	-111.5757610	2022-04-03 19:04:59.000	tcarlisle	4	119275771
9	1510139519	Great Western Express	40.5925372	-111.5614520	2022-04-03 19:04:59.000	tcarlisle	4	119275771
10	1510139526	Snake Creek Express	40.5831783	-111.5696420	2022-04-03 19:04:59.000	tcarlisle	4	119275771
11	565232100	Majestic	40.5907538	-111.5780940	2022-04-03 19:04:59.000	tcarlisle	4	119275771
12	1510562803	Baby Thuder Lift	40.5726008	-111.6706440	2022-03-09 23:28:07.000	tcarlisle	5	118298077
13	2632838779	Pioneer Lift	40.6236084	-111.5202620	2022-02-28 21:45:37.000	tcarlisle	3	117960373

Figure 14.6: OSM data updates to Utah ski lifts

You can now keep an eye on any changes in OSM, and even set up notifications using Amazon **Simple Notification Service (SNS)** to get real-time updates as contributions are made.

Using a visualization tool such as QuickSight provides a visual representation of the OSM data:

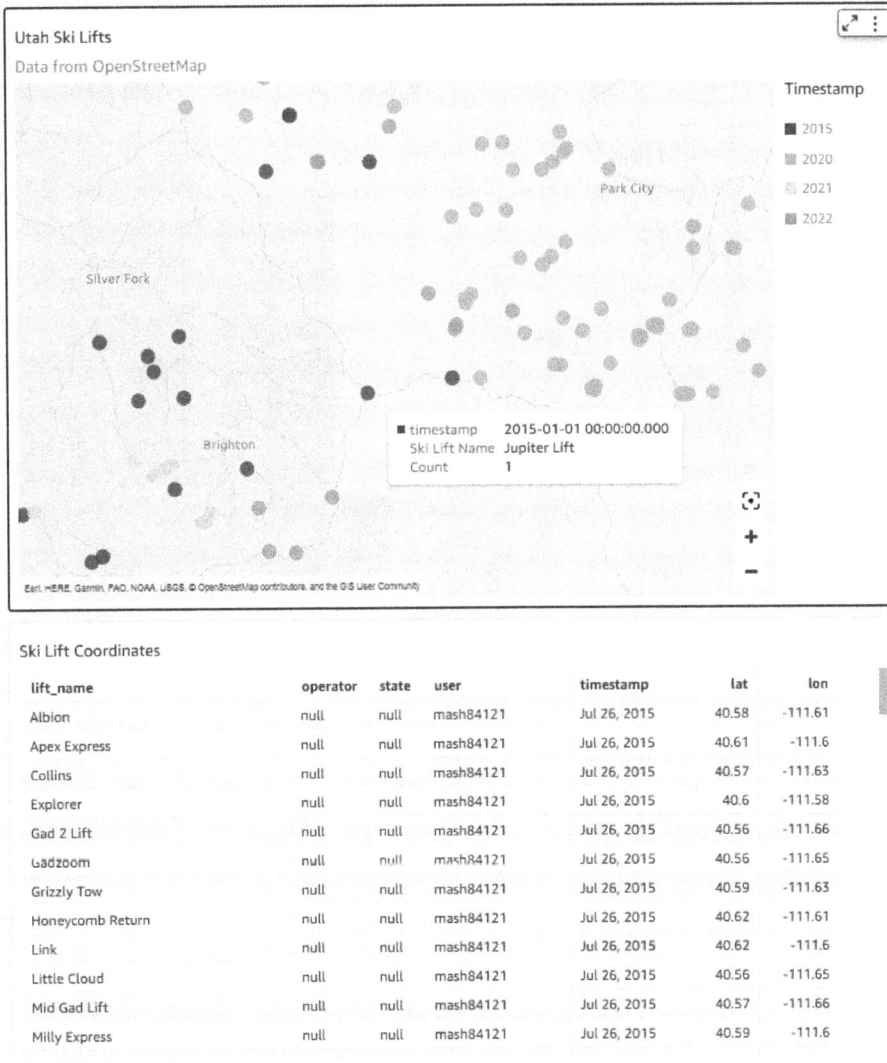

Figure 14.7: Example visualization of planet data

With all of these rich datasets provided by OSM, there are still areas that are light on geospatial data. Connectivity issues in developing regions make accurate surveying a challenge, and crowd-sourced data can often be the fastest and most reliable way to update your dataset. In the next section, we'll explore some of the great work being done around the world by geospatial technologists volunteering their time to help those in need.

The OSM community

One of the most benevolent and vibrant aspects of the OSM ecosphere is the community of dedicated groups that commit their time and energy to the cause of open source mapping. Dedicated service groups host events for geospatial practitioners to help with rapid mapping in areas of need. One such example is the **Humanitarian OpenStreetMap Team** (**HOT**), who help with mapping assistance using recent satellite imagery in underserved areas. The HOT team organized a massive effort after the 2023 earthquakes in Turkey and Syria to provide updated location insights to emergency responders.

Architectural considerations

When working with raw datasets that have large amounts of data, performance can be slower than desired as some basic queries can take 30 seconds or longer. A simple tactic for speeding up performance is to simply create an Athena table from the query results. You can limit your query to a bounding box of latitude and longitude values to refine the results further:

```
CREATE TABLE "skilifts-wasatch" AS
SELECT * FROM skilifts_vw
WHERE lat between 40 and 41
    AND lon between -112 and -111
```

This will capture a snapshot of the data from the view within the specified bounding box for fast querying. Any table that is created using this method should be managed and refreshed at the appropriate intervals. Using this approach can result in stale tables if not organized effectively. Despite the cautions, using this technique to search for a specific ski lift speeds up the query from around 20 seconds to well under a second.

One other consideration when using live open data is the durability of data schemas. Creating views in Amazon Athena is easy and can result in a quick proliferation of views if not managed properly. As useful views become shared among teams, analyses and dashboards may depend on certain elements of the presented data. Take the mountain peaks example from OSM we used earlier in this chapter. If an initial view of the data contains the Wikipedia column indicating the search term to use in a link, other teams with access to your data may build applications that leverage the URL linking capability. Subsequent versions of the view could impact these teams if the Wikipedia column were to be removed.

A best practice for all shared datasets is to tag your data and monitor usage using the built-in AWS tools for resource monitoring. By understanding how your data assets are used (or not used), you can make the best decisions for the future of your data platform. All teams are resource-constrained, so it only makes sense to spend your time wisely. Improve the areas that have the most gravity for workloads, and always be cognizant of making breaking changes. Through a profile of who relies on your datasets, you can have a smooth and well-communicated change process to continually enhance the available datasets.

Summary

OSM is quite literally an entire world of information that is free and available for a wide variety of uses. Because this data is hosted on Amazon S3, the data can be easily accessed and incorporated along with your proprietary geospatial data. This chapter showed you the basics with some examples, and I encourage you to spend some time browsing the wealth of data that can be used in your location-based analytics and visualizations.

Direct data access to features and attributes is tremendously valuable, as we showed in this chapter. However, many geospatial data challenges require map services to provide high performance, availability, and reliability for frequently requested map images. Map and feature services can amplify your organization's ability to quickly serve high-quality GIS maps to a wide variety of consumers. Mobile apps can cache local copies of map service and feature data to enable workers in no-/low-connectivity areas. The next chapter will describe how map and feature services can be launched and managed on AWS to expand your geospatial capabilities.

References

- *OpenStreetMap Public Data Set Now Available on AWS*: `https://aws.amazon.com/about-aws/whats-new/2017/06/openstreetmap-public-data-set-now-available-on-aws/`

- *Querying OpenStreetMap with Amazon Athena*: `https://aws.amazon.com/blogs/big-data/querying-openstreetmap-with-amazon-athena/`

- OpenStreetMap wiki – *Elements*: `https://wiki.openstreetmap.org/wiki/Elements`

- OpenStreetMap wiki – *Map features*: `https://wiki.openstreetmap.org/wiki/Map_features`

- HOT: `https://www.hotosm.org/`

- **Open Data Commons ODbL**: `https://opendatacommons.org/licenses/odbl/`

15

Feature Servers and Map Servers on AWS

In the last chapter, we learned about working with **OpenStreetMap** (**OSM**) with Amazon Location Service. In this chapter, we will cover Feature servers, which are queries against source data that return the points as individual objects displayed as a layer on a map. We will also cover Map servers, which can act like a feature service where it queries the source data but, instead of returning the individual points, it renders them as an image. Feature servers are great for analytics because you can perform calculations such as counting the number of points. Map servers are good for speed when you don't need analytics and you are trying to serve a map many times. It's easier for a user and a client application to download an image from a WMS than potentially over 50,000 individual points. OSM data is a common data source for Feature and Map servers around the world. It is one of the easiest datasets to get access to, as well as the cheapest to use as a base map on a map server; the former and the latter being because it's open source. The majority of base maps available are proprietary or locked down to only work with certain vendor products. Having OSM as an open source option makes it so anyone in the world can pull in streets, points of interest, or various boundaries, along with a plethora of other types of map features. There are trade-offs between the proprietary datasets and OSM though: OSM isn't usually the most up-to-date, as commercial datasets typically have significant investments to pull in local building data from every government in the world to incorporate changes quickly. In this chapter, we will talk about the different types of feature and map servers available, both commercial and open source. We will talk about the benefits, challenges, and capabilities of the two, and then finally, we will have a demo showing how to easily deploy GeoServer in a Docker container.

This chapter covers the following topics:

- Types of servers and deployment options
- Capabilities and cloud integrations
- Deploying a container on AWS with Elastic containers

Types of servers and deployment options

When it comes to choosing a geospatial server to serve geospatial data to clients, you have many offerings in the open source world, with QGIS Server, GeoServer, and MapServer all being popular choices. On the commercial side, the overwhelming majority will choose Esri's ArcGIS server. All of these options are supported on AWS and in various forms, containers, Kubernetes, and traditional EC2 instances. Deployment options also vary between implementations. ArcGIS has a few convenient methods of deployment, such as AWS CloudFormation templates, which can be modularly combined to customize the deployment. There is also the ArcGIS Cloud Builder tool available under downloads at myesri.com: `https://enterprise.arcgis.com/en/server/latest/cloud/amazon/arcgis-enterprise-cloud-builder-for-aws.htm`. This is by far the easiest way to deploy as it only requires an access key, secret key, SSL certificate, and license file. This tool has the option to deploy Enterprise on a single machine with multiple machine roles federated, such as imager server, geoanalytics, and so on.

For most of the open source options, I'd just recommend launching prebuilt containers as, with many open source projects, it's easy to run into dependency problems when you try to install directly into an operating system. Lastly, ArcGIS has a new Kubernetes offering, which comes with a deployment script to automate deploying into an existing AWS EKS cluster. In the next section, we will look at considerations and decision criteria for choosing your deployment option.

Capabilities and cloud integrations

Comparing the different implementations of map and feature servers would require a complicated matrix to show the thousands of capabilities between each. For your general map services and feature services, the open source implementations are more than enough. ArcGIS Server web services (map, feature, imagery, geoprocessing, and many more) have the benefit of being part of the most feature-rich offering as well as having seamless integration with other ArcGIS products in their ecosystem. Companies around the world that have chosen ArcGIS as their server and have publicly available services are typically only able to share between other ArcGIS environments. ArcGIS services are in a propriety Esri feature service format, which many client-side applications are unable to read. It's tricky, if not impossible, to pull these into most open source environments, making ArcGIS the only option for consuming them. But I think it's worth noting you get what you pay for, as the old adage goes; you can pay for a product upfront or you can get a product for free and pay for it with support hours. Both options have their pros and cons.

This is what a typical ArcGIS deployment looks like on AWS:

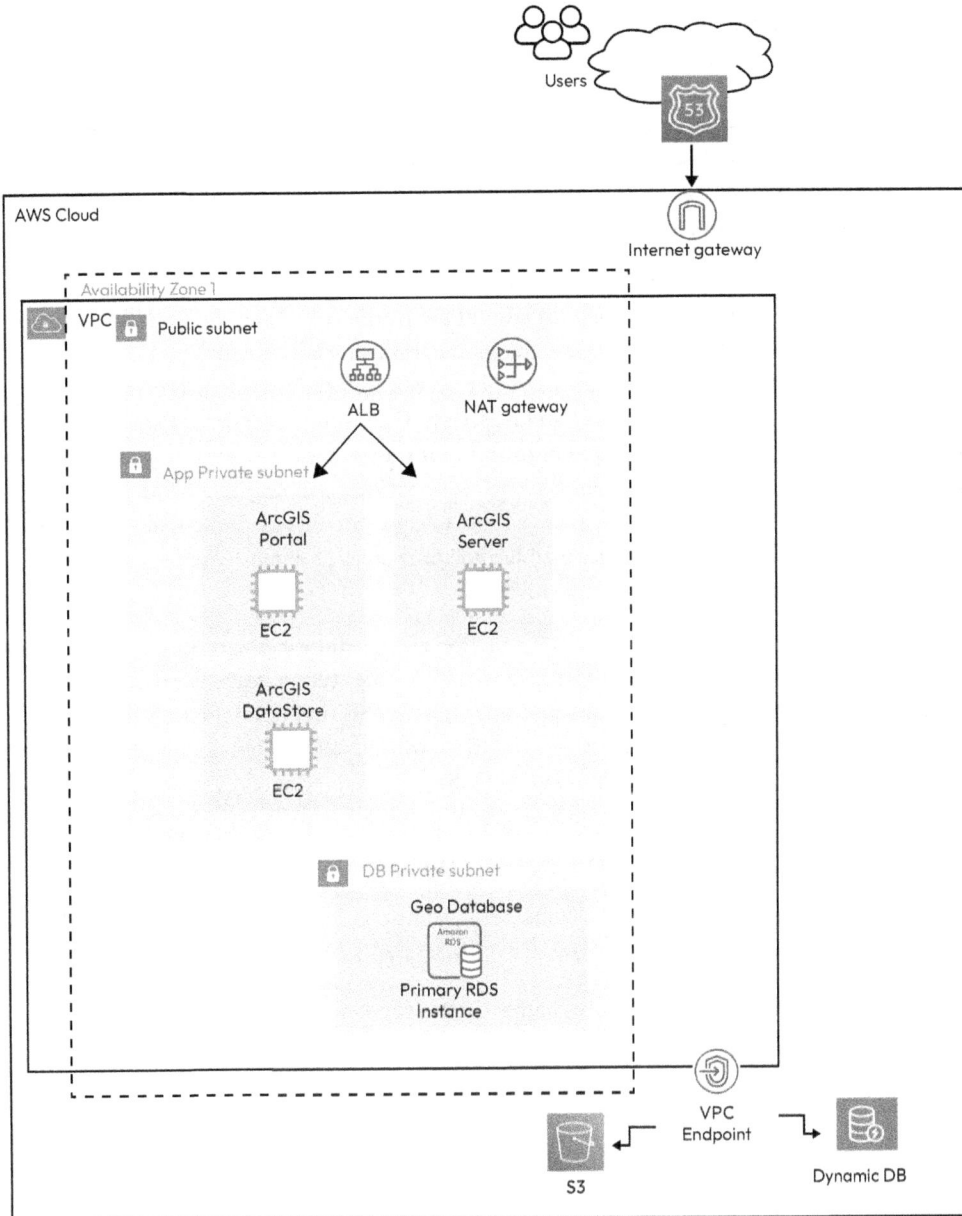

Figure 15.1: ArcGIS deployment structure on AWS

The main integrations that are important to these servers are their ability to take advantage of cloud-native services such as managed databases, data lakes, serverless, monitoring, logging, security, and the list goes on. Most of the implementations have support either directly or indirectly to take advantage of these, like with ArcGIS and data in Parquet on S3. Specifically, ArcGIS has limited support for reading vector data from S3 directly (note that ArcGIS's GeoAnalytics role does add capabilities here but requires additional infrastructure). A simple workaround though is to have Redshift mount the vector data in S3 as an external table, and then the data will show up in your ArcGIS environment as if it were sitting in a geodatabase. All of the implementations have great support for reading raster data from S3, either through an ArcGIS mosaic or through a VRT virtual raster.

A few other common services used include CloudFront, which is an Amazon **content distribution network (CDN)** to cache large tiles at edge pops around the world, AWS Web Application Firewall to protect service endpoints, and the API gateway to enforce throttling and identity/access capabilities. Lastly, on the operations side, AWS Systems Manager agents are used on the instances to perform various tasks such as OS patching or running ad hoc scripts. One common script is Esri's WebGISDR tool for backups, which is recommended in addition to instance backups. ArcGIS software at the instance level can be corrupted, and without a WebGISDR backup, you may be unable to export the data from a corrupted system. These services are a lot to take in and outside of the scope of this book but I wanted to give you an idea of what is possible and some areas to explore further as you look to secure, scale, and optimize your deployments on AWS.

In the previous paragraph, we talked about ArcGIS, but for a simple tutorial to get up and running that you can start with today, we will walk through how to deploy GeoServer on AWS. For our deployment, we will spin up an EC2 instance to download and stage our GeoServer container, we will upload the container to AWS Elastic Container Registry, and finally, we will launch the container on our Serverless Fargate service through **Elastic Container Service (ECS)**.

Deploying a container on AWS with ECR and EC2

So now that we know a little bit about what a container is, some common geospatial containers that we can deploy, and some AWS services we can use to deploy, let's walk through an example deployment:

1.   To create an ECR repository, click the orange **Create repository** button:

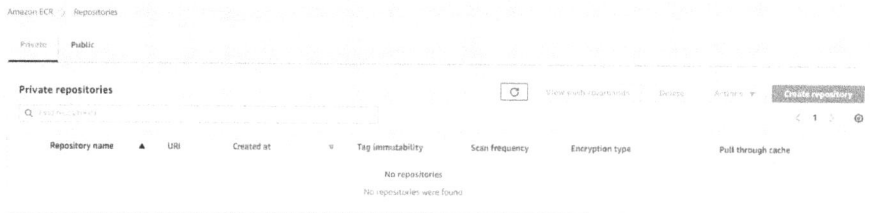

Figure 15.2: Creating an ECR repository

2. Select either **Public** or **Private**, type in a name, and click **Create repository**:

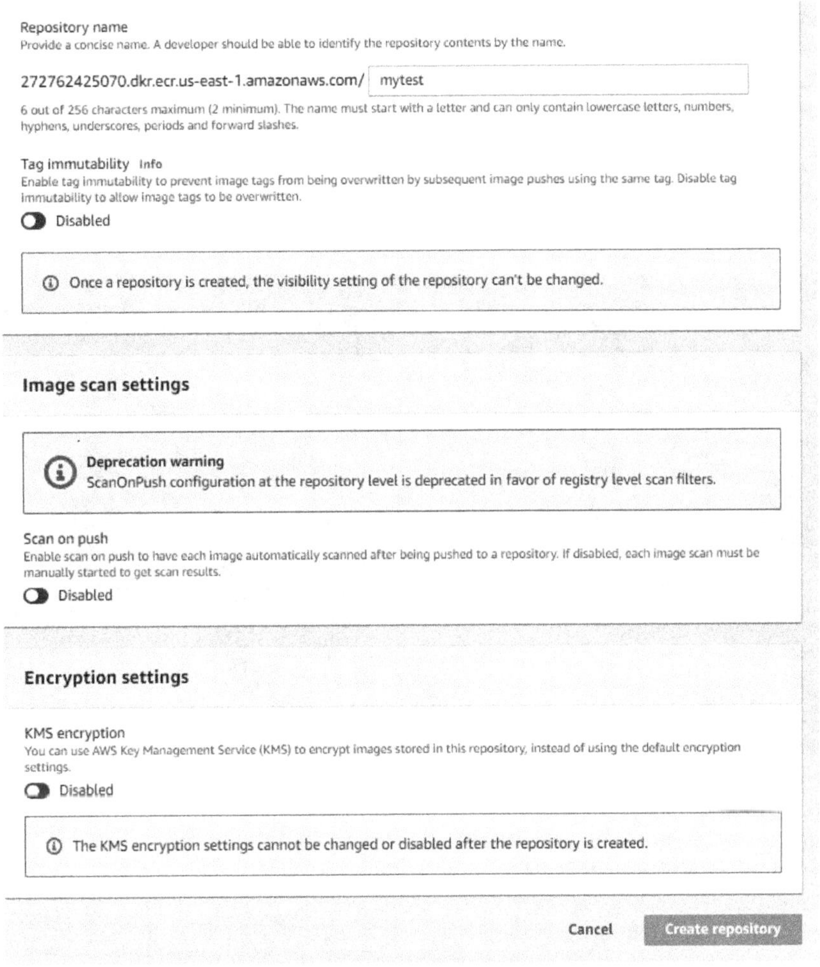

Repository name
Provide a concise name. A developer should be able to identify the repository contents by the name.

272762425070.dkr.ecr.us-east-1.amazonaws.com/   mytest

6 out of 256 characters maximum (2 minimum). The name must start with a letter and can only contain lowercase letters, numbers, hyphens, underscores, periods and forward slashes.

Tag immutability   Info
Enable tag immutability to prevent image tags from being overwritten by subsequent image pushes using the same tag. Disable tag immutability to allow image tags to be overwritten.

🔘 Disabled

ⓘ   Once a repository is created, the visibility setting of the repository can't be changed.

Image scan settings

ⓘ   **Deprecation warning**
ScanOnPush configuration at the repository level is deprecated in favor of registry level scan filters.

Scan on push
Enable scan on push to have each image automatically scanned after being pushed to a repository. If disabled, each image scan must be manually started to get scan results.

🔘 Disabled

Encryption settings

KMS encryption
You can use AWS Key Management Service (KMS) to encrypt images stored in this repository, instead of using the default encryption settings.

🔘 Disabled

ⓘ   The KMS encryption settings cannot be changed or disabled after the repository is created.

Cancel   **Create repository**

Figure 15.3: Settings for repository creation

3. Launch a t2.micro EC2 instance with Amazon Linux, a public IP address, and a security group open to 0.0.0.0/32 TCP port 8080:

https://docs.aws.amazon.com/cli/latest/userguide/cli-services-ec2-sg.html

Once you have the security group applied, go ahead and log in to your instance using either SSH or Systems Manager. I recommend Systems Manager for simplicity: https://docs.aws.amazon.com/AWSEC2/latest/UserGuide/session-manager.html.

4.   Use the following commands to install Docker:

```
sudo yum install docker -y
sudo usermod -a -G docker ec2-user
newgrp docker
sudo systemctl enable docker.service
sudo systemctl start docker.service
```

5.   Search for the GeoServer container:

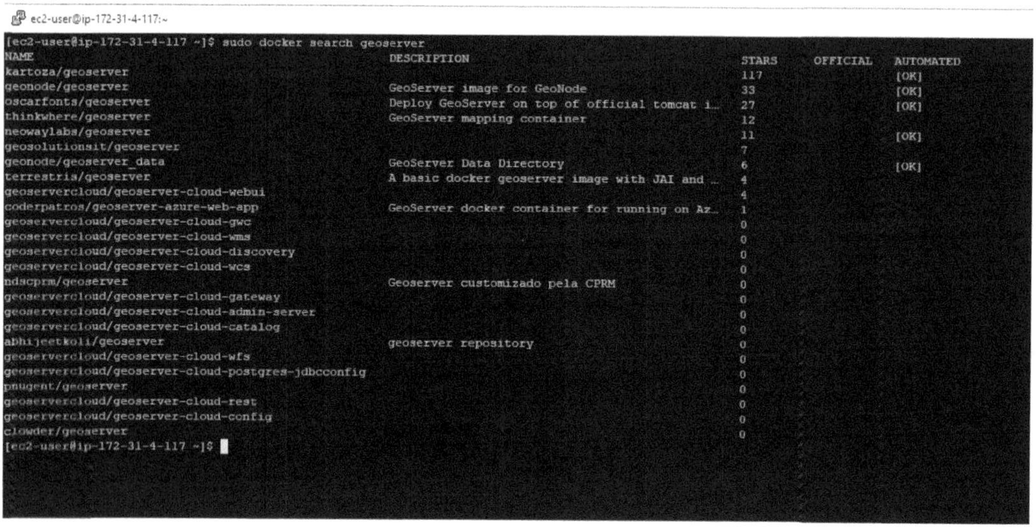

Figure 15.4: GeoServer Docker image search

6.   Pull down the `kartoza/geoserver` container:

> **Note**
>
> For more info about the container, check here: https://hub.docker.com/r/kartoza/geoserver.

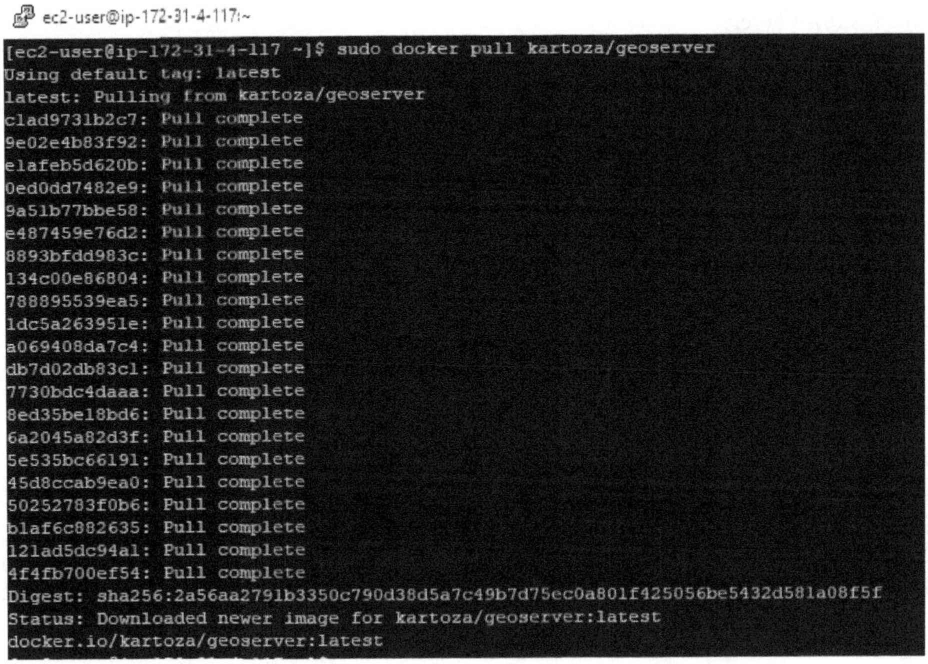

ec2-user@ip-172-31-4-117:~

```
[ec2-user@ip-172-31-4-117 ~]$ sudo docker pull kartoza/geoserver
Using default tag: latest
latest: Pulling from kartoza/geoserver
c1ad9731b2c7: Pull complete
9e02e4b83f92: Pull complete
e1afeb5d620b: Pull complete
0ed0dd7482e9: Pull complete
9a51b77bbe58: Pull complete
e487459e76d2: Pull complete
8893bfdd983c: Pull complete
134c00e86804: Pull complete
788895539ea5: Pull complete
1dc5a263951e: Pull complete
a069408da7c4: Pull complete
db7d02db83c1: Pull complete
7730bdc4daaa: Pull complete
8ed35be18bd6: Pull complete
6a2045a82d3f: Pull complete
5e535bc66191: Pull complete
45d8ccab9ea0: Pull complete
50252783f0b6: Pull complete
b1af6c882635: Pull complete
121ad5dc94a1: Pull complete
4f4fb700ef54: Pull complete
Digest: sha256:2a56aa2791b3350c790d38d5a7c49b7d75ec0a801f425056be5432d581a08f5f
Status: Downloaded newer image for kartoza/geoserver:latest
docker.io/kartoza/geoserver:latest
```

Figure 15.5: Pull completion messages from kartoza/geoserver

7. Run sudo docker images to get your current container's image ID:

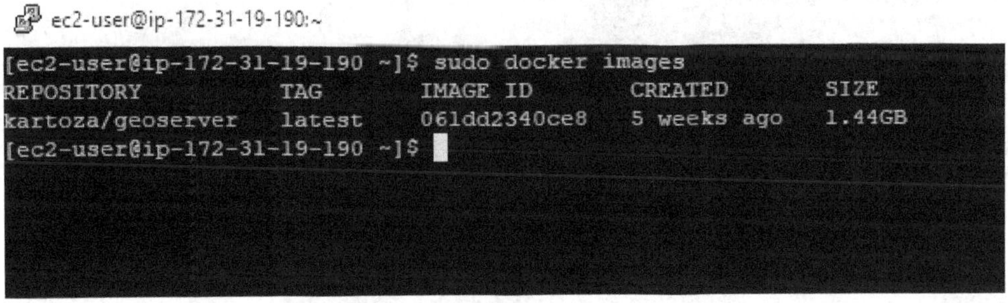

ec2-user@ip-172-31-19-190:~

```
[ec2-user@ip-172-31-19-190 ~]$ sudo docker images
REPOSITORY          TAG        IMAGE ID        CREATED       SIZE
kartoza/geoserver   latest     061dd2340ce8    5 weeks ago   1.44GB
[ec2-user@ip-172-31-19-190 ~]$
```

Figure 15.6: Getting the Docker image ID

8. Run the following command to add a tag to your image ID:

```
Docker tag <yourimageid> <youraccountnumber>.dkr.ecr.<region>.
amazonaws.com/geoserver:latest
```

This is shown here:

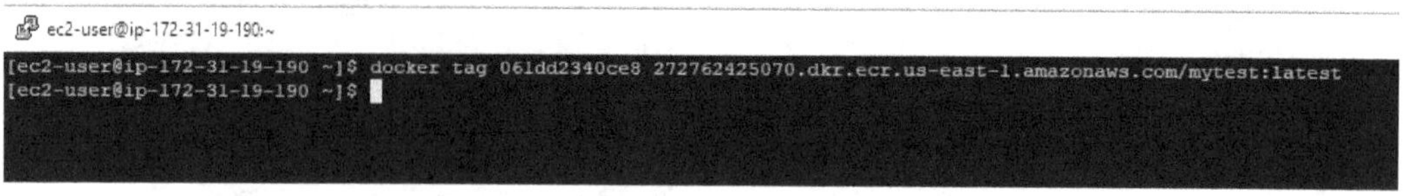

Figure 15.7: Tagging the Docker image ID

9. Run the following command to authenticate to your ECR registry (you may need to set up an AWS profile or an IAM role if using EC2):

```
https://docs.aws.amazon.com/AWSEC2/latest/UserGuide/iam-roles-
for-amazon-ec2.html
```

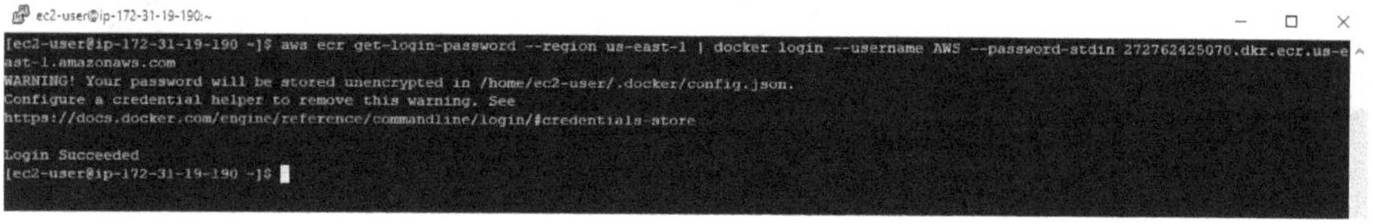

Figure 15.8: Authenticating to the registry

10. Now we are ready to push our image up to ECR:

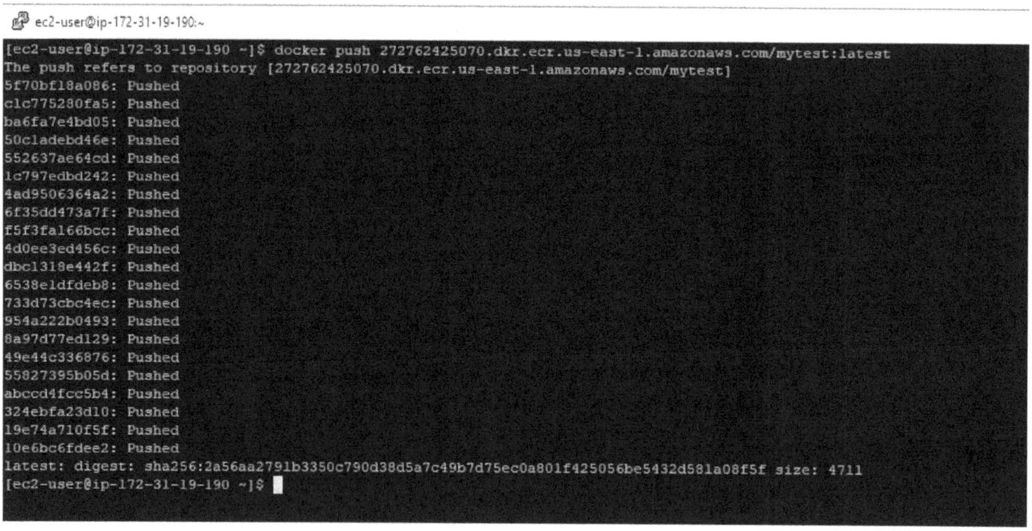

Figure 15.9: Pushing image to ECR

11. Create a variable with our repo information:

```
repo=$(aws ecr describe-repositories --region us-east-1 --query
'repositories[0].repositoryUri'|tr -d '"');
```

12. Run the following command to create an ECS cluster:

```
aws ecs create-cluster -region <yourregion>
```

ec2-user@ip-172-31-19-190:~

```
[ec2-user@ip-172-31-19-190 ~]$ aws ecs create-cluster --region us-east-1
{
    "cluster": {
        "status": "ACTIVE",
        "defaultCapacityProviderStrategy": [],
        "statistics": [],
        "capacityProviders": [],
        "tags": [],
        "clusterName": "default",
        "settings": [
            {
                "name": "containerInsights",
                "value": "disabled"
            }
        ],
        "registeredContainerInstancesCount": 0,
        "pendingTasksCount": 0,
        "runningTasksCount": 0,
        "activeServicesCount": 0,
        "clusterArn": "arn:aws:ecs:us-east-1:272762425070:cluster/default"
    }
}
[ec2-user@ip-172-31-19-190 ~]$
```

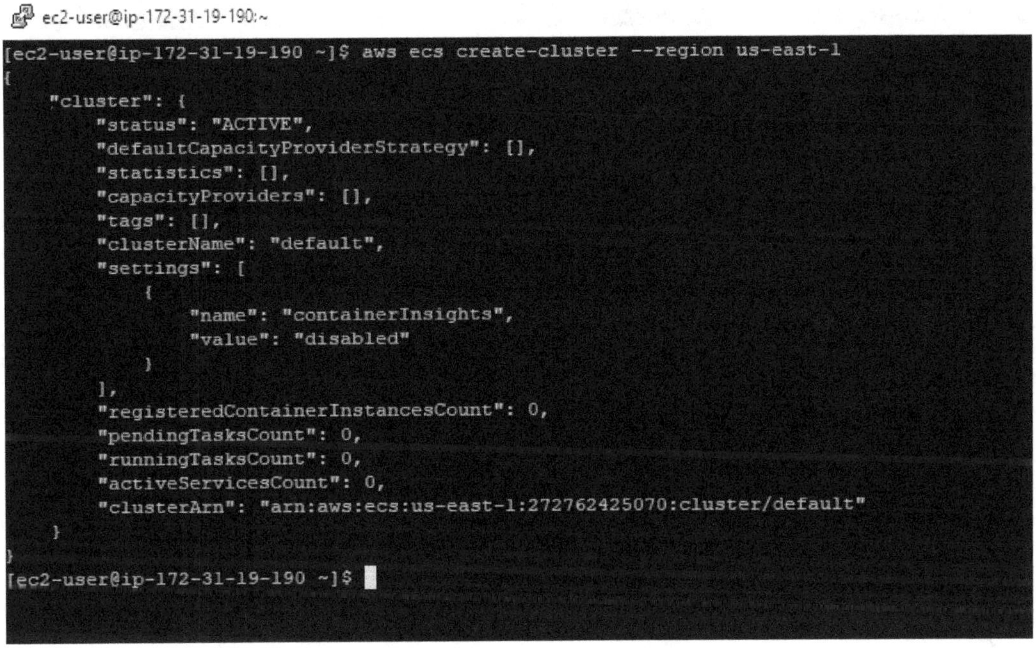

Figure 15.10: Creating an ECS cluster

13. Run the following command to create a task definition. Because we are using Fargate, which requires task and service definitions to run containers, we create the task definition with this command. More information is available at https://awscli.amazonaws.com/v2/documentation/api/latest/reference/ecs/register-task-definition.html:

```
aws ecs register-task-definition --family test --container-
definitions "[{\"name\": \"mytest\",\"image\":
\"$repo\",\"memory\": 128,\"portMappings\": [{\"protocol\":
\"tcp\",\"containerPort\": 80,\"hostPort\": 0}]}]" --region
us-east-1
```

14. Run the following command to start your container:

```
sudo docker run -e GEOSERVER_ADMIN_USER=packt -e GEOSERVER_
ADMIN_PASSWORD=packt -p 8080:8080 -d -t kartoza/geoserver
```

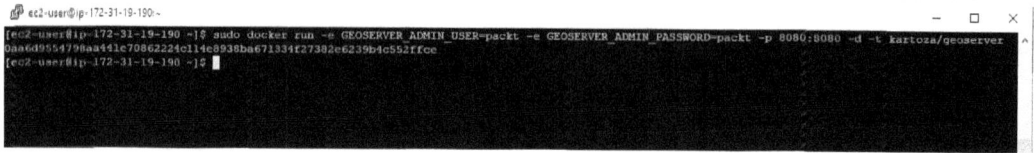

Figure 15.11: Starting the container

15. Now open a web browser and connect to the public IP of your EC2 instance on port 8080:

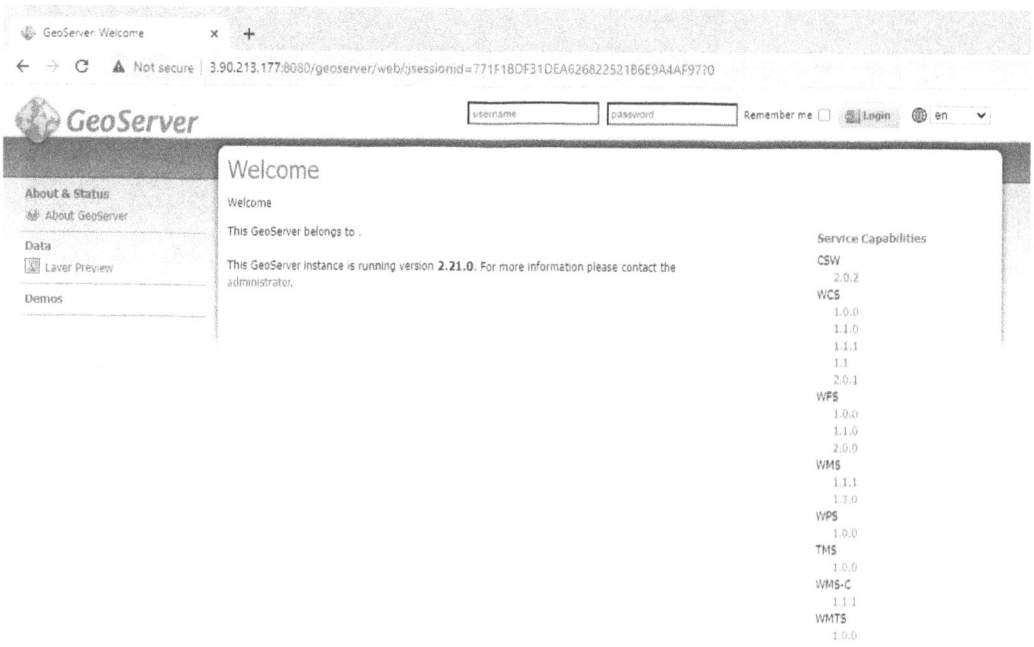

Figure 15.12: Running a GeoServer instance

Congratulations! You have now launched GeoServer on Fargate on AWS, so you can now navigate through the GUI and easily select a data source to host as a service. Keep in mind that containers are not persistent by default, so any changes you make here will be wiped out when the container is restarted. For persistence, you would need to script the feature service set up in the Docker file or attach a persistent volume.

Summary

In this chapter, we learned about which feature servers and map servers are available on AWS and a few deployment options for each. We also learned about a few common AWS service integrations that you can use to help manage, optimize, and secure your deployment.

In the next chapter, we will learn about a powerful and free imagery dataset called Sentinel on AWS.

Further reading

- `https://geoserver.org/`
- `https://www.arcgis.com/index.html`

16

Satellite and Aerial Imagery on AWS

In the previous chapter, we learned about Feature and Map servers. There are many different types of geospatial servers, including GeoEvent, which is used for streaming data, GeoAnalytics for big data and vector analysis, image services for image processing, and raster analytics. Image servers are used to stitch together and reproject image sets to be displayed on your map. In this chapter, we will talk about some of the imagery datasets that are available on AWS.

We will cover the following topics:

- Imagery options
- Sentinel
- Landsat
- NAIP
- Demonstrating imagery using AWS

Imagery options

In *Chapter 13*, we talked about Open Data on AWS. As part of this, we have several satellite datasets available. In this chapter, we will talk about Sentinel, Landsat, and NAIP. However, many other satellite datasets are available, such as those for weather, radar, and other sensors, as well as derivatives of satellite imagery, such as ESA WorldCover.

Sentinel

The Sentinel satellites were launched as part of the European Space Agency and through the Copernicus Program and consist of several satellites in various stages of deployment and production. Sentinel-1A was the first of the satellites to launch, in 2014, followed by 2A and 2B in 2015 and 2017, respectively.

These are the satellites we will use in our demo. Missions are planned out to 2025 with Sentinel6A and 6B. The Sentinel 2 satellites we will be working with collect 13 different spectral bands and have a revisit time of around 2 times per 10 days but with different angles. Sentinel 2 collects imagery at spatial resolutions of 10m, 20m, and 60m and is by far the most popular imagery dataset, given its high quality and low revisit time frame. Sentinel imagery is available in a few different buckets in the AWS Open Data Registry, but the two most common buckets are the Level 1C scenes at `s3://sentinel-s2-l1c/` and the Level 2A scenes at `s3://sentinel-s2-l2a/`. The Level 1C scenes provide orthorectified **Top of Atmosphere** (**TOA**) imagery, while the Level 2A scenes provide orthorectified **Bottom of Atmosphere** (**BOA**) imagery. These are essentially two different imagery products that serve different analysis needs. BOA will have some atmospheric corrections applied that aren't in the TOA product. You may want to make some corrections to TOA and use that as your starting point for analysis. Regardless of which dataset you choose, AWS has several publications, examples, and tutorials for using Sentinel imagery, such as for detecting deforestation and Near Real-Time Crop Conditions.

Landsat

Landsat was launched in 1972 and its satellites collect imagery across several spectral bands with resolutions ranging from 15m to 60m. Landsat satellites make a complete orbit every 16 days and have an 8-day cycle for repeat coverage. Landsat imagery is available on AWS through the Registry of Open Data, in the `s3://usgs-landsat/collection02/` bucket. The Registry Of Open Data also has a list of usage examples for different workflows and analyses that can be done with the data, such as those for exploring Chilean wildfires.

NAIP

The **National Agriculture Imagery Program** (**NAIP**) was established in 2003 and originally had a revisit cycle of five years. This was changed to three years in 2009. NAIP has a different revisit cycle because it's not satellite-based. NAIP imagery is produced through aerial photography or via plane. With the transition to three years, imagery is now collected by flying a plane over the United States every three years. There are pros and cons to this as the data quickly becomes out of date. However, because it is collected from a plane, the images are much higher resolution than if they were taken by satellite. NAIP imagery can have up to 1m resolution and is available on AWS for free. This would be more difficult to achieve via satellite given how much larger imagery scenes are when they're taken via satellite. NAIP imagery is located in the `s3://naip-source/` bucket. Some published use cases can be found in the AWS Open Data Registry, such as Urban Tree Detection. This use case makes sense given the high resolution of the imagery – you can get a much clearer picture of trees than what would be possible with Sentinel or Landsat.

Architectural considerations

Since these datasets are hosted on the AWS Open Data Registry, not many architectural considerations need to be made since you can't modify the origin bucket. However, there are still some design patterns you may want to consider.

Demonstrating satellite imagery using AWS

In this demo, we will pull down a few bands from Sentinel imagery on AWS, merge them, and assign the bands to display true color in open source QGIS. We will use the AWS S3 CLI to copy the images locally for editing:

1. To get started, install QGIS and the AWS CLI on either an Amazon workspace, an EC2 instance, or your local laptop. If you're installing the AWS CLI on a workspace or a local laptop, you will also need to generate an IAM user and run the `aws configure` command to assign your access key and secret key. See `https://docs.aws.amazon.com/IAM/latest/UserGuide/id_users_create.html` and `https://docs.aws.amazon.com/cli/latest/userguide/cli-configure-files.html` for additional information.

   Once these pieces are in place, we are ready to start downloading the images.

2. Run the following commands to copy the images to your machine. Note that these commands have the requester pays flag, which means you, the requester, will pay a few pennies for the network to download the image:

```
D:\Users\myuser>aws s3 cp --request-payer requester s3://
sentinel-s2-l1c/tiles/51/H/WE/2021/6/8/0/B01.jp2 ./2021-B01.jp2
D:\Users\myuser>aws s3 cp --request-payer requester s3://
sentinel-s2-l1c/tiles/51/H/WE/2021/6/8/0/B02.jp2 ./2021-B02.jp2
D:\Users\myuser>aws s3 cp --request-payer requester s3://
sentinel-s2-l1c/tiles/51/H/WE/2021/6/8/0/B03.jp2 ./2021-B03.jp2
D:\Users\myuser>aws s3 cp --request-payer requester s3://
sentinel-s2-l1c/tiles/51/H/WE/2021/6/8/0/B04.jp2 ./2021-B04.jp2
D:\Users\myuser>aws s3 cp --request-payer requester s3://
sentinel-s2-l1c/tiles/51/H/WE/2023/2/3/0/B01.jp2 ./2023-B01.jp2
D:\Users\myuser>aws s3 cp --request-payer requester s3://
sentinel-s2-l1c/tiles/51/H/WE/2023/2/3/0/B02.jp2 ./2023-B02.jp2
D:\Users\myuser>aws s3 cp --request-payer requester s3://
sentinel-s2-l1c/tiles/51/H/WE/2023/2/3/0/B03.jp2 ./2023-B03.jp2
D:\Users\myuser>aws s3 cp --request-payer requester s3://
sentinel-s2-l1c/tiles/51/H/WE/2023/2/3/0/B04.jp2 ./2023-B04.jp2
```

   With that, we have downloaded the same scene for two different years and we have downloaded bands 1–4, with 2, 3, and 4 being our RGB bands.

3. Next, open QGIS. From here, we can use raster functions to create VRTs or merge. VRTs are nice because we can visualize the data directly from S3 without copying it. For this example, we will use merge, which will merge all the images into a single image. VRTs are typically faster for visualizing and we don't need to copy the files down locally. However, any time you scroll to the scene in the world, you are essentially merging on the fly, which uses extra compute cycles.

To do this, select **Raster** > **Miscellaneous** > **Merge**:

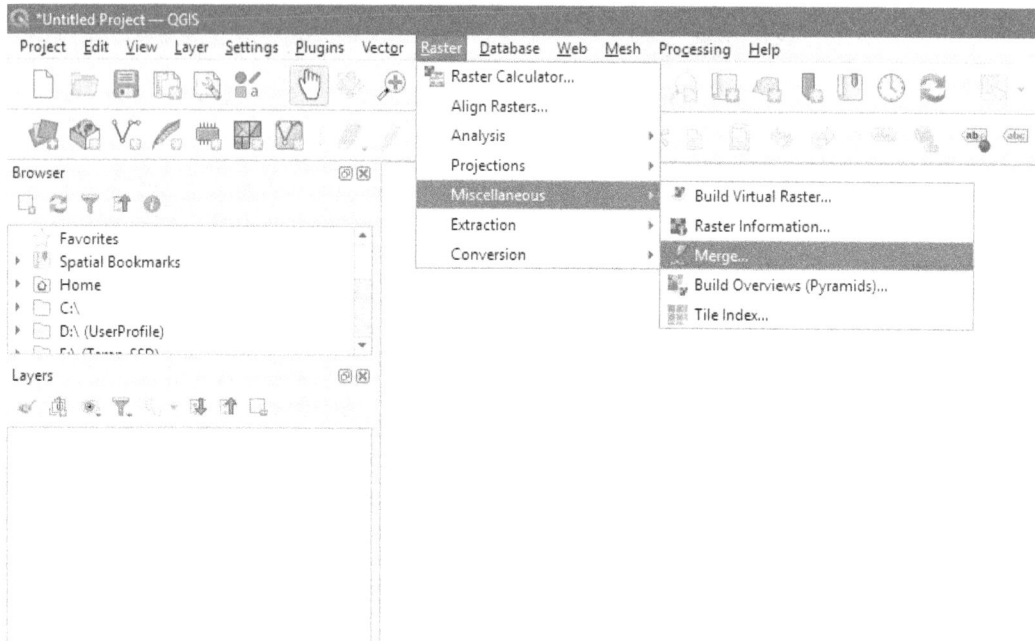

Figure 16.1: Merging images in QGIS

4. Click **Merge…** and navigate to one of the scenes you downloaded. Select the four 2021 bands to upload them, then click **OK**. Next, check the **Place each input file into a separate band** box and click **Run**:

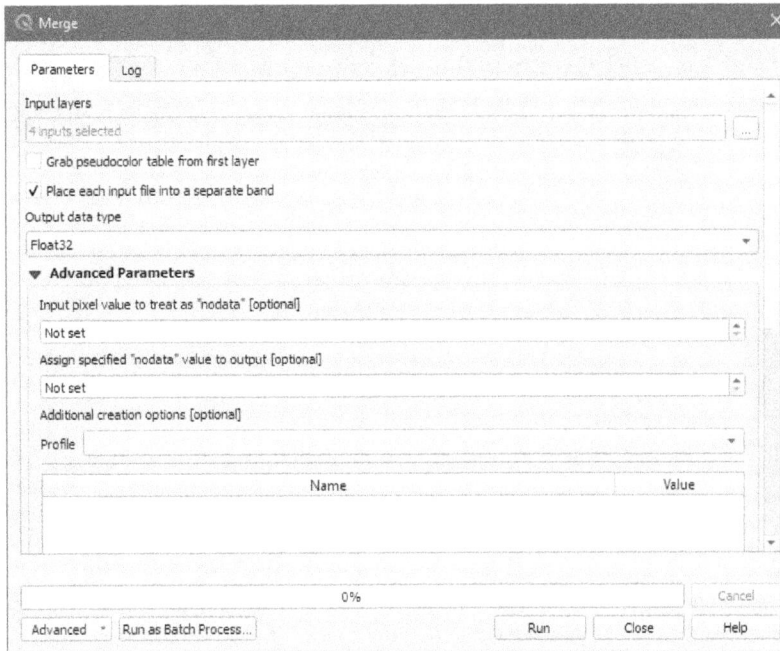

Figure 16.2: Merge parameters

5. When it completes, you will see your scene on the map. Click **Close** and repeat these steps for the 2023 scene.

6. Once you have the two scenes loaded, we can adjust their colors. Select one of your layers and click **Properties**. You can also click **Rename** to name them 2021 and 2023 as I have:

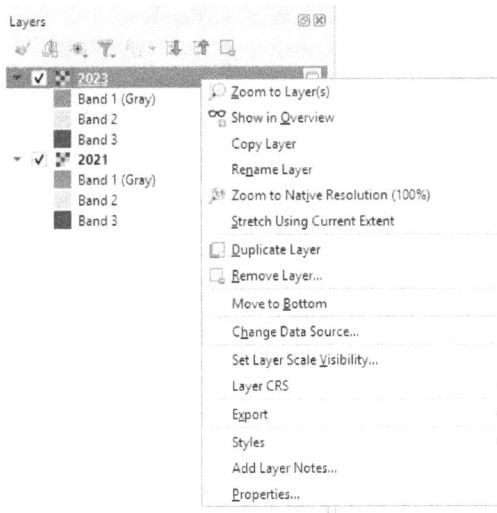

Figure 16.3: Updating the bands

7. Under **Symbology**, select **Band 4** for the red band, **Band 3** for the green band, and **Band 2** for the blue band. Then, click **Ok**. Repeat this step for your other layer:

Figure 16.4: Band properties

Congratulations – you have completed this tutorial! You can now toggle between the two layers we added and see any differences the satellite may have picked up, such as cloud cover or changes in vegetation. You may also want to filter out **Band 2** and **Band 3** since **Band 4** is best to track vegetation:

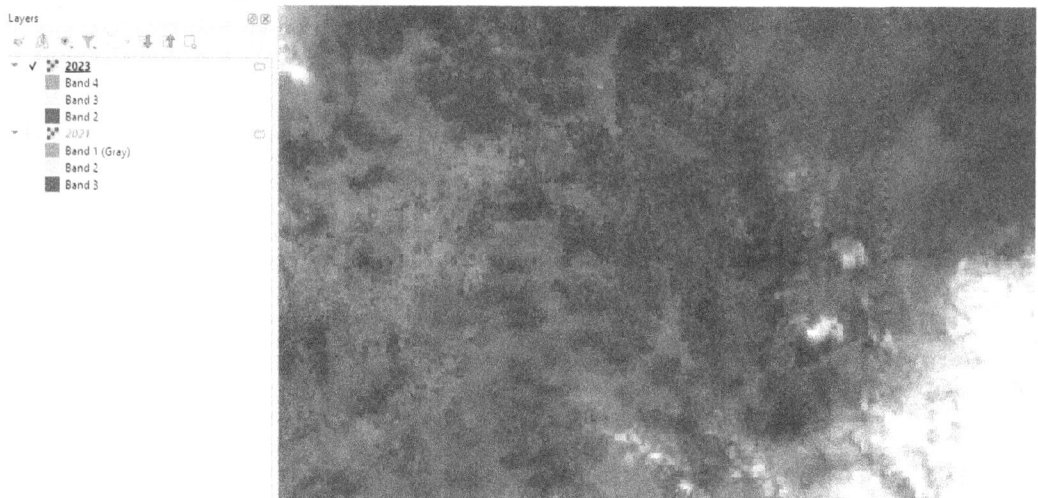

Figure 16.5: Final output

Summary

In this chapter, we learned about the different imagery products available on AWS and some of the differences between the datasets available. We completed a tutorial on how to load sentinel imagery into QGIS for analysis and how to work with the different bands available in the imagery. Before this data was available on AWS, it was challenging to access and analyze it. There wasn't easy access or the ability to work with the data in place; the only option was to download massive imagery files over the slow internet to the small amount of storage on a laptop. Not only does AWS provide the storage for this data but it also provides native tools such as SageMaker Geospatial to work with the data all in one place.

References

The following are the references for this chapter:

- United States Geological Survey: https://www.usgs.gov

- Landsat satellite information: https://en.wikipedia.org/wiki/Landsat_program

- AWS Open Data program: https://registry.opendata.aws/

- Example showing wildfires: https://www.gearthblog.com/blog/archives/2017/02/exploring-chile-wildfires-landsat-sentinel-2-imagery.html

- Additional imagery information: https://en.wikipedia.org/wiki/National_Agriculture_Imagery_Program

- Example showing tree detection: https://github.com/jonathanventura/urban-tree-detection

- Sentinel 2 satellite information: https://en.wikipedia.org/wiki/Sentinel-2

- The Copernicus space program information: https://en.wikipedia.org/wiki/Copernicus_Programme

- AWS deforestation example: https://github.com/aws-samples/aws-sms1-geospatial-analysis-deforestation/

- AWS example lab using Sagemaker Geospatial: https://aws.amazon.com/blogs/apn/tcs-digital-farming-generates-near-real-time-insights-on-crop-conditions-for-actionable-decision-making/

Index

A

Active Directory (AD) 32
Adaptive Server Enterprise (ASE) 33
Advanced Query Accelerator (AQUA) 46
algorithms
  used, in geospatial ML 161, 162
Amazon AppStream 8
Amazon Aurora database 6
  connecting to 65, 66
Amazon DocumentDB 6, 38
Amazon DynamoDB 6, 39
Amazon Elastic Block Store (EBS) 5, 33
Amazon Elastic Compute Cloud (EC2) 5, 33
  R, setting up on 129-138
  RStudio, setting up on 129-138
  used, for deploying container
    on AWS 228-234
Amazon Elastic Container Service
  (ECS) 34, 36, 111, 228
Amazon Elastic File System (EFS) 34
Amazon Elastic Kubernetes
  Service (EKS) 34
Amazon FSx service 34
Amazon Kinesis Agent 30
Amazon Kinesis Data Firehose 30
Amazon Kinesis Data Streams 29
Amazon Kinesis Producer Library (KPL) 30
Amazon Location Place Index 41

Amazon Location Service 40
Amazon Location Service
  Route Calculator 41
Amazon Location Tracker 41
Amazon Lookout for Equipment (L4E) 20
Amazon Machine Image (AMI) 5, 31, 138
Amazon Managed Grafana 40
Amazon MSK 29
Amazon OpenSearch Service 6, 38
Amazon Redshift 6, 37
Amazon Relational Database Service
  (Amazon RDS) 5, 39, 58
Amazon SageMaker
  RStudio, configuring on 139-152
  RStudio, using on 138-153
  used, for geospatial ML 162, 163
Amazon SageMaker Canvas 38
Amazon Simple Notification Service (SNS) 7
Amazon Simple Storage Service
  (S3) 5, 26, 81, 181
Amazon Sustainability Data
  Initiative (ASDI) 29
  reference link 29
Amazon Web Services (AWS) 4, 57, 159
  OSM, accessing from 214-217
  used, for demonstrating satellite
    imagery 239-242

Amazon WorkSpaces 8
Apache Kafka 29
API Gateway
   using, in Python 83
ArcGIS Cloud Builder
   reference link 226
ArcGIS deployment structure on AWS 227
architectural considerations 78, 174, 239
Athena 37
   architectural considerations 103
   AWS service integration 102
   configuring 94-96, 181, 182
   federated queries with 208, 209
   setting up 93
   spatial functions, using 100-102
Attribute values 178
Aurora Capacity Units (ACUs) 60
automated ML (AutoML) 160
Availability Zone (AZ) 5
AWS account
   using 206
AWS account team
   leveraging 8
AWS AppSync 36
AWS Auto Scaling 12
AWS cloud
   queries and transformations 72-77
AWS Database Migration Service
   (AWS DMS) 32
AWS Data Exchange 29
AWS Fargate 34, 36
AWS Glue 31
AWS Key Management Service
   (AWS KMS) 26
AWS Lambda 36
AWS Marketplace geospatial dataset
   example 204

AWS Migration Accelerate
   Program (MAP) 8
AWS ML
   background 159, 160
AWS modern data architecture
   pillars 26, 27
AWS OpsHub 31
AWS service integration 160, 161
AWS services 110
AWS services, deployment options
      for containers 111
   Elastic Container Service (ECS) 111
   Elastic Kubernetes Service (EKS) 111
AWS Snow Family 30

B

base map layer 40
Bottom of Atmosphere (BOA) 238
business-to-business (B2B) file
   transfer service 31

C

change data capture (CDC) 33
changeset 213
Classless Inter-Domain Routing (CIDR) 65
cloud
   geospatial data, storing 5, 6
cloud computing 4
Cloud Optimized GeoTiff (COG) 19
command-line interface (CLI) 206
comma-separated values (CSV) file 181
Comprehensive R Archive
   Network (CRAN) 127
Computerized Maintenance Management
   System (CMMS) 209

container on AWS
  deploying, with EC2 228-234
  deploying, with ECR 228-234
containers 107, 108
  deploying 111-114
  GDAL 109
  GeoServer 110
  portability 109
  reference link 230
  scaling 108
  updating 110
content distribution network (CDN) 228
cost management, in cloud 9
  end user compute services 12, 13
  file-based data 11
  geodatabase servers 10
  geospatial application servers 11
  hardware provisioning 10
CRUD operations 39

D

data
  normalizing 20, 21
database
  setting up 58-65
data source
  Athena, configuring 181, 182
  connecting to 180
  QuickSight, configuring 183-187
Desktop-as-a-Service (DaaS) 8
disaster recovery (DR) 10
distributed copy (DistCp) command 31

E

Earth Observation job (EOJ) 163
Elastic Container Registry (ECR) 110
  used, for deploying container
    on AWS 228-234
Elastic Kubernetes Service (EKS) 111
Elastic Map Reduce (EMR) 115, 116
  geospatial, applying to 117, 118
  launching 118-125
EMRFS 117
EMR Studio 36
Enterprise Data Warehouses (EDWs) 27
Enterprise Resource Planning (ERP) 209
Extended WKB (EWKB) 37
Extended WKT (EWKT) 37
**Extract, Transform, and Load
    (ETL) 11, 30, 159**

F

feature servers
  capabilities 226-228
federated queries
  with Athena 208, 209
Field wells section 191
file formats 18-20
filled maps 194-196

G

GDAL 109
**Geographic Information System
    (GIS) 3, 58, 128**
Geometry Data 178
GeoPandas 118, 161

GeoParquet 19

GeoPlatform 29

GeoServer 110

geospatial

applying, to EMR 117

geospatial applications 82

geospatial data 27

analyzing, with RStudio 153-156

loading 69-72

quality, impact on 15, 16

storing, in cloud 5, 6

visualizing 172-174, 177-180

visualizing, with RStudio 153-156

geospatial data formats 97

JSON-encoded geospatial data 97-99

Well-Known Text (WKT) 97

geospatial data lake 27

geospatial data lake architecture

data analytics and insights 37-39

data collection and ingestion layer 29-32

data processing and transformation 34-36

data storage layer 33, 34

data visualization and mapping 40, 41

designing, with modern data

architecture 27, 28

geospatial data management

best practices 8, 9

geospatial data processing 166-170

notebook step details 171

geospatial data strategy

AWS account team, leveraging 8

building 6, 7

data consumption 7, 8

unauthorized access, preventing 7

geospatial ML, with SageMaker 162, 163

geospatial query 96

running 48-55

GIS file formats 5

GML (Geography Markup Language) 33

Grafana 40

H

Hadoop Distributed File System
(HDFS) 30, 117

Hadoop frameworks 115-117

EMRFS 117

Hexagonal Hierarchical Geospatial
Indexing System (H3) 38

high-performance computing (HPC) 34

HiveQL (Hive Query Language) 36

Humanitarian OpenStreetMap
Team (HOT) 222

I

Identity and Access Management
(IAM) 7, 139, 180

imputing/forward-filling 20

Infrastructure as a Service (IaaS) 6

infrastructure as code (IaC) 57

integrated development environment
(IDE) 36, 129

Intelligent-Tiering 11

Internet Small Computer Systems
Interface (iSCSI) 32

IoT Device Shadow 18

J

JavaScript Object Notation (JSON) 178

JSON-encoded geospatial data 97-99

JSON Web Token (JWT) 83

L

lab activities
prerequisites 57, 58
Lambda function 36
using, in Python 83
Landsat satellites 238
libraries
used, in geospatial ML 161, 162
LoRaWAN 17
low earth orbit (LEO) satellites 17

M

machine learning (ML) service 38
Mahout 115
Map Reduce 117
map servers
capabilities 226
cloud integrations 228
modern data architecture
overview 25, 26
Multi-Availability Zone (Multi-AZ) 58
multiple data classes
analyzing 207, 208

N

National Agriculture Imagery
Program (NAIP) 238
near real time 18
Network File System (NFS) 31

O

object storage 82
OGR 109
Online Analytical Processing (OLAP) 44

Online Transaction Processing (OLTP) 44
open data 201
aerial photography 201, 202
analyzing 206
AWS account, using 206
contour lines of elevation data 203
modern applications 203
modern satellites 203
multiple data classes, analyzing 207, 208
Open Database License (ODbl) 214
Open Data on AWS
benefits 209, 210
references 205
Open Geospatial Consortium (OGC) 33
Open Source Geospatial
Foundation (OSGeo) 69
OpenStreetMap (OSM) 29, 211
accessing, from AWS 214-217
architectural considerations 222
benefits 214
community 222
data structure 211-213
nodes 212
relations 212
tags 212
ways 212
Optimized Row Columnar (ORC) 37
Oracle Enterprise Edition (EE) 39
Oracle Standard Edition 2 (SE2) 39
over the air (OTA) 17
Overture map
URL 109

P

pandas 161
Parquet 37
point map 190-193

PostGIS extension
installing 66-68
Public Geodata 29
Python
with API Gateway 83
with Lambda 83

Q

QGIS 37
quality
impact, on geospatial data 15, 16
Quality of Service (QOS) 18
QuickSight 40
collaboration 198
configuring 183-187
overview 180
reports 198
QuickSight dashboard
with map 196, 197
QuickSight user guide
reference link 183

R

R 127
setting up, on Amazon EC2 129-138
Random Cut Forest (RCF) 162
Redshift 44
Advanced Query Accelerator (AQUA) 46, 47
geohashing support 46
geospatial support 47
partitioning 44
Spectrum 45
Redshift cluster
launching 48-55
Registry of Open Data on AWS
accessing 204

relational database management
system (RDBMS) 5
Requester Pays model 204-206
R geospatial data analysis
ecosystem 127-129
RStudio
setting up, on Amazon EC2 129-138
used, for analyzing geospatial data 153-156
used, for visualizing geospatial data 153-156
using, on Amazon SageMaker 138-153

S

S3 Glacier Deep Archive storage class 11
S3 Standard 11
S3 web hosting 82
SageMaker Geospatial example
deploying 163
geospatial data processing 166-170
geospatial data visualization 172-174
one-time environment setup 164-166
SageMaker Notebooks 161
SageMaker Studio notebook, using with
SageMaker geospatial image
reference link 169
satellite connections 17
satellite imagery
demonstrating, with AWS 239-242
options 237
satellite imagery, options
Landsat satellites 238
NAIP 238
Sentinel satellites 237, 238
Schema Conversion Tool (SCT) 33
Sentinel satellites 237, 238
serialization/deserialization (SerDe) 97
serverless 81
services 81, 82
websites, with S3 82

serverless geospatial application
deploying 84-90
serverless hosting
performance, considering 83
security, considering 83
Server Message Block (SMB) 31
servers
deployment options 226
types 226
server-side encryption (SSE) 26
Simple Notification Service (SNS) 103
Single Sign On (SSO) 7
ski lift scout application 218-221
spatial functions 100-102
accessor functions 101
aggregation functions 101
Bing tile functions 101
constructor functions 100
geospatial relationship functions 100
operation functions 101
spatial query
structure 99
Spatial Type (ST) 100
SPICE 40, 180
store once, use many pattern 209
streaming data 18
Structured Query Language (SQL) 181
systems integrator (SI) 8

T

temporal dimensions
considering 21, 22
Top of Atmosphere (TOA) 238
transmission methods 17

U

unauthorized access
preventing 7
Unique Key 178
User-Defined Functions (UDFs) 37, 47

V

virtual hard disk (vHD) 107
Virtual Private Cloud (VPC) 139
visualization layout, QuickSight 187
features and controls 188, 189
filled maps 194-196
point map 190-193

W

Web Feature Service (WFS) 110
Web Map Service (WMS) 110
Well-Known Binary (WKB) 35
Well-Known Text (WKT) 35, 97, 116, 180
Wi-Fi 17

‹packt›

Packtpub.com

Subscribe to our online digital library for full access to over 7,000 books and videos, as well as industry leading tools to help you plan your personal development and advance your career. For more information, please visit our website.

Why subscribe?

- Spend less time learning and more time coding with practical eBooks and Videos from over 4,000 industry professionals
- Improve your learning with Skill Plans built especially for you
- Get a free eBook or video every month
- Fully searchable for easy access to vital information
- Copy and paste, print, and bookmark content

Did you know that Packt offers eBook versions of every book published, with PDF and ePub files available? You can upgrade to the eBook version at packtpub.com and as a print book customer, you are entitled to a discount on the eBook copy. Get in touch with us at customercare@packtpub.com for more details.

At www.packtpub.com, you can also read a collection of free technical articles, sign up for a range of free newsletters, and receive exclusive discounts and offers on Packt books and eBooks.

Other Books You May Enjoy

If you enjoyed this book, you may be interested in these other books by Packt:

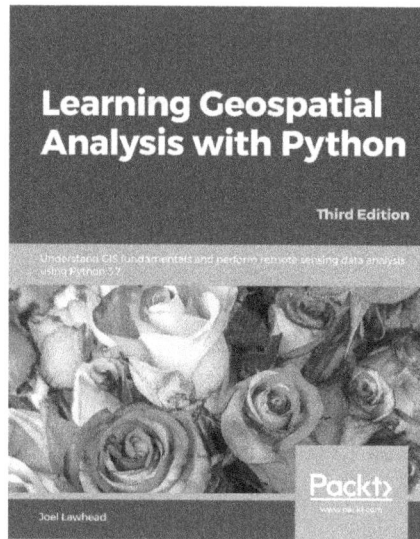

Learning Geospatial Analysis with Python - Third Edition

Joel Lawhead

ISBN: 9781789959277

- Automate geospatial analysis workflows using Python
- Code the simplest possible GIS in just 60 lines of Python
- Create thematic maps with Python tools such as PyShp, OGR, and the Python Imaging Library
- Understand the different formats that geospatial data comes in
- Produce elevation contours using Python tools
- Create flood inundation models
- Apply geospatial analysis to real-time data tracking and storm chasing

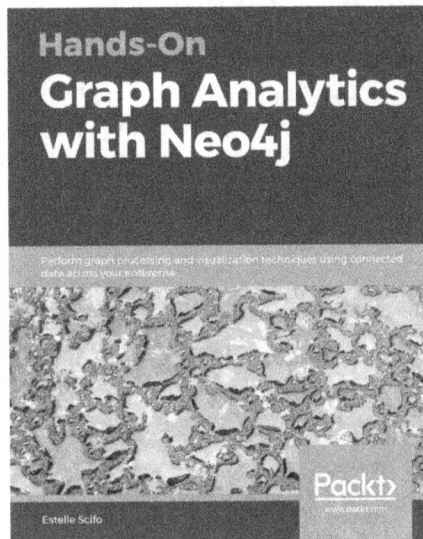

Hands-On Graph Analytics with Neo4j

Estelle Scifo

ISBN: 9781839212611

- Become well-versed with Neo4j graph database building blocks, nodes, and relationships
- Discover how to create, update, and delete nodes and relationships using Cypher querying
- Use graphs to improve web search and recommendations
- Understand graph algorithms such as pathfinding, spatial search, centrality, and community detection
- Find out different steps to integrate graphs in a normal machine learning pipeline
- Formulate a link prediction problem in the context of machine learning
- Implement graph embedding algorithms such as DeepWalk, and use them in Neo4j graphs

Packt is searching for authors like you

If you're interested in becoming an author for Packt, please visit `authors.packtpub.com` and apply today. We have worked with thousands of developers and tech professionals, just like you, to help them share their insight with the global tech community. You can make a general application, apply for a specific hot topic that we are recruiting an author for, or submit your own idea.

Share Your Thoughts

Now you've finished *Geospatial Data Analytics on AWS*, we'd love to hear your thoughts! Scan the QR code below to go straight to the Amazon review page for this book and share your feedback or leave a review on the site that you purchased it from.

`https://packt.link/r/1-804-61382-7`

Your review is important to us and the tech community and will help us make sure we're delivering excellent quality content.

Download a free PDF copy of this book

Thanks for purchasing this book!

Do you like to read on the go but are unable to carry your print books everywhere?

Is your eBook purchase not compatible with the device of your choice?

Don't worry, now with every Packt book you get a DRM-free PDF version of that book at no cost.

Read anywhere, any place, on any device. Search, copy, and paste code from your favorite technical books directly into your application.

The perks don't stop there, you can get exclusive access to discounts, newsletters, and great free content in your inbox daily

Follow these simple steps to get the benefits:

1. Scan the QR code or visit the link below

https://packt.link/free-ebook/9781804613825

2. Submit your proof of purchase
3. That's it! We'll send your free PDF and other benefits to your email directly

Printed in the USA
CPSIA information can be obtained
at www.ICGtesting.com
JSHW062225270923
49290JS00009B/29

9 781804 613825